The Novels of Theodore Dreiser:
A Critical Study

The
Novels
of
Theodore
Dreiser

A CRITICAL STUDY

by Donald Pizer

UNIVERSITY OF MINNESOTA
PRESS, MINNEAPOLIS

Copyright © 1976 by the University of Minnesota.
All rights reserved.
Printed in the United States of America
at NAPCO Graphic Arts, Inc., New Berlin, Wisconsin
Published in Canada by Burns & MacEachern Limited,
Don Mills, Ontario

Library of Congress Catalog Card Number 75-20769

ISBN 0-8166-0768-0

Second Printing, 1977

For Karin and Ann

Preface

THIS BOOK IS PRIMARILY about Dreiser's eight published novels. Dreiser's life, times, and ideas and his work in other forms enter my discussion when these matters contribute to the understanding of the origin and nature of a particular novel but are otherwise not fully examined. In the Introduction, however, I use four stories which Dreiser wrote in the summer of 1899—his first significant efforts at fiction—to summarize his beliefs and his fictional interests and techniques at the beginning of his career as a novelist and to anticipate some of the principal directions of that career.

My book has two major aims—to establish the facts of the sources and composition of each of Dreiser's novels and to study the themes and form of the completed work. My intent has not been to construct a genetic history of each novel merely to make available such a history but rather to relate what can be discovered about the factual reality of a novel to its imaginative reality. Although the fulfillment of these aims has resulted in a long book, I offer my conclusions with some modesty. Dreiser left behind a mass of manuscript material, much of it bearing directly on the genesis of his novels and much of it hitherto not fully examined. And Dreiser himself, as a man and as a writer, is a complex and difficult figure. So if I write fully about matters of composition or theme, I do so out of a conviction that there is profit in attempting to establish the history and quality of each novel at some length in order to present a foundation of fact and opinion for correction or amplification by future scholars and critics. Finally, I have sought to avoid a schematized view of Dreiser which posits a single overriding theme or direction in his work. Much Dreiser criticism of the past has been weakened by a tendency to sacrifice the distinctiveness of particular novels for a symmetrical interpretation of his career as a whole. Some themes occupied Dreiser more than others, and some fictional techniques appear in his work more often than others. But as a remarkably uneven writer whose work in fiction spans five decades, Dreiser deserves examination primarily on the basis of the individuality and worth of each of his novels.

My work has been aided over the years by many individuals and institutions, and it is a pleasure to record my thanks. In particular, Mrs. Neda Westlake, Curator of the Theodore Dreiser Collection of the University of Pennsylvania Library, has been a bulwark of resourcefulness and cooperativeness. Without her good will and expertise, I probably would not have embarked on this study, and I certainly would not have brought it to a timely conclusion. Richard Lehan, Ellen Moers, and Robert H. Elias have shared their knowledge of Dreiser with me on several important occasions. I am especially indebted to Professor Elias for making available to me his private collection of notes and for a careful scrutiny of my manuscript. I have also profited greatly from the editorial skill of my wife, Carol H. Pizer, and from the criticism of Griffith Dudding and Marvin Morillo. I have benefited in various ways from the knowledge and interest of the late Lloyd Arvidson, Anne Freudenberg, Gerhard Friedrich, Philip L. Gerber, Robert W. Hill, W. J. Keith, Kenneth A. Lohf, Peter Lyon, David C. Mearns, David J. Nordloh, David A. Randall, W. A. Swanberg, and Mrs. Waldo R. Wedel.

For permission to consult their Dreiser holdings and to quote from unpublished material in their collections, I wish to thank the University of Pennsylvania Library, the Lilly Library of Indiana University, the University of Virginia Library, the Yale University Library, Columbia University Library, Cornell University Library, the University of Illinois Library, the New York Public Library, and the Library of Congress. In addition, I have received much aid from the staffs of the library of the University of California at Los Angeles and the Tulane University Library. Mr. Harold J. Dies has generously granted me permission to quote from unpublished Dreiser material not in the University of Pennsylvania Dreiser Collection, and the University of Pennsylvania has granted me permission to quote from material in the Dreiser Collection. A portion of my Introduction has appeared in *Essays Mostly on Periodical Publishing in America: A Collection in Honor of Clarence Gohdes*, ed. James Woodress (Durham, N.C.: Duke University Press, 1973), and is republished by permission of Duke University Press.

At different stages in my work, I have benefited from grants in aid of research by the American Philosophical Society, the Tulane University Council on Research, and the American Council of Learned Societies. I wish especially to note the crucial role of an ACLS Fellowship in making possible a year's leave for the writing of this book.

Contents

The Novels of Theodore Dreiser:
A Critical Study

Introduction:
A Summer at Maumee

A S H A S O F T E N been noted, Theodore Dreiser's personal background differs significantly from that of most American writers of his generation. Unlike Hamlin Garland, Stephen Crane, and Frank Norris, who were of Protestant, Anglo-Saxon heritage and whose families had been long settled in America, Dreiser was the son of a Catholic German immigrant. And unlike the middle-class youth of these figures (including Garland, whose family owned their own land no matter how severe their labors), Dreiser spent his boyhood moving fron one Indiana town to another with his large and impoverished family while his father sought work as a millhand or watchman. Although he made his way up from these humble origins by the classic formula of luck and pluck, Dreiser's later awareness of both the rarity of the rise and the pervasiveness of the Alger myth of success contributed to the bitter caricature of that myth in *An American Tragedy*.

A dreamy, moody youth full of romantic ideals and the biting pull of sex, Dreiser broke into newspaper work in Chicago in 1892 by strength of will and with the aid of a sympathetic editor. His more than two years as a reporter—principally in St. Louis and Pittsburgh—played a major role in shaping his creative imagination. As he later recalled, his work as a newspaperman brought him his first "real contact with life—murders, arson, rape, sodomy, bribery, corruption, trickery and false witness in every conceivable form."[1] But despite his immersion in the lower depths, that part of Dreiser which was "a seeker of beauty" and "to whom everything romantic appeals"[2] was not destroyed or dismayed by this

3

experience but rather learned to coexist, so to speak, with the part that was fully aware of every kind and degree of human degradation. The two qualities often unite in his fiction to produce one of his most characteristic ironic effects: Hurstwood dies in a Bowery flophouse while Carrie sits quietly brooding upon her quest for beauty and happiness; or, in the final chapters of *The Stoic* (written just before his death), Cowperwood's fortune is dissipated by trickery and bad faith while Berenice discovers the beauty and joy to be derived from aiding the weak and poor.

Dreiser the "aspirant" was drawn to the bright, exciting world of New York. In late 1894 he left his safe job on the *Pittsburg Dispatch* and moved to New York with the intent of continuing his newspaper career. A few disheartening months as a space-rate reporter for the *New York World*, however, led him to forswear newspaper work forever, and several more months of unemployment resulted in almost complete discouragement. But in mid-1895 his brother Paul, a successful songwriter, began a new magazine called *Ev'ry Month* and installed Dreiser as editor. Since the magazine was established primarily to promote the songs of Paul's music publishing firm, Dreiser was permitted considerable discretion in the selection of material for the nonmusical portion of each issue. He used this freedom to write a lengthy monthly column called "Reflections," and signed "The Prophet," in which he commented solemnly on issues of the day and on philosophical and social matters in general.[3] The two years in which Dreiser edited and contributed to *Ev'ry Month* gave him a firm sense of the contemporary magazine market, and in late 1897 he gave up editing for the more profitable work of free-lance magazine writing. His principal outlets were the new ten-cent mass circulation journals then beginning to displace the traditional, often stuffy monthlies. He quickly mastered the formula for the preparation of simply written, fully illustrated articles about famous people, well-known places, and current events, and became one of the leading "magazinists" of the day. He had little interest in fiction and devoted most of his writing outside of journalism to a sizable number of conventional, high-minded poems.

The best account of Dreiser's beginnings as a writer of fiction is by Dreiser himself in a letter to H. L. Mencken in 1916:

It was he [Arthur Henry] who persuaded me to write my first short story. This is literally true. He nagged until I did, saying he saw short stories in me. I wrote one finally, sitting in the same room with him in a house on the Maumee River, at Maumee, Ohio, outside Toledo. This was in the summer of 1898 [1899]. After each paragraph I blushed for my folly—it seemed so asinine. He insisted on my going on—that it was good—and I thought he was kidding me, that it was rotten, but that he wanted to let me down easy. Finally, HE took [it], had it typewritten and sent it to *Ainslee's*. They sent me a check for $75. Thus I began.

The above is exact and sacredly true.

Then he began to ding-dong about a novel. I must write a novel, I must write a novel. By then I had written four short stories or five, and sold them all:
1. "Of the Shining Slave Makers"
2. "The Door of the Butcher Rogaum"
3. "The World and the Bubble"
4. "Nigger Jeff"
5. "When the Old Century Was New"[4]

Despite his avowal of exactness to Mencken, Dreiser's memory played him false in his recollection that the visit to Maumee occurred in the summer of 1898 (there is no doubt that it was 1899) and that his work of that summer represented his first efforts at fiction. He had attempted to write short stories during the winter of 1894–95,[5] and he had published at least one fictional sketch in *Ev'ry Month*. [6] Moreover, he had sold none, not all, of his Maumee stories by the time he began to write *Sister Carrie* in October 1899. Dreiser's correspondence reveals that both *Harper's Monthly* and the *Century* declined "The Shining Slave Makers," for example,[7] and that "Nigger Jeff" was not accepted by *Ainslee's* until the summer of 1900.[8] Because of these and other rejections, and because of the usual delay between acceptance and publication, the four stories were not published until 1901, from eighteen to thirty months after their composition. (I say four stories because "The World and the Bubble" has never been identified in either published or manuscript form.) The original titles of the stories and the journals in which they appeared are:

"When the Old Century Was New," *Pearson's*, XI (January 1901), 131–40.

"The Shining Slave Makers," *Ainslee's*, VII (June 1901), 445–50.

"Nigger Jeff," *Ainslee's*, VIII (November 1901), 366–75.

"Butcher Rogaum's Door," *Reedy's Mirror*, XI (December 12, 1901), 15–17.[9]

Dreiser was correct, however, in stressing the importance of his work during that summer in Maumee. For the first time since his abortive attempts of the winter of 1894–95, he was seeking to shape his interests and ideas into fictional form. He was now no longer young or inexperienced. At twenty-eight he had known grinding poverty and exhilarating success. He had spent much of his boyhood in the semirural Midwest, but he had also been both a penniless jobseeker and a minor celebrity in two great cities. A bumbling, shy, awkward adolescent, he had acquired the tact and tenacity necessary to interview such giants of his day as Andrew Carnegie and Philip Armour. Relatively uneducated despite a year at Indiana University, he had been deeply affected in his mid-twenties by the "naturalistic philosophy" of Spencer, Darwin, and Huxley and by the fiction of Balzac and Hardy. His more than 150 articles and editorials of 1895–99 reveal a writer with ideas or opinions on almost every matter of interest to Americans of the 1890s and with knowledge on subjects ranging from interior decorating to battleship construction. In short, though Dreiser's four Maumee stories are uneven in quality, from the almost worthless "When the Old Century Was New" to the powerful "Nigger Jeff," they are far from juvenilia. Rather, they reveal Dreiser working with subject matter, themes, and forms which were to reappear in his novels from *Sister Carrie* to *The Stoic*. It is this aspect of the four stories—their usefulness in isolating and clarifying significant characteristics of Dreiser's novels—that I intend to discuss at some length.

««««««««««««««««««««««««««««

"When the Old Century Was New" is set in the Manhattan of 1801. We follow William Walton, a prosperous young merchant, as he engages in the activities of a spring day, a day which closes with his successful proposal of marriage to a young belle of the town. The story is basically a historical romance, a form much in vogue at the turn of the century. Dreiser introduces much detail about costume and about specific historical figures, places, and events of early nineteenth-century New York, and he knits the whole together with a light love plot flavored with faintly archaic speech. "The Shining Slave Makers" is in the form of a dream vision. McEwen has taken refuge in a park from the heat and turmoil of the city. He discovers a number of ants at his feet, and as he studies their actions he finds himself transformed into a member of the tribe he has been observing, the Shining Slave Makers. He joins in their hunt for food and in their battles and is at last mortally wounded. As he is about to die, he again finds himself in the park, gazing at armies of warring ants. "Nigger Jeff" is primarily an initiation story. A lighthearted young St. Louis newspaperman is sent to a rural village to investigate reports that a Negro who has attacked a white girl may be lynched. In pursuit of his story, he follows a mob and observes the capture and hanging of a terrified Negro. The next day he visits the home of the Negro and encounters his grief-stricken mother. The reporter now senses the tragic nature of the events he has been observing and determines that he will try to embody this quality in his story. "Butcher Rogaum's Door" is in part a New York local color story. Rogaum, a German-American Bleecker Street butcher, attempts to rule his family with an iron hand. His young daughter Theresa rebels by staying out late with her beau, and Rogaum locks her out. Both Theresa and Rogaum soon regret their actions. She is frightened by her boyfriend's insistence that she run away with him, and Rogaum begins to worry. He becomes terrified when he encounters a dying young prostitute on his doorstep and momentarily mistakes her for his daughter. But Theresa is found by the police before any harm comes to her, and she and her family are reunited.

Although each of the four stories can be placed in a distinctive genre of short fiction, all rely on one of two kinds of subject matter. "When the Old Century Was New" and "The Shining Slave Makers" depend heavily on research. The Dreiser of 1899 who had written articles on "Japanese Home Life" and "Electricity in the Household"[10] could also turn to historical accounts of New York and to scientific treatises on ant life for his new ventures in fiction. Indeed, Dreiser was incensed when an editorial assistant of the *Century* questioned the accuracy of his material in "The Shining Slave Makers" and cited Sir John Lubbock's *Ants, Bees, and Wasps* as his source.[11] The two stories also reveal the way Dreiser was to incorporate research material into his novels. The method of "When the Old Century Was New" is self-conscious and forced, as it frequently is in the Cowperwood trilogy. Almost every prominent historical figure of the time—from John Adams and Jefferson to Aaron Burr—is awkwardly squeezed into the brief compass of the story. And several blocks of historical detail—notably an account of New York's ineffective fire-fighting equipment—have the disconcerting effect of unassimilated note-taking. In "The Shining Slave Makers," however, our acquisition of knowledge about ant life is inseparable from McEwen's experiences. As in

Dreiser's use of the Gillette case in *An American Tragedy*, research in this instance is a source of theme and form rather than a way to flesh out a thin narrative.

"Nigger Jeff" and "Butcher Rogaum's Door" derive primarily from personal experience. Dreiser had reported a rural lynching in the fall of 1893 while a St. Louis newspaperman,[12] and he was familiar with lower Manhattan street life as a resident of the area since late 1894. But both stories are also autobiographical in a more significant sense. It was Dreiser himself who had begun to realize the tragic nature of life when as a young reporter he had repeatedly encountered the consequences of human inadequacy. His account of his newspaper years in *A Book About Myself* abounds in memories of the failures in life whom he met in connection with his reporting—the slothful and inept, the drunken and the sexually perverse, the weak in every possible faculty of mind and body. Always for Dreiser there was the shock of recognition—the terrifying thought that he too might be weak or inept in some vital function and therefore also be crushed. And it was Dreiser himself who had observed in his own family the constant clash between thick-skulled parental authoritarianism and rebellious youth eager for life. Much of the account of his youth in *Dawn* is devoted to the innumerable conflicts between his four older sisters, who were "pagan" in their interests and desires, and his angry, bitter, and morally doctrinaire father.

These two kinds of material—research and personal experience—were to be Dreiser's principal resources as a novelist. Sometimes the research element is paramount, as in the Cowperwood trilogy with its detailed and thinly veiled account of Philadelphia and Chicago business and political history. In other works autobiography is the major source, as in Dreiser's close use of his family history in *Jennie Gerhardt* and of his own marriage in *The "Genius."* His best novels are a skillful blend of the two. In *Sister Carrie* and *An American Tragedy* a solid base of historical detail is lent emotional power by Dreiser's projection of his own experiences and longings into his major figures.

〰〰〰〰〰〰〰〰〰〰〰〰〰〰〰〰〰〰〰〰〰〰

"The Shining Slave Makers" appears to be a straightforward Darwinian allegory. The conventions of the dream vision form of the story permit

McEwen to have a double existence. His initial responses to the conditions of ant life, after he discovers that he has become a Shining Slave Maker, are still human. He expects other ants to share their food with him, and he sympathizes with victims of disaster. He quickly adapts, however, to a life of continuous struggle for food and for superiority in battle and becomes a prodigious and merciless warrior. McEwen's absorption of the ethics of ant life seems to demonstrate that man, in an animal situation, will quickly discover within himself the animal characteristics necessary to survive in that situation.

Thus, an obvious theme in "The Shining Slave Makers" is that the rule of force characterizes all life, both human and nonhuman. To the weary McEwen, seeking refuge from the "toil of the burning streets," nature—as represented by a park bench under a shady tree—is a sanctuary. But to McEwen the Shining Slave Maker, the paths and grass of the park are boulder-strewn hazards and a "jungle." The seeming difference between human and animal (or insect) life is only a difference in point of view, with man's false sense of superiority deriving from his failure to understand that he too is an inseparable part of nature. In reality, man is still subject both to the hazards of nature and to the "naturalness" of social life—that is, to a cold winter and to the struggle for existence within society. Dreiser stated these truisms of Social Darwinism explicitly in many of his *Ev'ry Month* editorial comments. "Nature," he wrote in February 1897, during a severe winter, "has by storm, sleet, and hunger weeded out the weaklings and the incompetents before offering the gentle springtime and the luxuriant summer to those fit ones who by strength and good fortune have withstood the inclemencies, and have thus managed to survive."[13] And in explanation of the Trust as a natural phenomenon, he wrote the following month: "The principle of life . . . is that the higher form shall live by the death of the lower, and the trust is laying down claim to be the higher. If it is not, there are the oppressed free to defend themselves; and if they do not, they merely admit their degradation."[14]

But to explicate "The Shining Slave Makers" merely as an illustration of a Darwinian ethic is to oversimplify both the story and Dreiser's ideas in general. For the story contains two distinctively Dreiserian qualifications of a crude Social Darwinism, qualifications which represent a permanent and important complex of themes in Dreiser's thought and writing. One such modification arises from McEwen's relationship with his fellow Slave

Maker Ermi. Soon after becoming an ant, McEwen rescues Ermi from death at the hands of ants from a rival tribe. Ermi responds with gratitude and affection, and the two ants become inseparable, fighting side by side with a brother-in-arms camaraderie and loyalty. At the close of the story, in a reversal of the initial situation, Ermi aids McEwen as he is about to be overcome. Friendship is therefore posited by Dreiser as both a practical need and an emotionally satisfying condition within the harsh reality of a world of struggle and death.

The sources of Dreiser's knowledge of "naturalistic" philosophy are well known, but it is less widely known that Dreiser drew upon these sources not only for the obvious Social Darwinism of "The Shining Slave Makers" but also for the complicating qualification represented by the relationship between McEwen and Ermi. In an oft-quoted passage in *A Book About Myself*, Dreiser recalled his reading of Huxley, Tyndall, and Spencer in the summer of 1894 when he was a Pittsburgh reporter. In particular, he remembered the impact of Herbert Spencer's *First Principles*. Spencer, he wrote, had blown him "intellectually, to bits" by destroying the last vestiges of his belief in immutable, supernaturally sanctioned moral laws.[15] The supernatural, Spencer had declared, was "unknowable." Only the natural could be known, and nature was a history of the evolutionary movement of all life—caused by the persistence of force—from the simple to the complex, the unspecialized to the specialized. Within this movement men had little significance. They were merely minor elements in a vast mechanistic process, a process which for mankind now took the distinctive shape of a struggle for existence in society rather than in nature.

In his recollections of his response to Spencer's beliefs, Dreiser thus stressed a negative effect. That is, he recalled primarily that Spencer's introductory section on the unknowable had destroyed the last traces of his conventional religiosity. But Dreiser also responded fully to Spencer's more affirmative idea of "equation" and made the idea the foundation of almost all of his later thought and of much of his discursive and creative writing. His failure to acknowledge this debt in his autobiography—though he does cite it in his philosophical essays—is an understandable consequence of the greater impact initially of Spencer as a destructive rather than as a constructive influence.[16]

Although Dreiser used the term "equation" throughout his career to refer to the central principle of a mechanistic universe, and though Spencer himself used the term occasionally, Dreiser was really drawing upon the idea which Spencer more commonly called "rhythm."[17] To Spencer, all reality is an expression of force (or energy), though force may take the corollary shapes of space, time, matter, or motion. Force always exists in "antagonistic forms," since "any force manifested, implies an equal antecedent force from which it derived, and against which it is a reaction."[18] Thus, the persistence of force—in the guise of rhythmic motion—is the prime mover of all life, since rhythmic motion causes all change, from the universal tendency toward complexity in all life to the fine gradations of hierarchy and power within society. Put more simply, Spencer maintained that the existence of strength posits the existence of weakness, but that weakness, in reaction to excessive strength, will develop a self-protecting power which will eventually redress the balance that nature strives for but never fully achieves. The constant fluctuation between opposites is change or rhythm or equation. Dreiser himself briefly summarized the process by which persistence of force leads to equation in an unpublished essay of 1916–19 called "Concerning Good and Evil":

Something which exists originally as force or matter or both wills to move (or must so will, or, more simply, *must move*), yet in order to do so must divide, replacing unity with variety and still retaining a unity of sorts. There follows, as a matter of course, all the elaborated phases or methods of adjustment indicated by chemistry and physics and the processes of evolution—equations of two or more movements or substances, and so—life. In order that one thing may not impinge upon another too destructively, equation is necessary.[19]

Spencer tended to write about the history of evolution in animal terms. It had been a process sparked initially by the goal of self-preservation, and strength and guile had been the principal means of achieving that goal, whether for beast, man, family, or tribe. But when Spencer discussed the future of social evolution, he introduced an important moral element. He developed this distinction between the past and future most clearly and fully in his *Data of Ethics* (always one of his most influential books), though it is present as well in almost all his other writing, including *First Principles*. He began with two premises: first, that "we regard as good the conduct furthering self-preservation, and as bad the conduct tending to self-destruction"; and, second, that "the conduct to which we apply the name good, is the relatively more evolved conduct; and that bad is the name we apply to conduct which is relatively less evolved." In other words, all conduct at any time is to be measured against the aim of self-preservation, but the nature of self-preservative acts is itself evolving. As society evolves, "simple" acts of self-preservation, such as physical strength and family loyalty, become less "efficient" than complex ones, such as consciousness of others and social cooperativeness. Men at present are still guided by egotism, Spencer believed, because society was still dominated by an older form of evolution, but men were also increasingly recognizing the greater social efficacy of conscious altruism and "harmonious cooperation." In Spencer's specialized terminology, "the general truth disclosed by the study of evolving conduct . . . that for the better preservation of life the primitive, simple, presentative feelings must be controlled by the later-evolved, compound, and representative feelings, has thus come, in the course of civilization, to be recognized by men."[20] In practice, therefore, Spencerian morality contained a built-in paradox which made it adaptable to varied uses. Spencer's beliefs could be used to justify the presence of a struggle-for-existence ethic in contemporary society because struggle had produced the present level of social and moral civilization and was necessary for still further advance. But his ideas could also be used to celebrate all signs of the realization of Christian idealism in man's personal and social life as evidence of the true direction of evolutionary progress.

Many liberal clergymen of the 1880s and 1890s seized upon this paradox in Spencer's thought in order to reconcile evolutionary science and religious thought, and in particular to use the rising fortunes of the former to bolster the sagging hold of the latter. It is probable that Dreiser encountered and absorbed Spencer's ethical ideas in popular form even before he distilled them from Spencer's difficult and wordy prose. During the early 1890s, he had been attracted by several of the nondenominational preachers who lectured to large audiences in downtown Chicago halls on Sunday afternoons. He especially recalled his enthusiasm for the sermons of the Reverend Frank Gunsaulus, one of the most influential and popular Chicago clergymen of his day, who was widely known for his "liberal" theology.[21]

The influence upon Dreiser of Spencer's mating of an amoral and a moral conception of life was both profound and complex. Initially, Dreiser expressed the two halves of this union overtly, both in his philosophical writing and in his fiction. As his career advanced, however, his philosophical speculations were increasingly characterized by a full-blown amoralism, while his fiction became the principal vehicle for a covert and oblique moralism. There is thus a three-fold difficulty in sorting out Dreiser's ideas about the moral significance of life: they differ in overt expression at different moments of his career; they appear in his fiction in covert forms which appear to contradict his overt expression at that time; and they involve at all times the paradox of a world both moral and amoral.

Initially, however, a clear combination of "low" and "high" thinking—of accepting the amoralism of the struggle for existence while applauding all evidence of man's moral nature—characterizes much of Dreiser's philosophical commentary in his *Ev'ry Month* columns. For example, in June 1896, he noted that

all must die that [man] may live—fruits, flowers, animals and vegetables. The very hills must be torn to give him homes of stone, and the forests destroyed that he may have the beauty of ornamental carving about him. He must step in where others have failed, crowd out the old and feeble, override the desires and hopes of others, who also wish for success, and so on, until death. This is the law, cold, hard, immutable—the law of self-preservation, and upon it all must take their stand and press forward so or die. It is hard to think that such must be the condition of living, but nevertheless such it must be, and all honor to him who fights bravest but with as much charity and as many tears as the dread of failure will permit.[22]

Beneath the conventional rhetoric of this passage—the rhetoric of Darwinian apologists and liberal clergymen—lies Dreiser's characteristic and permanent mélange of a cold-blooded endorsement of destruction as a principle of life and a warm responsiveness to those human qualities which aid in the relief of pain and suffering. In "The Shining Slave Makers," for example, the relationship between Ermi and McEwen is in part an illustration of the mechanistic power of tribal loyalty to bind members of the tribe into an effective destructive force. But the relationship is also one of sympathy and unselfishness and thus has the emotional coloration of a "good" which is good for reasons other than tribal. Like most men of this time, Dreiser found that the image of social life as a struggle for existence was apt and convincing. But he had also found that his mother's all-embracing love was a powerful compensating force in the midst of the poverty and flux which was his youth. And he had discovered within the cutthroat competitiveness of the New York journalistic scene an immensely satisfying relationship with Arthur Henry. Thus, Dreiser's responsiveness to threads of moral idealism in the popular philosophy and religion of his day suggests that his disbelief was always to be accompanied by a will to believe. Indeed, the depth of disbelief in Dreiser at any moment in his career usually measures the strength of his search for belief. "I catch no meaning from all I have seen," he wrote in a famous statement of 1928,[23] as he was about to set out on a decade-long search for the roots of all meaning in contemporary science. From his earliest *Ev'ry Month* editorials of 1895 to his death in 1945, Dreiser argued that experience was chaotic, directionless, and valueless. At the same time, though in various ways and with various degrees of self-awareness, he sought to find evidence that it had both meaning and value.

In addition to the moral element introduced into "The Shining Slave Makers" by the friendship between McEwen and Ermi, Dreiser qualified the Darwinism of the story in yet another important way. McEwen's initial horror at the ruthlessness of ant life soon passes. He begins to "revel" in the "sport" of pillaging and killing, and develops a "lust" for warfare. At the end of the story, when his dream is over and he views the warring ants at his feet, he at first wishes to aid the Shining Slave Makers, to continue in some way to battle for them. "Then came reason, and with it sorrow—a vague, sad something out of far-off things." Dreiser in this instance was dramatizing what he was often to call the "color" of the "game" of life. Though life is a constant equation, the conflict which arises out of this equation is responsible for the richness and excitement of experience, both for the participant and for the artist-observer. Thus, McEwen paradoxically does not welcome his escape from death as an ant but rather views it with "sorrow." And so Dreiser can call his 1923 collection of sketches about the poverty and hardship of New York life *The Color of a Great City*. "The game [of life] is open, free, a thrashing, glorious scene," he wrote in his essay "Equation Inevitable."[24] And it is Dreiser's aesthetic of "thrashing" which underlies such basic structures in his fiction as Carrie's rise and Hurstwood's fall, or Cowperwood pitted against the massed wealth and power of the financiers of Chicago.

As Dreiser's career advanced, he came to acknowledge openly that struggle and its consequences were a source of aesthetic value. He told an interviewer in 1907,

Every human being is intensely interesting. If the human being has ideals, the struggle and the attempt to realize those ideals, the going back on his own trail, the failure, the success, the reason for the individual failure, the individual success—all these things are interesting; interesting even when there are no ideals, where there is only the personal desire to survive, the fight to win, the stretching out of the fingers to grasp—these are the things I want to write about.[25]

In 1929, he stated this aesthetic of chaos even more strikingly:

What we plainly see is birth and death—the result of chemic and electrophysical processes of which at bottom we know exactly nothing. And beyond that—murder, the chase, life living on life, the individual sustaining himself at the expense of every other, and wishing not to die. And then beauty, beauty, beauty, which seems to derive as much and more from this internecine and wholly heartless struggle as from any other thing. And yet, beauty, beauty, beauty—the entire process, to the human eye at least, aesthetic in its results if by no means entirely so in its processes.[26]

"The Shining Slave Makers" thus contains not merely a single strand of Dreiser's Darwinism but three interwoven strands. Most obviously, Dreiser dramatizes life as a struggle for existence in order to invalidate a conventional belief in man's moral superiority to all other creatures. But Dreiser also finds expressions of moral behavior and sentiment in experience, even though he separates such expression from its traditional base in volition. And finally, he views the entire chaotic flux of life as beautiful. These three strands are almost always found together in Dreiser's writing, though—as I have noted—their presence varies in degree, form, and explicitness. For example, one of Dreiser's principal motives in the Cowperwood trilogy is to celebrate the amoralism of the struggle for existence at the expense of a traditional moralism, while much of his writing of the 1930s is devoted to redressing an equation which has shifted too much in favor of the Cowperwoods of the world. But always there is for Dreiser the beauty which is inseparable from conflict, a beauty which is both a sensitivity to physical symmetry and grace and an intuitive responsiveness to the fullness and richness of life. Toward the close of his career, as reflected in the final sections of *The Bulwark* and *The Stoic*, beauty becomes both aesthetic and moral. Celebrating all life as beautiful, Dreiser absorbs and resolves all ethical dilemmas and paradoxes within a faith in the transcendent goodness of the inexplicable force which makes for beauty in life.

But I am of course running ahead too far and too swiftly. And I am overclarifying and overabstracting Dreiser's early thought and expression by isolating too neatly these three thematic threads in "The Shining Slave Makers." It should nevertheless be apparent that Dreiser did not begin to write *Sister Carrie* in the fall of 1899 with his ideas as unformed as was his notion of his plot at that point. Rather, he had already shaped in his mind the beliefs which could give rise to an affirmative portrayal of a promiscuous girl who was seeking to rise in a world of struggle and to a depiction of an awesome beauty in the collapse of a man who had failed to hold his place in that world.

ccccccccccccccccccccccccccccc

Despite the superficiality of "When the Old Century Was New," it too anticipates several of Dreiser's major themes. The story dramatizes above all the thesis that life is impermanent. New York in 1801 is the capital of the country, Wall Street is only semiurban, and the Bowery is completely rural. Moreover, by setting the story exactly 100 years before its publication date, Dreiser enforces the moral that the New York of 1901, with its seemingly indestructible solidity, will also someday disappear or be changed. Dreiser's belief in the importance of change in human affairs is of course closely related to his evolutionary ideas. "No thing is fixed," he stated again and again in various ways throughout his career, "only a balance is maintained."[27]

Both as an idea and as a fictional theme dramatized by the device of a changing cityscape, the concept of transience or impermanence is a nineteenth-century truism. Dreiser, however, as in his representation of the idea of the struggle for existence in "The Shining Slave Makers," qualifies the concept in several distinctive ways and thereby makes it one of the significant and compelling themes in his fiction. First, in the minds of most Americans of Dreiser's day, the idea of change was indistinguishable from the idea of progress—progress in material life, in social justice, and in a fuller expression of man's ethical potential. To Dreiser, however, material advance by any one person or any segment of society was always at the expense of some other person or segment, and man's nature was a permanent reservoir of conflicting emotions, some conventionally called evil, others good. "Each new generation, new century," he wrote in 1927, "brings new customs, new ideas, new theories, but misery, weakness, incapacities, poverty, side by side with happiness, strength, power, wealth, always have, and no doubt, always will exist."²⁸ In "When the Old Century Was New," Dreiser therefore ironically undercuts the reader's expectation that a century's change is a century's progress. Young Walton at one point passes "the Collect [the city's reservoir], where is now the Tombs [the central prison of New York]." And as he walks along the idyllic Bowery at the end of the story, Dreiser comments:

Here young Walton, as so many others before him, strolled and hummed, thinking of all that life and the young city held for him. Here he planned to build that mansion of his own—far out, indeed, above Broome Street. He had no inkling, as he pondered, of what a century might bring forth. The crush and stress and wretchedness fast treading upon this path of loveliness he could not see.

Thus, everything changes and everything is the same in Dreiser's fiction. Carrie rises and Hurstwood falls, but bums beg in Chicago at the opening of the novel and in New York at its close. Cowperwood builds great street railway systems, but conniving and cheating mark every step of his career. Clyde goes to his fate, but a new Clyde, his cousin Russell, is to be pressed by Clyde's parents and by society into the same mold of restrictive moralism which led Clyde to rebel so violently.

Dreiser's ironic portrayal of the impermanent and permanent in life has yet another important characteristic. Young Walton is unaware of the process of change that will destroy the idyllic Bowery and make it yet another setting for the permanent human condition of wretchedness. Although he is living in the future, it is a future of his own imagining, of his hopes for a lovely bride, a proud home, and unending happiness. His "poetic mind" is "set dreaming" by the bucolic landscape, and he dreams of fulfillment of his hopes and expectations. To Dreiser the capacity to dream is the sustaining basis of life in a world characterized by the impermanence of purposeless change and the permanence of human weakness and misery. Dreams, of course, are not fulfilled, but they are a source of both strength and tragedy—a source, that is, of the significant and moving in life. "It is because we can and do dream—and must, at times—" Dreiser wrote in 1916, "and because of our dreams and the fact that they must so often be shattered, that we have art and the joy of this thing called Life."²⁹ For Dreiser's seeking or questing characters—Carrie, Jennie, Eugene, and Clyde—the material world has great importance, for they place much of their hope in the expectation of the gain of a loved one or of a desired object or goal. Yet the unyielding force in their lives is their unending dream of happiness or beauty or love, a dream which is both intangible and changeless.

♫♫♫♫♫♫♫♫♫♫♫♫♫♫♫♫♫♫♫♫♫

In "Butcher Rogaum's Door," Dreiser again used the city as a source of imagery and plot. To Dreiser, the city, with its sharp contrasts in conditions of life, dramatized more powerfully than any other phase of American experience the truth that the world was made up of the rich and powerful and the poor and oppressed. Moreover, the city, because it promised so much and delivered so little, was an apt field of action for the process by which the youthful aspirant to love, happiness, fame, and fortune discovers that hope is seldom fulfilled. It was an apt setting, in short, for the move from illusion to disillusion which marks all life.

Dreiser had himself, of course, experienced these various phases of city life by the time he began to write fiction in the summer of 1899. As a boy visiting Chicago for the first time in 1884, he had found the city " a veritable miracle of pleasing sensations and astounding and fascinating scenes. The spirit of Chicago flowed into me and made me ecstatic. Its personality was different from anything I had ever known; it was a compound of hope and joy in existence, intense hope and intense joy."[30] But Dreiser's years of struggle in Chicago and New York, and his close observation, as a newspaperman, of the cruelty and heartlessness of city life, led him to qualify his early response and to recognize the poverty and degradation beneath the luxury and beauty of the city.

Of course, the city as an example of the immense and increasing distance between the two worlds of the haves and have-nots had been a conventional theme in nineteenth-century European imaginative and social writing. During the 1890s, the theme received new life in America because of the combined effect of Jacob Riis's influential study of the New York poor, *How the Other Half Lives* (1890), and the widespread distress in the cities caused by the severe depression of 1893–94. In addition, the city had already served as a metaphor for the expression of two widely divergent yet complementary views of American life. To many commentators on American social life, the dramatic juxtaposition of wealth and poverty in a large metropolis was an example of the struggle for existence in operation. In the popular imagination, however, though the city was a place of danger, it was also the setting for the fulfillment of the Alger myth of success, in which youthful energy and perseverance found their just reward in good fortune.

These pervasive beliefs and assumptions of the 1890s about the city, as well as Dreiser's own experience, were powerfully affirmed and united for Dreiser in the novels of Balzac when he encountered them in the summer of 1894 while a Pittsburgh reporter. For Balzac's fiction expressed in a heady combination of sensational plot and authorial enthusiasm a Paris of gross contrasts in every phase of life but a Paris as well which to the young man from the provinces is a fortress to be conquered, a jewel to admire, a wine to intoxicate—a world, in short, of infinite beauty and delight as long as the heart and spirit have the strength and desire to seek. To both Balzac and Dreiser, the city was the supreme example of the richness and variety of experience, from failure and suicide to success and fame. It was the color of life.[31]

As I have already suggested in connection with Dreiser's treatment of the themes of struggle and change, one of his characteristic strengths as a writer was his ability to reshape the hackneyed into the complex and distinctive. He achieves this effect in his depiction of the city by his introduction of the theme of beauty into his portrayal. Thus, "Butcher Rogaum's Door" dramatizes, as an obvious theme, the dual possibilities of city life. Two New York girls seek romance in the form of youthful admirers. Both are locked out by their fathers, but one, Emily, becomes a prostitute and at twenty-one commits suicide on Rogaum's doorstep when her lover deserts her, while the other, Theresa, is saved from seduction when a policeman finds her and arranges for her return to her parents. In these parallel lives which eventually move in opposite directions because of the roles of strength or chance in determining one's fortune in the city, Dreiser crudely anticipates the careers of Carrie and Hurstwood and of Clyde and Gilbert.

But Theresa is more than simply a figure who illustrates one of the possibilities of city life. Like Carrie and Clyde and all of Dreiser's seekers, she partakes of two worlds—an external world which has an objective reality and an interior world which is the subjective, imaginative product of her need for beauty and happiness. Theresa's street is a commonplace working-class thoroughfare, but to her, because of her powerful desire to experience life, it is a place of romance and beauty. She "loved to walk up and down the . . . street, where were voices and laughter, and occasionally moonlight streaming down." And in this setting of laughter, voices, and moonlight, she finds someone whom she believes to be a lover, someone who urges her to escape the narrow, restrictive world of her parents' home. In Theresa, Dreiser begins to sketch one of his great themes—the power of the youthful, questing imagination to create the beautiful and desirable out of the tawdry and cheap. In an article "Christmas in the Tenements," published in 1902, he clearly spelled out this theme:

Over in the Bowery, that great thoroughfare which caters to the vanity and desire for amusement of all this submerged tenth, may be found a whirl of illusion, the glory of which, to these sweaters in the earthly treadmill, may not be eclipsed by anything that Broadway or Fifth Avenue can show. Sawdust and tinsel, the long rope of hemlock and the wreath of holly, lights, music, dancing, voices, singing, all these have here combined to produce a splendid night flower and glittering show piece, the beauty of which is as a magnet to the hearts of the weary.[32]

So Carrie and Clyde find in Chicago and Kansas City an Arabian Nights wonderland, a world of excitement and beauty which is primarily the product of their need for the exciting and beautiful. Dreiser's tone in rendering this distinction between the objective and subjective reality of the city takes its coloration from such key words in the above passage as "illusion," "magnet," and "beauty." To an observer who is no longer young or inexperienced or desiring, the "beauty" of the Bowery is merely tinsel and sawdust and cheap revelry in degrading surroundings. But to an observer who can sense the strength of the "magnetic" pull of desire, the "illusion" of "beauty" has a powerful and moving reality of its own.

Helen Dreiser once remarked that Dreiser "often read more beauty into things than existed,"[33] while Roger Asselineau has noted that "what Dreiser means by beauty is not plastic beauty, but the mysterious presence behind appearances of something wonderful which escapes his senses."[34] Both of these comments are in part true. Theresa is like Dreiser in that she has seen in Bleecker Street a beauty which is not objectively there. But she is also like Dreiser in that her intuitive discovery of beauty in the street resembles a religious experience in which man overcomes the limits of the senses in order to create an imaginative construct which pleases and satisfies. Dreiser's response to Theresa's vision of the beautiful thus blends two attitudes—compassion for the inevitable destruction of illusion by disillusion and acceptance of the emotional and psychological reality of illusion itself.

Which is another way of saying that Dreiser's epistemology contains a deep vein of romanticism. He shared not only the romantic poet's wonder and delight in the common realities of life but also his faith in the validity of the personal truth encapsulated in those realities. Dreiser's characters, like Wordsworth, also "perceive" and "half create." But because the focus of their vision is a cityscape rather than a landscape, the stream, field, tree, and flower of the poet become, in Dreiser's fiction, a street, theatre, hotel, and mansion. Nevertheless, Dreiser's world still has the resources of a romantic iconography. Man, in his fiction, still creates images of worship out of his immediate setting and then, through the imaginative strength of desire, transforms them into spiritual truth.

ⱲⱲⱲⱲⱲⱲⱲⱲⱲⱲⱲⱲⱲⱲⱲⱲⱲⱲⱲⱲ

"Butcher Rogaum's Door" contains a scene in which a policeman learns that Emily has committed suicide because she had been deserted by her lover. Though an experienced and hardened officer, he cannot help thinking, "Wonderful, wonderful. . . . Great, surging, maddening passion, that would rather die in a doorway than lose." Dreiser himself had seen many such incidents during his years as a reporter, and he too had seldom failed to respond with wonder at the tragic force that was human passion. In "Nigger Jeff," passion is narrowed to sexual hunger, and its victim is an ignorant Negro rather than a beautiful young girl. Jeff's animal sexuality and repellent stupidity, however, increase rather than lessen the usefulness of the story as an introduction to the sense of the tragic in Dreiser's work.

Davies, the young newspaperman who is sent to investigate reports of a sexual assault at Pleasant Valley, is at first a passive observer of the events leading up to the lynching. With professional rather than personal interest, he follows the mob which is pursuing the sheriff and Jeff and then views the successful ruse by which the attacked girl's father tricks and overpowers the sheriff. But after the mob drags the blubbering, terrified Jeff from the jail, Davies uncontrollably "clapped his hands over his mouth and worked his fingers convulsively." "Sick at heart," he accompanies the mob back to Pleasant Valley. The hanging itself stuns him into a deep torpor.

By the close of the story, after he has also visited Jeff's cabin and encountered his weeping mother, Davies has experienced a wide range of character and emotion—the competent, strong-willed sheriff, the cowardly mob, the father intent on vengeance, and above all the terrified Jeff and his heartbroken mother.

Davies's encounter with the sorrowing mother is the key scene in the story, since it reveals to him both the depth and the meaning of his own response to the lynching. As he views Jeff's body, he hears a noise in the room:

Greatly disturbed, he hesitated, and then as his eyes strained he caught the shadow of something. It was in the extreme corner, huddled up, dark, almost indistinguishable, crouching against the cold walls.

"Oh, Oh, Oh," was repeated, even more plaintively than before.

Davies began to understand. He approached lightly. Then he made out an old black mammy, doubled up and weeping. She was in the very niche of the corner, her head sunk on her knees, her tears falling, her body rocking to and fro.

On leaving the cabin, Davies "swelled with feeling and pathos. . . . The night, the tragedy, the grief, he saw it all.

" 'I'll get that in,' he exclaimed, feelingly. 'I'll get it all in.' "

"Nigger Jeff" is thus a story in which the viewer of an action comes into knowledge of the tragic realities of life. And since the observer is a reporter who will attempt to "get it all in," the story is also the dramatization of the birth of an aesthetic. That is, Davies discovers not only the nature and force of some of man's deepest emotions but also that these emotions and their consequences can and should be made part of a tragic vision of experience.

One such emotion is sexual desire. It is the first flush of spring, and Jeff, a poor, ignorant Negro, attacks a white girl—a girl who knows him and whom he meets in a lane. " 'Before God, boss, I didn't mean to. . . . I didn't go to do it,' " he cries to the mob. Although sexual desire may not lead to the destruction of such a figure as Frank Cowperwood, it is nevertheless a dominant, uncontrollable force in almost all of Dreiser's principal male characters. Hurstwood, Lester Kane, Eugene Witla, and Clyde Griffiths are at its mercy.

Another of man's deepest emotions is the unthinking love and loyalty which exists within a family and particularly between a parent and a child.

When Davies arrives at Jeff's home after the lynching, he asks the Negro's sister why Jeff had returned to the cabin after the attack, since the waiting sheriff had easily captured him there.

"To see us," said the girl.
"Well, did he want anything? He didn't come just to see you, did he?"
"Yes, suh," said the girl, "he come to say good-by." Her voice wavered.
"Didn't he know he might get caught?" asked Davies.
"Yes, suh, I think he did."
She stood very quietly, holding the poor battered lamp up, and looking down.
"Well, what did he have to say?" asked Davies.
"He said he wanted tuh see motha'. He was a-goin' away."

The son come back to say good-bye to the mother, the mother mourning over the son's body—here is emotion which in its overpowering intensity parallels the sex drive itself. It is the force which binds the Gerhardt family together, which is the final refuge of Clyde Griffiths, and which creates the tragic tension of Solon Barnes's loss of his children. In "Nigger Jeff," the force appears not only in the relationship between Jeff and his mother but also in the figure of the assaulted girl's father. Although Dreiser depicts the mob as cowardly and sensation-seeking, he respects the motives of the father. Both victim and avenger are caught up in the same inexplicable emotional oneness which is a family.

Like most of Dreiser's characters, the principal figures in "Nigger Jeff" have little of the heroic about them. Even the sheriff loses his potential for such a role once he is easily tricked by the mob and complacently accepts its victory. Jeff himself is described at the moment of his capture by the mob as a "groveling, foaming brute." But the major figures in "Nigger Jeff," despite their often grotesque inadequacies, feel and suffer, and the young reporter comes to realize the "tragedy" of their fate. To Dreiser, tragedy arises out of such realities of life as human desire and familial love. These realities do not lend "nobility" to his characters; like Jeff, they are often weak and contemptible even while suffering their fate. But their capacity to feel combined with their incapacity to act wisely or well is to Dreiser the very stuff of man's tragic nature. The realization which the young reporter must "get in" thus involves not only the truths of lust and of mother love but also the truth that the experience of these emotions lends meaning and poignancy to every class and condition of man. "Sometimes,"

Dreiser was to write about a weak but tragic character in *The Financier*, "the mediocre and the inefficient attain to a classic stature when dignified by pain" (p. 480).

In Dreiser's best novels, the themes of the power of sex and the lure of the beautiful join to produce his most characteristic expression of man's tragic nature. Hurstwood and Carrie are, to Dreiser, tragic figures, the first reaching out for life in the form of Carrie but unable to hold what he has won, the second desiring and gaining the beautiful but discovering that once gained it is no longer desirable or beautiful. These two principal kinds of human desire, the sexual and the aesthetic, appear in a single character in the only work of fiction which Dreiser explicitly called a tragedy. The tragedy of Clyde Griffiths, crudely put, is that of a seeker of sex and beauty who is destroyed by weaknesses within himself and his society as he attempts to fulfill his quest.

Dreiser's strength as a tragic writer resides in part in his ability to identify himself with the victims of desire in his fiction. In *Dawn*, Dreiser depicted sexual desire and family love as two of the compelling emotions of his own youth. He described the sexuality of his boyhood in Warsaw as "the molten, sputtering main theme pulsating and winding like a great river within the depths of my inner self."[35] And around the fixed point of Sarah Dreiser's all-encompassing love there circled the indivisible unity that was the Dreiser family.

Thus in "Nigger Jeff" Dreiser is not only Davies, the young reporter who is beginning to discover something about life, but is also Jeff, the victim of life's deepest emotions. In his characterization of Jeff, Dreiser had depicted the failings of an uneducated Negro farmhand, but he had also acknowledged Jeff's humanity. That is, Dreiser had reached down into his own inmost nature and had found in his own sexual compulsions and familial loyalties a tragic potential. This double identification, in which the artist-observer recognizes within himself the same drives and needs which have overwhelmed the tragic protagonist, is revealed fully in a sentence omitted from the published version of the story but present in its manuscript. Immediately following "the night, the tragedy, the grief, [Davies] saw it all," there appears in the manuscript, "it was spring no less than sorrow that ran whispering in his blood."[36] Spring and sorrow, sex and mother love—these sound deeply resonant chords within Dreiser whether he is in the guise of artist-observer in "Nigger Jeff," autobiographical narrator in *Dawn*, or seemingly neutral authorial voice in *An American*

Tragedy. Dreiser shares with all major tragic writers the ability to find within himself that identification with man's most powerful yet destructive emotions which makes for understanding and compassion. He is not only Jeff and Davies but will also be Carrie and Hurstwood, Jennie and Lester, Clyde and Roberta, and Stewart and Solon.

ᵉᵉᵉᵉᵉᵉᵉᵉᵉᵉᵉᵉᵉᵉᵉᵉᵉᵉᵉᵉᵉᵉᵉᵉᵉᵉᵉᵉᵉᵉᵉᵉᵉ

Dreiser's basic tendency as a novelist was to establish a clear central structure (Hurstwood's fall and Carrie's rise; Cowperwood's alternating business and love affairs; Clyde's parallel life in Kansas City and Lycurgus; Solon's double life as businessman and Quaker), to pursue this structure to its seeming conclusion (death or an emotional stasis), yet to suggest both by authorial commentary and by a powerful symbol within the narrative (a rocking chair, deep-sea fish, a street scene, a brook) that life is essentially circular, that it moves in endless repetitive patterns. Frequently this circular pattern involves a seeker or quester—sometimes driven by desire, sometimes by other motives—who finds at the end of the novel that he has returned to where he started: Carrie still seeking beauty and happiness; Jennie once again alone despite her immense capacity to love; Cowperwood's millions gone; Clyde still walled in; Solon returning to the simplicity of absolute faith. It is possible to visualize Dreiser's novels as a graphic irony—the characters believe they are pushing forward but they are really moving in a circle. Dreiser's early short stories anticipate this basic structure but do not achieve it fully in any one instance. "The Shining Slave Makers" offers the best example. The story has a single important character relationship, that of McEwen and Ermi; its "inner" time scheme is complete in that it comprises McEwen's life as an ant; and it has a double circular form—an inner circle of the initial rescue of Ermi by McEwen and the reversal of this event at the conclusion of McEwen's activities as an ant, and an outer circle of the awake-dream-awake structure. And though McEwen is hardly a seeker, his movement from ebullient participation in ant life to sorrowful resignation at the end of the story is a typical spiritual voyage for a Dreiser protagonist.

Another pervasive structure in Dreiser's novels is best illustrated by "Butcher Rogaum's Door." The three principal figures in the story—Rogaum, Theresa, and Almerting—can be characterized as a well-meaning but ignorant and authoritarian parent, a youth seeking the wonder and excitement of life, and a seducer who takes advantage of the conflict between parent and child. Rogaum, blind to the needs of youth, drives Theresa to rebellion, and she is almost seduced by Almerting. This triangle and the narrative which derives from it constitute an archetypal structure within the world of Dreiser's novels, though it is a structure which appears in increasingly complex and displaced forms. It is present in Carrie's departure from the Hansons' and her seduction by Drouet, in Clyde's rebellion against his parents and his seduction by the pleasures associated with the Green-Davidson hotel, in Roberta's parallel experience with her parents and Lycurgus, and in Solon's unworldly authoritarianism which drives his children into various kinds of worldliness while he himself comes to realize that he too has been seduced by a form of worldliness.

A third significant characteristic of the form of Dreiser's early stories is their tendency toward the parody of sentimental or hackneyed narrative patterns. In "The Shining Slave Makers," the relationship between McEwen and Ermi is an unconscious caricature of the "comrades in arms" motif in the historical romance, complete with a battlefield farewell and death scene. In "Butcher Rogaum's Door," Theresa's adventures are parallel to those of the poor but honest working girl who faces the dangers of the city in sentimental popular fiction. And in "When the Old Century Was New," Walton's experiences among the elite of New York are in the mode of the high-society romance popularized by Anthony Hope and Richard Harding Davis. Throughout his career as a novelist Dreiser was to rely on similar formulas, particularly those of the seduced country girl in *Sister Carrie* and *Jennie Gerhardt* and the Horatio Alger myth of success in the Cowperwood trilogy, *The "Genius," * and *An American Tragedy.* In most instances, he both used the myth and reversed some of its traditional assumptions. Carrie "rises" not only despite her seduction but also because of it, and Clyde finds neither luck nor pluck in his attempt to succeed. Like many major American novelists, Dreiser used the mythic center of American life as a base from which to remold myth into patterns more closely resembling experience as he knew it.

The various overlapping structures which I have been discussing constitute in their totality the formalistic expression of Dreiser's basic cast of mind, a cast which can best be called ironic. For though Dreiser seldom engages in verbal irony, he habitually relies in his fiction on an intricately interwoven series of narrative or structural ironies. That is, he constantly juxtaposes the true nature of a situation and a character's estimation of it in order to reveal the weaknesses either in the character's values or in ours, a revelation which is at once theme and form in his work. So McEwen awakens from imminent death as a warrior ant but sorrows rather than rejoices at his escape. Walton, planning his idyllic country home, is unaware of the misery and ugliness which progress will bring to his retreat. Rogaum locks his daughter out and discovers on his doorstep a dying girl whose father had locked her out a few years earlier. And Jeff is trapped and destroyed not only by lust but by his love for his mother. On the one hand, these are the conventional ironies of all fiction. Fiction—because it is a temporal rather than a spatial art, and because it dramatizes the difference between what characters believe and what the author knows—is inherently ironic. On the other hand, Dreiser's ironic formulas in his short stories look forward to a bolder and more intense reliance on this particular characteristic of fiction than is usual in most novels. Like Stephen Crane, Dreiser translated an uneasy mixture of iconoclasm and unconventional belief into a structural principle. But whereas for Crane this principle was a subtle and complex modulation in authorial tone, imagery, and diction, for Dreiser it was an equally sophisticated ordering of events within an extended narrative. Dreiser labored to perfect this technique throughout his career as a writer of fiction, and after some twenty-five years he achieved in *An American Tragedy* a novel whose structural approximation of his deeply ironic view of life results in a work of complex beauty.

PART ONE

Sister Carrie

MOST OF THE GENERAL and many of the specific sources of *Sister Carrie* have been known for some years. Scholars have noted that Dreiser drew loosely upon the experiences of his sister Emma and her lover L. A. Hopkins for his account of Carrie and Hurstwood in Chicago, that much of Dreiser's own sense of the wonder and terror and mystery of life enters into his characterization of Carrie adrift in Chicago and Hurstwood going under in New York, and that he borrowed directly from the work of George Ade and Augustin Daly. Recently, Ellen Moers devoted almost half of her *Two Dreisers* to a detailed study of Dreiser's reliance upon such diverse sources as the theatrical activities of his brother Paul, the pseudo-scientific theories of Elmer Gates, and the photography of Alfred Stieglitz. It would thus be possible to devote an entire book to a discussion of the origin of *Sister Carrie*, but I would like to confine myself to a detailed study of the sources of four specific aspects of the novel: the narrative of the rise of Carrie and the fall of Hurstwood, the character of Carrie, the streetcar strike, and the amateur theatrical, *Under the Gaslight*, in which Carrie stars. I have not chosen these examples at random. Rather, they illustrate a range of subject from the basic structure of the novel to its most complex character to specific scenes and incidents. They illustrate as well the variation in Dreiser's method from his almost literal yet subtly transformed use of a particular source to his fusing of a large number of influences into a single fictional element. The examples have been chosen, in short, to reveal some of the basic influences upon the novel; to illustrate the diversity of Dreiser's sources; and to suggest how Dreiser successfully but also occasionally ineptly shaped the crude blocks of his original material into a finished work of art.

Emma Dreiser, the prettiest of the five Dreiser sisters, was eight years older than Theodore. As a young girl in the small town of Sullivan, Indiana, she and her sisters Mame, Theresa, and Sylvia had been deeply interested in boys. By their late teens, they had had a series of affairs with well-to-do older men—manufacturers and store proprietors, town dignitaries and professional men—many of whom supported them for various periods. They were, Dreiser recalled, "not so much calculating as vain and unthinking."[1] Like her sisters, Emma felt stifled by the limitations of small-town life, by her father's moralism, and by the tediousness of the jobs open to young unskilled girls. After a number of affairs in Sullivan, she ran away to Chicago at eighteen or nineteen. When Dreiser saw her again in Chicago in the summer of 1884, she was twenty-one and was living contentedly with an architect. Sometime the following fall, after Theodore and most of the Dreiser family had settled in Warsaw, Indiana, Emma began in Chicago a more serious and portentous affair with Hopkins. A man of about forty, with a wife and daughter on the West Side, Hopkins had worked for fourteen years for Chapin and Gore, a firm which owned a number of Chicago saloons.

Throughout the winter of 1885–86, Hopkins visited Emma in a house maintained by her sister Theresa.[2] (Theresa was herself being kept by a middle-aged lover.) Since Hopkins frequently spent the night with Emma, his wife became increasingly incensed. On the night of Thursday, February 11, she employed a Pinkerton detective to follow Hopkins. With several witnesses in tow in order to gather evidence for a divorce proceeding, she burst in upon the sleeping couple. On Sunday the fourteenth, Hopkins, one of whose duties was to close the main warehouse of Chapin and Gore on alternate Sundays, absconded with $3500 in cash and $200 in jewelry which had been left in the firm's safe. Earlier that day an express wagon had called at Theresa's house and had removed Emma's trunk to a railway station, where it had been claimed by Hopkins. Immediately after the theft, he and Emma left Chicago on a train for Montreal, accompanied by her trunk.

In Montreal, Hopkins, whether motivated by fear, police pressure, or a change of heart, arranged to return the jewelry and most of the cash to Chapin and Gore, after which he and Emma went on to New York. There he became associated with the corrupt Tammany organization and for a time flourished in a soft job with the sanitation department.[3] He and Emma had two children and she became stout. But by the time Dreiser visited the couple for the first time in the summer of 1894 in their West 15th Street flat, their fortunes were on the decline. The Lexow investigations of 1894 had temporarily destroyed Tammany's power, and Hopkins had lost his job. For a time he and Emma had supported themselves by renting out rooms to prostitutes. Hopkins, who was now permanently unemployed, frequently mistreated Emma and was also unfaithful to her. Thoroughly sick of her life with Hopkins, she persuaded Dreiser during the winter of 1894–95 to aid her in a ruse to free herself from him. Dreiser, who had moved from Pittsburgh to New York that November and was living with the Hopkinses, pretended that he had to return to Pittsburgh in order to find work. After moving out, he had a friend mail a letter from Pittsburgh in which Dreiser asked Emma to come live with him. She thereupon seemingly left for Pittsburgh, though in reality she moved to another New York apartment.[4] Dreiser never saw Hopkins again, but he continued to see much of Emma and her children and aided them financially when he could.

Such, in bare outline, is the story of Emma and Hopkins. Dreiser had learned of it in various ways—from family conversation in Warsaw soon after the scandal of the elopement; from Paul in St. Louis in 1893; and from Emma herself in New York in 1894. Out of his awareness of the events in Chicago and his knowledge of Emma and Hopkins in New York Dreiser shaped a narrative rather different from what had actually occurred. The affair between Hopkins and Emma was from the beginning tawdry and occasionally comic. Hopkins was a lower-middle-class clerk, Emma a girl of considerable sexual experience, and their relationship had culminated in a scene out of a French bedroom farce. When discovered by Mrs. Hopkins in bed with Emma, Hopkins had cried out, " 'My God! Ma . . . is that you!' "[5] From farce the affair had moved in the direction of cliché: the planned robbery and elopement to escape the wrath of Mrs. Hopkins, the sorry decline of Hopkins into a sordid dependency and of Emma into a premature middle age, and the final separation. Dreiser transformed this unpromising material in three ways. He raised the social and moral level of the Chicago portion of the story; he created an almost totally new narrative for Carrie and Hurstwood in New York; and he deepened the characters of both figures.

For the "trusted employee"[6] who lives on the unfashionable West Side, Dreiser substituted the prosperous and respected upper-middle-class manager who keeps a well-appointed house on the North Side, the best section of Chicago. And for Emma, Dreiser substituted the comparatively fresh and innocent Carrie, a girl whose only previous fall was occasioned primarily by necessity. Most of all, Dreiser introduced moral depth and complexity into the theft and elopement. Instead of being merely a carefully planned event, in which fear and desire were apparently the principal motives, Hurstwood's theft and his abduction of Carrie are also characterized by indecision and the force of circumstance. Although *Sister Carrie* was often attacked during Dreiser's early career for its vulgarity and immorality, Dreiser's reshaping of his principal source was in the direction of "raising" and "refining" both his basic narrative and the thematic potential of that narrative.

The consequences of this process of heightening and cleansing can be clearly seen in Dreiser's almost complete neglect of Hopkins's and Emma's later experiences in his account of Hurstwood and Carrie in New York. The major similarity between Emma and Carrie is that they both have pleasure-loving temperaments. In Emma, this quality expressed itself primarily in shallow, indiscriminate sexual alliances. As Dreiser recalled Emma in *Dawn*, she resembles above all Drouet in that both have a good-natured, pleasure-seeking amoral attitude toward life. In his depiction of Carrie, however, Dreiser purified and elevated this aspect of character into a questing drive to fulfill herself and into an inherent ability to move others to appreciate the depths of human feeling. In short, Emma's sexuality matures not into the stout, defeated woman Dreiser encountered in 1894 but into the seeker of beauty and happiness and the actress of potential greatness who is the Carrie of the last chapters of the novel.

Hopkins underwent an analogous yet somewhat different transformation. Dreiser, of course, knew him only from his brief visit to New York in the summer of 1894 and from his few months' residence in the Hopkins flat during the winter of 1894–95. But from this impression of a listless middle-aged man, once successful in a minor way but now gone to seed, he created one of the most moving narratives in American fiction. The Hurstwood of New York is far from a literal study of Hopkins. For the details and emotional reality of Hurstwood's fall, Dreiser depended primarily upon both his own experience and a generic fear within the Dreiser family. Dreiser's father had been a successful mill owner, but he had failed in middle age and Theodore was raised in a home pervaded by the memory of better times and the nervous tension arising from a man who knew he was a failure. During the winter of 1894–95, while he was living with the Hopkinses, Dreiser himself began to fear that his career might duplicate his father's. A top-flight reporter in the comparatively small worlds of St. Louis and Pittsburgh, he had found himself unappreciated and unwanted by New York newspapers. By the late winter he was out of a job, and as he wandered the city hall newspaper area, he began to project his fears about the future into an identification of himself with the bums who frequented City Hall Park. One day, after visiting several offices with no success, he rested for a moment in the park.

About me on the benches of the park was, even in this gray, chill December weather, that large company of bums, loafers, tramps, idlers, the flotsam and jetsam of the great city's whirl and strife to be seen there today. I presume I looked at them and then considered myself and these great offices, and it was then that the idea of Hurstwood was born. The city seemed so huge and cruel. . . . At four in the afternoon I dubiously turned my steps northward along the great, bustling, solidly commercial Broadway to Fifteenth Street, walking all the way and staring into the shops.[7]

Dreiser's recollection is of an initial association of himself with the principal symbol of failure in American life, the Bowery bum, and then of a further association of his own restless wanderings through a rich and luxurious city with those of a Bowery derelict. It is associations of this kind which inform Dreiser's account of Hurstwood's decline in New York, for whatever Hopkins's state when Emma left him in early 1895 and Dreiser lost touch with him forever, he had not reached the condition of the Hurstwood who turns on the gas in a Bowery flophouse.

Thus, the entire New York half of *Sister Carrie*, with its closely observed and interwoven accounts of Hurstwood's gradual decline and Carrie's successful theatrical career, emerged primarily not out of Dreiser's knowledge of the New York life of Hopkins and Emma but out of the distinctive direction he had given his reshaping of Emma's and Hopkins's lives and characters in the Chicago portion of the novel. Dreiser did not merely retell the story of Hopkins and Emma in Chicago and then invent a new plot for the New York phase of their experience. Rather, he created from the first characters whose artistic temperament and whose apparent strength and position required denouements involving the pathos of success and the tragedy of failure instead of the commonplace, dreary, inconclusive fates of Emma and Hopkins.

Though Hurstwood is one of Dreiser's most effective portraits, Carrie is by far the more complex figure. Her complexity, as well as some of the discrepancies and weaknesses in her characterization, have their source in part in the diversity of influences affecting Dreiser's depiction of her. He relied initially, of course, on a base of Emma's physical attractiveness and erratic sex life. But for Carrie's essential nature—her capacity to dream and hope for the future and her emotional strength—he drew primarily upon his recollection of his mother and upon himself. It was Dreiser who had responded with wonder and desire to the possibilities of life represented by Chicago and New York and who, after much initial difficulty, had gained success. (His swift climb to success in 1898 as a magazine writer is comparable to Carrie's rapid rise as a comic opera star; his turn to the novel form is comparable to Carrie's projected undertaking of more serious dramatic roles.) And it was Dreiser's mother who had emanated an emotional responsiveness to life which Dreiser again and again character-ized as "pagan." Her all-embracing love had brooked no moral question-ing, and her faith in life had lent her a resiliency which often took the form of cloudy dreams and hopes of a better life in the future. Carrie, of course, is an artist, and her artistic temperament contains an element of deep-grained selfishness absent in Sarah Dreiser. But Carrie's moodiness, her amoral quest for the fulfillment of her desires, and her core of emotional power reflect some of the most striking personal qualities both of Dreiser's mother and of Dreiser himself. The pathos which Dreiser sought to introduce in scene after scene of Carrie dreaming in her rocking chair derives both from Dreiser's own strongly developed sense of self-pity as a never-to-be-fulfilled seeker of happiness and, even more significantly, from his compassionate awareness of the kind of temperament he identified above all with his beloved mother.

Carrie's successful career as an actress represents, of course, Dreiser's attempt to find a satisfactory fictional vehicle for the expression of both her emotional power and her will to succeed. From his days as a stage-struck adolescent in Chicago, Dreiser had been fascinated by the theatre. He had turned this absorption to professional use as a play reviewer for the *St. Louis Globe-Democrat* during 1893–94 and as the author of a theatrical column for *Ev'ry Month* during 1895–96. Allied to Dreiser's interest in the stage was his life-long absorption in the feminine artistic temperament. *Ev'ry Month* was primarily a woman's magazine (its subtitle, after January 1897, was "The Woman's Magazine of Literature and Music"), and many of its features were about woman musicians, authors, lawyers, and so on. It was also a magazine whose principal commercial purpose was to popularize the songs which were the major attraction of each issue. Thus, for more than two years Dreiser was at the center of a seething world in which the Broadway success of a song or an actress was a fairy-tale-come-true. Carrie's theatrical career thus derives from Dreiser's *Ev'ry Month* years in two senses. He acquired in the offices of Howley, Haviland, & Company, as well as through his brother Paul, who was the principal asset of that firm, an intimate knowledge of the musical-comedy world in which Carrie so quickly rises.[8] And as he compared the lives of the women he had known—and particularly the women of his own family—with those of the many actresses he was meeting both professionally and socially, he decided, as he later put it in *A Traveler at Forty*, "that the stage is almost the only ideal outlet for the artistic temperament of a talented and beautiful woman."[9] Carrie becomes an actress in New York not merely because it is a career in which a woman can succeed rapidly but because the stage represents the best "objective correlative" of her essential nature.

Dreiser's depiction of Carrie as initially a fresh, illusioned seeker of life's bounty and finally a worldly wise actress has a heavy touch of the sentimental, even of the lachrymose. In his youth Dreiser had been an avid reader of the sentimental novels which filled the cheap weekly newspapers of the time,[10] and as he grew older he came to know the work of such popular sentimental authors as Bertha M. Clay, Laura Jean Libbey, E. P. Roe, and Albert Ross. In later life he frequently cited the success of these writers as evidence of the low state of American popular taste.[11] Both his early fascination and his later contempt for the sentimental heroine affect his portrait of Carrie. The overlay of the sentimental in Carrie is most evident when Dreiser deals closely with her sexual fall. Because Carrie's initial situation closely resembles that of the innocent young girl from the country who is seduced by the city villain, Dreiser falls unconsciously into the language of absolute morality of the sentimental novelist. "When a girl leaves her home at eighteen," he tells us early in the first chapter, "she does one of two things. Either she falls into saving hands and becomes better, or she rapidly assumes the cosmopolitan standard of virtue and becomes worse" (p. 2). Moreover, the basic pattern of Carrie's fall (she is a victim first of need and then of deceit), as well as Dreiser's use of such stock devices as the mock marriage, bring the novel close to such best sellers of the day as Bertha M. Clay's *Dora Thorne* (1883) and *A True Magdalen* (1886), E. P. Roe's *Barriers Burned Away* (1872), and Laura Jean Libbey's *A Fatal Wooing* (1883) and *Only a Mechanic's Daughter* (1892).[12] Yet despite Dreiser's apparent acceptance of the absolute sexual ethics of sentimental fiction, he attempts throughout the novel to dissociate Carrie from the traditional consequences of a sexual fall—disgrace, a tormented conscience, pregnancy, and death. Although Carrie is a "fallen woman," she suffers few of the pangs and none of the misfortunes of the type.

Much of our difficulty in responding correctly to Carrie stems from Dreiser's unresolved mixture of parody and acceptance of the myth of seduction and from his wavering reliance upon different threads of self-identification in her characterization at different points in the novel. During the Chicago portion of *Sister Carrie*, Carrie's situation as a soul in travail dominates her characterization. Although her later emergence as an independent and powerful spirit is anticipated by her Avery Hall success, in Chicago she is above all a "half-equipped little knight" who is "adrift on the sea of life"—two pervasive images which firmly associate her with the plight of the sentimental heroine. Dreiser's chapter titles are also in this vein. Carrie as a "spirit" in peril and Hurstwood as the "flesh" in pursuit make explicit the moral stereotypes of the sentimental novel within which Carrie and Hurstwood are in part functioning. But as Carrie develops as an artist in New York and as she comes under the influence of Ames, Dreiser increasingly finds in her qualities of maturity similar to those of his own early New York years. Whereas in Chicago she was a reader of the novels of Bertha M. Clay, as was Dreiser in his youth, in New York she is led by Ames to pursue the works of Balzac and Hardy,[13] precisely the same authors who had most affected Dreiser's own development.[14] Thus, because Carrie's early naïveté resembles Dreiser's notion of his youth, he half-patronizes her when she arrives in Chicago. The image of a "half-equipped little knight" reflects this attitude of mind as well as her situation as a seduced country girl. And because Carrie's development into a conscious seeker of beauty closely resembles Dreiser's mature conception of himself, he rather gushingly overidentifies with her at the close of the novel.

In their revision of *Sister Carrie*, Dreiser and Arthur Henry seemed to have realized some of these discrepancies in the depiction of Carrie and to have attempted to correct them. In order to conclude the novel on the note of pathos which dominated his early characterization of Carrie, Dreiser rewrote the conclusion and added a Balzacian epilogue in which Carrie, alone in her rocking chair, broods about the future. Considered in relation to the form of the novel, the scene is successful, since it reintroduces a theme and a symbol which Dreiser had earlier developed with some fullness. But the language of the scene is that of Dreiser at his sentimental worst—the language of "harps in the wind," of "titled ambassadors of comfort and peace," and above all of "a lone sheep bell o'er some quiet landscape." Dreiser returns, in short, with an anomalous abruptness to the hackneyed and clichéd language of pathos which had characterized his depiction of Carrie in Chicago. Moreover, Dreiser and Henry cut and revised many of the passages in the Chicago section of the novel which deal with Carrie's limitations, since these passages present too fully or emphatically qualities in her character which are neglected or contradicted by her later development. So, for example, while living with Drouet, Carrie listens to a neighbor play a pathetic melody on the piano. In Chapter XI of the holograph, Carrie is described as follows: "She was not delicately moulded in sentiment and yet there was enough in her of what is commonly known as feeling to cause her to answer with vague ruminations to certain wistful chords."[15] In the typescript, however, Dreiser revised the passage to read: "She was delicately moulded in sentiment, and answered with vague ruminations to certain wistful chords."

Yet despite revisions of this kind, Carrie still emerges from the pages of the novel as neither completely focused nor convincing. As a figure compounded out of Emma, out of the sentimental heroine, and out of Dreiser's own view of himself at various moments in his career, she reveals more the diverse and often unharmonious strands of her origin than a single controlling characterization.

In contrast with his difficulties with Carrie, Dreiser's narrative of one of the most powerful episodes in the novel—the Brooklyn streetcar strike—illustrates his ability to combine the personal and the documentary into an effective fictional reality. Strikes by public transportation workers were common in the 1890s. While wandering through the Midwest in the spring of 1894 in search of work as a reporter, Dreiser acquired a temporary job in Toledo, which was in the midst of a streetcar strike. His assignment was to ride as a passenger on a car manned by scabs and managerial staff and to report his experiences. His long account, which appeared in the *Toledo Blade* on March 24, is semijocular in tone.[16] The strike was comparatively nonviolent, and Dreiser had not as yet encountered the appalling conditions of the Pittsburgh steelworkers which were for the first time to lead him to question the well-being of the American working man. Nor had he as yet experienced his own unemployment and subsequent depression in the winter of 1894–95. He could therefore easily fall into a mock-heroic tone as he described the adventures of the car and its occupants.

In January 1895, however, when Dreiser was out of work and, like Hurstwood, was spending much of his time reading newspapers, there was a fully reported and much more serious streetcar strike in Brooklyn. Cars were overturned and burned, scabs beaten, and there were open clashes between the strikers and the state militia. In writing the strike chapters of *Sister Carrie*, Dreiser drew upon both incidents. He relied upon his Toledo experience for the basic narrative of Hurstwood's taking a car out into the hostile streets. But for almost all other details he turned to the Brooklyn strike. And like the trained researcher he had become during his free-lance magazine years, he did not depend on his memory of the events of January 1895, but rather looked up reports of the strike in the New York newspapers of that period. Thus, details of geography and weather of the Brooklyn strike, the exact nature of the strikers' demands, and the mood and actions of the mob,[17] all combined with Dreiser's renewed—and no doubt reinterpreted—memory of the Toledo car ride and strike atmosphere to create one of the best portrayals of industrial violence in American fiction to that time.

In the course of his narrative of the strike, Dreiser printed verbatim a circular published in the *New York Times* of January 15, 1895, in which the Atlantic Avenue Railway offered work to strike-breakers. Although the circular contributes a note of documentary authenticity to Dreiser's account, its principal effect is more significant. Hurstwood reads the circular and is moved to respond to it at a point when Carrie's suggestion that he has been stealing from the grocery money has piqued him into a last, desperate desire to reassert his independence and manhood. But of course his action is both foolhardy and inconsequential, since a career as a scab is more a futile gesture than a means toward self-assertion and self-renewal. Dreiser's skill as a documentary novelist—a skill which was to reach its peak in *An American Tragedy*—lay not merely in his ability to research apt incidents. It lay rather in his ability to infuse these incidents both with a personal emotion derived from his own experience and with a thematic thrust closely related to a basic direction of the novel. Although *Sister Carrie* contains a vivid account of a strike, the novel does not explore the problem of social justice posed by the industrial violence of the 1890s—a problem which had occupied William Dean Howells in his depiction of a similar strike in *A Hazard of New Fortunes* and which had led Dreiser to explicit comments in several of his *Ev'ry Month* editorials.[18] Dreiser's intent, rather, was to establish dramatically the futility of Hurstwood's attempt to reclaim himself. This theme emerges starkly and forcefully from the juxtaposition of the deceptive neutrality of the circular and the emotional reality of such scenes as Hurstwood surrounded by a derisive crowd of strikers in a cold, bleak Brooklyn street and Hurstwood back in the warm comfort of the flat and his rocking chair close to the radiator where he can read about the strike in his newspaper.

Dreiser appears to use his sources even more literally in his reliance on Augustin Daly's *Under the Gaslight* as the play in which Carrie gains success in an amateur theatrical. Daly's famous melodrama, first produced in 1867, had been published in 1895, and Dreiser turned to this version for his verbatim quotes. With some minor exceptions, he was faithful to the plot and dialogue of the play, both in the rehearsal scenes and in the actual performance on the evening of the Elks' benefit. Yet by a careful selection of material, Dreiser shaped the plot and dialogue of *Under the Gaslight* into a subtle and ironic commentary on the themes and characters of *Sister Carrie*. Thus, he omitted almost all the comedy and physical melodrama of the play, including its two most popular features—a comic Civil War veteran named Snorkey and a scene in which the heroine, Laura, chops her way out of a railway shed in order to save Snorkey, who has been tied to the rails by the villain. Dreiser focused instead on the role of Laura, the noble-spirited, self-sacrificing society girl who, when revealed to be of low birth, is rejected both by her fiancé and society. Even within this narrowing down of the play, Dreiser pruned carefully, for he omitted the last act, in which Laura is proven to be genuinely high born and in which she and her fiancé Ray are reunited. His intent was to stress, through cutting and through judiciously selected dialogue, the selfless idealism, born of love and superior to all social distinctions, which Laura represents, and then to play upon the relationship between this melodramatic sentiment and the "real" sentiments embodied in the themes and action of the novel.

One such interplay involves the ironic resemblance between the outrageously contrived melodramatic situations of the play and the seemingly commonplace yet equally melodramatic reality of the lives of Carrie, Hurstwood, and Drouet. Instead of the secret births, hidden identities, and last-minute revelations and rescues of the play, we have the "real" melodrama of Carrie performing under an assumed name while her two lovers—one of whom is living with her but has refused to marry her, the other of whom secretly desires her but has not told her he is married—sit side by side in a box and admire her performance. A second large irony emerges out of Carrie's identification with Laura's situation as a woman who has been spurned by society because of her low origins yet who is able to act with a generosity of spirit in releasing her lover for a more suitable match. Not only Carrie but also Drouet and Hurstwood catch fire at the high moralism of Laura's speeches. Yet all three figures live by a code of selfish amoralism, a code shaped by the drive to fulfill desire without thought of the consequences to others. Each, indeed, is living by that code at the very moment he is luxuriating in the warmth of an identification with noble sentiments nobly expressed.

The performance of *Under the Gaslight* at Avery Hall contributes in several other ways to the characterization of Carrie and Hurstwood and to the advancement of the plot of the Chicago portion of the novel. But I have introduced Dreiser's use of *Under the Gaslight* at this time primarily to make the point that at his best Dreiser had the ability to adopt a source almost literally and yet to manipulate and mold his seemingly inert matter into new shapes expressive of layer upon layer of implication for the novel in which the borrowing occurs. Dreiser's technique in these instances of his use of his sources can perhaps best be described as that of eclectic absorption. That is, he had the novelist's ability to use everything in his experience, from his vague memory of a romance read in adolescence to a document scrupulously researched, yet to transform all into something essentially new and unique. Like Henry James's ideal novelist, Dreiser was one on whom nothing was lost. But also in Jamesian terms, the result of this assimilative strength was a personal impression of life.

ꞔꞔꞔꞔꞔꞔꞔꞔꞔꞔꞔꞔꞔꞔꞔꞔꞔꞔꞔꞔꞔꞔꞔꞔꞔꞔ

In his May 13, 1916, letter to Mencken, in which he described his beginnings as a short-story writer, Dreiser went on to recount the history of the composition of *Sister Carrie*. After he had completed his initial group

of stories at Maumee, he recalled, Arthur Henry had begun
to ding-dong about a novel. I must write a novel, I must write a
novel. . . . He had a novel in mind—*A Princess of Arcady* (Doubleday
Page—1900—same year as *Carrie*). He wanted to write it but he needed
me, he confessed, to help him. Finally—September 1899 I took a piece of
yellow paper and to please him wrote down a title at random—*Sister
Carrie*—and began. From September to Oct. 15th or thereabouts I wrote
steadily to where Carrie met Hurstwood. Then I quit, disgusted. I thought
it was rotten. I neglected it for two months, when under pressure from him
again I began because curiously he had quit and couldn't go on. (Isn't that
strange?) Then I started and laughed at myself for being a fool. Jan. 25th or
thereabouts I quit again, just before Hurstwood steals the money, because
I couldn't think how to have him do it. Two months more of idleness. I was
through with the book apparently. Actually I never expected to finish it.

About March 1 he got after me again and under pressure I returned to
it. This time I nearly stopped because of various irritating circumstances—money principally—but since he was there to watch I pressed on
and finally got it done. I took an intense interest in the last few [chapters]
much more so than in anything which had gone before. After it was done
considerable cutting was suggested by Henry and this was done. I think all
of 40,000 words came out. Anyhow there is the history.[19]

Sister Carrie was published on November 8, 1900, a little more than a year
after Dreiser wrote its title on a blank sheet of small-sized yellow paper.
Though not all the events of that year which bear on the composition of
Sister Carrie are known, we nevertheless have a clearer picture of the history
of the writing of this work than for any other Dreiser novel.

One of the provocative details in Dreiser's account of the composition
of *Sister Carrie* is his insistence that he began the novel with no other plan
than a randomly selected title. In a 1930 conversation with Dorothy
Dudley he made this claim even more explicitly than in this earlier letter to
Mencken. "Yes," he told her, "My mind was a blank except for the name. I
had no idea who or what she was to be. I have often thought there was
something mystic about it, as if I were being used, like a medium."[20] Yet in
1938, in reply to a series of questions by Michael Kowan about his writing
habits, he wrote, "I cannot imagine myself ever sitting down and figuring
out a plot without the characters, their emotions, environment, and the
ensuing scenes being quite clear in my mind at the time."[21] A reconciliation between these two theories of composition—the mystic and the fully
preconceived—perhaps lies in the title "Sister Carrie." Emma Dreiser's
full name was Emma Wilhelmina, and she was frequently called Minnie

within the Dreiser family. Dreiser's "at random" title echoes both his own sister's name and relationship and Balzac's family novels, such as *Cousine Bette* and *Père Goriot*. In these novels the familial adjective correctly implies a family novel—a novel in which the relationship of Bette and Goriot to their families is a major subject in the work. For Dreiser, however, the title "Sister Carrie" was immediately evocative of—and no doubt stimulated by—the story of his own sister. By writing the title Dreiser was signifying that he wished to write a Balzacian novel about the adventures of his sister Emma, and with the title on the page before him he thus had immediately at hand "the characters, their emotions, environment, and the ensuing scenes." For in Emma and her architect lover and Hopkins, and in the theft and elopement of Hopkins and Emma, he had a base of character and narrative sufficient for him to begin swiftly and with apparent ease that process of reshaping his sources which for Dreiser was the act of writing fiction.

Dreiser began the novel in September or October (he cited both dates at various times) and worked steadily to the close of Chapter IX,[22] at which point Hurstwood is about to call on Carrie and Drouet for the first time.[23] After a break of almost two months, he returned to the novel and wrote another seventeen chapters, reaching but not writing Chapter XXVII, in which Hurstwood steals the money. During this second interruption, in late January, he made an extensive reporting trip. In mid-February, he returned once more to the novel and writing rapidly completed it in late March. Ellen Moers therefore posits three six-week writing spurts and two major interruptions. She and other scholars discount Dreiser's recollection in 1930 of a third interruption, during the writing of the account of Hurstwood's decline. He stopped work, he recalled, because he "felt unworthy to write all that. It seemed too big, too baffling."[24] Miss Moers and others suggest that Dreiser in this instance was confusing his intense involvement with Hurstwood's fate (correctly recalled in his 1916 letter to Mencken) with an interruption.

Dreiser's difficulties with the composition of these major episodes—the first meeting between Carrie and Hurstwood and Hurstwood's theft—were undoubtedly the result of his need to go beyond his sources at points where his sources were still providing the structural framework of the novel. The cheap adultery and planned robbery and elopement of Emma and Hopkins were no longer relevant to his themes or to his characterization of Carrie and Hurstwood as the novel took shape under his pencil. Emma, for example, undoubtedly knew, while living with Hopkins, that he was a married man with a family, and Hopkins, of course, carefully planned the theft. But Dreiser, from the very opening of the novel, had stressed the themes of Carrie's "innocence" and Hurstwood's lack of foresight. His task, therefore, was to create new plot situations to accommodate his recasting of his central characters. His interruptions represent a creative hiatus familiar to most writers, a halt in composition while the subconscious wrestles with the dilemma that caused the interruption. On both occasions, when he returned to the novel he had solved the problem. Hurstwood disguises his marriage from Carrie, a deception which preserves her innocence. And his theft is a closely woven account of the role of fear, desire, and accident in human affairs rather than a narrative of a preconceived crime.

In his recollections of the composition of *Sister Carrie*, Dreiser stressed the importance of Arthur Henry in encouraging him to take up the novel again after these long interruptions. The holograph of the novel reveals that Henry played a similar though less important role at other stages as well. It appears that at several additional points when Dreiser had difficulty continuing, Henry would read to that point and then pick up the plot for a few pages, after which Dreiser would again proceed. There are three such sections in Henry's handwriting: a passage toward the opening of Chapter XX involving the Hurstwood household; the first four pages of Chapter XLVI, later cut, which concern Hurstwood's efforts to sell the furniture which Carrie left behind when she deserted him; and a brief section of Chapter L on the Fleishmann breadline. The presence of these passages in Henry's hand reveals his close involvement in the first draft as well as in the revision stage of *Sister Carrie*. This early involvement reached a peak in the composition of the conclusion of the novel.

On the final page of the original holograph version of the conclusion of *Sister Carrie*, Dreiser wrote, "The End. Thursday, March 29—1900." This version differs from the published conclusion in two important ways. It contains a long section, almost thirty holograph pages, at the close of Chapter XLIX (the next-to-last chapter of the holograph), on the relationship between Ames and Carrie and on Carrie's growth under Ames's tutelage. And it ends with the death of Hurstwood rather than with the epilogue on Carrie which presently concludes the novel. The fullest account by Dreiser of his revision of this original conclusion occurs in a 1907 interview. He told the reporter:

There is one odd circumstance about the book. When I finished it I felt that it was not done. It was a continuous strip of life to me that seemed to be driven onward by those logical forces that had impelled the book to motion. The narrative, I felt, was finished, but not completed. The problem in my mind was not to round it out with literary grace, but to lead the story to a point, an elevation where it could be left and yet continue into the future. The story had to stop, and yet I wanted in the final picture to suggest the continuation of Carrie's fate along the lines of established truths.

The note, the exact impression that I sought, evaded me. The drain of sustained imagination was beginning to tell. Finally, with notebook and pencil I made a trip to the Palisades, hoping that the change of scene would bring out just what I was trying to express.

Finding a broad, overhanging shelf, I stretched out flat on my back and allowed my thoughts to wander—gave them a sort of open air holiday.

Two hours passed in a delicious mental drifting. Then suddenly came the inspiration of its own accord. I reached for my notebook and pencil and wrote. And when I left the Palisades "Sister Carrie" was completed.[25]

Considerably more, however, was involved in the revision of the conclusion than a single sustained imaginative effort on the Palisades. As Dreiser suggested in his 1907 interview, the principal weakness of the original conclusion was that Ames and Hurstwood received too much attention—Ames as the instructor of Carrie, Hurstwood by his death. This initial version left Carrie out in an emotional and narrative limbo, even though the novel begins with her arrival in Chicago and is essentially her story. Both Dreiser and Henry realized this structural weakness, and their revision was a cooperative effort. They began by sharply compressing the long Ames-Carrie section into the five printed pages it now occupies. In addition, they decided that the final two paragraphs of the initial version of the Ames-Carrie section, an effusion on Carrie which begins "Oh blind striving of the human heart," could serve as the basis for a much longer meditation on Carrie's past, present, and future life, and that this expanded rhapsody should be placed in the climactic position of an informal epilogue after Hurstwood's death. Henry and Dreiser then jotted down a number of notes in which they tried to sum up their final impressions of Carrie's career.[26] In Henry's hand, for example, is the note "Ames is not a matrimonial possibility. That is not his significance. Had she never seen him after his first [appearance] the effect would have been great—in as much as he opened up for her a further vista." And in Dreiser's hand is the comment, "Carrie is an illustration of the by what devious ways one who feels, rather than reasons, may be led in the pursuit of beauty." Using these notes, Dreiser wrote—whether on the Palisades or elsewhere—a draft of the Balzacian epilogue on Carrie which now concludes the novel. Henry then made a fair copy of this draft, a copy which includes various verbal revisions, and it is this fair copy which became the text for the conclusion as published.[27]

Dreiser's and Henry's revision of the conclusion of *Sister Carrie* significantly altered the theme as well as the form of this portion of the novel. The cut and compressed material dealing with Ames and Carrie strongly suggested a burgeoning romance between the two figures, while the epilogue stressed Carrie's loneliness and unhappiness. The revision thus returned Carrie to her role as a pathetic heroine despite her "rise" in New York.

Except for the major revision of the conclusion, the holograph version of *Sister Carrie* shows little sign of extensive reworking.[28] The manuscript contains many minor verbal changes—some by Henry, though most by Dreiser—but these are primarily in the direction of verbal tidiness. Few revisions or cancellations involve more than a line.[29] In short, Dreiser was satisfied with the work as it stood and was anxious to get it into typescript and off to a publisher. In the fall of 1899, Henry and Dreiser had become friendly with Miss Anna Mallon, who ran a typing agency on lower Broadway. Henry soon began to court Miss Mallon, and when she received the holograph of *Sister Carrie* in April 1900, she undertook the typing herself and completed it with dispatch and correctness. With the typescript before them, Dreiser and Henry cut the novel extensively. Their motive was no doubt salability. The novel as published in the first edition by Doubleday, Page runs 557 pages. The 40,000 words which Dreiser and Henry cut (Dreiser's more or less accurate estimate) represent approximately 120 additional printed pages, a difference in length which, in a first novel by an unknown writer, would probably have led most publishers to turn down the novel out of hand. It was no doubt Henry who played the major role in suggesting a sharp reduction in length. As a former newspaper editor who had been editing much of Dreiser's magazine work of 1899–1900, he was aware of the advantages of judicious compression and of the wordiness of much of Dreiser's writing.

In later years Dreiser differed in his accounts of who actually did the cutting of *Sister Carrie*. In his letter to Mencken, for example, he implied that it was Henry. However, on other occasions he stated that both he and Henry were responsible. He wrote to Louis Filler in 1937, for example,

As for *Sister Carrie* being cut, it happened this way. When I finished the book, I realized it was too long, and I went over it and marked what I thought should be cut out. Then I consulted with a friend, Arthur Henry, who suggested other cuts, and whenever I agreed with him I cut the book. It was thus shortened to its present length.[30]

The typescript does not offer conclusive proof of responsibility because of the way in which lengthy sections were deleted. The longest omissions, sometimes as much as seven or eight typed pages, were made by literally cutting out the section involved and then pasting or pinning together the remaining portions of the typescript. Shorter cuts, from several paragraphs to a sentence, were made by x-ing out the passage being deleted. A characteristic of this second kind of deletion suggests that it was indeed Henry who was responsible for much of the cutting, for the omitted passages frequently have verbal corrections in Dreiser's hand. The sequence of editing, in other words, seems to have been first a verbal revision by Dreiser, with perhaps some cutting, and then a major shortening by Henry, including many passages which Dreiser had initially revised but not deleted.

Dreiser's and Henry's attempt to shorten *Sister Carrie* had a number of effects on the theme and form of the novel. As far as form is concerned, many of their cuts involved repetitious or overdeveloped material whose omission aided the fictional pace and balance of the novel. For example, the Chicago portion was cut more extensively than the New York section because it contained much discursive commentary on Carrie and Hurstwood which both clogged the fictional movement and overextended the first half of the novel. Other omissions, in both portions of the novel, eliminated or condensed overdeveloped characters, scenes, or authorial description. Thus, the two writers cut much of the material involving Mrs. Hale, Carrie's rooming-house neighbor in Chicago who instructs her in the ways of the city, and Mrs. Wilson, a New York neighbor who aids Carrie in finding a theatrical position. Both blocks of material are flabby; they contain a number of scenes of little dramatic or thematic thrust. In their revision, Dreiser and Henry compressed the Mrs. Hale material and eliminated the role of Mrs. Wilson entirely. Moreover, some scenes, such as the Avery Hall amateur theatrical, were severely cut because their length was too great within their fictional context. Others, such as Drouet taking Carrie for a carriage ride, were omitted because they were too close in theme and effect to similar scenes—in this instance, a carriage ride involving Mrs. Hale and Carrie. Finally, Dreiser and Henry cut obviously overextended or repetitious authorial comment—a brief essay on New York in the 1890s, for example, or a too frequent reminder that Carrie and Drouet are but "thinly bound."

The most important deletions in the typescript are the passages of authorial commentary which bear directly on the characterization of Carrie and Hurstwood. Many of these deletions are related to the obvious but significant fact that Dreiser wrote the Chicago portion of the novel first. Dreiser and Henry had been dissatisfied with the original conclusion of *Sister Carrie* because it failed to sum up adequately either Carrie's character or her life. In his new summation, Dreiser stated directly for the first time in the novel that the essential truth of Carrie's experience and temperament was her quest for beauty. This conception of Carrie is of course anticipated, even though not stated, throughout the novel. It is present in the Chicago portion in her expressive power at Avery Hall and in Dreiser's frequent comments about her emotional rather than intellectual strength. In New York it comes to the surface even more openly in her association with and response to Ames. But Dreiser's dissatisfaction with his initial conclusion and his struggle to articulate abstractly a conception of Carrie's ennobled sensibility reveal that his portrait of her in earlier portions of the novel may not have reflected this aspect of her character so clearly and so fully as he felt was warranted by his final estimation of her. In the Chicago portion of the novel, as I have already noted, he was in part characterizing Carrie in relation to Emma's rather soiled career and to Carrie's plight as a country girl in distress. Both of these aspects of Carrie's character led Dreiser to comment upon her sensibility in terms not entirely appropriate to a seeker of beauty and to involve her in incidents whose tonal quality also clashed with this view of her character.

Thus, Dreiser's and Henry's revision of the typescript occasionally represents their attempt to modify an earlier, less favorable estimation of Carrie in order to avoid contradictions between this earlier characterization and Dreiser's later apotheosis of her artistic temperament. The passage already noted in which Dreiser changed his initial comment that "Carrie was not delicately moulded in sentiment" to its opposite is one such example. In most instances, however, omissions which have the effect of "refining" Carrie's nature are inseparable from the basic intent of the revision of the typescript—to shorten the novel—and appear to be more a byproduct of that intent than a desire to revise her characterization radically. For example, Dreiser and Henry cut from Chapter XXVI of the typescript a long section, about fourteen pages in the holograph, describing in detail Carrie's attempt to get a job after she and Drouet have separated and after she has written to Hurstwood dismissing him. The account ends in a scene in which an obviously salacious-minded store owner offers her a position which tempts her despite its dangers. The section was cut primarily because it is repetitious both in action and theme. Dreiser had devoted a full chapter earlier in the novel to Carrie's job-hunting in Chicago, and Chapter XXVI itself contains a lengthy section on Carrie's attempt to discover how one obtains a theatrical position, a section which includes a stage manager who is also interested in her personally. It is no news to us at this point in the novel that men are interested in Carrie and that given their skill and her need she will succumb. Nevertheless, there is a coarse texture to Carrie's encounter with the store owner, a coarseness which, though it does not taint Carrie, adheres to her sufficiently to have probably encouraged a response by Dreiser and Henry, in the light of Carrie's New York rise, that the incident was especially extraneous and repetitious.

Some of the cuts involving Hurstwood in the Chicago portion of the novel seem to have a similar complex motivation. For example, in a passage cut from Chapter XIV, Dreiser commented at length on the failure of men in Hurstwood's position to realize that the fulfillment of illicit sexual desire is fraught with danger. "When after error, pain falls like a lash," Dreiser summed up, "they do not comprehend that their suffering is due to misbehavior." No doubt Dreiser and Henry cut this passage because of its discursiveness and length. But another, perhaps unconscious motive might have been that the tone of righteous judgment in the analysis of Hurstwood clashed with the initially neutral but eventually compassionate tone which characterizes Dreiser's depiction of Hurstwood's fall in New York. Again, as in the cuts involving Carrie, the omission does not reflect a major change in theme. Hurstwood's New York decline is itself an implicit judgment upon his lack of foresight in Chicago. Rather, Dreiser and Henry now found Dreiser's earlier hectoring tone inappropriate to the tragic force of Hurstwood's later fall.[31]

Dreiser submitted the heavily cut typescript of *Sister Carrie* to

Harper's in April.[32] When that firm promptly rejected the novel, he turned, in early May, to Doubleday, Page. Frank Norris was a part-time reader for Doubleday, Page, and largely on the strength of his enthusiastic endorsement of the novel, the firm accepted it for publication, even though Frank N. Doubleday was in Europe at the time. Dreiser's controversy with Doubleday, Page over the publication of *Sister Carrie* is one of the most famous incidents in American literary history, but the controversy is pertinent to this study only insofar as it influenced Dreiser's published work. Paradoxically, that influence is more evident in the tortured composition history of *Jennie Gerhardt* and in several of the themes of *The "Genius"* than in *Sister Carrie*. But there are, nevertheless, a number of ways in which *Sister Carrie* reflects Dreiser's difficulties with Doubleday, Page.

Even before Frank Doubleday returned from Europe in July and became intent on not publishing the novel, the firm had reservations about the work and was suggesting changes.[33] Walter H. Page, the junior partner, and Henry Lanier, a senior editor, were dissatisfied with the title, which, according to Arthur Henry, they thought not sufficiently "imposing and pretentious," and they had misgivings about Dreiser's Balzacian use of the names of living personages and actual business establishments, restaurants, and theatres. When Doubleday returned and the dispute over publication itself arose, these reservations became moot. They again became matters of contention when the firm finally agreed to honor its word and to publish the novel. The question of the title appears in the contract which was at last formally drawn up and signed on August 20, 1900, where it is "The Flesh and the Spirit" in an unknown hand and "or Sister Carrie" in Dreiser's.[34] Dreiser's use of real names also soon again became an issue.

Early in September, the typescript was returned to Dreiser with a personal letter from Doubleday himself. Doubleday conceded that the title of the novel should remain *Sister Carrie*, but he insisted that Dreiser remove profanity and that he should revise the names of living persons, etc. He went on to note that material of this kind as well as other passages about which the firm had doubts were noted in the margin by a question mark. Dreiser's response to this request was characteristic. In his reply to Doubleday, he wrote that he had cut "suggestive" lines noted by Doubleday's editor[35] and that he had changed such names as those of Francis Wilson, Charles Frohman, the Waldorf, the Morton House Hotel, the Broadway Central Hotel, and so on, but he attacked Doubleday's insistence that he revise other names as well as his request that he remove profanity. As a matter of fact, however, Dreiser did cut most of the profanity—principally some "damns"—but was wildly inconsistent in all other matters except that of the name of Hurstwood's Chicago saloon. Dreiser had called it Hannah and Hogg's because he mistakenly believed that this was the firm which had employed Hopkins. Once he made the change to Fitzgerald and Moy's, he was obliged, of course, to maintain this change throughout. In other instances involving names, he revised, for example, some allusions to Sherry's or the Waldorf, but let others remain unchanged,[36] and he omitted references to Francis Wilson and Lillian Russell, but retained those to Nat Goodwin, E. H. Sothern, and Joseph Jefferson.

There remains the vexing problem of the lachrymose chapter titles of *Sister Carrie*. Because they do not appear in the holograph and are entered in hand by Dreiser and Henry on the typescript, it has always been assumed that they were a late addition forced upon a reluctant author by a commercially minded publisher.[37] In fact, however, they appear to have been added by Dreiser and Henry during the process of cutting the typescript, before the book was submitted to Doubleday, Page. Because Dreiser was in Missouri visiting his wife's family from early July to mid-August, there is much extant correspondence between Dreiser and Henry (who was still in New York) and between Dreiser and Page on matters involving the novel. Though the issues of the title and names appear frequently in this correspondence, there is no mention of chapter titles. Moreover, the title which Doubleday, Page desired and which the firm included in the August 20 contract—"The Flesh and the Spirit"—can more reasonably be viewed as a response to the obvious allegorical use of the metaphors of Flesh and Spirit in the chapter titles than as a source of the metaphors. Dreiser was only once again to use chapter titles in a novel, and when *Sister Carrie* was published by Harper's in 1911, he regretted that he had neglected to use the opportunity to remove them.[38] It is therefore possible to surmise that though the wording of the poetical-allegorical titles is for the most part Dreiser's, the principal inspiration for their inclusion was Henry's. His was the more "poetic" temperament, Dreiser frequently noted, and in this instance Dreiser appears to have temporarily succumbed to the promptings of that temperament.

ᴄᴄᴄᴄᴄᴄᴄᴄᴄᴄᴄᴄᴄᴄᴄᴄᴄᴄᴄᴄᴄᴄᴄᴄᴄᴄᴄᴄᴄ

Almost all that is compelling and permanent in Dreiser's portrait of Carrie lies not in his sentimental and hackneyed overview of her as a spirit in travail—an overview expressed in the chapter titles and epilogue—but in his detailed dramatization of the actualities of her life as a young girl in the city.[39] Early in Chapter I, in a passage whose opening I have already cited, Dreiser introduces the theme of the role of the city in Carrie's life:

When a girl leaves her home at eighteen, she does one of two things. Either she falls into saving hands and becomes better, or she rapidly assumes the cosmopolitan standard of virtue and becomes worse. Of an intermediate balance, under the circumstances, there is no possibility. The city has its cunning wiles, no less than the infinitely smaller and more human tempter. There are large forces which allure with all the soulfulness of expression possible in the most cultured human. The gleam of a thousand lights is often as effective as the persuasive light in a wooing and fascinating eye. Half the undoing of the unsophisticated and natural mind is accomplished by forces wholly superhuman. A blare of sound, a roar of life, a vast array of human hives, appeal to the astonished senses in equivocal terms. Without a counsellor at hand to whisper cautious interpretations, what falsehoods may not these things breathe into the unguarded ear! Unrecognized for what they are, their beauty, like music, too often relaxes, then weakens, then perverts the simpler human perceptions. (p. 2)

The principal significance of this passage is Dreiser's characterization of the city as tempter and seducer.[40] Its lights and sounds speak with "superhuman" force to the "unguarded" ear of this new Eve. The city is thus a symbol of experience, and to the innocent it symbolizes above all the wonder of experience, of life, which lies before them. It seems to promise happiness, beauty, excitement, if one will only taste of the apple. It is therefore life, in this instance life in the guise of the city, which is the universal seducer of mankind. But the language of seduction, though it renders the force and appeal of the city for the innocent, is misleading in its moral implications. Carrie, as Eve, "falls" not because she is weak or because her human tempters, Drouet and Hurstwood, are evil, but because the apple is beyond resistance in its attraction. And life, though it is filled with terror and mystery as well as wonder, is not evil.

The Chicago portion of *Sister Carrie* is pervaded by scenes and incidents whose metaphoric intent is to enforce the emotional logic of Carrie's seduction by the city as an inevitable but morally elevating rather than degrading event. Initially, she encounters two cities. The first, which she instinctively rejects because it harks back to the sterility of Columbia City, is that of the Hansons' drab flat and dull lives, of oppressive factory labor, of unfashionable, shabby clothes, and above all of cold—the physical cold of the approaching winter and the chill emptiness of the Hansons' emotional life. The second is that of her dreams—a night city of theatres and restaurants, of physical warmth and comfort and good clothes. It is this second city which woos Carrie in the person of Drouet and which has a sensual and sexual attraction for her that Drouet himself lacks. Sometimes, indeed, Drouet is bypassed, and the physical objects of the city appear to address Carrie directly. "Fine clothes," for Carrie, "were a vast persuasion; they spoke tenderly and Jesuitically for themselves" (p. 111).

Dreiser's open and extensive use of an imagery of sexuality in describing Carrie's response to the city and his thin and covert suggestion of sensuality in his account of Carrie's relations with Drouet and Hurstwood are not the result of his simpleminded transference of a woman's sexual responsiveness from humans to objects because of the publishing restrictions of the day. His full exploration of woman's sexuality in the opening portions of *Jennie Gerhardt*, which he began soon after completing *Sister Carrie*, indicates that Dreiser had little hesitation in introducing the fact of feminine sensuality if that fact was appropriate to his themes. In *Sister Carrie*, however, Dreiser wished to communicate above all Carrie's desire for life. He introduced the sexual into this theme not merely as a metaphor of desire but as a condition of desire.

Of course, the objects which attract Carrie for most of the novel are not in themselves beautiful or even admirable. Dreiser realized that he had the difficult task of dramatizing the importance and worth of Carrie's longing despite the superficiality of that which she specifically desires—a modish jacket, an evening at a music-hall theatre, a warm restaurant. In a long discursive passage which was cut from the opening of Chapter XI, he attempted to explain and defend Carrie's desire. "The things that appeal to desire," he began, "are not always noble objects. Let us not confuse this with selfishness. It is more virtuous than that." In Carrie's case, he continued, her naïveté and limited experience combined to focus her desires on "fine clothes, rich food, [and] superior residence." Since these were not readily available, she unconsciously sought a way to make them available.

It must next be considered that if desire be ripe in the mind and no channel of satisfaction is provided, if there be ambition, however weakly, and it is not schooled in lovely principle and precept, if no way be shown, be sure it will learn a way of the world. Need it be said that the lesson of the latter is not always uplifting.

This deleted passage clarifies an occasionally misunderstood theme in Dreiser's characterization of Carrie. Some readers, finding her drawn to elegant tan jackets and observing that she accepts the sexual attentions of Drouet to gain such baubles, have concluded that she is not only shallow but also a gold digger. Dreiser, however, was attempting to represent a much more complex and genuinely pathetic theme—that the desiring imagination has the ability to create beauty out of the tawdry and to transform the illicit into the virtuous while in pursuit of the tawdry. By cutting his discursive analysis of this theme, he demanded of his readers a sympathetic identification with the worth and depth of the first powerful stirrings of Carrie's imagination of desire despite the "ignoble" and "not always uplifting" circumstances of the fulfillment of desire.

Because Dreiser portrayed Carrie as living illicitly with Drouet and Hurstwood in her pursuit of beauty, he felt compelled to enter the deep waters of the morality of her action. (Of course, she herself naïvely believes that she is married to Hurstwood, but to the reader their relationship is adulterous and therefore involves her ethical wisdom if not her absolute guilt.) At this point in his career Dreiser had not reached the conscious amoralism of The *"Genius"* and the Cowperwood trilogy, in which the satisfaction of sexual desire is openly characterized as part of a larger quest for the fulfillment of beauty or power. In *Sister Carrie* his ideas were more hesitant and his fictional expression therefore more indirect. This obliqueness sometimes deepens his themes and sometimes muddies them. I have already noted one way in which Dreiser attempts to come to grips with the moral problem posed by Carrie's "fall"—that in which the superhuman attraction of the apple absolves Eve from blame. Two other important ways are Dreiser's discursive grappling with the problem of evil in various philosophical passages in the novel and his dramatic portrayal of a spiritual rise in Carrie despite her sexual fall.

Dreiser summarized his philosophical speculations about Carrie's moral nature in his epilogue when he commented that "Not evil, but longing for that which is better, more often directs the steps of the erring. Not evil, but goodness more often allures the feeling mind unused to reason" (p. 556). His fullest and most complex apologies, however, occur at the openings of Chapters VIII and X, just before and after Carrie begins to live with Drouet. At the close of Chapter VII, Carrie has left the Hansons' flat at Drouet's urging and has moved to a room which he has taken for her. In nineteenth-century sentimental terms, she is soon to decide that a comfortable existence as a fallen woman is preferable to the hard life of a poor but honest working girl. Dreiser begins Chapter VIII with a lengthy commentary on Carrie's action:

Among the forces which sweep and play throughout the universe, untutored man is but a wisp in the wind. Our civilisation is still in a middle stage, scarcely beast, in that it is no longer wholly guided by instinct; scarcely human, in that it is not yet wholly guided by reason. On the tiger no responsibility rests. We see him aligned by nature with the forces of life—he is born into their keeping and without thought he is protected. We see man far removed from the lairs of the jungles, his innate instincts dulled by too near an approach to free-will, his free-will not sufficiently developed to replace his instincts and afford him perfect guidance. He is becoming too wise to hearken always to instincts and desires; he is still too weak to always prevail against them. As a beast, the forces of life aligned him with them; as a man, he has not yet wholly learned to align himself with the forces. In this intermediate stage he wavers—neither drawn in harmony with nature by his instincts nor yet wisely putting himself into harmony by his own free-will. He is even as a wisp in the wind, moved by every breath of passion, acting now by his will and now by his instincts, erring with one, only to retrieve by the other, falling by one, only to rise by the other—a creature of incalculable variability. We have the consolation of knowing that evolution is ever in action, that the ideal is a light that cannot fail. He will not forever balance thus between good and evil. When this jangle of free-will and instinct shall have been adjusted, when perfect understanding has given the former the power to replace the latter entirely, man will no longer vary. The needle of understanding will yet point steadfast and unwavering to the distant pole of truth.

 In Carrie—as in how many of our worldlings do they not?—instinct and reason, desire and understanding, were at war for the mastery. She followed whither her craving led. She was as yet more drawn than she drew. (pp. 83–84)

The philosophy of this passage combines Spencerian evolutionary ideas and popular "ethical culture" thought, a combination much in vogue among liberal, nondenominational clergymen in the 1890s. Man is pictured as a dualistic creature. He still responds instinctively to life because of his animal heritage, yet he is also capable of rational choice. Nature is the norm: if man were entirely instinctive in his actions, he would be in accord with that norm; if by free will he could choose the way of nature, he would also be acting correctly. Evolution is progressing in the direction of complete rational choice of nature's way. But at present man often finds himself divided and misled because of the conflicting pulls of instinct and reason.[41]

The passage, as becomes obvious in the short concluding paragraph, is an apology for Carrie's impending choice of an immoral life with Drouet. Carrie will sense the "wrongness" of the decision, Dreiser implies, because of the glimmerings of reason. But she is dominated by her instinctive needs—by the fact that Drouet represents at this point the full, rich life of Chicago which her imagination has pictured and that he will supply shelter, warmth, clothing, and food (as well as appreciation and a kind of love) on a level far superior to that offered by the Hansons and on a level commensurate with her "craving for pleasure." These instinctive needs associate Carrie with "the tiger [on whom] no responsibility rests"; but they do not dissociate her actions from moral judgment. Man's "reason" permits him to recognize that Drouet is an inadequate—that is, immoral—fulfillment of Carrie's instinctive needs. Carrie herself, however, finds her instinctive needs too strong, her reason undeveloped, and so she "followed whither her craving led. She was as yet more drawn than she drew."

Dreiser's attempt in the passage is to free Carrie from moral responsibility for her action—to suggest that not only Carrie but most men at this stage of evolutionary development are more led (and misled) than leading. But the passage also judges Carrie's action even though it does not judge Carrie herself. Going to live with Drouet—that is, sexual immorality—is not the "way of nature," Dreiser implies. Someday, when evolution has progressed further, the "ideal" and the "distant pole of truth" will unwaveringly guide man, and the unmistakable implication is that they will not guide him toward sexual promiscuity.

Less frequently discussed than this passage, but even more significant as a revelation of Dreiser's moral ideas in *Sister Carrie*, is the passage which appears early in Chapter X. Carrie is now living with Drouet, and Dreiser comments:

In the light of the world's attitude toward woman and her duties, the nature of Carrie's mental state deserves consideration. Actions such as hers are measured by an arbitrary scale. Society possesses a conventional standard whereby it judges all things. All men should be good, all men virtuous. Wherefore, villain, hast thou failed?

For all the liberal analysis of Spencer and our modern naturalistic philosophers, we have but an infantile perception of morals. There is more in the subject than mere conformity to a law of evolution. It is yet deeper than conformity to things of earth alone. It is more involved than we, as yet, perceive. Answer, first, why the heart thrills; explain wherefore some plaintive note goes wandering about the world, undying; make clear the rose's subtle alchemy evolving its ruddy lamp in light and rain. In the essence of these facts lie the first principle of morals. (p. 101)

Underlying this passage is Dreiser's belief that there are three different kinds of moral principles and that these exist in a hierarchal order. The first and lowest is the conventional moralism which judges Carrie in absolute terms. Minnie's dream, in which she sees Carrie falling into a pit or abyss, is a symbolic rendering of a conventional view of her liaison with Drouet. The second is Spencer's "liberal analysis" which Dreiser had seemingly endorsed at the opening of Chapter VIII but which he now finds limited because it only apologizes for Carrie without defending her. The last and least understood morality is that which derives from the heart or "feeling mind"; it is a morality which finds a rationale for action in an emotional response to the beauties of life. Both echoing and rejecting Spencer, Dreiser claims that this rather than conventional or evolutionary morality is the true "first principle" of ethics.

These three modes of moral judgment, the social, evolutionary, and aesthetic, appear in various contexts in the novel. The first mode is not merely a weapon of the self-righteous. Minnie, for example, though she condemns her sister, also sympathizes with her. And Carrie herself has a conscience, even though it "was only an average little conscience, a thing which represented the world, her past environment, habit, convention, in a confused way" (p. 103). It is the conventional moralism of Carrie's conscience which leads her to raise the question of marriage with both Drouet and Hurstwood. And it is characteristic of Dreiser's ironic treatment of conventional morality throughout the novel that she is only saved from the blighting effect of a marriage to either man by their reluctance to marry a girl they had already won.

Dreiser's evolutionary moral ideas appear primarily in the philosophical comments at the beginning of Chapter VIII and in a parallel passage in Chapter XXVII on Hurstwood's dilemma as he stands before the open safe. Dreiser's seeming endorsement of an evolutionary morality has to be qualified, however, by his more inclusive philosophical statement at the beginning of Chapter X and by his depiction of Carrie in later portions of the novel. As I will discuss at some length, Carrie's two illicit relationships are in fact the opposite of what Dreiser suggested about such relationships in Chapter VIII. They are moral rather than immoral, since they contribute to Carrie's "spiritual" development. The evolutionary morality of Chapter VIII must therefore be interpreted in relation to its limited and eventually qualified role in the novel as a whole. It moves us from the conventional morality of Minnie's dream at the close of Chapter VII to a more liberal ethical view, one which stresses the lack of responsibility of most men (including Hurstwood) for their actions. But it too will give way to another, even more liberal ethical position, one which is particularly attuned to an aesthetic sensibility such as Carrie's.

What I have called Dreiser's aesthetic morality appears in his overt characterization of Carrie, in his depiction of her relationship with Drouet, Hurstwood, and Ames, and in Ames's comments on art. By the end of the novel both the reader and Carrie have become aware of the ethical imperatives of an aesthetic sensibility in quest of beauty.

Carrie's response to Drouet, Hurstwood, and Ames is conditioned by two overlapping criteria—the relation of each figure to that in the city which she covets, and his relation to that which she has dismissed as wanting. The three men are therefore like rungs in a ladder, an image which Dreiser himself used. They are in hierarchal relationship to the quality of life which they represent and to Carrie's progress upward in understanding and values. Drouet has a twofold initial appeal to Carrie. Both on the train and in her encounter with him in downtown Chicago when she is out of work, he is the Chicago she desires—the Chicago of good clothes, fine restaurants, and the theatre. Moreover, by the time Drouet presses two soft $10 bills into her hand, he is far superior in Carrie's mind both to the crudely salacious factory workers and street loungers who have accosted her and to the dull emptiness of Sven Hanson. Thus, when Carrie is faced with the pressures of want and of a threatened enforced return to Columbia City, she can without difficulty accept living with Drouet and can indeed for a time find in him her desired comfort and ease.

Soon after they are settled in their Ogden Place flat, however, Carrie realizes that Drouet lacks the "keenest sensibilities" (p. 105). In addition, now that she has reached a certain plateau of worldly comfort, she is able to glance about her and to recognize the height of the mountain still before her and the inadequacies of Drouet as a guide. Mrs. Hale serves as a mentor who introduces Carrie to splendors of the city far above the aspirations of a Drouet but not the dreams of a Carrie. Hurstwood's arrival on the scene is parallel to that of Drouet earlier. He is a man of greater material substance and personal power than Drouet, as well as superior taste, experience, and sophistication, and Carrie "instinctively felt that he was stronger and higher" (p. 121). In addition, Hurstwood represents a fuller emotional life than she had known with Drouet. Unlike Drouet, he is responsive in Chicago to her potential depth as an actress, and he overwhelms her with the intensity of his desire for her. Drouet had won her in part because she needed him, but part of Hurstwood's appeal is that he needs her. His passion "exercised an influence over her, sufficient almost to delude her into the belief that she was possessed of a lively passion for him" (p. 222). Hurstwood, however, represents for Carrie less the excitement of a passionate lover than a means toward the fulfillment of her muddy and ever-changing notion of the beautiful and desirable. "She wanted pleasure, she wanted position," Dreiser tells us, "and yet she was confused as to what these things might be. Every hour the kaleidoscope of human affairs threw a new lustre upon something, and therewith it became for her the desired—the all. Another shift of the box, and some other had become the beautiful, the perfect" (p. 159).

So in her responsiveness to Hurstwood's interest in her, as in her receptiveness to Drouet during their crucial lunch in downtown Chicago, she permits the "warmth" of that which the man represents to obscure and lessen her moral qualms. Of course, Hurstwood's appeal is dampened by Carrie's discovery that he is married. With Drouet a "rung put behind" (p. 241) and Hurstwood discredited, Carrie faces the dismaying prospect of beginning again her struggles as an unemployed and unskilled working girl. Although she has dismissed both Drouet and Hurstwood, she does not wish to return to the condition of the Hansons, to the lascivious advances of shop owners, to hard, poorly paid labor, and perhaps even to Columbia City. She does not want Drouet and Hurstwood, but she needs the "comfort and ease" which they represent.

When Hurstwood tricks her into accompanying him on the train, Carrie is therefore in the same position as in the early stages of her relationship with Drouet. Again there is the same powerful combination of expediency and a temporary responsiveness to an attractive figure. Inside the train, as in the restaurant with Drouet, Carrie is confronted by an attentive, desiring man and his compelling world—in this instance, a comfortable Pullman on its way to the wondrous cities of the East. "Montreal and New York! Even now she was speeding toward those great, strange lands, and could see them if she liked" (p. 300). Outside it is cold and raining, and to leave the train would also mean a return to the difficulties of a struggle to exist in Chicago. Carrie's not getting off the train is thus a paradigm of the way in which she reaches decisions. In one sense, she does not make a decision. The train pulls into a station, and Carrie, confused and troubled, does not act. But in this instance, as in many others, her nonaction is equivalent to her drifting in the direction she subconsciously desires—to move up to the next rung with Hurstwood despite her anger and bitterness at his deception. As Dreiser remarks at one point, "Carrie had little power of initiative; but, nevertheless, she seemed ever capable of getting herself into the tide of change where she would be easily borne along" (p. 339). She cannot consciously choose because her reasoning power is weak and underdeveloped and leaves her helpless when she is confronted by a difficult decision or problem. But her instinctive sense of the appropriate direction her life should take acts as a force that places her in positions in which others will choose that direction for her. Thus, once the train is underway again, Carrie's spirits lighten, as though she had indeed taken a decisive and advantageous step. "She did not feel herself defeated at all. Neither was she blasted in hope. The great city held much" (p. 305). And in Montreal she accepts Hurstwood as a lover without thought or question or passion, since she had already accepted him on the train as a necessary adjunct of the new life which the cities of the East appeared to promise. "There was no great passion in her, but the drift of things, and this man's proximity created a semblance of affec-tion. . . . True love she had never felt for him" (p. 316).

The Chicago pattern of a spiritual move upward represented by a change in material possessions and male admirers is repeated in New York. The process begins, as it did in Chicago when Drouet had won her, with a period of seeming placidity and contentment, though the period is much more extended in this instance. But beneath this surface contentment, Carrie's nature begins to stir. Hurstwood, in the larger world of New York and without the fine manners of courtship, begins to lessen in her estimation. In a movement which ends only at the close of the novel, when she finds in him the spectre of complete poverty, he begins to go down in the scale of her values. At first, his care in money matters and his references to brighter prospects in the future merely recall Drouet. But later, the silent, morose Hurstwood, sitting by the radiator in their drab flat and reading his newspaper, conjures up in her mind distinct recollections of Hanson.

Carrie also finds in New York a mentor parallel to Mrs. Hale in Chicago. Mrs. Vance introduces Carrie to a New York world which she had dreamed of but which Hurstwood had been incapable of providing—that of fashionable Broadway and of Sherry's. And she also meets, through Mrs. Vance, a high-minded young intellectual, Ames, who, though he can partake of this world (unlike Hurstwood), has little interest in it and indeed is above it (unlike Carrie). A serious-minded engineer from Indianapolis, Ames has nothing of the "dashing lady's man" about him (p. 350). He does not seek to attract Carrie, and yet Carrie finds something attractive in him—his superiority of mind. "He seemed wiser than Hurstwood, saner and brighter than Drouet" (p. 357). He disparages the notion that wealth means happiness and is enthusiastic about the art of acting. When Carrie returns from her dinner at Sherry's with the Vances and Ames, she rocks and thinks. "Through a fog of longing and conflicting desires she was beginning to see. . . . She was rocking, and beginning to see" (p. 359).

Although she is moved and stimulated by Ames's ideas, Carrie cannot make use of them as yet, since she has neither wealth to question nor an art to pursue. Throughout the remainder of her New York career, however, as Hurstwood sinks to apathy and as she gains success, she regards Ames and his beliefs as an "ideal." (Dreiser uses this term repeatedly.) Carrie's desire to leave Hurstwood must therefore be viewed in the context of the basic "drift" of her life if it is to be properly understood. Her immediate motive, as always with Carrie, seems both selfish and slight. She wishes to keep more of her salary in order to buy clothes. But as in Chicago, clothes are primarily a metaphor for the freedom and for the upward movement of the spirit which have always impelled Carrie. Hurstwood's New York "gloom" (another oft-used word) has become a prison of the spirit for Carrie, who finds only outside their flat both the present "brightness" of her Broadway life and future hopes of achieving the "ideal" represented by Ames and his beliefs. In a passage cut from the typescript of Chapter XLII, Dreiser describes Carrie's response to the temporary absence of Hurstwood during his strikebreaking adventure in a way which anticipates the underlying motive for her later desertion of him. "With him there passed out of the flat a great shadow. In its place came hopes for the future—hopes of freedom from annoyance and money drain. . . . It was not because hardheartedness was a characteristic of her nature. It was weariness and an ache for change." Of course, Carrie does indeed want to be free of money worries and to have fine clothes. But above all she wants to be free of the death of the spirit which life with Hurstwood has become, and it is this powerful though inexpressible desire which informs her conscious motives.

Very quickly after leaving Hurstwood, Carrie achieves the wealth and position she had always desired—$150 a week in salary, a luxurious apartment, applause, and admirers. Almost as quickly, she discovers that these do not satisfy her, that she is as lonely and as unhappy as ever. She finds that the men who pursue her are unbearably shallow. They "did not talk of anything that lifted her above the common run of clothes and material success" (p. 489). Ames, however, does talk above the common run, and when she encounters him again she is properly uplifted.

Of course, the entire third rung of Carrie's rise, after she leaves Hurstwood, is weakened by Dreiser's oversevere foreshortening of the conclusion of his very long novel. Carrie rises too quickly; she is too quickly dissatisfied with what she has gained; and, most of all, her relationship with Ames is insufficiently developed given its importance in her growth. Dreiser intended from the first to deal rather abruptly with Carrie's rise to stardom and with her discontent; he did not describe these moments in her life fully in the holograph and then cut them in the typescript in order to foreshorten the conclusion. But, as I noted earlier, he did in his first draft write a more extended account of Carrie's final two meetings with Ames. The heavily cut published version of these meetings unfortunately only suggests the meaning of Ames's ideals and the impact they are to have on Carrie's life. It would be best, therefore, to sketch this suggestion as it appears in the published novel and then to fill out the theme by recourse to the fuller expression of it in the original draft.[42]

In the published work, Ames is not impressed with Carrie's success in musical comedy when they meet again at the close of the novel. Rather, he is disappointed that she has not undertaken the more serious roles of "comedy-drama."[43] (During the 1890s, any serious play not a traditional tragedy was a "comedy-drama.") Ames's interest in her dramatic powers and his conception of acting as an art sound for Carrie "the old call of the ideal" (p. 534). His encouragement "unlocked the door to a new desire" (p. 536), to achieve the kind of artistry which he admires. She now realizes that she has not pursued the potential for dramatic effect and power which she had discovered in herself at Avery Hall. They soon meet again, and Ames uses the occasion to explain the nature of her strength as an actress. It is her ability to express human longing. She must, he tells her, make this "valuable to others" (p. 537). She has been given her power for this purpose, and if she does not use it for this end, it will disappear.

Although Carrie comes away from these interviews moved by Ames's "lofty" sentiments and his interest in "forwarding all good causes" (p. 538), the nature and source of these sentiments and causes are obscure. They are much clearer, however, in the holograph version of Carrie's lengthy conversations with Ames. In their first interview, having earlier started Carrie "on a course of reading which would improve her," Ames discourses on Balzac, who is one of his recommended authors. Although he approves highly of Balzac, he is critical of his belief "that happiness lies in wealth and position." Rather, Ames tells her,

"Your happiness is within yourself wholly. When I was quite young, I felt as if I were ill-used because other boys were dressed better than I was, were more sprightly with girls than I, and I grieved and grieved, but now I'm over that. I have found out that everyone is more or less dissatisfied. No one has exactly what his heart wishes."

Nevertheless, Ames tells Carrie, her art—her acting ability—can be a permanent solace to her if it is preserved by proper use. Her power of sympathetic expression depends on her sympathetic response to life. " 'You can't remain tender and sympathetic and desire to serve the world without having it show in your face and your art. If you want to do most, do good. Serve the many. Be kind and humanitarian. Then you can't help but be great.' "

Carrie is deeply responsive to this advice. She realizes that the goal he offers her is "not money—he did not mean that. Not clothes—how far was he from their pretension. Not applause—not even that—but goodness—labor for others." Because of Ames's instruction, she is again, when they part, "the old mournful Carrie, the desireful Carrie—unsatisfied." The conclusion of their last interview is followed in the holograph by the two paragraphs on Carrie which Dreiser later expanded into the full epilogue, paragraphs which begin, "Oh blind striving of the human heart. Onward, onward, it saith, and where beauty leads there it follows."[44]

Ames's idealism, as fleshed out in the holograph, is a composite of various beliefs about success, art, and happiness which Dreiser had encountered during the previous few years. First, Ames's values reflect the notion of success which Dreiser had had expressed to him again and again in his interviews with various great men for *Success* magazine during 1898–99. Material success, these figures had told him, was less important than spiritual peace and happiness, and these states could best be achieved by the use of one's wealth or position or talent to aid others.[45] This conventional apology for success by the successful, which Dreiser appears to have taken with an appropriate grain of salt, had received far more significant endorsement by Tolstoy during the 1890s. Tolstoy's neo-Christian tracts *What to Do?* and *What Is Art?* had a greater influence upon American intellectuals of that decade than did his novels. Howells in particular had been deeply affected by Tolstoy's thought, and Dreiser himself had read and responded to Tolstoy as early as 1889 during his year at Indiana University.[46] By the time Dreiser interviewed Howells for *Success* in early 1898 and then for *Ainslee's* in 1899, he had absorbed enough Tolstoy to comment upon and—in *Ainslee's*—to endorse Howells's interest in Tolstoy's neo-Christian beliefs.[47] Indeed, Dreiser himself appears to have viewed his own literary mentors before the writing of *Sister Carrie* in an ascending order of spirituality, with Tolstoy the culminating figure. He told an interviewer in 1911, "Balzac lasted me a year or two, then came Hardy, and after him, Tolstoy."[48] The Tolstoyean idea which Ames reflects in his idealism is thus appropriately one which Howells had stressed in his essay on Tolstoy in *My Literary Passions*—an essay which Dreiser had quoted in his March 1899 article on Howells in *Ainslee's*. Tolstoy, Howells had written in his essay, had taught him that it was necessary to see life "not as a chase of a forever impossible personal happiness, but as a field for endeavor toward the happiness of the whole human family."[49]

The "lofty" sentiments and "good causes" which Carrie responds to and accepts are thus primarily an adaptation of a traditional Christian idealism to art and the artist. Carrie now realizes that material comforts do not bring inner peace and happiness and that her spirit demands a higher calling, one in which the pursuit of beauty becomes primarily an attempt to aid others rather than herself. She is to become a kind of ascetic idealist, we sense, and our final impression of her life is that it will be appropriately asexual. Earlier, she had departed Hurstwood's bed before deserting him entirely. And when she left him $20 with her farewell note, she was in a sense lifting the sexual encumbrance on her life represented by the $20 which Drouet had given her in the Chicago restaurant. She now wishes to live free of temporary, impeding entanglements while she continues to seek beauty. So she lives with Lola and conducts the final phases of her acquaintance with Ames on a level of high thinking and mutual respect.

Ames and Carrie in the concluding chapter of the novel represent Dreiser's idealized concept, in 1900, of his own life and career. Carrie by the close of the novel has reached Dreiser's notion of the stage of development he himself had reached during 1894–95. She is dreamy and inarticulate, but she has begun to discover the great truths of life and will undertake the expression of these truths through her art. Ames is the Dreiser of 1895–99. Though young, Ames is both a man of ideas and a success as an engineer. He is the Dreiser who was at once the speculative, idealistic "Prophet" of *Ev'ry Month* and the successful editor and free-lance writer. Carrie and Ames thus blend into an honorific self-portrait of Dreiser as both a soulful artist, driven by a quest for beauty, and a practical, successful man of affairs who is also a speculative thinker. The two figures merge most clearly in the ideal of art which they share—an ideal which Ames expresses and which Carrie is to exemplify.

Dreiser thus viewed affirmatively Carrie's development from the naïve, ignorant girl who meets Drouet on the train to the noble-minded though unhappy actress who embraces Ames's high idealism. Much in his narrative of her career represents his attempt to structure the themes of her spiritual development by a close rendering of the daily occurrences of her life. His principal structural device, of course, is the "ladder" of Drouet, Hurstwood, and Ames. Though it appears to be an obvious device, Dreiser handles it with considerable subtlety. For example, one of Carrie's major characteristics is that she lives primarily in the future. Her dreamy nature and her rocking are intended to signify her discontent with the present and her hope for the future. Her three relationships therefore represent, among other themes, her unconscious desire to discover a similar temperament, one which will confirm the validity of her own inner life. Drouet lives only in the present; for him the now is all. Hurstwood in New York lives primarily in the past as he seeks to blot out his misfortunes and gloom by the memory of his earlier position and comfort. Part of Carrie's responsiveness to Ames therefore derives from her sense that he too lives in the future and that he does so in the "deep" way which has been implicit though inexplicable in Carrie's repeated exclamation, "I will be happy."

Dreiser also introduces a thematically functional "bookish" element into Carrie's "ladder" relationship with Drouet, Hurstwood, and Ames.[50] Drouet is interested in the popular theatre and in cheap romances, such as those by Bertha M. Clay that Carrie acquires from him early in the novel. Hurstwood has no literary tastes or interests; he is concerned only with the relative fame or importance of the "personalities" who frequent Fitzgerald and Moy's. The melodrama and sentimentality of *Under the Gaslight* appropriately characterize the permanent level of taste of both Drouet and Hurstwood and the temporary level which Carrie has reached under their tutelage. In Ames, however, Carrie encounters a man who is contemptuous of the popular romance, however successful, and who instructs her in the worth of Balzac (Hardy as well in the holograph) and in the significance of serious drama.

In addition to the "ladder" of Drouet, Hurstwood, and Ames, Dreiser's principal means of structuring Carrie's career is his constantly recurring symbol of the rocking chair. Carrie rocking and dreaming of the future is an apt and compelling symbol of the role of dream in our lives and of Carrie's distinctive quality as a character. The openness yet poetic force and suggestiveness of the symbol is in sharp contrast to the contrived and unconvincing allegory of Carrie's life presented in the chapter titles and the epilogue. Occasionally, the rocking chair has been interpreted primarily as a symbol of circularity because Carrie rocks on her first night in Chicago and again at the close of the novel in her New York apartment.[51] It is suggested that Dreiser means us to understand that nothing has really happened to Carrie, that though her outer condition has changed she is essentially the same both morally and spiritually. The symbol does indeed function partly in this way, but its principal emphasis is not the negative one of nothing changed and therefore nothing gained. Its stress is rather the positive theme that Carrie continues to have the ability to wonder about herself and the future, that her imaginative response to life has not been dulled by experience. Although she has not achieved the happiness that she thought accompanied the life she desired and which she now has, she will continue to search. Ames has indicated the next step, and there will be still other rungs of hope beyond him. And at whatever stop she momentarily rests, she will always have the inner force which is her ability to dream, a force which is bold and free. She will always be the dreamer, Dreiser says, and though her dreams take an earthly shape controlled by her world, she has acquired meaning and stature and significance because of her capacity to dream and rock and thereby to question life and to pursue it. Thus Carrie seeks to fulfill each new venture and gain each object as though these were the only realities in life, and yet by her dissatisfaction with and questioning of what she has gained to imply the greater reality of the mind and spirit that dreams and rocks. The rocking chair goes nowhere but it moves, and in that paradox lies Dreiser's involvement with Carrie and his attempt to communicate the nature and intensity of her quest. For in his mind too the world is both solid and unknowable, and man is ever pursuing and never finding.

But though Dreiser clearly intended that Carrie be the principal and the most appealing figure in the novel, many readers have found her less satisfying as a fictional character than Hurstwood or even Drouet. The major reason for this response is Dreiser's not wholly successful attempt to attribute an aesthetic sensibility and a spiritual development to an inarticulate country girl with commonplace tastes and little moral awareness. In a passage which was cut from Chapter XII, Dreiser described the unvoiced thoughts of Carrie and Hurstwood. He then asked the reader that he not be "quarrelled with" for attempting to represent the "psychological truths" of two such seemingly commonplace individuals. "The great forces of nature must not be arrogated by the intellectual alone," he continued, for they can be found in the "commonest moulds." The "force of nature" which Dreiser wished to capture in Carrie was, of course, that of the instinctive, emotional, dreaming seeker of beauty and happiness—the character of the romantic heroine as artist. But Dreiser was for the most part both too honest and too inept in his depiction of Carrie for his portrait to be successful.

He is inept in several ways, but most obviously, perhaps, in the aura of the sentimental with which he surrounds Carrie. This quality is most evident in the imagery and diction of the chapter titles and epilogue, but it is also present throughout the Chicago portion of the novel, in which Carrie is repeatedly characterized as a soldier of fortune, a little toiler, and a ship atoss on a stormy sea. As I will discuss more fully later, Dreiser often stands at some distance from his hackneyed and clichéd language of the pathetic, and this language also has a function in the total effect of the novel which at least clarifies, if not completely justifies, its presence. Nevertheless, one of its immediate effects is to weaken our recognition that a character so superficially described can also be a figure of depth and complexity.

In addition, Dreiser fails to create an acceptable "objective correlative" of Carrie's depth and growth as an artist, particularly at the close of the novel. Carrie discovers at the Avery Hall theatrical her power as an actress. She has, Dreiser tells us, the quality of "emotional greatness" (p. 410), a quality which is the necessary basis of all art in that the artist must be moved by beauty if he is to recreate beauty. And because of her circumstances as a woman in the late nineteenth century, and because of the distinctive form which her aesthetic sense takes, acting is the mode of art which she adopts. For Dreiser, it should be clear, acting is not merely an "imitative" or "performing" art. Both in his account of Carrie's effect on her Avery Hall audience and in Ames's later speeches on the nature of the actor, Dreiser attributes to the actor a power found in all art—the power to move and therefore to transform. When Carrie holds her audience at Avery Hall, it is with "the magic of passion, which will yet dissolve the world" (p. 201). And as Ames tells Carrie, she is a potentially great actress because the world sees in her "a natural expression of its longing. . . . Most people are not capable of voicing their feelings. They depend upon others. That is what genius is for. One man expresses their desires for them in music another one in poetry; another one in a play" (p. 537).

But Carrie's one moment of emotional power as an actress occurs too early in the novel for it to vitalize our response to Ames's recognition of her artistic potential. And Ames, as every reader of *Sister Carrie*, including Dreiser,[52] has recognized, is inadequately portrayed to serve either as an acceptable spokesman for the most significant abstract ideas in the novel or as a figure who has the power to perceive Carrie's true nature and ability. His weakness as a fictional character thus almost completely undermines Dreiser's theme that Carrie has developed. In his high-mindedness he is like the twenty-four-year-old Dreiser who as the "Prophet" had declaimed ennobling "Reflections" from the pulpit offered by *Ev'ry Month*. In short, he is too much the prig. There is something of Dreiser in both Drouet and Hurstwood, but there is too much of what Dreiser thought he was (or should be) in Ames. Moreover, Ames fails to convince because, unlike Drouet and Hurstwood, who are fully realized dramatic figures, he is almost entirely a spokesman. Since he has no depth or identity except as an instructor of Carrie, her responsiveness to him as an exemplum of the higher life lacks the convincingness of her earlier identification of her aspirations with Drouet and Hurstwood. Of course, Dreiser's severe foreshortening of Ames's role may have been instinctively correct. It is a nice question whether a spokesman of what is essentially a neo-Platonic idealism could be believably developed in the character of an Indiana engineer advising a young New York actress at dinner parties. We may thus be better off with a weak but briefly sketched Ames than with a fuller portrait.

Finally, Dreiser's epilogue is a poor summary of Carrie's basic nature. For most of the novel Carrie is an aspiring artist. She has grown and matured, and with Ames's help will mature further, but her level of development does not warrant the high lyricism of Dreiser's apostrophizing conclusion. The conclusion, in other words, constitutes too sudden a reversal of tone, as Dreiser abruptly shifts from an authorial voice which has been dispassionately aware of Carrie's obvious limitations to one which emotionally identifies itself with the goal of her aspirations. As a result of this reversal, we fail to accept fully the strength and depth which Dreiser attributes to Carrie. One way to explain this important lapse in tone in the epilogue is to note again the "chronology" of self-identification at the close of the novel. Carrie and Ames in the concluding pages are, as I have suggested, the Dreiser of 1894–95 and 1895–99; but the Carrie of the epilogue is the Dreiser of "now." She is the Dreiser who, in the composition of *Sister Carrie*, has set out on a difficult artistic career, a career devoted to high ends but nevertheless capable of being misunderstood by the world, and who therefore views himself melodramatically and sentimentally in his self-analysis as an artist. The epilogue thus anticipates the weaknesses of *The "Genius"* when Dreiser again attempted to dramatize the "now" of his artistic nature.

Carrie's appeal as a fictional character suffers, however, not only from Dreiser's ineptness, particularly in the closing chapters of the novel, but also, paradoxically, from his integrity of vision. Throughout most of the novel, Carrie's conscious motivation is to escape drabness, poverty, and gloom and to gain ease, comfort, and contentment. It is only when she has acquired wealth and position that she consciously undertakes to develop her artistic potential. One does not have to be a hard-line Marxist to accept the truthfulness of Dreiser's depiction of Carrie's interest in bread first and art second. And for Carrie, it should be recalled, bread is also good clothes and comfortable rooms and surroundings—that which subconsciously feeds the spirit while it provides for the body. Nevertheless, Dreiser's honesty in recounting Carrie's flush of joy and excitement as she acquires a new outfit or visits a fashionable restaurant works against our assumptions about the artist as romantic hero. Like Thoreau, we expect that our artists will go up garret and starve for their art. But Carrie doesn't like to starve, and she doesn't know that she is an artist; as a result, we find ourselves unconvinced when Dreiser at the close of the novel announces that she is in effect a romantic artist.

Moreover, Carrie is often placid, narrow, shallow, and selfish in her personal life. Her one major emotional outburst occurs when she discovers that Hurstwood is married; otherwise she seems to lack the quality of "emotional greatness" Dreiser attributes to her. And though she is not hardhearted, her sympathy for the difficulties of others is superficial and fleeting. Her principal interest is usually a firm self-interest. In these instances of personal shallowness Dreiser was attempting, though perhaps not consciously, to distinguish between the professional and personal life of the artist. Carrie's "emotional greatness" does not lie in her histrionic reaction to the events of her own life; it lies rather in her ability to sense the emotional realities of life and to communicate them to others through her art. She displays this ability at Avery Hall when she holds and moves the audience despite the shallowness of the play, and she displays it as well on Broadway, for such a discriminating viewer as Ames, despite her superficial roles. In addition, Carrie's ability to project herself into an emotional reality does not mean that she can make this reality operative in her own life. She can portray Laura's self-sacrificing faithfulness at the moment she herself wishes to discard Drouet for Hurstwood, and she can respond to the same noble quality in Père Goriot when she has all but dismissed the derelict Hurstwood from her mind. When she discovers that Hurstwood is married, she is concerned almost entirely with her own plight, not Hurstwood's or Drouet's. And her failure to understand the cause of Hurstwood's later collapse is in part a failure of compassion. In short, she is like Dreiser himself: she is an artist who is capable of communicating in her art the essential tragedy of life and therefore the need for compassion, but she is narrow and selfish in her dealings with others. In Carrie's emotional isolation, Dreiser was anticipating the clearly presented theme in *The "Genius"* that an emotional economy and selfishness are necessary for the survival of the artist as artist. (Indeed, Carrie's final asexuality is a rough approximation of Witla's discovery of the handicap which sex represents for the artist.) But in *Sister Carrie* this theme is less explicit. As a result of both its implicitness and its radical honesty, the theme is often misunderstood as Dreiser's failure to satisfactorily dramatize Carrie's "emotional greatness."

Carrie is thus one of Dreiser's most complex fictional characters. Created out of a large number of not always successfully reconciled sources and influences—from Emma Dreiser's Chicago adventures to the Dreiser who had just completed an "advanced" novel, from the midcentury stereotype of the sentimental heroine in distress to the contemporary vogue of the artist as Tolstoyean Christian—Carrie is not surprisingly a characterization that does not always jell. But she is not the single-faceted figure she has often been taken to be. She is not merely a representation of Dreiser's attempt to reverse Victorian assumptions of sexual morality, and her career is not simply an example of the need for illusion if one is to survive in a world of struggle. Although her characterization contains both of these themes, her nature defies easy classification. For in Carrie Dreiser sought to depict less a character's confusion about life than the very confusion at the center of life itself—the seeming haphazard but subterraneanly directed currents of experience, the amoral need most individuals have to fulfill themselves in a world controlled by moral assumptions, and the pathetically superficial but moving instances of man's pursuit of beauty. But if one has to have a single "handle" by which to interpret Carrie, perhaps she is above all the artist. Like so many other writers of his day, Dreiser found that the role of the artist was a deeply satisfying and flexible metaphor for the expression of his response to the meaning of life and to experience as he had found it.

⸲⸲⸲⸲⸲⸲⸲⸲⸲⸲⸲⸲⸲⸲⸲⸲⸲⸲⸲⸲⸲⸲⸲⸲⸲⸲⸲

Dreiser's portrait of Hurstwood is more fictionally compelling than that of Carrie not because it is less complex (though it is so) but because Dreiser had a firmer and more conscious recognition of the effects he wished to achieve. Since Hurstwood is so memorable a figure, there is a tendency in discussions of *Sister Carrie* to isolate his nature and fate from the moral context of the work as a whole. Hurstwood's character, however, is in fact best approached initially in relation to the fully elaborated ethical ideas present in Dreiser's depiction of Carrie.

In broad terms, Hurstwood and Carrie lead similar emotional lives in Chicago. He, too, is confronted by two worlds—a sterile, empty family life, and the youth and attractiveness of Carrie. Like Carrie's "craving for pleasure," his instinctive reaching out for happiness becomes the dominant force in his life, overriding all ethical and rational guides. Dreiser's depiction of Hurstwood's all-consuming desire for happiness, at the point of his most intense desire for Carrie, contains both the conventional moral terminology and the key phrase "She would be happy" which he had used for Carrie. "His passion had gotten to that stage now where it was no longer coloured with reason. . . . He would make a try for Paradise, whatever might be the result. He would be happy, by the Lord, if it cost all honesty of statement, all abandonment of truth" (p. 225).

The most significant moment in Hurstwood's life is that of his hesitation in front of the safe. With the money in his hand, the safe still open, and the desire to escape his wife and win Carrie strong within him, he is like Carrie in Chapters VII, VIII, and IX when she is drawn to accept what Drouet represents—escape and happiness—though she senses the "wrong" of doing so and still has the option of refusing him. Again, as in Carrie's period of crisis, Hurstwood engages in an internal debate, and again Dreiser himself comments philosophically on the role of instinct in ethical decisions.

Yet despite these important similarities, Hurstwood differs from Carrie in the vital fact that his moral life is one of indecision and accident rather than of purposeful drift. Dreiser's discussion of the role of instinct in Hurstwood's dilemma during the theft scene pinpoints the nature of this difference. "The dullest specimen of humanity," Dreiser tells us,

when drawn by desire toward evil, is recalled by a sense of right . . . proportionate in power and strength to his evil tendency. We must remember that it may not be a knowledge of right, for no knowledge of right is predicated of the animal's instinctive recoil at evil. Men are still led by instinct before they are regulated by knowledge. It is instinct which recalls the criminal—it is instinct (where highly organized reasoning is absent) which gives the criminal his feeling of danger, his fear of wrong. (p. 287)

Carrie's ethical dilemma had been characterized by a weak, undeveloped reason which failed to sufficiently inform or strengthen her moral sense, and by a powerful, instinctive "craving for pleasure" which controlled her actions. In Hurstwood, however, reason as an ethical force is not present.

He had decided much earlier that any action would be justified if it would win Carrie. His dilemma consists rather of the opposing pulls of two instinctive forces—a desire for Carrie and a fear of capture. Carrie, because the struggle within her was one-sided, drifted easily in the direction of fulfilling her instinctive need. But Hurstwood is torn by two conflicting and equally powerful instincts. He therefore "could not bring himself to act definitely. . . . He was drawn by such a keen desire for Carrie, driven by such a state of turmoil in his own affairs that he thought constantly it would be best, and yet he wavered. He did not know what evil might result from it to him—how soon he might come to grief" (p. 288). Thus, "the true ethics of the situation never once occurred to him" (p. 288) because "true ethics" involve a conscious moral sense which should reasonably conclude that taking someone else's money is wrong.

The accidental closing of the safe is therefore but one of several significant characteristics of the theft scene.[53] Dreiser did not wish to dramatize by that event the overriding importance of a single fatalistic action in our lives. He wished rather to represent the ineluctable moral complexity of acts which appear to be clear-cut instances of wrong. Hurstwood before the safe is in an intolerable position. His wife has just successfully blackmailed him and Carrie has just dismissed him, though not, he feels, irrevocably. His dominant impulse is to relieve the pressure upon him—to escape his wife and to win Carrie. To flee with the money and Carrie appears to be a solution to his difficulties. The clicking shut of the safe transforms indecision into action, but though the click is a fortuitous event it is only one in a series of fortuitous events which seem to be compelling Hurstwood to reach a decision: the unusually large amount of money left in the safe this particular evening, the safe left unlocked by the cashier, and Hurstwood's uncharacteristic action of looking in the money drawer ("quite a superfluous action, which another time might not have happened at all") (p. 284).

The weight of the principal factors in Carrie and Hurstwood's crucial moral acts is thus different. Carrie meets Drouet in downtown Chicago by chance, but the fortuitousness of this event lacks the heavy emphasis which chance receives in Hurstwood's theft. Carrie has some faint glimmerings of "reason"; Hurstwood is confronted by two conflicting instinctive desires. Yet despite these major differences, Carrie's acceptance of Drouet and Hurstwood's theft dramatize the same essential ethical reality—that conscious decision-making has little to do with the most important moments in our moral lives. In a letter to Walter H. Page during the controversy over the publication of *Sister Carrie*, Dreiser wrote that the novel "deals with the firm insistence of law, the elements of chance and sub-conscious direction."[54] The element of "law" in the lives of Carrie and Hurstwood consists largely of Dreiser's own overlay of philosophical commentary. Men, we are told in relation to Carrie, will some day reach the "distant pole of truth" and will be able to choose rationally the good life; and there is a "true ethics" in Hurstwood's theft even if Hurstwood does not realize its nature. Dreiser's radical breakthrough in his depiction of man's moral nature occurs not in these explicit comments but in his dramatization of the ways in which chance and subconscious desire blend into event. One figure drifts, the other is precipitated into action; but neither makes a choice in the conventional sense of choice.

In his philosophical commentary on Carrie and Hurstwood, Dreiser was drawing upon the simplistic distinction in evolutionary moralism between the dominance of animalistic instinct in the past and the coming glory of rational choice in the future in order to structure and understand the immensely complex realities of human motivation and action. He was seeking to salvage some remnant of conventional moral affirmation in the face of the overwhelming amorality of action itself. The crucial difference between these morally significant events in *Sister Carrie* and the parallel event in *An American Tragedy* of the death of Roberta lies not in Dreiser's dramatic rendering of an ethically complex and ambiguous action but in his later conscious acceptance of the amorality underlying such actions.

Dreiser's success in portraying Hurstwood, however, derives less from the power of individual scenes, such as the theft, than from the suggestiveness and cumulative weight of his depiction of Hurstwood's entire career. Much of that career stands in exact juxtaposition to Carrie's not only in the obvious sense of her rise and his fall but in the more significant and less immediately apparent sense that her life moves in the direction of the exposure of her essential strength while his moves in the direction of the exposure of his essential weakness.

Because Carrie and Drouet admire Hurstwood in Chicago, and because he is an imposing figure as manager of a large and prosperous saloon and as head of a middle-class household, it has sometimes been assumed that Dreiser himself admires the accomplishments and strength of the Chicago Hurstwood. This is a misreading, for Dreiser above all wishes to represent in Hurstwood the facade of strength which middle-class roles provide the weak man. Hurstwood's decline in New York is a result of the loss of that facade and of the full impact of the harshness of the struggle for life upon his defenseless weakness.

Dreiser's initial description of Hurstwood in his splendor as manager of Fitzgerald and Moy's subtly renders the superficiality of that role and the limitations of the man disguised by it. To Drouet, Hurstwood appeared to be "very successful." He has a "good, stout constitution, an active manner, and a solid, substantial air, which was composed in part of his fine clothes, his clean linen, his jewels, and, above all, his own sense of his importance." He is "shrewd and clever in many little things" and is "capable of creating a good impression." His position at the saloon is "fairly important—a kind of stewardship which was imposing, but lacked financial control." He has a "little office" where he keeps his "simple accounts," for the major executive and financial matters of the business are handled by Fitzgerald and Moy. He keeps a "neat trap, has his wife and two children, who were well established in a neat house on the North Side near Lincoln Park." Dreiser completes this portrait in controlled irony by summing up Hurstwood as "a very acceptable individual of our great American upper class—the first grade below the luxuriously rich" (pp. 49–50).

Class labels were not as firmly set at the turn of the century as they are today, and it is clear that in Hurstwood Dreiser is characterizing above all a particular kind of middle-class figure. Hurstwood is a man whose entire life is built upon his effect on others. His role at Fitzgerald and Moy's is that of "front man"—to make a good impression and to establish an air of hospitality and of interest in the affairs of the customers. Beyond this role, his duties and responsibilities are slight. His profession, in short, is to appear successful—"to make a good impression"—and his "neat home" in the right part of town, with the correct complement of a wife and two children, is part of his profession. But beneath the roles of manager and head of household, Hurstwood has neither power nor strength. At work, he makes no important decisions; at home, when his authority is challenged, he "walks away" instead of fighting (p. 93).

The high point of Hurstwood's career as "a very successful and well-known man about town" occurs during the Avery Hall performance. His superficial acquaintance with the minor lights of Chicago has made the affair an occasion, with him at its center as organizer and brightest luminary. But on the day following the performance he is for the first time put under intense pressure. Hitherto, he had been borne effortlessly forward in life by deep grooves of habit and position. His new role of seducer, however, requires that he be fresh and innovative. Initially, because his victims are the unsophisticated Carrie and the blithe and superficial Drouet, he appears to have successfully developed these talents. He is the classic "friend of the family" who seduces the wife and cuckolds the husband. But immediately after the performance, Carrie discovers that he is married, and his wife becomes convinced that he is having an affair. His response to his wife's ferocity is an outward resolution and anger but an inner indecisiveness which permits her greater resourcefulness to win the day. And his response to the dilemma presented by his desire for Carrie and her dismissal of him is to wait and to hope. Although he is "keenly alive to the difficulties of his situation," he can only hope "over and over that some solution would offer itself" (p. 258). The " 'I don't know' " (p. 263) which he mutters to himself at the end of his week of inaction not only echoes Carrie's earlier outward indecisiveness but reflects a far deeper core of enervating inertia. He is "rescued" from this state only by blundering into an action which he almost immediately regrets.

Dreiser places his account of Hurstwood's desire for Carrie in the context of the sexual realities of a middle-class marriage. Married when very young, Hurstwood now lives in a state of bland indifference with his "cold, self-centered" wife and his social-climbing children (p. 123). He has had his minor, sordid affairs in distant cities, but he is deeply conscious of the need to avoid scandal because of his position and his family. Carrie's appeal for Hurstwood is thus "the ancient attraction of the fresh for the stale. . . . He looked into her pretty face and felt the subtle waves of young life radiating therefrom" (pp. 116–17). At home, Hurstwood is viewed as merely a grudging provider of funds; to Carrie, he is all the world. At home, he is confronted by his wife's growing hate; with Carrie there is burgeoning love. Hurstwood's fatal error is that he does not realize, as Dreiser realizes, that "the life of the resort . . . was his life" (p. 97). He does not realize, in other words, that the sources of his well-being are not in the fire and excitement of youth but in the tame middle-class roles which he must sacrifice if he is to attempt to gain what youth appears to offer him. Hurstwood's fall is therefore not primarily a tragedy of chance, of the accidental closing of the safe. It is principally the tragedy of a man who thinks he is impregnable but who then is discovered to be weak when his desires drive him outside the protection of his roles. It is a tragedy so basic to human nature and experience that our response to it is less the shock than the unthinking flow of recognition.

From the moment that Hurstwood arrives in New York and realizes that he must consider the minor expense of taking a cab from the station to a hotel, he is marked as a doomed man. He declines not merely because he is too old to begin again in a great city the battle for "place and comfort" or because his psychological depression causes a physiological condition which affects his capacity to act (the infamous anastates-katastates passage). The principal cause both of his failure to pursue energetically a new career and of his depression is his lack of strength. Hurstwood is a man without a center. He has no resources of morality, belief, or ambition to draw upon. He has only his memories of Chicago and his present emptiness. Dreiser renders his decline in New York by depicting it both dramatically and through metaphor as a retreat from the demands of the present into the past and into his own inner vacuum.

Hurstwood's decline, as befits a middle-class tragedy, is gradual, with an initial period of only minor and scarcely perceptible change. His new business venture, however, is indeed only a business rather than a place to shine among "notabilities." And his concern about money restricts his and Carrie's social life and therefore his absorption in his effect on others. Gradually, he loses interest in his business, in Carrie, and in his surroundings and appearance. He begins to brood and to be "gloomy." When the lease on the Warren Street saloon is not renewed, Hurstwood's position is similar to his earlier state when Carrie and Mrs. Hurstwood made their parallel discoveries after the Avery Hall performance. Again he must act quickly and decisively, either to reinvest his small capital or to acquire a position in which he can augment his capital. Now, however, he has neither the pull of his desire for Carrie nor the willfullness of his wife to make indecisiveness intolerable. Although he makes some gestures toward investment and job-hunting, he finds it easier to wait for the dilemma of employment to resolve itself than to accept a position which is beneath his conception of his own worth.

Chapter XXXV, "The Passage of Effort: The Visage of Care," is the key narrative in the metaphysics of Hurstwood's fall. It is winter, and after a halfhearted effort at job-hunting, Hurstwood takes refuge in a hotel lobby, where "he could forget, in a measure, the weariness of the street and his tiresome searches" (p. 384). After a few days of lobby-sitting, a blizzard drives Hurstwood to the more secure refuge of the flat. There he finds a niche near the radiator where he can rock and read the newspaper. He helps Carrie with some of the household chores during the blizzard. When the storm is over, he stops pretending to himself (though not to Carrie) that he is looking for a job and again seeks out the lobby of the Broadway Central Hotel. But a chance meeting with an old Chicago acquaintance drives him from this sanctuary, and a cold forces him into another prolonged stay in the flat. Even though he soon recovers from his illness, he remains permanently at its level of physical effort and personal appearance. He wears his old clothes around the flat, does not shave, and assumes more and more of the trivial labors of housekeeping. Carrie is now thoroughly disgusted with him and after a quarrel moves out of their bedroom. They never sleep together again.

The chapter contains almost all the symbolic strands which communicate the emotional reality of Hurstwood's decline. The outer world is both demanding and indifferent and is therefore cold. Inactivity—the lobbies and the flat—is undemanding and is therefore warm and, paradoxically, life-sustaining. The rocking chair, the newspaper, and the radiator become the centers of life for Hurstwood. The motion of the chair, the vicarious experience of events in the newspaper, and the warmth of the radiator constitute a seeming participation in life while actually representing a means of withdrawing from it. Since Hurstwood now lives more and more within himself, his personal appearance and the withdrawal of sex are unimportant to him. Since he wishes to obliterate time, he is drawn to the mind-numbing routine of household duties for reasons other than the ostensible one of saving on expenses. He fears such reminders of the difference between his past and present states as the chance encounter with a Chicago friend, but he begins to live more and more in memories of the past. Eventually, his waking life is to be punctuated by daydreams of past moments of social triumph. " 'You're a dandy, Hurstwood' " (p. 476), he repeats out loud at one point as he relives such a moment.

These motifs of a search for oblivion mingle with those which measure the speed and angle of Hurstwood's decline. At first the principal variant is the degree of difference between Hurstwood's outward commitment to find a position and his inward disinclination. But his decline is soon measured by three additional major motifs: his cash on hand, from the $700 with which he leaves the Warren Street venture to the few cents he has in his pocket as a Bowery derelict; his clothes, from the still presentable suit with which he initially looks for a job to the beggar's rags of his last days; and his dwellings, from the small but comfortable flat which he and Carrie share to his final resting place in a tiny flophouse room.

While Hurstwood and Carrie are still living together, her bitterness and contempt occasionally goad him into a brief but ineffectual attempt to recover and assert the strength and sense of position he believed he had in the past. He indulges in a fine and expensive dinner at the Morton House to prove to himself (and Carrie) that he is still a gentleman, and he tries his hand at poker to demonstrate his cool superiority to others. His two days as a scab represent a last, futile attempt to demonstrate to Carrie and to himself that he is an honest seeker of work and a man. Once Carrie leaves him, however, there is no need to prove anything to himself or to her, and his life quickly settles into a pattern of keeping alive by an ever-decreasing amount of effort. He moves from laborer to active beggar to passive recipient of charity. He becomes less a person than a thing, an object to be fed and housed by the efforts of others. In the crowded free-soup lines and Bowery flophouses, he is friendless and isolated. In a world in which the present constantly impinges upon him because of his present needs, he lives more and more in the past. Only his apparently indestructible inertia keeps him alive. And finally inertia is not enough in the face of his need for oblivion and his desire to escape from the incessant cold which life has become for him. Before turning on the gas, "he reviewed nothing, but merely hesitated." He then does turn it on. " 'What's the use,' he said, weakly, as he stretched himself to rest" (p. 554).

Dreiser himself, in 1907, called *Sister Carrie* the story of "the tragedy of a man's life,"[55] and many readers have responded to Hurstwood's decline with a depth and intensity of compassion traditionally associated with the effect of tragedy. Yet Hurstwood is not a tragic figure in any conventional sense. In Chicago, he is the butt of a semicomic irony, since he is the man of seeming worldly power who is overcome by his wife in the sanctuary of his own home. There are elements of dignity in the New York Hurstwood because he is a man of some pride. He is embarrassed when he meets old Chicago friends, is irritated by Carrie's goading about a job, and later does not seek out Carrie for aid as long as he has some money of his own. But these are not ennobling characteristics. Rather, I think that we respond to Hurstwood's fall as a tragic event because as Dreiser unfolds the story of his gradual decline and decay we begin to recognize the modern

everyman in his condition—how dependent we all are on the class-deter-
mined roles and grooved ways of our lives for our emotional and spiritual
well-being. In other words, we begin to respond with pity and fear, for we
are experiencing a version of medieval tragedy—a fall from high place as
the universal forces of "circumstance" and "subconscious direction" have
their day. And because we ourselves are also creatures of place—that is, we
are middle-class—we can sense the tragic import for our own lives in the
fall of a Hurstwood.

ͼͼͼͼͼͼͼͼͼͼͼͼͼͼͼͼͼͼͼͼͼͼͼͼͼͼ

In a review of Ford Madox Ford's *The Good Soldier* in 1915, Dreiser
praised the theme of Ford's daring study of sexual passion but dealt harshly
with its experimental form. Ford, it will be recalled, had used the device of
a muddled first-person narrator who wanders back and forth in time as he
tells his story and who lacks insight into the meaning of what he is telling.
Dreiser found this device exasperating and proceeded to advise Ford on
how the novel should have been constructed.

Personally, I would have suggested . . . that he begin at the beginning . . . not at the beginning as some tertiary or quadrutiary character
in the book sees it. . . . Of far more importance is it that, once begun, it
should go forward in a more or less direct line, or at least that it should
retain one's uninterrupted interest. This is not the case in this book. The
interlacings, the cross references, the re-re-references to all sorts of things
which subsequently are told somewhere in full, irritate one to the point of
one's laying down the book.[56]

Dreiser's advice implies that he did not understand the possible subleties in
the art of fiction, that his insistence upon a third-person narrator telling a
chronologically progressive story is that of a naïve taste for a simple story
simply told. A distinction has to be made, however, between Dreiser's
discomfort when encountering experimental techniques and his sophisticated use of a major form of the nineteenth-century novel—the third-person "biographical" narrative—a form in which the "naturalness" of the
storytelling technique occasionally blurs our appreciation of the author's
skillful handling of such matters as structural "interlacings," narrative
voice, and symbolic imagery.

To describe the structure of *Sister Carrie* appears to be an exercise in stating the obvious: Carrie rises and Hurstwood falls. Yet this over-arching construct rests on many smaller units, and it is from this solid support that the overall form of the novel acquires substance and power. For example, as I have noted, Carrie's rise is in part plotted on the hierarchal positions of Drouet, Hurstwood, and Ames. In addition, the distinctive social realities of New York and Chicago play important roles in the shaping of the fates of Carrie and Hurstwood. Thus, three major inter-twined structural strands are usually present at any one moment in the novel: Carrie's rise in relation to Hurstwood's fall, Chicago events in relation to New York events, and Carrie's association with one of the three men in her life in relation to the other two. Occasionally, Dreiser com-ments directly on the connection among these various strands, most often when Carrie's pathetic Chicago condition contrasts so obviously with the circumstances of Drouet's and Hurstwood's lives. His principal technique, however, is to permit this intertwined structural core to express theme obliquely and ironically through incident and symbol.

For example, the rocking chair is associated initially with Carrie alone and appears to be primarily a symbol of her dreaming nature and of her quest for happiness, for it is while rocking before an open window that she is melancholy about the present and vows happiness for the future. Yet Drouet and Hurstwood also use the chair—Drouet in the scene after he and Carrie have parted and he is baffled by the resistance and anger he has encountered in the usually docile Carrie, and Hurstwood on the many occasions in New York when he sits reading his newspaper by the radiator. The symbol thus not only characterizes Carrie but also structures her relationship to Drouet and Hurstwood in Chicago and New York. The rocking chair is in part a symbol of mental repose, but Carrie's affirmative and "poetic" use of repose in order to dream is rendered as intrinsically superior both to Drouet's ineffectual use of it to solve the problems of the present and to Hurstwood's later use of it to escape these problems. When Hurstwood sits by the radiator rocking while Carrie prepares supper in the kitchen, the symbol not only comments upon Hurstwood at that moment but also ironically implies the vast difference between what Carrie contin-ues to be in New York, despite the outer drabness of her life, and what Hurstwood has revealed himself to be.

There are, of course, some flaws in the masonry supporting the basic structure of Carrie's rise and Hurstwood's fall. The principal weakness is not, as Mencken believed, that *Sister Carrie* is "broken-backed" because of

Hurstwood's prominence in the New York portion of the novel.[57] Mencken was responding primarily to the power of Dreiser's depiction of Hurstwood in New York rather than to a structural fault in that depiction. Dreiser gives equal attention to Carrie and Hurstwood in New York, either following Carrie in one chapter and Hurstwood in another or interweaving accounts of their activities in a single chapter. Dreiser's failure is not in the architectonics of the novel as a whole or in the New York section in particular but in his inability to characterize Carrie and Ames in New York with the depth he brought to his account of Hurstwood's decline. Put another way, his plan of the structure of the novel was adequate but his execution of that part of the narrative involving Carrie in New York was unequal to his execution of other parts.

One of the least noticed but most successful formal characteristics of *Sister Carrie* is Dreiser's use of a distinctive and appropriate narrative pace for each of the two major portions of the novel. In Chicago, events are initially slow-paced and are keyed to the seasons rather than to a specific chronology of action. Carrie arrives in midsummer, she and Drouet begin to live together in the fall, and Hurstwood becomes deeply interested in her during the winter. The Avery Hall performance in the spring, however, marks a sharp and full halt to this mood of drift. The elaborate deceits which had permitted the Hurstwood-Carrie-Drouet triangle to move slowly toward a climax are suddenly exposed, as Drouet discovers that Hurstwood is interested in Carrie, Carrie discovers that Hurstwood is married, and Mrs. Hurstwood discovers that Hurstwood is interested in another woman. The narrative now becomes tightly structured and relies on a precise chronology. This chronology begins on the day after the play, with Dreiser's presentation of the three parallel discovery scenes. He then moves on to a carefully interwoven narrative of the exact movements of Carrie and Hurstwood during the week following the performance, a week which ends with the theft and abduction. During this week, time suddenly becomes important both to Carrie and Hurstwood, since she faces a dwindling supply of money and he is confronted by his wife's ultimatum.

Dreiser handles the complex time-scheme and constantly shifting scenes of the climactic week in Chicago with surprising skill for a comparative novice in the intricacies of narrative form. He goes astray, however, in a number of unbelievable plot details which arise out of his need to solve the narrative problems introduced by his triangle. We are expected to accept that Drouet could believe that he had told Carrie about Hurstwood's marriage and that the subject had never come up again, that Hurstwood had placed all his property in his wife's name, and that Carrie could think that a married man could legally remarry simply by assuming a new name. Yet, all in all, except for the Montreal marriage, I do not think that we are troubled by these illogicalities. They function, rather, somewhat like the illogic of Huck and Jim seeking freedom by going downriver. The effective portrayal of the emotional reality of Hurstwood's dilemma and Carrie's need creates an emotional "logic" which renders insignificant these minor aberrations in probability.

The New York portion of the novel is plotless in comparison to the intrigues and the closely intertwined events of the Chicago half. Carrie's rise and Hurstwood's fall in this new setting appear to be self-generated rather than to involve the influence of other characters or to be the result of a series of causally linked incidents. Moreover, this portion of the novel has an effect of timelessness, particularly after Hurstwood loses his saloon. As in the opening chapters of the novel, change is primarily emotional change and appears to occur within a permanent distinctive season. Hurstwood's collapse exists in a timeless winter landscape, and Carrie's life in the Elfland of the theatre is set against a backdrop of spring. Both the plotlessness and the timelessness of the New York half of *Sister Carrie* contribute to the impression of inevitability in the closing section of the novel—an impression of figures moving relentlessly and almost effortlessly to fates which have already been determined by their characters and circumstances. This impression is one of Dreiser's most characteristic and powerful effects as a novelist, and in *Sister Carrie* he had already mastered the technical resources necessary to achieve it.

For many readers, the most significant aspect of Dreiser's fictional technique is his distinctive "voice" as a narrator. In *Sister Carrie*, as in all his other novels, Dreiser tells his story in the third person and permits himself complete freedom both in what he knows and how he goes about informing us of what he knows. He is a third-person omniscient narrator who informs the reader directly about the characters and their situations and addresses him on philosophical and social themes arising out of the substance of the novel. Unlike many of his contemporaries on both sides of the Atlantic, Dreiser accepted rather than rejected the dominant role of an authorial presence in the art of storytelling.

Dreiser's point-of-view technique initially suggests a solid though occasionally clumsy competence. For most scenes, he centers his attention on the major character of greatest importance in the scene and then describes that character's actions and thoughts doggedly and consistently. For example, the arrival of Carrie and Drouet in Chicago clearly calls for an emphasis on Carrie's impressions, while our initial impression of Hurstwood at Fitzgerald and Moy's demands the admiring point of view of Drouet. Occasionally, he is more adventurous, with some success. When Carrie determines to leave Hurstwood, Dreiser narrates her departure indirectly through Hurstwood's actions, following him as he unsuspectingly takes a long walk and then returns to find Carrie gone. And for two of the climaxes of the novel—the day following the Avery Hall performance and the night of Hurstwood's suicide—he adopts a panoramic method, in which he shifts from one disparate thread of action to another in order to render the theme of the complementary nature of experience.

As a novelist, Dreiser was of course committed to an attempt to represent the relationship of a character's inner life to outer reality. Broadly speaking, this relationship is what the novel is all about, though both the mode of representation and the nature of the relationship are capable of infinite variation. As an omniscient novelist writing in the nineteenth-century tradition of direct authorial analysis of his characters, Dreiser appears to rely primarily on authorial summary to render the response of his characters to their worlds. It is primarily when engaged in such commentary that Dreiser's prose becomes most turgid and circumlocutory. Fortunately, he did not depend exclusively on this technique but used as well a number of other means to define the emotional reality he wished to depict. Carrie, for example, is almost inarticulate, both in speech and in her own self-analysis. Her responses are usually limited to a smile, a frown, or a noncommittal reply. Beneath her surface placidity, however, she has an emotional nature which Dreiser communicates by investing the commonplace events and scenes of her life with an emotional meaning appropriate to her temperament. Thus, on the night that Drouet sleeps with Carrie for the first time, he and Carrie go to the theatre. Carrie is troubled by the cold evening and December sky and is further disturbed when she catches a glimpse of one of the girls from her shoe factory. At the theatre, she is moved by its spectacle of wealth and magnificence. " 'Isn't it fine,' said Carrie. . . . Once she looked up, her even teeth glistening through her smiling lips" (p. 88). After the theatre, she and Drouet have supper in a restaurant—an occasion which "went off with considerable warmth" (p. 89)—and then return to Carrie's room. By means of a series of brief vignettes, Dreiser has captured the nature and intensity of Carrie's emotional life at this moment—the fear which she associates with cold and the factory, the excitement of life represented by the theatre, and her association of Drouet both with this excitement and with a warm refuge from want.[58]

Passages of this kind are not isolated occurrences but are rather the very warp and woof of Dreiser's fiction. Often, however, their emotional reference point is less immediately available than in the theatre passage I have just cited. For example, Carrie returns to her drab New York flat and finds Hurstwood sitting by the radiator reading his newspaper. The sight throws her into a mood of despair, a mood which has its origin—unknown to her and unexplained by Dreiser—in her subconscious recollection of the dour Hanson reading his newspaper each evening while waiting for his supper. If Hurstwood is Hanson, Carrie is becoming Minnie—a role which had repelled her from her earliest Chicago days. It is the emotional weight upon Carrie's subconscious of a series of such discrete "physical" moments in her relationship with Hurstwood in New York which compels her to leave him, though she consciously attributes her motive to a need for new clothes.

Dreiser's two most distinctive authorial voices are those of a seemingly dispassionate chronicler of event and background and of a fussy commentator on his characters' actions and on the philosophical issues inherent in their actions. This second authorial voice is most apparent at the opening of a chapter, when Dreiser will frequently preface a scene with a lengthy discursive comment on a general topic related to the narrative. Dreiser's role as philosophical commentator in his novels arises out of his acceptance of the nineteenth-century convention of the novelist as an epic narrator who not only represents but also discusses the underlying truths of society and human nature. More particularly, of course, Dreiser found in Balzac a compelling example of the novelist in the guise of self-confident "seer and . . . genius."[59] After being "fascinated" by this aspect of Balzac in 1894, Dreiser had had two years' practice in philosophical speculation during his occupation of the role of "Prophet." In his *Ev'ry Month* column he frequently used a popular assumption as a straw man in order to introduce a seemingly novel or radical truth. So, in *Sister Carrie*, we have brief essays on the "true meaning" of money, of clothes, of ethics, and of travel. Occasionally, as in his comments on the true meaning of the home which open Chapter IX, he also adopts the tone of an *Ev'ry Month* "Reflection" at its most fulsomely homiletic.

The underlying function of many of Dreiser's philosophical comments, however, is less to establish a particular abstract truth which should guide our rational consideration of an incident or character than to elicit from us a sentiment which aids Dreiser fictionally at the moment in question. An obvious and characteristic example is the passage on evolutionary moralism opening Chapter VIII, which I have already discussed at some length. As I noted earlier, the abstract philosophy of the passage is contravened both by Dreiser's own statements on an aesthetic moralism in Chapter X and by his portrait of Carrie's illicit relationships as ultimately moral rather than immoral since they contribute to her spiritual development. Yet the passage does play a necessary and successful role in its immediate fictional context. Dreiser had just depicted his heroine at an early stage of her career and at an early point in the novel as about to begin a promiscuous life. His philosophical comments, however, assert that Carrie is not responsible for her actions and suggest that most women would have acted as she did. The passage, in short, for all its quasiphilosophical diction and tone is primarily a means of maintaining Carrie as a sympathetic character, of assuring the reader (in particular the reader of 1900) that despite her imminent "fall" she is still worthy of compassionate interest and of hope for success. Put another way, Dreiser's comments serve primarily the aesthetic function of contributing to the characterization of Carrie rather than the philosophical function of stating an abstract truth.

Most of Dreiser's other philosophical comments in *Sister Carrie* are similar in their divided allegiance to abstract statement and narrative persuasion, including those comments cast in psuedoscientific terms, such as the notorious anastates-katastates passage. Dreiser's philosophical authorial voice is thus analogous to his voice as a seemingly dispassionate chronicler of setting and action. Whether Dreiser is describing the rise of the department store or discussing the "philosophy" of clothes or narrating Carrie's response to clothes in a department store, he is characterizing Carrie. And out of this device of several lenses with a single focus there emerges an important though paradoxical Dreiserian effect—our impression of the author's complete absorption in and identification with his central characters despite his relatively scant attention to interior analysis and his lengthy, seemingly "neutral" passages of social history and abstract philosophy. We have in Dreiser on the one hand a relaxed narrative, compared to that of James or Conrad, because of the principally "exterior" action and the large blocks of authorial commentary and description not focused directly on the characters. Yet we have on the other a sense that the author's "looming presence"[60] is one of deep and constant identification with his characters' underlying natures and that each discursive social detail or general idea is in fact a kind of metaphoric link between his understanding and their psychic reality.

For many readers, the most objectionable characteristic of Dreiser's fictional form is the hackneyed and clichéd language present in all his authorial voices. For some obscure reason, Dreiser's failures in diction appear to arouse greater irritation than his failures in syntax despite his frequently tortured and awkward sentence structure. It is his journalist's ear for the inevitable phrase or expression which grates upon the sensibilities of the modern reader and which constitutes for many readers a major obstacle to an appreciation of his work. There are several conventional explanations of Dreiser's verbal ineptness: that his poverty of style signifies his poverty of mind, that his prose is an appropriate analogue of his "crude" subject matter, and (most recently) that his style is of minor or secondary interest because fiction communicates primarily through scene. Although each of these explanations has a degree of validity, I would like to approach Dreiser's verbal style from the somewhat different direction of the possible aesthetic function of the hackneyed and clichéd in his omniscient point-of-view technique and in his plots.

Throughout the nineteenth century, authors used the freedom permitted the third-person omniscient narrator to slip into a verbal style appropriate to the intrinsic nature of a character when describing the responses and reflections of that character. This technique permitted writers as different as Dickens and Flaubert to establish an impression of authorial closeness to the figure involved, yet to maintain as well an ironic distance because of the inadequacies or peculiarities of the style adopted. Many instances of the hackneyed and clichéd in Dreiser's diction can be viewed as a fuzzy approximation of this technique. When Dreiser comments in his own voice about "a little tan jacket . . . which was all the rage that fall" (p. 76), or "a really gorgeous saloon" (p. 48), or "a temple of gastronomy" (p. 352), he does so in the context of a character's response to the jacket, saloon, and restaurant. The careful reader does not need the phrase "from a Chicago standpoint" immediately after "a really gorgeous saloon" to realize that the saloon is "gorgeous" because Drouet and Hurstwood, not Dreiser, think it so. Dreiser makes it abundantly clear in the novel as a whole that he is aware of the limitations of taste of his major figures. Often, then, the most blatant and infamous of Dreiser's verbal gaucheries, such as "a truly swell saloon" (p. 48), must be viewed in terms of the technique of "tonality" or "indirect discourse," a technique in which the narrative voice assumes a verbal style appropriate to the character on whom the voice is focused.

Yet if Dreiser's diction functions in this way, why does his verbal style offend a class of readers who should recognize and respond appropriately to this not uncommon technique? The answer lies in two characteristics of Dreiser's style. His hackneyed and clichéd diction occurs frequently when he is not engaged in a form of indirect discourse, as in his description of the New York theatre district. And it occurs when he is identifying fully rather than semiironically with his characters, as in his epilogue on Carrie—a passage which is almost a vade mecum of the nineteenth-century literary cliché. Dreiser's verbal style in these passages causes the reader to question the degree of tonality and ironic distance elsewhere in the novel and to attribute all inadequacies of diction to Dreiser himself. This attribution is particularly apt to occur in reading *Sister Carrie*, for Dreiser's technique for the rendering of indirect discourse in his first novel was not as clearly discernible as it was to become in *An American Tragedy*, where he used a series of easily recognizable syntactical and verbal signs to indicate a shift into a verbal style appropriate to a character.

Dreiser's technique of tonality thus accounts for only a portion of his clichéd diction. The remainder of it can best be understood in relation to his plots, a relationship suggested both by the hackneyed nature of his basic plots and by the similarity between his hackneyed diction and that found in the "bookish" and "literary" narrative voice of the popular romance. Almost all of Dreiser's plots, as I noted earlier, have their origin in popular literature—the plight of the seduced country or working girl in *Sister Carrie* and *Jennie Gerhardt*, the Alger myth of success in the Cowperwood trilogy, the romance of the artist in *The "Genius."* In each instance, however, Dreiser reverses the basic moral assumption of the popular myth. Thus, in *Sister Carrie*, Carrie is redeemed not by God in death but by her own unending quest for pleasure, and she rises not because she is honest or plucky but because she has the native shrewdness to allow others to ferry her in the direction she wishes to take. But despite this reversal, a segment of Dreiser's creative imagination was committed to his original clichéd plot. When Dreiser falls into the violin vibrato of the epilogue, he is writing in felt response to Carrie's situation as a sentimental heroine, as a maiden who has been in distress and who will continue to be in distress. The underlying hard self-sufficiency of Carrie does not negate Dreiser's response to her as a noble-spirited heroine who has suffered and has been misunderstood.

Which is a way of saying that Dreiser found that clichéd myths were often simultaneously true and false and that his hackneyed language represents his unconscious adaptation of his diction to what he felt was true in particular myths. As a newspaper reporter, he had discovered that country boys and girls are indeed tricked when they come to the city, that middle-aged men do leave their families for young girls, that businessmen go bankrupt because they overreach themselves, and that artists attempt to lead Bohemian lives. And he had found, both as a reporter and as a reader of romances, that the conventional language for such narratives was that of cliché and euphemism. Dreiser's reversal of the moral values conventionally brought to bear upon these narratives is one direction of his fiction; another is his acceptance of the narratives as event. The reader recognizing Dreiser's ambivalent use of his mythic sources should therefore respond to his hackneyed and clichéd diction primarily as a base from which Dreiser will push off to undermine the moral themes adhering to that base.

Because Dreiser works against the grain of his diction, his novels appear rough and unfinished, as though the author knew neither his own mind nor the proper language in which to express his mind. For example, when Dreiser calls Carrie a "harp in the wind" (p. 555), he wished to achieve a pathetic effect, but that effect is undermined by our realization that in the course of her career she has vibrated crudely and awkwardly as well as pathetically. It is thus undeniable that Dreiser's clichéd and hackneyed diction is a flaw in his fiction. Almost all readers respond to it as a failure in artistry, and an effect of this kind indeed means a failure in artistry.

Dreiser's images and symbols resemble his authorial voices in that they vary from those imposed upon the character (parallel to his philosophical comments) to those which arise implicitly out of the narrative (parallel to his descriptive passages). The most common metaphors imposed on Carrie are those which arise from the sea.[61] Metaphors of Carrie as a boat adrift on troubled waters or as a small craft in search of a safe harbor during a storm dominate the imagery of the first half of the novel. Dreiser was always at his worst in this kind of imagery. Its obviousness makes each use of it beyond the first painfully repetitious and it also represents Dreiser at his most patronizing toward Carrie. Moreover, like Dreiser's comments on Carrie's moral dilemma early in the novel, it tends to falsify her situation in order to gain a pathetic effect. For no matter how storm-battered she may be, Carrie has a heavy ballast of self-interest to keep her from capsizing, and her subconscious motivation is well-charted whatever her appearance of drifting.

Dreiser is much more successful as a symbolic than as a metaphoric writer. Some of his symbols are, of course, as repetitious and occasionally even as hackneyed as his sea imagery. But in this instance both their obviousness and repetitiousness are often functional in the overall narrative of the novel. They frequently are what E. K. Brown, in his *Rhythm in the Novel*, has called rhythmical symbols because their constant reappearance in various contexts structures change and difference in character and situation during the course of the novel. The rocking chair, as a symbol of dream for Carrie in Chicago and of escape for Hurstwood in New York, is an obvious example of a rhythmical symbol. And there is also the important symbolic role of the theatre as an ascending form of illusion for Carrie, from merely an escape from the troubled sea of life to a source of material plenty and therefore happiness to the highest kind of illusion, the practice of an art.

Both the rocking chair and the theatre are self-evident symbols because their distinctiveness calls attention to their symbolic role. In many ways, however, Dreiser is at his best as a symbolic writer when his symbols arise out of the texture of everyday life, when he involves us in the symbolic significance of clothes, money, dwellings, physical contact, and heat and cold. Because some readers approach Dreiser with a disinclination to allow him any subtlety of technique, they occasionally fail to recognize this powerful current of "realistic" symbolism in his novels. I use the term "symbolism" in connection with these objects and actions because they are not merely the solid stuff of verisimilitude but are also, as a result of Dreiser's elaborate patterning of them through repetition and cross-reference, a means of complementing and reinforcing the principal themes of the novel.

The most obvious and well-known symbol of this kind in *Sister Carrie* is that of clothes—clothes as an index of taste and social position and—for

Carrie—of a naïve but moving desire for that which is fine and pleasing in life. Money is a somewhat more subtle though still readily apparent symbol. Dreiser's characters often are fascinated by the physical reality of money—the two soft ten-dollar bills that Drouet slips into Carrie's hand, for example, or the large bills, their denominations carefully noted by Dreiser, which Carrie receives on the occasion of her first $150 a week salary payment—because the physical transfer of money is an act which promises so much for both the body and the spirit that it either entails or suggests the sexual. Interiors of dwellings also serve an important symbolic role. (*Sister Carrie* resembles a play more than a film; we visualize Chicago and New York primarily as a series of interiors.) The careers of the principal figures can be charted on a graph of the various dwellings between the Hansons' flat and a luxurious Waldorf apartment and between Fitzgerald and Moy's well-appointed bar and a 15¢ a night flophouse cubicle. Dreiser's depiction of Hurstwood's decline contains his most successful use of realistic symbols. The detailed rendering of the physical substance of Hurstwood's decay—his clothes, activities, rooms, and appearance—creates out of the circumstantial objects of a man's life a highly structured pattern of event and object which communicates above all a moving psychological and emotional reality.

Dreiser's symbolism of the commonplace also clarifies themes which are otherwise open to misunderstanding. Although Dreiser tells us explicitly that Carrie is not a gold digger (p. 269), some critics of the novel have viewed her as both sexually cold and as a user of men. This reading is based on an interpretation of Carrie as hard and cold because she wishes to be free of a man once she had recognized his personal and material limitations. But a close reading of the scenes in which she succumbs to Drouet and Hurstwood reveals the innate sexuality of her interest in these figures at the moment of their greatest appeal to her. In the mode of the nineteenth-century novelist, Dreiser expresses her interest not as an open passion but as a covert sensuality which she communicates to her prospective lover by eye and touch. When Drouet during the restaurant scene responds sympathetically to her plight and she is moved by his kindness, "every little while her eyes would meet his, and by that means the interchanging current of feeling would be fully connected" (p. 68). And in an action which she does not repel, "he put his larger, warmer hand" (p. 69) over her hand as it lies on the table. Dreiser's symbolism in this instance carefully defines and qualifies the nature of Carrie's sexual response to Drouet. It is above all the response of gratitude, of the weak unit for the aid of the larger and stronger. It is not a fiery sexuality but it is nevertheless genuine and is a significant element in Carrie's acceptance of Drouet.

The current of sex between Hurstwood and Carrie in Chicago is stronger and, because unfulfilled, more lasting. When she and Drouet accompany Hurstwood to the theatre, "several times their eyes accidentally met, and then there poured into her such a flood of feeling as she had never before experienced" (p. 121). As they part at the end of the evening, Hurstwood takes her hand, "and a current of feeling swept from one to the other" (p. 122). When Hurstwood calls upon her during Drouet's absence, "the growing desire he felt for her lay upon her spirit as a gentle hand" (p. 131), and he indeed does take her hand, gently, in the course of the meeting. By the time they have their climactic interview in the park on the day following the Avery Hall performance, Carrie has begun to respond to this powerful current of sexuality. Basking in the "warmth of his feeling, which was as a grateful blaze to one who is cold" (p. 142), she finds herself "in a fine glow, mentally and physically" (p. 145). Carrie is not in love with either Drouet or Hurstwood. But her acceptance of both men as lovers is made easier for her by the covert sexuality of her response to their desire, whether it be the responsiveness of gratitude or of partial reciprocation of an intense desire.

Carrie's early relations with Drouet and Hurstwood involve a symbolism of sexual warmth which is part of a larger pattern of heat and cold symbolism in the novel as a whole. In Chicago, it is the emotional frigidity of the Hansons' life and the physical cold of an oncoming winter which make Drouet's enveloping warmth so attractive to Carrie. Warmth is therefore an image of life for Carrie. She requires its effect of physical comfort and well-being if other parts of her nature are to flower and flourish. In New York, Hurstwood paradoxically reverses the heat-cold symbolism of Carrie's Chicago life. Warmth is Hurstwood's refuge from the cold of an inhospitable world, as it was for Carrie. But for Hurstwood warmth is destructive rather than life-giving. He is willing to find a permanent rather than a temporary sanctuary in the warmth of the flat and the radiator, and in the closing days of his life his desire to escape the cold moves appropriately toward the act of suicide. Both Carrie and Hurstwood wish to avoid the cold but for different reasons. Cold represents spiritual emptiness for her, the need for effort for him. Warmth is therefore life for her, death for him.

The conclusion of *Sister Carrie* rests on this paradox as well as on Dreiser's finely controlled symbolic use of the Bowery and Broadway. Carrie has ascended to the warmth of Broadway, where she has a comfortable dressing room and apartment and where her name appears in lights. Hurstwood has descended to the cold of the Bowery. He is alone, penniless, and hungry. She has found the wonder, he the terror of the city. Each of the four vignettes which conclude the novel draws upon some aspect of this symbolism. The conclusion begins with a description of a snowstorm in the two worlds of the city. "Along Broadway men picked their way in ulsters and umbrellas. Along the Bowery, men slouched through it with collars and hats pulled over their ears" (p. 548). In her "comfortable chambers at the Waldorf" (p. 548), Carrie is reading *Père Goriot* and is moved by it sufficiently to sympathize with "the people who haven't anything to-night" (p. 549). But she does not think of Hurstwood. She is still the Carrie who played the faithful Laura so convincingly at the moment she was becoming deeply interested in Hurstwood; she is capable of responding to the noble sentiments and tragedies of life as long as that response does not impinge on self-interest. Her last reflection in the novel is that she will have to take a coach to the theatre. She may sympathize with those affected by the storm but her immediate concern is the effect of the storm on her.

The second vignette briefly displays Drouet in his New York hotel. He is occupied with thoughts of entertainments for the evening that "will shut out the snow and gloom of life" (p. 549). The third vignette abruptly returns us to the closed, vacuous world of Mrs. Hurstwood, whom we have not met since her last bitter argument with Hurstwood in Chicago. She has succeeded in arranging a good match for her daughter Jessica, and she and the newly married couple are in a Pullman en route to New York and then to Rome in order to escape the cold of a Midwest winter. The final vignette is that of Hurstwood. A few days earlier he had attempted to approach Carrie in her Broadway theatre but had been dismissed by a doorman without seeing her. Now, he is waiting in the cold for a flophouse to open.[62] There is no longer any warmth for him to escape into; there is only death. He opens the gas but does not light it.

The four concluding vignettes are in part an adaptation of the nineteenth-century convention of an authorial summing up of the fates of the principal characters in a novel. But they are also dramatic scenes which contain the dominant symbolic motifs of the novel, motifs which rise to a finely orchestrated finale. The search for comfort, pleasure, social posi tion, and love has been for each of the major figures in the vignettes a search for warmth. The pursuit of warmth results in temporary human connec- tions, but eventually the pursuit estranges men from each other as each figure shapes his life, or is shaped by life, in relation to the distinctive nature of his seeking. For some, fulfillment is a simple matter of a Pullman and Rome or a good dinner and an evening at the theatre. For others, it may take the far more complex form of an aesthetic sympathy for those in the cold and a complementary concern for one's own personal warmth, or it may take the deeply tragic form of a despairing acceptance of permanent cold as the only possible source of warmth.

Dreiser's epilogue is thus one characteristic of his art: an inept attempt to sum up his portrayal of Carrie. His four concluding vignettes are another: a moving and complex representation, through scene and symbol, of the principal themes of the novel.

Jennie Gerhardt

D U R I N G T H E S U M M E R of 1900, while Dreiser was in the midst of his controversy with Doubleday, Page over the publication of *Sister Carrie*, he noted in a letter to Arthur Henry that he was planning to write a second novel that winter.[1] Despite his chagrin at the "suppression" of *Sister Carrie* by Doubleday, Page upon its appearance in November, and despite increasing financial worries as he produced fewer and fewer potboiling articles, he began his new project on January 6, 1901.[2] By February 2 he had completed nine chapters of *Jennie Gerhardt*, writing in pencil on the same kind of yellow half sheets he had used in the composition of *Sister Carrie*. He apparently continued to write at approximately this speed or a little faster (the tenth chapter is the last which bears a date), for on April 16 he wrote George P. Brett, an editor at Macmillan's, offering him the novel and suggesting an advance

so that I might go forward with the work and complete it by midsummer. I have already written more than forty chapters, but an error in character analysis makes me wish to throw aside everything from my fifteenth chapter on and rewrite it with a view to making it more truthful and appealing. I shall save considerable of that which is already done, but the new parts will necessitate three and perhaps four months additional labor.[3]

Dreiser's initial and in part discarded draft of *Jennie Gerhardt* is extant in several forms. He preserved the first thirty chapters as an integral text, though portions of the text are heavily revised and other sections are missing. Fragments of approximately the next twenty chapters are also present in cannibalized form in a later manuscript of the novel. In addition, some time before Dreiser decided that he had to rewrite much of the novel, he had Anna Mallon prepare a typescript of the first thirty chapters of his holograph, a typescript which incorporates the revisions Dreiser was making in the holograph concurrent with his composition.[4] Although Dreiser was later to edit this typescript severely and to discard almost all of it after Chapter XIII, it is preserved complete in an additional fair-copy typescript.

It is possible to comment with some confidence about the dating and length of these various versions of the first draft of *Jennie Gerhardt*. The holograph, in its complete form, ran to approximately Chapter XLVII or XLVIII (Chapter XXXIII of the published sixty-two-chapter novel), since its last preserved fragment—the interview between Lester and Robert in Chicago—occurs at this point and since this length corresponds roughly to Dreiser's estimation in his letter to Brett. The typescript prepared by Miss Mallon was probably made concurrent with Dreiser's composition of the holograph. It is unlikely that he would have had it prepared after April 16, by which date he had decided to revise the novel extensively, and it is even more unlikely that it could have been prepared after June, since Dreiser quarreled with Henry and Miss Mallon in July and thereafter did not employ her as a typist. The thirty chapters typed by Miss Mallon include the two seductions of Jennie and close at the end of Chapter XXIII of the published work, when Lester and Jennie return from New York. The fair-copy typescript of these thirty chapters is the most difficult of the early drafts to date. Since it reflects Dreiser's first and principally verbal revision of Miss Mallon's typescript, he perhaps had it prepared in March or early April—before he decided to revise the novel fully—to show prospective publishers in his pursuit of an advance. In any case, the dating of this version is not too significant, for whatever its date it is a slightly revised version of the first thirty chapters of Dreiser's initial draft of *Jennie Gerhardt*.

The surviving portions of the first draft reveal that Dreiser undoubtedly referred to the characterization of Jennie when he wrote Brett that "an error in character analysis" made him wish to rewrite most of the novel. As had been true of *Sister Carrie* and as was to be true of several of Dreiser's later novels, he hobbled his imagination early in the composition of *Jennie Gerhardt* by an overreliance on his sources. In the writing of *Jennie Gerhardt*, these sources were primarily his own family background and Hardy's *Tess of the D'Urbervilles*.

For the basic plot of *Jennie Gerhardt*, Dreiser relied principally on the experiences of his sister Mary, who was generally called Mame within the Dreiser family.[5] Ten years older than Dreiser, Mame had been seduced at sixteen by a prominent and middle-aged Terre Haute lawyer whom Dreiser called Colonel Silsby in *Dawn*. The Dreiser family fortunes were at a low ebb during their Terre Haute years of 1870–79. John Dreiser was usually unemployed, Paul and Rome were in trouble with the law on several occasions, and the older girls were interested in men who could buy them things. The Dreisers of Terre Haute, as recalled in *Dawn*, and the Gerhardts of Columbus, as portrayed in *Jennie Gerhardt*, lead parallel lives both broadly and in such details as the mothers taking in laundry from a local hotel and the boys throwing down coal from railway cars. And, most pertinent of all, Paul had been arrested for theft, Colonel Silsby had intervened on his behalf, and Mame had subsequently been seduced by the colonel.

In the summer of 1879, Sarah Dreiser moved with part of the family to Sullivan, Indiana, leaving John, Mame, and several of the other girls temporarily behind in Terre Haute. That winter Mame joined her mother in Sullivan, pregnant. Silsby had unsuccessfully attempted to arrange for an abortion and had refused to marry her.[6] Mame remained with her mother until a stillborn child was delivered in April 1880 and then moved to Chicago. There she found work in a boardinghouse which was also apparently a gambling club. Within a short time, she began to live with Austin Brennan, a bluff, hard-living man, fourteen years her senior, who traveled for his family's Rochester dry-goods firm. After years of living together, primarily in Chicago, they were married sometime in the mid-1880s. Brennan's family were well-to-do and conservative, with social pretensions, and though Mame visited them in Rochester both before and after her marriage, she was apparently not welcomed. She therefore frequently lived with the Dreiser family—first in Warsaw and after 1887 in Chicago—where Brennan would join her for lengthy periods. In the late 1890s, however, she and Brennan finally settled in Rochester, and when John Dreiser died late in 1900, it was at their Rochester home. Soon afterward they moved to New York City, and though Brennan was in poor circumstances during his later years, they remained a faithful couple until his death in 1928.

Dreiser drew upon the experiences of other members of the Dreiser family besides Mame. The Terre Haute difficulties of his two older brothers Paul and Rome—the first spent some time in jail, the second was a gambler—were coalesced into the character and experiences of Dreiser's initial portrayal of Bass. Mame's illegitimate child had died and she and Brennan were childless, but another sister, Sylvia, had had a child by the son of a prominent Warsaw family in 1886. Because of the danger of a local scandal, she had gone to New York to have the child at the home of her sister Emma. She had returned to Warsaw, and after a brief stay had left the child with the Dreisers, where John Dreiser soon became attached to it.

Since Dreiser was only seven when the family left Terre Haute, he probably knew Colonel Silsby only from family legend. But he did know Brennan personally, first in Warsaw and then more fully in Chicago and New York. Brennan's Rochester connections, as reported at length by Mame, served as a base for Dreiser's portrait of the Kanes of Cincinnati.[7] There seems to be no specific source, however, for Letty Gerald. There was no such figure in Brennan's life, as far as we know. But of course she is a stock figure of the sentimental novel—the worldly upper-class "other woman" who woos the hero away from the poor working girl—and Dreiser appears to have filled in that stock part from a variety of other sources.

Mame's career appealed to Dreiser as the base for a novel because it could be adapted to demonstrate, as had Emma's, that a woman's instinctive nature created its own moral truth whatever the conventional social and moral attitude toward her actions. Dreiser had reshaped Emma's experiences to represent one aspect of this large theme—that of the woman as seeking artist; he could remold Mame's to express another—that of the woman as the spirit of generosity. In Dreiser's recasting of Emma's life, Balzac had played a major role by suggesting how a biographical narrative could be transformed into fiction; for Mame, Hardy's *Tess of the D'Urbervilles* served much the same purpose.

"After Balzac, (1894), came first Hardy (1896)," Dreiser once wrote Mencken.[8] In 1902 he thought that Hardy was "the greatest figure in all English literature,"[9] and in later years he characterized him as a tragic writer equal to Euripides and Sophocles.[10] Such novels as *Tess of the D'Urbervilles* and *Jude the Obscure* left a permanent mark on Dreiser's portrayal of the tragic nature of life. He was above all moved by Hardy's youthful figures who bring to experience a craving for life and a responsiveness to beauty but who are tragically handicapped by social restrictions, by the uncontrollable power of desire, and by a cosmic force which catches all men up in a web of action not of their own making.

Hardy's *Tess* had provoked much discussion in the midnineties of the once taboo theme of whether a "good" girl who has sinned can "live down" that experience and gain and hold the love of a good man.[11] Except for its denouement in a successful marriage, Mame's life has a striking, though essentially superficial, resemblance to that of Tess. Both were girls from poor, working-class families who had been seduced, when young and inexperienced, by a family benefactor. Their disgrace was made known to the world by a pregnancy, but despite this handicap they had won the love of another and far better man. Mame, however, though apparently a large and good-natured woman, was clearly no Tess. Like her sister Emma, she was in her youth as much pursuer as pursued, and she was also frequently domineering and vain.[12] The recasting of Mame into a figure resembling Tess was no doubt encouraged by the ready availability within the Dreiser family of a woman with many of Tess's qualities. For in his memory of Sarah Dreiser her son had at hand a powerfully evocative example of the worth and stature of the instinctively generous nature, of the temperament which reaches out to give to those in need, whatever their circumstances or condition. The emotional reality for Dreiser of Sarah Dreiser as the spirit of the mother incarnate no doubt led him to accept and to affirm Hardy's association of Tess with a spirit in nature which gives without question of propriety or convention—of a spirit, to be more particular, whose sexuality is thus "moral" whatever the common judgment of that quality.

Dreiser's principal reshaping of Mame's story in his first draft was therefore to introduce the theme of her association with nature and the natural and to cast her in the Tess-like role of a "pure woman" whose only fault, whatever her sexual sins, is her liberality of spirit.[13] Jennie, he tells us in this draft, possesses "the larger generosity of nature itself—the body that could not save itself, because it could not refuse to give" (Chapter XI).[14] Jennie thus reaches out instinctively to sacrifice herself for the good of the Gerhardt family. She gives herself to Brander in an impulsive, thankful reaction to his efforts to save Bass, and she accepts Kane as a lover primarily because he is the only hope for the Gerhardts at that point. The first draft of *Jennie* dramatizes a simple moral theme. Jennie is the "good" of this theme. Hers is the "naturally sacrificial and sympathetic temperament" which faces every call to service without any really serious consideration of the interest of self. Although the first law of nature seems truly to be that of self-preservation, and the responsibility of every individual for himself is a demonstrable physical truth, yet there is this strange errant sympathy in life, which wanders about thoughtful only for the woes of others. (Chapter XXII)

The "evil" of the theme is the moralism which condemns Jennie on the basis of the superficial circumstances of her life. "She had bitten the apple," Dreiser notes, "and the gates of a world-arranged and regulated Eden had already closed against her" (Chapter XI). Thus, her "unseeking simplicity" is to be "ground between the upper and nether millstones of society and convention" (Chapter XI).

Dreiser's initial conception of the novel stressed the moral melodrama and easily gained pathos of Jennie's plight as a betrayed and misjudged child of nature. His initial characterizations of Brander and Lester Kane in part reflect this simplistic theme. Neither is the conventional seducer of sentimental fiction—or indeed of Hardy, whose Alex D'Urberville is drawn from Victorian melodrama. Nevertheless, Brander and Kane are cast primarily in sexual roles. Brander, like Hurstwood, is age responding to the "fresh bloom" of youth. And Kane is portrayed as a character who can still be roused by the piquancy of the chase despite his world-weary rejection of almost all other pursuits and values. Neither Brander nor Lester is purposely cruel, but both are self-centered and their principal fictional role was therefore as a foil to Jennie's all-encompassing generosity.

Dreiser seems to have realized the poverty of his characterization of Jennie sometime in the spring of 1901, after he had completed approximately half of the novel in this first draft. Both this recognition and his failure to interest a publisher in subsidizing his revision led him to put the novel aside. But in the fall came good news and renewed hope and enthusiasm. *Sister Carrie* had been published in England in late July and by September had received a number of favorable reviews. Heartened by this reception, Dreiser again made the rounds of publishers, seeking now both a new American edition of *Carrie* and an advance in order to finish *Jennie*. By late October he had reached an agreement with J. F. Taylor and Company; the firm was to subsidize him through the completion of *Jennie* and were then to publish both it and *Sister Carrie*. [15]

Armed with the confidence and cash of Taylor, Dreiser and Sallie moved to Virginia in November in order to live cheaply and quietly while he worked on *Jennie*. Dreiser began his revision by heavily editing and cutting the first thirteen chapters of Miss Mallon's thirty-chapter typescript. At Chapter XIV he began a new holograph (in ink on 8 x 11 paper) at the point when Jennie meets Lester while working at Mrs. Bracebridge's home (Chapter XVI of the published novel). He included in this new holograph, however, material from all his other first draft forms—that is, he pasted in passages of varying length from the pencil holograph, the first typescript, and the carbon of the fair copy of the first typescript.

Dreiser began his laborious and complicated process of revision full of hope. "No great stretch of ground has been covered," he wrote Taylor on November 25, "but I have regained my full interest in the idea."[16] The work went at a snail's pace, however. By late April 1902, he had only the initial ten chapters to send to Taylor,[17] and by June he had reached only the early adventures of the Gerhardts in Cleveland.[18] The reason for this uncharacteristic slowness of composition was that Dreiser had begun to experience periods of hypochondria and depression in the fall of 1901, just as he was about to plunge back into *Jennie Gerhardt*, and that these soon increased so rapidly in severity and length that his work on the novel became more and more sporadic.

In July 1902, after some eight months of wandering through the South in search of health, Dreiser settled in Philadelphia. Here, too, he alternated between extensive periods of absorption in his physical and nervous condition and occasional periods of work.[19] By late December he admitted defeat to J. F. Taylor and Company, promising to return their advances when he could.[20] Almost destitute, he returned to New York in February 1903. Just before he reached the lowest point in his decline, he wrote Ripley Hitchcock, an editor who had expressed an interest in *Jennie*, that "a long illness—quite a year and a half—of nervous prostration—has completely destroyed all my original plans and I still have the novel you read, in part [apparently the fair-copy typescript], only three quarters or there abouts concluded and with no immediate prospects of finishing this spring, as I had hoped."[21]

When Dreiser put aside this second version of *Jennie Gerhardt* in late 1902 or early 1903, he had reached approximately the point when the relationship between Lester and Letty Gerald is beginning to deepen. As we can tell from a comparison of this second version of the novel and his first drafts, Dreiser's revision had been both thematic and structural. Most

of all, he had reshaped his account of Jennie's sexual fall to introduce
several new themes. Jennie, in this new version, remains a deeply emotional, self-sacrificing creature of nature, but her emotional life—particularly
with Lester—now has a stronger element of responsive sexuality than was
true of her earlier characterization. She is no longer merely acted upon but
also has a sense of the possibilities of life which expresses itself initially in
her sexual response to a man of Lester's strength and experience and later in
her own developing and ultimately profound understanding of life.
Dreiser had transformed his earlier union of Mame's adventures and the
pathos of Tess's dilemma into a study of the significant phases in the
emotional life of a woman of innate power.

Dreiser's revision also involved strengthening the portrayal of his
other major figures. For example, he introduced into his account of
Brander's desire for Jennie several key paragraphs in which Brander's
response includes his recognition of her potential depth as well as her
youthful beauty—a recognition which makes explicit in Brander's mind
the moral dilemma posed by his desire.[22] By deepening his characterization of Jennie, in other words, Dreiser was strengthening his characterization of those who love her. In particular, his full and powerful depiction of
Kane in the second half of the novel arises directly from the difficulties
imposed upon Kane's life by his realization of the depth and intensity of
Jennie's nature.

Because his new conception of Jennie now stressed her later development, much of Dreiser's initial revision and recasting of his first draft
involved the cutting and telescoping of the narrative of the two seductions.
He cut much of his lengthy account of Bass's difficulties in order to proceed
more swiftly to the climax of Jennie's relationship with Brander. And he
introduced Lester into the novel some seven chapters earlier than he had
initially and also compressed severely the account of Lester's winning of
Jennie.[23] Because of these revisions in the narrative structure, the two
seductions in the second version of *Jennie Gerhardt* have a less significant
thematic role and fictional impact than in the first. Their piquancy is
blunted by the swiftness with which they occur, and their thematic weight
is reduced by the far greater burden of material—almost two-thirds of the
novel—devoted to Jennie's development after her fall.

This, then, was the revision which Dreiser began in November 1901
and which he brought to three-quarters completion by February 1903. It
took him almost a year to recover from his collapse. When he began his

literary career again in early 1904, he devoted himself primarily to editorial work. Although he occasionally expressed a desire to complete *Jennie Gerhardt*, and although he perhaps made a few gestures in that direction, he seems not to have worked on the novel for over seven years.[24] His enforced resignation as editor of the Butterick publications in mid-October 1910, however, transformed desire into action. He determined to finish *Jennie Gerhardt* as quickly as possible so that he could hurry on to other novels and thereby discover if he could have a successful career as a novelist. He turned to the manuscript he had revised and rewritten between the fall of 1901 and early 1903 and, because of its advanced state of composition and his own sense of urgency, was able to complete the novel within two months. *Jennie Gerhardt* was put in typescript in December[25] and by early January was being read in that form by several of Dreiser's friends.

At this point the already complex history of the composition of *Jennie Gerhardt* grows even more complex and mysterious. Both Fremont Rider and Lillian Rosenthal, who read typescripts of *Jennie* in early January 1911, criticized the novel because of its "happy ending" in which, after much anguish and travail, Lester and Jennie are reunited and marry. "It occurs to me," Miss Rosenthal wrote on January 25, "that if Lester had married Letty, the tragedy of Jennie would have been greater. Poignancy is a necessity in this story and it can only be maintained by persistent want on the part of Jennie. The loss of Lester would insure this."[26] Again, as in his first draft, Dreiser had been led astray by his sources, for the marriage and long life together of Mame and Brennan, after years of separation and of rejection by the Rochester Brennans, had indeed been a happy ending. But the criticism of Miss Rosenthal and Rider[27] led Dreiser to agree immediately that the emotional logic of his portrayal of Jennie and Lester required that they be irreversibly separated. He quickly decided to recast the concluding third of the novel. But instead of revising either of his typescripts, he again turned to the battered and much-traveled manuscript which had served as his working copy since November 1901. When Dreiser began this revision in late January 1911, one copy of his typescript was in England for consideration by an English publisher,[28] and the other was apparently also unavailable. In any case, beginning with midway in Chapter XXXIV (Chapter XXXVI of the published novel), Dreiser revised his manuscript to reflect the eventual permanent separation of Jennie and Lester. He marked on the cover sheets of the chapters which followed either "old-corrected" or "new"; almost all the chapters from XLIX of the manuscript, when Letty is increasingly prominent, are marked "new." Again working swiftly, Dreiser completed this second major revision within a month. In a letter to Mencken on February 24 he announced that he had just finished *Jennie*,[29] and by mid-March he had had the second half of the novel retyped and friends were again reading the book in typescript form.[30]

The new typescript of *Jennie Gerhardt* was approximately 725 pages long. A number of Dreiser's friends who read the novel in this form during the spring of 1901 suggested that the work would benefit from cutting.[31] In April, Harper's accepted the novel but apparently insisted upon some compression. So in the summer of 1911 Dreiser put aside his research for *The Financier* and spent several weeks cutting some 25,000 words from the novel.[32] Sacrificed were some Dreiserian commentary and considerable detail involving the Gerhardts' Cleveland misfortunes and the Kanes' financial activities. Although Mencken, who had read the uncut "tragic ending" manuscript, was initially disturbed by the extent of these omissions, both he and Dreiser soon agreed that they contributed to the pace of the novel without detracting from the nature or impact of its themes.[33]

《《《《《《《《《《《《《《《《《《《《《《《《《《《《《《《《《《《

Jennie Gerhardt consists of two unequal narrative segments, each of which is itself made up of two parts. The first segment, twenty-three chapters of the sixty-two-chapter novel, tells of Jennie's seductions, first by Senator Brander and then by Lester Kane. The remainder of the novel deals with Jennie's life with Lester. This segment divides roughly into an upward movement culminating in the happy ménage at Hyde Park and a downward movement which includes the separation of Lester and Jennie and the deaths of Vesta and Lester.

The first portion of the novel, that devoted to the seduction of Jennie by Senator Brander, is the least successful because of its blatant theme of natural generosity and goodness misunderstood and mistreated by the rigid social and religious moralism which passes for righteousness in the world. A large, full-bodied girl with a dreamy, poetic temperament, Jennie resembles Carrie in that she is a creature of emotion rather than reason. But unlike Carrie, the beauty which she finds in life and nature moves her to give rather than to take; hers is the large expansiveness of nature itself and not the necessary protective self-interest of the artist seeking to find and express the beauty in nature.

Although Dreiser anticipates this characterization in his first-chapter comments on Jennie's "innate affection" and "poetic mind" (p. 1), he states it most fully in the second chapter, which is cast in the form of a prose-poem. "The spirit of Jennie—who shall express it" (p. 15), he begins, and then makes the attempt himself by means of a series of brief vignettes and images which reveal her spirit to be essentially that of nature itself at its most beautiful and pure:

When the soft, low call of the wood-doves, those spirits of the summer, came out of the distance, she would incline her head and listen, the whole spiritual quality of it dropping like silver bubbles into her own great heart.

Where the sunlight was warm and the shadows flecked with its splendid radiance she delighted to wonder at the pattern of it, to walk where it was most golden, and follow with instinctive appreciation the holy corridors of the trees. (pp. 16–17)

Dreiser's theme in such passages is less that of a religion of nature than of a natural religion; her spirit does not so much learn goodness from nature as find confirmed in natural beauty its own inherent goodness. But such a spirit, though it is at home in nature, is an anomaly in the world of men, a "world of flesh into which has been woven pride and greed [which] looks askance at the idealist, the dreamer" (p. 15). In particular, the world of men cannot understand the instinctive generosity of natural virtue, since the world of men buys and sells rather than gives. Jennie is held in contempt by society, Dreiser tells us at a later point, because she "had not sought to hold herself dear" (p. 93).

The novel thus begins on the edge of moral allegory. Jennie, whose warm and generous spirit reflects a natural religion, is to be judged and punished for her expression of that spirit by the narrow and prohibitive absolutes of social morality and formal religion, as personified by Dr. Ellswanger, Pastor Wendt, and old Gerhardt. And, of course, what better way to dramatize a moral allegory than by a sexual fall, one in which the reality of Jennie's innocence and virtue is poised against the illusion of wickedness imposed upon her because she has broken a commandment and violated a social law. The birth of Jennie's illegitimate child completes the allegory. Though born in what the world believes to be sin, the child is in truth a product of the beneficent "processes of the all-mother" (p. 98). To both Jennie and Dreiser, the birth is a confirmation of the beauty and goodness of the generative principle in life, and Jennie is not only unsullied but uplifted and strengthened by the experience.

In the context of turn-of-the-century morality and fiction, Dreiser's themes in this opening portion of *Jennie Gerhardt* have integrity and force. Like Hardy, he was drawing upon an idea present in both romantic poetry and evolutionary thought—the belief that man was part and parcel of the processes of nature—in order to raise to tragic stature a poor servant girl who was a living example of this idea. In particular, both writers sought to deal with the physical and psychological realities of sex in relation to this idea, and thus both wrote seduction stories which included much lyric prose on the heroine's affinity to nature. In Dreiser's hands, however, the story and the prose descend to the bathetic and lachrymose. His purple passages sound every cliché and hackneyed metaphor in nineteenth-century romantic poetry. And the personae and plot of Jennie's initial seduction could serve as a model for a "classic" sentimental novel: the poor but honest workingman's daughter, the upper-class family benefactor, the precipitating family crisis requiring the benefactor's aid, the pregnancy which follows his taking advantage of her gratitude, the desertion of the heroine by the lover and the resulting family and social obloquy. In short, the novel is pushed in the direction of the dead-end simplicity and sentimentality of a woman's magazine romance by Dreiser's lush initial characterization of Jennie and by her situation as a victim of her own virtue and of chance.

Dreiser saves the novel from this fate in two ways. He soon shifts its direction—initially and to a slight degree in the second seduction and then completely in the major segment dealing with Lester and Jennie after her second "fall." And he introduces even into the first portion of the novel a number of themes which relieve and indeed undermine its otherwise bathetic tone and action. For example, he endows Jennie with the same moving quality he had given Carrie—the wonder and excitement of an impressionable sensibility as it encounters for the first time the material beauty and splendors of life. The early chapters thus evoke with considerable power the emotional reality of two worlds—the Gerhardt home, with its sickness and poverty and eight people crowded into a few rooms, and the imposing elegance and plush of the Columbus House, with its warmth and light and its color and music. "How beautiful life must be for the rich"

(p. 29), Jennie thinks at one point, and her thought has all the evocative naïveté of social innocence at its most penetrating. Jennie's response to Brander, like that of Carrie to Drouet and Hurstwood, is therefore inseparable from the dawning of her aesthetic sensibility. His room to her is a place of "wonder," and she associates it with the "heavenly" and "magical" (pp. 14, 37)—in short, with an exultation of the spirit related to an Arabian Nights elevation of the poor beggar boy to a realm of riches and beauty. The richness of the carpet, the brightness and warmth of the room, the comfort and good taste of its furnishings—all to Jennie have the beauty of nature itself. Her response to beauty has a Keatsian depth and complexity, for the sensuous moves her spirit in whatever context she finds it. Dreiser has in this instance taken a conventional aspect of the seduction formula—the social superiority and therefore grandeur of the Lord—and transformed it into an effective and distinctively Dreiserian theme.

Dreiser also raises the seduction from its bathetic base by endowing Jennie and Brander with "human" characteristics within their stereotyped roles. Although Jennie is "beauty in distress" from her appearance in Chapter I in the hotel lobby with her mother until the birth of the dead Brander's illegitimate child in Chapter XI, the relationship between Brander and Jennie is itself complex and moving rather than superficial and formulistic. Establishing a motif which is to recur throughout the novel, Dreiser tells us that Jennie finds Brander's room a "home" for her spirit. The room is a place of gaiety and of human contact and exchange where Jennie's natural warmth has an outlet and where her qualities are appreciated. The repeated meetings of Brander and Jennie in his room thus occur within several overlapping emotional contexts. The two figures are a kind of provincial Othello and Desdemona. He is the experienced, world-weary warrior (political in this instance) who has "received his hard knocks and endured his losses" and therefore has an aura "which touched and awakened the sympathies of the imaginative" (p. 20). And she is the youthful innocent whose association with Brander represents her first contact with the world at large. Their propinquity, and her admiration and sympathy and his response to her natural affection and freshness, encourage the growth of love. But Brander and Jennie are also father and daughter. Their attachment therefore involves not only the affection of the protected for the protector but the more complex emotion of the provoking innocence of the daughter and the subconscious guilt of the father. When Brander announces to Jennie his generous plans for her and the Gerhardts, "reaching up impulsively, she put her arms around him. 'You're so good to me,' she said with the loving tone of a daughter" (p. 53).

Jennie is thus not a seduced rural maid and Brander is not a cunning upper-class villain despite the overt structuring of their relationship within this sentimental formula and despite old Gerhardt's almost immediate belief that Jennie has suffered a fate worse than death. Brander has an intense need and desire for Jennie coupled with an almost equally powerful sense of parental responsibility for her. And his one act of sex with her occurs not as a planned seduction in which he seeks payment for his efforts as a family benefactor (though their lovemaking has this appearance), but rather has its principal source in Jennie's impulsive response to the deepest strain in her nature, her thankfulness at his generosity.

The passage from Richard Jefferies, the nineteenth-century English nature mystic, which concludes the chapter in which Brander and Jennie make love in his room, has several purposes.[34] Most obviously, it is a form of paraphrasis—a transition from a scene in which Brander is kissing Jennie to the opening of the next chapter, at which point we find that Jennie has "fallen." But because the lengthy quotation deals with the theme of the long, slow process by which the beauty of a woman evolves in nature through many generations, and because Dreiser concludes the passage with his query "if all beauty were passing, and you were given these things to hold in your arms before the world slipped away, would you give them up?" (p. 77), the quotation summarizes the essential nature of the relationship between Jennie and Brander. For beneath the lush and hackneyed prose of Jefferies's apostrophe to natural beauty lies the dramatic truth of the sexual impulses which have brought Jennie and Brander together. As Randolph Bourne noted many years ago, one of Dreiser's major contributions to American fiction was that for the first time "he made sex human."[35] Even more remarkable than the achievement itself is that he was able to do so while laboring under the handicaps of his poetizing of Jennie's character and his adherence to the plot formula of the seduction myth.

Jennie's seduction by Lester Kane, the principal event of the second portion of the first segment of the novel, has many of the same characteristics as her seduction by Brander. The Gerhardt family has moved from Columbus to Cleveland in order to begin a new life, and Jennie finds work in the cultivated, upper-class home of the Bracebridges. Again, as with the

Columbus House, her taste and awareness are improved by her contact with a new and "higher" world, but again a step upward in knowledge brings the danger of sex. Lester Kane pursues the chase with vigor and is aided by another Gerhardt family crisis, one caused by the accidental burning of old Gerhardt's hands. Jennie is again placed in the sacrificial role of appealing for aid to a man who desires her, and again his aid is followed by her acceptance of the man as a lover.

The similarity between the two seductions is in fact only superficial. They differ in most important aspects, and these differences constitute some of the most significant themes in the novel. Kane is no conscience-stricken, fatherly benefactor but an aggressively virile man of thirty-six. And Jennie now has the experience to recognize immediately Lester's sexual interest in her. The sexual basis of their response to each other is not covert and repressed, as it was throughout most of Jennie's meetings with Brander; it is a conscious and electric force in their awareness from the moment Kane sees Jennie at work at Mrs. Bracebridge's home. Moreover, Jennie's and Lester's interest in each other is not based primarily on role, as had been true for Jennie and Brander, for whom the realities of experience and innocence, father and daughter, and benefactor and beneficiary had been more vital than their distinctive qualities as individuals. Rather, the love of Jennie and Lester is to Dreiser the consequence of their essential beings. Kane is a vigorously possessive male. His " 'You belong to me' " to Jennie echoes exactly Brander's statement (pp. 79, 130), but Kane means exclusive proprietorship rather than the protection which Brander intends. Kane's powerful drive to possess and to hold is matched by Jennie's instinctive desire to be possessed and to be held. His is the masculine principle of iron, hers the feminine one of softness. In a passage heavy with sexual imagery, Dreiser describes the inevitable attraction that a Jennie will have for a Lester:

It is a curious characteristic of the non-defensive disposition that it is like a honey-jar to flies. Nothing is brought to it and much is taken away. Around a soft, yielding, unselfish disposition men swarm naturally. They sense this generosity, this non-protective attitude from afar. A girl like Jennie is like a comfortable fire to the average masculine mind; they gravitate to it, seek its sympathy, yearn to possess it. (p. 126)

Each senses the basic nature of the other. "She was the kind of woman who was made for a man—one man," Lester thinks. "All her attitude toward sex was bound up with love, tenderness, service" (p. 144). And when Lester kisses Jennie for the first time, "She was horrified, stunned, like a bird in the grasp of a cat; but through it all something tremendously vital and insistent was speaking to her" (p. 130).

Dreiser was seeking to depict in the love between Jennie and Lester one kind of sexual and temperamental compatibility. Jennie and Lester are drawn to each other not only by a "magnetic" desire (p. 131) which might blaze and then die but by permanent needs—the need of the strong man whose strength derives in part from the act of possession, and the need of the "soft, yielding" woman (p. 138) whose deepest emotional life lies in the act of being possessed, in the giving of herself not only sexually but in every other way. The seduction plot is therefore now extraneous except for its efficiency in bringing together Jennie and Lester rapidly and outside of marriage. Their relationship is primarily that of mutual responsiveness, of a "natural affinity" (p. 131), despite its shape of an experienced benefactor taking advantage of a girl in need. When Jennie agrees to give herself to Lester, she is "sorrowful" because of the illicit circumstances of her acceptance, but her "yes" is spoken "with a strange thrill of affection" (p. 166).

Besides lacking the quality of betrayed innocence, the relationship between Jennie and Lester also lacks the earlier melodramatic elements of the loss of the benefactor, a pregnancy, and public exposure. Jennie and Lester begin to live together, and they soon discover more about each other and about the difficulties which their relationship entails. Put another way, Dreiser has moved the novel from the theme of Jennie as a betrayed child of nature to that of two human beings involved in the complex interaction between their love and the social reality which is the context of that love.

A major cause of this new direction in *Jennie Gerhardt* is the importance which Lester Kane now assumes in the story. In a long passage in Chapter XVII, Dreiser characterizes Lester as a New Man. Like Dreiser, Lester is a first-generation American and a lapsed Catholic whose response to the complexity, variety, and speed of communication of ideas in the modern world has been a loss both of faith and of fixed beliefs. "Life was not proved to him" (p. 133), Dreiser tells us. Lester is a Henry Adams who has been reading Herbert Spencer, for he has been "confused by the multiplicity of things, the vastness of the panorama of life, the glitter of its details, the unsubstantial nature of its forms, the uncertainty of their justification" (pp. 132–33). His response to this confusion and loss has been to turn inward to his own interests and desires and away from all institutionalized forms of belief and behavior. Max Nordau, in his widely read and discussed *Degeneration* (1895), had dealt with this phenomenon and had stressed the personal neuroticism which he believed was one of its major characteristics. But Dreiser, though he alludes to the "insomnia, melancholia, and insanity" (p. 132) caused by the impact of modern life and thought upon the reflective mind, casts Kane in a different, more positive mold. Lester's doubts take the complementary forms of a desire to satisfy his "animal" nature (p. 133) and a desire to preserve his personal freedom. Physical need is the only certainty in an otherwise unstable universe; and freedom is necessary to escape the restrictions imposed upon life by those who believe. The two join in Lester's attitude toward women in a way which is crucial for Jennie: "He wanted the comfort of feminine companionship, but he was more and more disinclined to give up his personal liberty in order to obtain it" (p. 136).

The initial impression we have of Lester is therefore of a man who is strengthened rather than weakened by his realization of the multiplicity of life because his insight has led him to cultivate a primitive self-interest and an emotional integrity. But the combination of doubt and self-interest in Lester's makeup also contributes to a basic weakness in his character despite his appearance of unassailable strength. Because he is a man of reflective insight, he realizes that there are few matters in the world worth one's intense preoccupation. Most beliefs are false and most difficulties will sort themselves out in time.

He flattered himself that he had a grasp upon a right method of living, a method which was nothing more than a quiet acceptance of social conditions as they were, tempered by a little personal judgment as to the right and wrong of individual conduct. Not to fuss and fume, not to cry out about anything, not to be mawkishly sentimental; to be vigorous and sustain your personality intact—such was his theory of life, and he was satisfied that it was a good one. (p. 135)

In short, Lester is an unbeliever but he is not a fighter.

Moreover, Lester is confined by the same animal self-interest which is the source of his apparent independence and strength. He is a man who desires and needs above all the "comforts" of life. Dreiser means by this term, which he uses again and again in the novel to designate that which preeminently attracts and holds Lester, a kind of sensuous ease of body and mind. This ease takes many forms, from Lester's delight in "the luxury of love" which he finds in Jennie to his pleasure in the "homey" atmosphere of his family's Cincinnati house to his satisfaction in living and working among wealthy and cultivated men and women.

Dreiser thus characterizes Lester as a man whose strength and independence seem adequate to wrench his life with Jennie out of the pattern to which its irregular origin and their different social classes have apparently destined it but whose basic inclinations are nevertheless toward an accommodation with his world rather than a struggle against it. Kane's tragic fate has two major characteristics. He is the New Man who, with some pride, believes himself free of conventional forms and institutions but who discovers that they nevertheless control him both materially and spiritually. And his belief in freedom as the one firm principle in life prevents him from securing Jennie irrevocably when he can still do so without facing a major challenge to his need for comfort. Unconsciously and subtly bound by the cords of his own temperament and ideas despite his seeming freedom and power, Kane makes his way through life increasingly puzzled by its paradoxes and ultimately dismayed by its meaninglessness.

Because Jennie's primary desire in life is to give of herself, and because in Lester she has found a satisfactory fulfillment of that need, she appears to be a static figure in the latter portion of *Jennie Gerhardt*. In fact, however, she both grows and acts, and her development and initiative contribute to the tragic irony that as the washerwoman's daughter matures intellectually and socially into a fit mate for Lester, the possibility of achieving a permanent union gradually lessens.

The matrix of Jennie's growth is now the world of men rather than of nature. From her experience at Mrs. Bracebridge's and from her early life and travels with Lester, she quickly acquires adeptness and assurance in dress, deportment, and social custom. And, more significantly, she acquires from Lester himself a knowledge of the structure of society and of life. By the time she and Lester go abroad, some ten years after their meeting in Cleveland, she is not only an appropriate and admired companion for him but can appreciate the tragic meaning of the ancient civilizations of Europe and Africa which they visit. She now shares Lester's breadth of vision. Although she clings to the ideal of marriage, she has otherwise adopted his moral relativism, particularly in matters of sex and religion (pp. 197, 310).

From the opening pages of the novel, those encountering Jennie have sensed her indefinable largeness of temperament. Both Dreiser and his characters attach a constantly recurring dual motif to this quality. Jennie is not only a "good" woman but a "big" woman. At first, these characteristics are rendered primarily by her large-souled generosity. But by the close of the novel, she has also developed in perception, not only in "philosophical" matters but in her judgment of others. She continues to be generous to all whom she meets, but she now understands consciously as well as instinctively whom or what she is responding to. When old Gerhardt dies, she weeps not only because she loves him and has long since forgiven him but because she now sees his life in "perspective" and realizes its hardships and difficulties (p. 347). And when she and Lester face the crisis created by Archibald Kane's will, it is Jennie who has a fuller recognition of Lester's essential character than anyone else in the novel. "He cared, in his way," she realizes. "He could not care for any one enthusiastically and demonstratively. He could care enough to seize her and take her to himself as he had, but he could not care enough to keep her if something more important appeared" (p. 361).

Jennie thus moves from her earlier simplicity as a symbolic equivalent of nature's generosity to a figure of some complexity. Though still cast in the pathetic role of the noble spirit hounded by the world, her actions within that role now have a hard as well as a soft edge. Her deception of Lester about Vesta, her unconscious attempts to force him into marriage by leaving him, and her later bitterness at his ready acceptance of her own suggestion of separation are the acts and emotions of a woman rather than a paragon.

At first Jennie and Lester have little difficulty, for Lester is circumspect and he and Jennie live together primarily at the Gerhardts' home in Cleveland. But when they move to Chicago their relationship becomes known—first vaguely by rumors and then fully and explicitly by Louise's accidental discovery of their flat. Lester initially believes that he can ignore the disapproval of his family and the world and live as he wishes to. But gradually he realizes that he must choose between Jennie and almost everything else he values in life—the familiar world of wealth and power in which he has flourished.

Dreiser weaves an elaborate ironic theme into his account of this long, drawn-out crisis in the lives of Jennie and Lester, a crisis which is the principal fictional event of the second half of the novel. Lester, the man of action and strength, is unable to make a decision. From his parents' discovery of his relationship with Jennie to the point ten years later when the provisions of his father's will must be faced, his characteristic response to his dilemma is to postpone a decision. It is Jennie, therefore, with her "soft, yielding" disposition, who must take the decisive step. Dreiser engages in some careful and indeed contrived plotting in order to make her aware of both the availability of Letty and the contents of the will. Jennie is thus placed in a position in which her innate self-sacrificial nature must express itself. The tragic irony in her persuasion of Lester that they must separate is not merely that it is she rather than Lester who is the motive force in this decision but also that her generosity in this instance is victorious over her instinctive recognition of the depth and permanence of their love for each other.

Jennie's mistake is not primarily an error in judgment. It is rather a flaw inseparable from the beneficent generosity which at once elevates her above the rest of mankind and lowers her self-estimation so severely that she may actually harm others as well as herself. Any attempt, however, to describe Jennie as a traditional tragic figure would falsify both her character and the aesthetic effect of her fate. For despite her one significant error, hers is primarily a tragedy of deprivation rather than of chaos resulting from an action. She is both the "good" woman who suffers because her nature and actions are not understood by the world and the universal mother whose children have left her or died. The first is the more obvious theme because it is introduced early in the novel and because its pathetic effect is close to the surface of the work. The second, however, becomes the deeper and more compelling theme as the novel progresses. Jennie's life consists in part of a constantly narrowing focus for her love. After the breakup of the Gerhardt family, she still has old Gerhardt, Lester, and Vesta. But one by one they depart until she is reduced to the artifice of adopting orphans. And they too will soon leave her, and then will come loveless "days and days in endless reiteration" (p. 431).

Jennie's loss of Lester, first through his departure and then his death, must therefore be seen in the context of her other losses. There are four major deaths in the novel—Mrs. Gerhardt, old Gerhardt, Vesta, and Lester—and at each Jennie is heartbroken and weeps. The causes of these deaths or separations—old age, illness, and social convention—represent the force that makes for transience in human relationships and in life itself. Jennie, Dreiser tells us, is someone for whom "life was made up of those mystic chords of sympathy and memory which bind up the transient elements of nature into a harmonious and enduring scene" (p. 368). The specific "scene" which Dreiser refers to in this passage is the house at Hyde Park where Jennie, Lester, Vesta, and old Gerhardt live harmoniously and happily, thus arresting for a brief period the impermanence of life. That this scene is destroyed by the death of old Gerhardt and the separation of Lester and Jennie and eventually has its last remnant of love removed by the death of Vesta represents the fragile and temporary hold we have on our moments of joy and fulfillment. The depth of our response to Jennie's life is thus conditioned not only by her limited circumstance as a woman wronged by men within a particular social reality but by her universal circumstance as a woman "wronged" by life itself. The frequent comment that Jennie is "merely" a figure of pathos rather than of tragedy is largely irrelevant.[36] She is a moving figure whose emotional life contains one of the great themes in all literature.

Lester's condition for several years after he and Jennie begin to live together is one of equilibrium as he successfully satisfies his desire for both freedom and "comfort." From the beginning, however, he recognizes the possible conflict between his unwillingness to "justify" his relationship with Jennie to his family (p. 174) and the great pleasure he derives from the order and power lent his life by his role in the family concern. "It was something," he reflects, "to be a factor in an institution so stable, so distinguished, so honestly worth while" (p. 176). Of these two worlds, it appears that Jennie's has the stronger hold on Lester, for his love increases as he comes to know her fully, and he delights in her deep vein of receptive sensuality and in her love for him. And he seems as well to be fully in control of his family and to be strong enough to resist any pressure that might be brought to bear upon his personal life from any direction.

Lester does not realize at this point, however, that men are limited by their social environments and that they court danger when they violate these limits. Dreiser introduces this theme overtly in a brief chapter-opening exercise on the theory of Social Darwinism. Animals, Dreiser notes, have their circumscribed spheres of possible life and so do men, though the boundaries for men are social rather than physical. "The opinions, pleas, and judgments of society serve as boundaries which are none the less real for being intangible" (p. 238). Man is not necessarily doomed when he crosses such a boundary, but he cannot live "comfortably" (p. 239)—a key term for Lester—when he does so. Lester thus resembles Hurstwood more than he does Frank Cowperwood. Like Hurstwood, he has reached out for the forbidden pleasures of life and in so doing has cut himself off from his safe and comfortable world. He is of course superior to Hurstwood in both intellect and position, but like him he nevertheless finds that he lacks the strength to begin a new life in an alien world in middle age. Hurstwood's step was irreversible, whereas Lester can and does turn back. But for either man to choose is to choose wrongly. Not to have possessed Carrie or not to have lived with Jennie would have been torture, but to choose love is also to choose failure.

Only a superhuman Cowperwood can avoid this universal dilemma, and as Dreiser makes clear early in *Jennie Gerhardt* when he compares Lester and his brother Robert, Lester is no Cowperwood. Lester is "bigger" than Robert in the same sense that Jennie is a "big" woman. He possesses a wide-ranging, sympathetic understanding of life while Robert is cold and sanctimonious. This difference is reflected in their business principles. "Lester was for building up trade through friendly relationship, concessions, personal contact, and favors. Robert was for pulling everything tight, cutting down the cost of production, and offering such financial inducements as would throttle competition" (p. 177). (Lester personifies a pre-Civil War capitalistic ideal, Robert the postwar reality.) In their battle for control of the company, a battle in which Lester's relationship with Jennie plays a vital role, Robert is victorious. He is "the clean, decisive man, Lester the man of doubts" (p. 236) who lacks the "subtlety," "guile," and "ruthlessness" (p. 300) necessary to succeed in great economic affairs.

An important revelation of Lester's limitations occurs in the incident involving his discovery of the existence of Jennie's illegitimate child, Vesta. On the surface, it seems that the discovery is beneficial. The last secret between Jennie and Lester is exposed, Lester soon becomes fond of the child, and his acceptance of its presence contributes to the establishment of the Hyde Park home where he and Jennie are so content for several years. But in the process of resolving Jennie's "offense" in having the child and in not revealing it, Lester reveals himself as a man powerfully conditioned by the assumptions of his class and sex despite his conception of himself as a New Man. "Jennie was before him as the criminal at the bar. He, the righteous, the moral, the pure of heart, was in the judgment seat. Now to sentence her—to make up his mind what course of action he should pursue" (p. 214). He decides to leave her but discovers that there is a major gap between "theorizing" about a decision and taking it in the face of the familiar "usage" of "comforts, appetites and passions" (p. 215). So he determines to let matters continue as they were, with the exception that Jennie must now clearly understand that there is no possibility of marriage. Thus, by revealing his susceptibility to conventional moralism, by his indecision, and by his failure to recognize the depth of his love for Jennie and therefore his need to marry her in order to forestall his social vulnerability, Lester has anticipated the doom of their relationship at the very moment that he has apparently given it new life.

The years that follow this incident expose fully the impossibility of Lester's situation given his character and circumstances. Gradually his relationship with Jennie becomes known, initially to Chicago friends and acquaintances and then to his family—first Louise, then Robert, and finally Archibald Kane himself, who, despite his fondness for Lester, has come under Robert's control. Both Archibald's will and a Sunday supplement "feature" about Lester and Jennie cruelly distort their love as well as place Lester in an intolerable position. The will is a testament to that aspect of social morality which judges a situation rather than individuals. Lester is to receive his full share of the estate if he leaves Jennie, a small legacy if he marries her, and—after three years—nothing at all if he continues to live with her outside of marriage. The newspaper account attempts "to frame up a Romeo and Juliet story in which Lester should appear as an ardent, self-sacrificing lover, and Jennie as a poor and lovely working-girl, lifted to great financial and social heights by the devotion of her millionaire lover" (p. 285). The will, in brief, misunderstands because it is based upon a conventional moralism, the story upon a conventional sentimentalism.

Lester's response to the pressures stemming from the disclosure of his relationship with Jennie is a permanent indecision. He has several opportunities to give her up—most notably when she herself tries to leave him after Louise's discovery—but he cannot bring himself to do so. But neither can he bring himself to marry her in the face of the scandal and family opposition that this step would entail. A solution finally offers itself in the fortuitous reappearance of Letty, an old admirer of his, at the point when he realizes that he must make a decision within the three years permitted by the will. Now a wealthy widow, Letty appears to offer the best of both worlds: a woman of cultivation and warmth, she is also eminently eligible and a suitable social match. Beleaguered by his family, by Letty (who has always wanted him), and by Jennie herself, he permits himself to be persuaded that there must be a separation.

Although Lester successfully implements this decision by his departure and by his marriage to Letty two years afterward, it does not bring him peace. True, he now assumes a major role in business and society. And his life with Letty is placid and satisfying. But despite his successful reestablishment of himself as a man of worldly authority, Lester is troubled and unhappy. He soon realizes that whatever Letty's attractions, Jennie is by far the "bigger" woman. And he is now fully conscious of having deeply wronged Jennie both in not marrying her when it was possible to do so early in their relationship and in leaving her. His years without Jennie thus contain a growing world-weariness and pessimism and a self-indulgent Epicureanism. Dreiser's brief account of these years and of Lester's death has an allegorical simplicity. Deprived of the "spiritual" bulwark of Jennie, Lester has sunk into despair and mere animalism. Crudely put, he has an empty soul and an overactive body, both of which contribute to his early death. At his deathbed, however, with Letty conveniently absent in Europe, he and Jennie are momentarily reunited. He expresses his sorrow and guilt, she her undying love, and they are at peace. Just before his death, she tells him about her life since their separation, and "He listened comfortably, for her voice was soothing to him" (p. 423). So Lester again gains a measure of "comfort" in this final moment.

For many readers, however, the most memorable and significant scene in the novel is not that of Lester's death, which has mawkish overtones, but rather that of his visit to Jennie after the death of Vesta. Deeply depressed by Vesta's death and by his realization that he erred in leaving Jennie, Lester tells her that

It isn't myself that's important in this transaction apparently; the individual doesn't count much in the situation. I don't know whether you see what I'm driving at, but all of us are more or less pawns. We're moved about like chessmen by circumstances over which we have no control. (p. 401)

This famous pronouncement, which has supplied several generations of literary historians with a ubiquitous image for the philosophical center of American naturalism, requires careful analysis both in its immediate context and in relation to the novel as a whole if it is to be properly understood.

Whatever the general truth of Lester's words, they represent a personal truth. His pawn image expresses both his sense of ineffectualness in the face of the central dilemma of his life and a covert supernaturalism which has characterized his thought throughout the novel despite his overt freethinking. Earlier he had attributed his difficulties merely to bad luck, as in the misadventure which allowed Louise to discover his living arrangements with Jennie (pp. 229–30). But by the time he and Jennie separate, he has elevated and generalized "fate" into a specific force which is at once social, supernatural, and (as far as he is concerned), malevolent:

It was only when the storms set in and the winds of adversity blew and he found himself facing the armed forces of convention that he realized he might be mistaken as to the value of his personality, that his private desires and opinions were as nothing in the face of a public conviction; that he was wrong. The race spirit, or social avatar, the "Zeitgeist" as the Germans term it, manifested itself as something having a system in charge, and the organization of society began to show itself to him as something based on possibly a spiritual, or, at least, supernatural counterpart. (pp. 373–74)

Lester's speculative statement that men are pawns in the control of circumstances is thus in part an explanation and a defense of his own conduct. In particular, it is a covert apology to Jennie for his failure to marry her when he could have done so. But it is also a powerful means of characterizing Lester. Throughout his life he had lived for the moment and had postponed making decisions about the direction of his life. But the decisionless flow of time contained an impetus of events which constituted an implicit and irreversible decision, and when Lester at last awoke to the fact that his life has been decided for him, he bitterly and angrily blamed fate.

Because Lester is a perceptive and on the whole an honest figure, his belief that men are pawns involves more than a rationalization of his own indecisiveness and ineffectuality. His belief also aptly characterizes social reality as that reality has been dramatized in the novel. The pressure of circumstance on Lester in his relationship with Jennie has indeed been intense, from their initial meeting within the convention of a seduction—a convention which appears to preclude marriage—to the later opposition of Lester's personal, business, and social worlds to the continuation of the relationship. In a passage cut from Chapter XL of the final holograph, Dreiser himself, as narrator, echoed Lester's attribution of superhuman powers to social force. "The conventions in their way," he wrote, "appear to be as inexorable in their workings as the laws of gravitation and expansion. There is a drift to society as a whole which pushes us on in a certain direction, careless of the individual, concerned only with the general result."

In his final position as one deeply puzzled by the insignificance of the individual, Lester therefore reflects a persistent strain in Dreiser's thought. Before making his pawn speech to Jennie, Lester had "looked down into Dearborn Street, the world of traffic below holding his attention. The great mass of trucks and vehicles, the counter streams of hurrying pedestrians, seemed like a puzzle. So shadows march in a dream" (p. 400). The scene effectively images both Lester's and Dreiser's belief that life is a helter-skelter of activity without meaning either for its observers or for the "shadows" who give it motion. As a New Man, aware of the direction of modern thought, Lester is able to give this view of life an appropriate philosophical framework. In the years that pass after Vesta's death, his view of life becomes "decidedly critical":

He could not make out what it was all about. In distant ages a queer thing had come to pass. There had started on its way in the form of evolution a minute cellular organism which had apparently reproduced itself by division, had early learned to combine itself with others, to organize itself into bodies, strange forms of fish, animals, and birds, and had finally learned to organize itself into man. Man, on his part, composed as he was of self-organizing cells, was pushing himself forward into comfort and different aspects of existence by means of union and organization with other men. Why? Heaven only knew. . . . Why should he complain, why worry, why speculate?—the world was going steadily forward of its own volition, whether he would or no. Truly it was. (pp. 404–405)

It must not be assumed, however, that Lester's pessimistic response to the "puzzle" of man's role in a mechanistic world is Dreiser's principal and only philosophical theme in *Jennie Gerhardt*. For Jennie, though not Lester's equal in formal knowledge or in experience, is his equal in the "bigness" of her responsiveness to the underlying reality of life, and she discovers not only puzzlement and frustration in life but also an ineradicable beauty. Dreiser therefore follows his comments on Lester's "critical" outlook with an account of Jennie's final evaluation of life, an account which suggests, because of its strategic location, that it has a weight and significance equal to Lester's beliefs. Jennie, Dreiser writes,

had never grasped the nature and character of specialized knowledge. History, physics, chemistry, botany, geology, and sociology were not fixed departments in her brain as they were in Lester's and Letty's. Instead there was the feeling that the world moved in some strange, unstable way. Apparently no one knew clearly what it was all about. People were born and died. Some believed that the world had been made six thousand years before; some that it was millions of years old. Was it all blind chance or was there some guiding intelligence—a God? Almost in spite of herself she felt there must be something—a higher power which produced all the beautiful things—the flowers, the stars, the trees, the grass. Nature was so beautiful! If at times life seemed cruel, yet this beauty still persisted. The thought comforted her; she fed upon it in her hours of secret loneliness. (p. 405)

Jennie's and Lester's complementary views of life represent Dreiser's own permanent unresolved conception of the paradox of existence. To both figures the world "was going steadily forward of its own volition," apparently guided by some unknowable supernatural power. Individuals counted for little in this process, but individuals of different temperaments might respond to the mechanism of life in different ways. One kind of temperament might be bitter and despairing, another might affirm the beauty which was inseparable from the inexplicable mystery of life. It has frequently been noted that Dreiser himself held both views at different stages of his career—that he stressed a cruelly indifferent mechanistic universe in *Hey Rub-a-Dub-Dub* and a mechanistic world of beauty in *The Bulwark*. It has not been as fully realized that he held the two positions simultaneously as well as consecutively and that he gave each position equal weight and dramatic expression in *Jennie Gerhardt* without resolving their "discrepancy." For to Dreiser there was no true discrepancy; there was only the reality of distinctive temperaments which might find truth in each position or, as in his own case, of a temperament which might find an element of truth in both. Dreiser's infamous philosophical inconsistency is thus frequently a product of his belief that experience is a "puzzle" to which one can respond in different ways, depending on one's makeup and experience. The "philosophy" of mechanism in Dreiser's novels is secondary to the fictional role of that concept as a metaphor of life against which various temperaments can define themselves. Or, to put the matter another way, Lester's belief in one kind of mechanistic philosophy and Jennie's in another are less significant fictionally than the depiction of Jennie as a woman of feeling and of Lester as a man of speculative indecision.

As in his best novels, Dreiser concludes *Jennie Gerhardt* with a series of tableaus which sum up in dramatic form many of the central themes in the novel. Lester has died, and the first tableau depicts the Chicago home of his sister, where his body is lying before being returned to Cincinnati. "It was curious to see him lying in the parlor of this alien residence, candles at his head and feet, burning sepulchrally, a silver cross upon his breast, caressed by his waxen fingers. He would have smiled if he could have seen himself, but the Kane family was too conventional, too set in its convictions, to find anything strange in this" (p. 425). The image, of course, is that of Lester bound and controlled by convention even in death. If permitted conscious-ness, he would be amused by the incongruity between his unbelief and the trappings of belief accompanying his death, but his quizzical puzzlement would not alter the fact that the rigidity and power of his family's conventional faith have controlled him in death as in life. The second tableau is that of the funeral mass for Lester in a Chicago church. Jennie, though present, has had to secrete herself in a corner of the church and does not participate in the service. Yet in spite of her isolation, she finds something mysterious and beautiful in the very religion which Lester had sought to discard as a bondage. "The gloom, the beauty of the windows, the whiteness of the altar, the golden flames of the candles impressed her. She was suffused with a sense of sorrow, loss, beauty, and mystery. Life in all its vagueness and uncertainty seemed typified by this scene" (p. 427). The third tableau is set in the railway station, where Lester's body is being loaded on a Cincinnati train. Again Lester is controlled by others and again Jennie observes the scene apart from Lester's relatives. But now the image projects as well a reality which silences all speculation about life—the raw finality of death as a force in the midst of life, a force which has bereft Jennie of mother, father, Vesta, and now Lester. " 'Hey, Jack!' " one baggageman calls to another. " 'Give us a hand here. There's a stiff outside!' " (p. 430). The train is drawn by a powerful black engine, "its smoke-stack throwing aloft a great black plume of smoke that fell back over the cars like a pall" (p. 431), yet the cars themselves are "brilliantly lighted" and contain "a dining car, set with white linen and silver, and a half dozen comfortable Pullmans" (p. 430). So man accommodates to death by continuing to live life at its fullest. But Jennie, alone at the station, "did not hear . . . anything . . . of the chatter and bustle around her. Before her was stretching a vista of lonely years down which she was steadily gazing" (p. 431).

Dreiser appended to this closing group of vignettes, which so su-perbly rehearse the dominant motifs in the lives of Jennie and Lester, a brief epilogue on Jennie called "In Passing" (pp. 432–33). In it, he attempted, as he had in the epilogue to *Sister Carrie*, to render poetically and discursively the career and essential nature of his heroine. Heavily and lugubriously he characterized Jennie as a kind of natural object whose life could not be judged by ordinary criteria of success and failure and whose wisdom of soul transcended understanding. The passage, like its equivalent in *Sister Carrie*, is both an unnecessary apology for his heroine's errant ways and a deflating simplification of her character. Fortunately, the epilogue was set up in print as a separate concluding chapter and could easily be dropped. Belatedly heeding the advice of such critics as James G. Huneker who had attacked the epilogue in the manuscript form of the novel,[37] Dreiser cut it from *Jennie Gerhardt* sometime after the first printing of 1911 and before Boni and Liveright reissued the novel in the early 1920s.[38] The novel is best read in its revised form, without the epilogue.

❦❦❦❦❦❦❦❦❦❦❦❦❦❦❦❦❦❦❦❦❦❦❦❦❦❦

There are a number of instructive similarities and differences between the form of *Jennie Gerhardt* and that of *Sister Carrie*. As in *Sister Carrie*, Dreiser's narrative contains an effective dramatic opening in which a young girl enters a new and expansive world; some contrivance in the solution of plot dilemmas; and an ending consisting of a finely grouped series of symbolic vignettes and an overwrought discursive epilogue. Again, segments of narrative often begin with a brief essay introducing a subject or situation, go on to the state of mind or condition of a particular character, move "inward," through indirect discourse, to a "dramatic" representation of the character's thoughts, and then present a dramatic scene in which the character is the principal focus of interest. Again, Dreiser is successful in his symbolic use of clothes, cash, and dwellings and is awkward and disconcerting (though somewhat less so) in his use of clichéd, sentimental, and pseudoscientific diction, particularly when writing about love or sex. Again, and perhaps most significantly, Dreiser communicates a sense of the causal force of time. As in the fall of Hurstwood in New York, the separation of Jennie and Lester is not only an anticipated but an inevitable event because Dreiser carefully and repetitiously details the mounting pressure upon them over the years, until time itself seems to be an agent of fate. And, finally, Dreiser achieves this sense of the inevitable in part by a rhythmic repetition of event and scene. For example, he juxtaposes Lester's rising level of confrontation with members of his family (from Louise to Robert to Archibald) and Jennie's increasing dependence upon Lester as her own family slips away.

The most important and suggestive similarities in form between the two novels, however, arise out of their parallel story lines of a young girl's sequential relationship with several men. Of course, there are three men in *Sister Carrie* and two in *Jennie Gerhardt*, but this difference is less significant than the similarity of a brief and inconclusive affair followed by a lengthy and tragic relationship. In both novels, the girl is sexually "ruined" by her affairs but nevertheless discovers through them her strength and abilities and rises in the world, though this rise is not accompanied by happiness. In both novels, the principal male figure moves from a self-confident sense of power and of oneness with his world to a self-destructive bitterness and emptiness. Through these parallels Dreiser seemed to be reaching out for a conception of human nature based on sex. His women maintain a steady pace of inner growth and an emotional integrity whatever their worldly status and despite their outward passivity. His men, though they appear to be independent and strong, are in reality dependent for their well-being on their social worlds. But as Dreiser's later novels make clear, this difference, though he may have depicted it in relation to sex in his early fiction, was to become in his mind a distinction between varying temperaments rather than between the sexes. Solon Barnes is closer to Jennie than to Lester, and Aileen Cowperwood is closer to Hurstwood than to Carrie.

Yet despite these significant similarities in the themes and form of the two novels, they have a very different emotional impact both in degree and in kind. These differences stem in part, of course, from the varying nature of the failure or decline of the principal characters in the two works. Whatever Carrie's unhappiness at the close of *Sister Carrie*, hers is not as tragic a fate as is Jennie's; and Lester, despite his dissatisfaction with his life after leaving Jennie, does not suffer as complete and compelling a fall as Hurstwood. In other words, in *Jennie Gerhardt* the emotional and narrative threads of the novel are combined in the character of Jennie, since she is both the central and the principal tragic figure in the novel, while in *Sister Carrie* they are divided between Hurstwood and Carrie. Moreover, Dreiser in *Jennie Gerhardt* not only focused more consistently on Jennie but was also more successful in dramatizing an effective "objective correlative" of her emotional nature. In *Sister Carrie*, Carrie's fall and rise are fully portrayed in relation to place, but Carrie's strength as an actress is less satisfactorily dramatized because of Dreiser's inadequate use of the stage for that purpose. In *Jennie Gerhardt*, Dreiser used the family both to shape the central themes and the structure of the novel and—once he put aside his early emphasis on Jennie's relationship with nature—to effectively render Jennie's emotional strength.

Jennie Gerhardt revolves around the relation of three families to each other and to Jennie. Initially, two families are juxtaposed—the Gerhardts and, after Lester's appearance, the Kanes. The two are similar in a number of ways despite their differences in wealth and position. Each is an immigrant family, but the Gerhardts are still European in their way of life. They speak German at home, their familial unity is characterized by patriarchal authoritarianism and matriarchal power, and old Gerhardt has a peasantlike religious dogmatism and a scrupulous honesty. The Kanes, however, have shrewdly adapted a capacity for hard work to the American entrepreneurial economy and have risen rapidly in the world. In the way-to-wealth formula Dreiser had encountered many times as an interviewer for *Success*, Archibald Kane had seen the need for a well-made product, had met the need, and had made a fortune. The two fathers thus represent the opposite poles of the assimilated and the unassimilated in American cultural life of the late nineteenth and early twentieth centuries—the immigrant who attempts, usually unsuccessfully, to preserve within his family the old and distant, and the immigrant who quickly adapts to the new and near at hand. These different kinds of response to American life have resulted, however, in a similarly rigid moralism in the two patriarchal figures. Old Gerhardt's moralism arises out of his desire to protect his family against an alien culture. His instinctive suspicion of Brander, despite Brander's avowed good intentions, is of this nature. Archibald's moralism stems not only from an innate conservatism but from a sense of good business practice. The good name of a family is a business asset which must be safeguarded. Jennie and Lester are therefore under parallel family pressure to contract safe and respectable marriages—that is, for each to marry within his religion and class. Later, when each has fallen—Jennie with Brander, and Lester with Jennie—old Gerhardt and Archibald respond with a similar combination of a sympathetic awareness of the worth and emotional depth of the errant child and a decision about the child's fate which is based on a moral absolutism. Dreiser's depiction of the Gerhardts and the Kanes reveals his compassionate understanding of the strengths and limitations of the family as an emotional reality and as a social institution. His principal intent in his portrayal of the two families was less to attack moral rigidity than to reveal the roots of that rigidity within one's deepest and therefore most confining values.

The relationship of Lester and Jennie to their families is subtle and significant. Each figure becomes an outcast as each goes his own way morally. But each also needs the emotional base of a family—Jennie to give of herself and Lester to have a "world which was back of him" (p. 223), a social foundation of power and security. As their love develops, however, their emotional roots within their own families provide less and less sustenance. The Gerhardts disintegrate as a family after the death of Mrs. Gerhardt. And the Kanes are increasingly hostile toward Lester as they discover more about his personal life. The response of Lester and Jennie is to set up a family unit of their own which both parodies a middle-class establishment and yet provides an emotional base in its own right. The movement toward mock respectability begins when Lester and Jennie pretend to the Gerhardt family that they have been married. For a time Jennie lives at home with her family, but when Lester moves to Chicago to begin a branch of the Kane family business, he establishes her in an apartment there. However, in Chicago several events persuade Lester that if he and Jennie are to live together they should do so "properly." He no longer needs to hide Jennie in an obscure corner, since the Kane family knows of their relationship; he has himself discovered the existence of Vesta; and old Gerhardt is living alone. He therefore rents a large house in the fashionable Chicago suburb of Hyde Park. He, Jennie, and Vesta settle down in their comfortable home, and soon old Gerhardt is persuaded by Jennie to join them.

For several years, despite being socially ostracized by their neighbors, the "family" of Lester, Jennie, Vesta, and old Gerhardt flourishes. The group has a "classic" middle-class configuration: the prosperous business-man husband, the homeloving and matronly wife, the charming child, and the crotchety but inwardly contented grandparent. The frugal Gerhardt and "spendthrift" Lester even indulge in some traditional domestic come-dy as they engage in a minor controversy over household expenses. Yet in reality each relationship within the family constitutes a moral outrage: the couple are unmarried, the child is illegitimate by another man, and the grandparent tacitly sanctions the ménage. Dreiser's parody of a middle-class family in the establishment at Hyde Park has a double edge. There is considerable irony in his study of Lester settling down contentedly to the life of a conservative family man despite his earlier resistance to marriage. But more vitally, Dreiser directs his irony outward against a false concept of family morality and therefore, by extension, against false concepts of morality within any social institution. Because there is happiness and emotional fulfillment in the Hyde Park home, the "family" living there is "moral" whatever its official status in social morality. Dreiser in this instance is again relying on one of his most pervasive and successful fictional techniques, that in which he both uses and undermines a cliché. Like the "seduction" of Jennie by Brander, the contented "family" at Hyde Park echoes a popular cliché while indicting the underlying assumptions of that cliché.

Since the Hyde Park family has no status in society, it cannot last, whatever its internal unity and success. The combination of widespread public exposure because of the newspaper story and increasing pressure from the Kane family ends these "dream years" for Jennie (p. 269). Old Gerhardt dies, Jennie and Lester decide they must separate, and thus this third family base disintegrates and with it all possibility of emotional fulfillment, of "comfort," both for Lester and Jennie. Both move on to more socially acceptable but less satisfactory family situations—Jennie alone except for Vesta and Lester with Letty.

The importance of the connection between Jennie's basic character and the structuring of the novel in relation to three families is nowhere more evident than in the parallel confessions of old Gerhardt, Lester, and Robert. Old Gerhardt's moralism was initially a powerful force in Jennie's life. He was an almost stereotyped portrait of the dogmatic religionist whose moment of bitter triumph occurs when he has an opportunity to drive his errant daughter from his home. But over the years he is not only reconciled to Jennie but comes to acknowledge her essential goodness and therefore his earlier error. He cannot completely square his beliefs and his feelings, for his is an irreconcilable conflict between a "conventional understanding of morality and [a] naturally sympathetic and fatherly disposition" (p. 117). Somewhat like Lester, the experience of a lifetime has led him to the unsatisfactory conclusion that life is "strange, and dark, and uncertain" (p. 245). Nevertheless, at his death, in a scene not so much borrowed from *King Lear* as reflecting an archetypal image of familial love, he asks forgiveness of Jennie, is told that there is nothing to forgive, and dies at one with her. Lester undergoes a parallel penitence. He, too, realizes that he has erred—both in not marrying Jennie and in leaving her—and suffers the anguish of his sense of having wronged her. At his death he too confesses to Jennie and is spiritually reunited with her. And finally Robert, as the years pass, comes to realize that he had wronged Lester—and indirectly Jennie—when he used his superior moral position to force Lester out of the family business. And he too confesses. The theme which Dreiser sought to express through these three confessions is the poignancy of the impossible contradictions of life which force men into choices which they later regret. So Gerhardt is torn between his beliefs and his love, and Lester and Robert between ambition and love. And it is Jennie who by representing love unalloyed—that is, love unsanctioned morally and unprofitable socially—demonstrates to Gerhardt, Lester, and Robert the priority of love in human affairs whatever the press of other demands and other needs.

The conclusion of *Jennie Gerhardt* thus has much of the emotional tension of a tragedy, though the principal figures of the novel cannot be described as conventional tragic heroes. This tragic effect arises in part from the sense of inevitability both in the separation of Jennie and Lester and in the emptiness which follows their separation. The effect is present as well in the deep and cumulative gloom caused by the deaths of Gerhardt, Vesta, and Lester. Yet parallel to these descending notes is the rising chord of the vindication of Jennie as a figure of emotional power and integrity, a vindication which receives its fullest dramatic expression in the parallel confessions of Gerhardt and Lester. Lester had said that only personality could be kept intact under the pressures of experience, that integrity plays no role in the "silly show" which is life (p. 401). But Jennie had maintained her integrity, that of her essential generosity, and the novel ends with that force intact if not triumphant.

On the whole, Dreiser is successful in structuring *Jennie Gerhardt* on the foundation of two moral families who dismiss love and an immoral family who seeks to preserve it. His portrait of the Kanes belies the frequent criticism—based primarily on *An American Tragedy*—that Dreiser could not satisfactorily depict life above that of the lower middle class, for he captures with precision the subtle variations between generations and between temperaments within a middle-class business family. And of course the Gerhardts have the particularized convincingness of Dreiser's memory of his own boyhood family life. His principal failures occur in those characters whom he created to complete the symmetry of his family structure—Vesta and Letty. Both are one-dimensional figures who were obviously manufactured to fulfill a particular role. Vesta is a latter-day Pearl; her function throughout the novel is to demonstrate the irony of sin, since she attracts not only the love of Jennie but also of old Gerhardt and Lester. And Letty, of course, is artificially shaped as a seemingly satisfactory alternative to Jennie. But these are minor flaws in the form of a novel which, despite its checkered prepublication history and despite its disconcerting early emphasis on Jennie as a child of nature, ranks as one of Dreiser's major achievements.

PART TWO

The "Genius"

D R E I S E R   B E G A N   W R I T I N G   The "Genius" in late December 1910, almost immediately after completing Jennie Gerhardt. For the next five months he worked intensively on the novel, interrupted only by the need to revise the conclusion of Jennie Gerhardt in February. By late April he had finished a lengthy holograph draft and by midsummer the draft was in typescript.[1] Harper's, which had in April accepted both Jennie Gerhardt and The "Genius,"[2] of course did not wish to publish simultaneously two long novels by the same author, and The "Genius" was put "on ice"[3] to await its turn. Jennie Gerhardt, because of Dreiser's need to cut it, was not published until October 1911, which meant that The "Genius" could not be published until the spring of 1912 at the earliest, with the fall of 1912 a more probable date. But Dreiser, working with the speed and energy characteristic of his literary affairs for almost a decade after leaving The Delineator, completed his research on The Financier by September 1911 and—despite a five-month trip to Europe—finished a first draft of the novel in late July 1912.[4] Harper's thereupon again opted to postpone publication of The "Genius," apparently finding a novel about a financier and his love life more attractive than one about an artist and his romances.

In December 1912, two months after the appearance of The Financier, Dreiser visited Chicago to do research for The Titan. He took a typescript of The "Genius" with him to be read by various Chicago friends, in particular by William Lengel, who had been his personal secretary during his Butterick days and who was now working in Chicago. When he returned to

133

New York in early February, he left the typescript behind to be read by Edgar Lee Masters and Floyd Dell, among others.[5] When Lengel finally returned the typescript in early May, it was lost in the mail.[6] Dreiser had apparently lost either the carbon or original of this typescript some time earlier, so now, almost two years after completing the novel, he was again left with only his original holograph.[7]

But even before this second loss, Dreiser had written Major F. T. Leigh of Harper's in February 1913, that "I reserve the right . . . to withdraw *The Genius* and substitute for it some completed work (novel) which I may then be anxious to see published first."[8] This "complete work" was no doubt *The Titan*, which Dreiser wished to see published first, though he had not written it as yet, because of its position as the second novel in the Cowperwood trilogy. With this desire in mind, Dreiser did not even bother to have *The "Genius"* retyped, but rather pushed ahead with his work on *The Titan*. He completed this second volume in his trilogy in November 1913 and then spent a busy winter revising it thoroughly for spring publication. Early in March, however, with the novel already in press, Harper's decided not to publish it because of Dreiser's possibly libelous account of Yerkes's mistress Emily Grigsby, the Berenice Fleming of the novel. A new publisher, John Lane, was soon secured for *The Titan*. And after some difficulty, Dreiser was able to convince Harper's to release *The "Genius"* as well for publication by John Lane.

Dreiser's dispute with Harper's over *The Titan* probably contributed to his desire to postpone completion of his trilogy and to publish *The "Genius."* But no doubt the major reason for his interruption of the trilogy was financial. It would be at least a year before he could complete his research for *The Stoic* and write the novel, while *The "Genius"* was on hand as a finished novel. In any case, he wrote Mencken on March 25, 1914, soon after reaching an agreement with John Lane on *The Titan*, that "I haven't done with the trilogy yet. One more volume—but not immediately. I am preparing *The Genius* of which more later."[9] By "preparing," Dreiser appears to have meant primarily a revision of the last two chapters and epilogue of the novel, for in the years between early 1911 and early 1914 he had become dissatisfied with the "happy ending" of his first version. In Dreiser's original conclusion (Chapter CIII of the holograph and Chapters XXVIII–XXIX and L'Envoi of Book III of the published novel) Eugene and Suzanne meet on Fifth Avenue four years after their enforced separation. Though neither seems to wish to renew their affair, they discover, during a visit by Suzanne to Eugene's studio, that they are still in love, and they are married six months later. In Dreiser's revision, Eugene decides not to greet Suzanne when they encounter each other on Fifth Avenue, since he realizes that they have now grown apart. Eugene's philosophical views and emotional life, however, are much the same in both versions. In both the 1911 and the 1914 drafts, he finds a resolution of his philosophical perplexity in Spencer's idea of the Unknowable and an emotional stability in his work and home, with his daughter Angela, in the 1914 revision, replacing Suzanne in a final scene of domestic contentment. In June 1914, after this revision, the novel underwent its second and last transformation from original holograph to typescript, this time with the preparation of two carbons to forestall any further disastrous losses.[10]

Except for its new conclusion, the novel which Dreiser had typed in mid-1914 was still the overlong, unedited work he had completed in April 1911. The three copies of the typescript had varying careers in the inevitable editing process which preceded publication. Early in the fall, the original was sent to an editor (perhaps Lengel, who was now in New York) to be cut for possible sale as a magazine serial.[11] In late November and early December, one carbon, completely unedited, was sent to Mencken in two installments for his opinion.[12] And a second carbon remained in Dreiser's hands for revision toward book publication.[13] The chronology of the editing of this second carbon is not clear, though several facts are known. First, Dreiser himself was actively engaged in editing the novel during the winter of 1914–15. He wrote Mencken on December 8, 1914, while Mencken was reading the unedited carbon, that "I am pruning and editing all the way through taking out a number [of] things which in the ms. you have stand as severe blemishes."[14] In addition, John Lane seemed to have had doubts about Dreiser's editorial skill after their experience with the massive *The Titan* and used two editors of their own. In London, Frederic Chapman worked primarily on style,[15] while in New York Floyd Dell, who had migrated from Chicago a year earlier, was hired specifically to cut the manuscript. As Dell recalled,

I would take out a large chunk of that mountainous manuscript, and go through it, crossing out with a light lead pencil such sentences, paragraphs, and pages as I thought could be spared; but when I returned for more, there sat Dreiser, with a large eraser, rescuing from oblivion such pages, paragraphs, and sentences as he felt could not be spared.[16]

Nevertheless, many of Dell's proposed cuts and Chapman's changes were accepted by Dreiser, as were the revisions suggested by Kirah Markham, who had begun living with Dreiser in Greenwich Village in mid-1914. In all, some 75,000 words were cut (approximately a fifth of the novel),[17] of which almost all were justified omissions on the grounds of repetitiousness and tediousness. Most of the cuts, aside from a few passages of sexual material slightly more explicit than those in the published novel, involve either details of Eugene's business experiences or Dreiser's discursive comments on Eugene's relations with Angela and Suzanne.

Two specific late changes, however, are worthy of note. In all of Dreiser's correspondence about *The "Genius"* up to late 1914, he spelled the title without quotation marks, and the title also appears in this form both on the holograph and on the original copy of the second typescript. But in late November 1914, when Dreiser sent an unedited carbon of the novel to Mencken, he noted that he had decided to change the title from *The Genius* to *The "Genius,"*[18] and it is this second title which appears on that carbon, on Dreiser's own carbon, and of course in the published book. (I shall discuss the significance of the quotation marks later.) Another late change was the division of the novel into three books. No manuscript or galley proof of the novel is so divided, although the published work is. This decision was apparently taken, with Dreiser's approval, when page proof was prepared, in order to divide a very long novel into shorter parts. The book which was published in early October 1915 was therefore the product of a characteristic process in the preparation of a Dreiser novel. Dreiser's first draft was initially revised by himself. Then, in typescript, it was extensively cut by himself and others, with Dreiser maintaining control of the editorial work of others at all stages in the process.

￼ᒋᒋᒋᒋᒋᒋᒋᒋᒋᒋᒋᒋᒋᒋᒋᒋᒋᒋᒋᒋᒋᒋᒋᒋᒋᒋ

The autobiographical impulse was always strong in Dreiser, though its intensity and form differed at various moments of his career. He wrote autobiographical sketches as early as the turn of the century, when he composed many of the pen portraits he later collected in *Twelve Men* (1919). And with his return to full-time authorship in 1910 there came a flow of heavily autobiographical travel books—*A Traveler at Forty* (1913) and *A Hoosier Holiday* (1916)—and of explicit autobiography. Although *Dawn* and

A Book About Myself were not published until 1931 and 1922 respectively, both were written between 1914 and 1920. And scattered throughout Dreiser's uncollected and unpublished work are many reminiscent and autobiographical fragments.

Yet the question still remains why Dreiser, once he had fulfilled his self-commitment to complete *Jennie Gerhardt*, turned to the writing of an autobiographical novel. An answer perhaps lies in the fact that *The "Genius,"* like *Jennie Gerhardt*, was unfinished business and that the particular nature of its business—to explain and to justify Dreiser as an artist—was again, in late 1910, paramount in his mind. In August 1943, in a confused and rambling account of his career to Mencken, Dreiser wrote that "in 1903, while dreaming of doing *Jennie Gerhardt*, I wrote 32 chapters of what was to be '*The Genius*,' and in 1907 or 1908 tore them up and burned them in order to do *Jennie Gerhardt*."[19] One would be inclined to dismiss this account were it not for the existence of fragments of an early manuscript of *The "Genius."* Dreiser's holograph of *A Book About Myself* is written in ink on large white sheets, but it contains as well lengthy sections on small yellow sheets, written in pencil, which are pasted in the larger, white sheet holograph. These pencilled sheets deal with Eugene's experiences as a St. Louis newspaperman, and they are so directly autobiographical that Dreiser was able to use them unrevised in *A Book About Myself* except for the change of "Eugene" to "I" and other appropriate pronoun changes.[20]

Since Dreiser stopped writing in pencil on small yellow sheets considerably before his return to full-time authorship in late 1910, this initial effort at an autobiographical novel probably does indeed date from 1901 or 1902, after he had completed *Sister Carrie* and while he was struggling with the composition of *Jennie Gerhardt*. And, of course, he did not destroy this lengthy fragment, as he recalled to Mencken, but rather disposed of much of it by embodying it in his autobiography of his newspaper days. The significance of this early attempt at an autobiographical novel does not lie in its role as a source for *The "Genius"*; except for some isolated passages (notably the letter from Dreiser's Chicago sweetheart Alice in *A Book About Myself* and Eugene's sweetheart Ruby in *The "Genius"*),[21] Dreiser did not use his 1901–2 fragment as a basis for his 1911 version. The important connection between the two attempts is that they occurred at parallel moments of crisis in Dreiser's career. On both occasions, Dreiser had just left the safety of a successful commercial career—earlier as a free-lance writer, later as an editor; on both occasions, he had left the sanctuary of marriage for the temptations and hazards of his response to youthful beauty and charm outside of marriage—earlier in a girl of eighteen with whom he became infatuated during the summer of 1901,[22] later in Thelma Cudlipp, the Suzanne Dale of *The "Genius."* Dreiser thus undertook an autobiographical novel in late 1910 to complete what he had abortively begun some ten years earlier under similar circumstances—to justify himself as a man who sought beauty in art and life despite the hardship and pain which this pursuit caused himself and others.

Dreiser's preparation in 1910 of a completely new version of *The "Genius"* can be explained on two grounds. The earlier version had of course concentrated on his experiences during the 1890s; he wished now to examine primarily his life and ideas since his emergence as an artist in 1900. And he had apparently decided that he could express his themes more readily through the persona of a painter than of a writer. *The "Genius"* therefore has two major sources—Dreiser's own life to late 1910 and his knowledge of the lives, artistic interests, and ideals of a number of young painters of his own time.

The principal difference between Eugene Witla and Dreiser is not that one is a painter and the other a writer, for Dreiser was exceptionally apt in translating his experiences and beliefs as author and editor into those of Witla as painter and art director. Rather, the major difference is the total absence from Witla's life of the subject matter of *Dawn.* Unlike Dreiser's own poverty-stricken boyhood in a German-American Catholic family, Witla's youth is bland and middle-class. Indeed, after the three opening chapters, we hear little of Eugene's family and background. Dreiser's neglect of his own early life in his portrayal of Eugene was not the result of embarrassment; in a few years he was to deal so frankly with his boyhood in *Dawn* that the book could not be published for over a decade. Rather, his creation of a colorless, swiftly narrated youth for Eugene reveals his principal focus in the novel—the exploration not of the genesis of an artist but of his mature temperament and conflicts.

However, when Eugene becomes, very early in the novel, a Chicago illustrator, Dreiser's life does become the major source of *The "Genius."* The parallels between Eugene's experiences and Dreiser's could be rehearsed in great detail, since *The "Genius"* chronicles, with few exceptions, most of the important and many of the minor events of Dreiser's life between 1892 and

1910.[23] But since my interest in the novel is critical rather than biographical, I will merely note the major parallels between Dreiser and Eugene: that each rises swiftly in journalism and then exhibits great promise as an artist; that a long-delayed marriage to a deeply sensual but conventional woman is followed by a nervous breakdown which is overcome by a period as a manual laborer; and that a second successful commercial career is interrupted by a desire to escape the limitations of marriage and to live a free artistic and sexual life. In short, though Dreiser reshaped freely the details of his life, he added little of significance that is "new" except at the opening and close of the novel—that is, except for Eugene's boyhood and Angela's death.

It was relatively easy for Dreiser to transpose his experiences into those of a painter because he had known artists from almost the beginning of his career.[24] While a St. Louis reporter, his two closest friends had been newspaper illustrators, and once installed as editor of *Ev'ry Month* in 1895, he was in the midst of the New York world of young magazine illustrators who were striving to emerge as artists. One such figure, W. L. Sonntag, attracted Dreiser greatly, and it was probably from him—or so Dreiser recalled in a later article—[25]that he first learned of the growing attempt by young American artists to capture in oil the vitality and beauty of the commonplace scenes and occurrences of a great American city. By the turn of the century, Dreiser knew a number of artists with aims of this kind. Later, after their famous 1908 exhibit, these figures were known as The Eight and, still later, as The Ashcan School. But when Dreiser encountered them at the turn of the century as illustrators of his articles or as fellow contributors to *Ainslee's*, they were merely a group of young Philadelphians who had moved to New York and were attempting to combine work for the popular magazines with their own innovations in city genre painting. Dreiser appears to have known George Luks, William Glackens, and Everett Shinn best of all, and to have responded in particular to Shinn's bold and energetic oils of New York street life.[26] In 1911, with the perspective gained by a decade, Dreiser had little difficulty associating the general direction of his own creative work with the efforts of these young artists. Indeed, in many of his New York sketches of 1898–1909, later collected in *The Color of a Great City* (1923), he had attempted to create in prose an effect similar to that achieved by a Shinn, Glackens, or Robert Henri street scene. By early 1910 this identification was complete. Dreiser wrote at that time two prose sketches so close to a typical cityscape by an Ashcan School painter that in *The "Genius"* he was able to draw upon one of them—"Six O'Clock"—for a description of a painting by Eugene.[27]

Although Shinn served as the principal source of Dreiser's detailed account of Witla's art career—in particular Shinn's New York exhibitions and Paris journey—Dreiser was attempting to render a general rather than a specific art experience and art ideal. He was concerned with art that arose out of the artist's close observation of American city life and the artist's attempt to communicate the reality—that is, the beauty—of that life.[28] His own career, as reporter, magazine writer, and novelist, had led him to believe in the validity and strength of art of this kind, and in the careers and work of The Eight he found a remarkably parallel experience and ideal.

((((((((((((((((((((((((((((((((

The distinctive and permanent element in Eugene's character is his artistic temperament. Whatever role he plays at particular moments in the novel, he is at heart emotional rather than intellectual, nebulous rather than decisive, a dreamer rather than a man of action. Above all he is responsive to beauty in its two complementary forms of natural beauty, including the "natural" beauty of the city, and "of beauty in the form of the face of a woman" (p. 295). As a young art student in Chicago, Eugene is free and happy in his pursuit of beauty. He is beginning to find himself as an artist and his emotional life is his own. He does not realize, however, the dangers inherent in his adoration of feminine beauty. His infatuation with a girl in his hometown had illustrated the possessiveness of women in love. And his brief affairs with Margaret and Ruby in Chicago had revealed that sexual desire alone cannot sustain love. But despite these experiences he deceives himself into believing that in Angela Blue he has met a woman whose possessive love offers no danger to his career and whose physical desirability represents a noble and compatible nature as well as a sensual fulfillment.

Angela's strength and danger lie in her joining of an ironclad conventionalism, a deep sexuality, and a "sympathetic attitude" (p. 80). The first prevents Eugene's early conquest and subsequent disillusionment, and the last two are the source of her permanent hold upon him. Both frustrated and trapped by Angela's nature, Eugene does the "right thing" after a six-year engagement and one sexual encounter and marries her. Once married and free to possess her without restraint, he becomes entirely "carnal" (p. 288) in his desire and surrenders to an excess of sexual activity that is the primary cause of his nervous collapse.[29] Dreiser's ironic reversal of the conventional notion of marriage as a moral institution is complemented throughout the novel by his accounts of Eugene's extramarital affairs. Marriage is a prison of sensuality for Eugene, whereas in his affairs with Christina in Book I, Carlotta in Book II, and Suzanne in Book III he finds women of a more refined sensibility. Unlike Angela, who does not share Eugene's interests in art, nature, or philosophy, they are women of an appropriate aesthetic temperament and intellectual depth. They appeal to Eugene's "finer" nature as well as to his sexuality. And best of all, they conceive of their relationship with Eugene as one of freedom rather than confinement.

But despite this ironic characterization of marriage, Dreiser portrays as well the deep need within Eugene for a protective and possessive force whatever the apparent destructiveness of that force. Paradoxically, although Dreiser does not depict his early life in *The "Genius,"* he does dramatize the powerful shaping influence of his home and his mother upon him in the guise of Eugene's desire for Angela and her hold upon him. Angela's appeal to Eugene is always greatest when he encounters her within the placidity and well-ordered routine of the Blue home. There, her stable values, her deep concern for Eugene, and her suppressed sexuality constitute in their complex emotional reality all which Dreiser had found most compelling and powerful in his mother and which had been lacking in every other aspect of his youth. The sense of guilt with which Dreiser portrays Eugene's sexual "overindulgence" with Angela thus has deeper roots than a conventional vampire theme in which the artist is drained of his creativity by his grosser appetites. Dreiser was depicting as well the combination of dependence and fear, of need and anxiety, which characterized his entire sexual life and which no doubt was a major cause of his "varietistic" career.

Although Eugene wishes to be recognized and acclaimed as a painter, material success is not his principal goal until he is recovering from his collapse. Then he decides that art has brought him nothing and that it is success which he desires. He determines to stop being a "brooding sentimentalist" and to "behave" himself (p. 394)—that is, to suppress his artistic nature. For some years he competes successfully in the world of advertizing and magazine publishing and rises to a high position. During this period he remains faithful to Angela. The artificiality and impossibility of his attempt to curb his basic nature, however, becomes apparent when he falls in love with Suzanne. Stimulated by her youthful beauty and what Dreiser wishes us to believe is her "soulfulness," he determines not only to escape from Angela but to return to art. " 'You have changed me so completely,' " he tells Suzanne, " 'made me over into the artist again. From now on I can paint again' " (p. 542). Angela and Suzanne's mother are of course opposed to this liberating union. Both are superficially successful—Angela through her pregnancy and Mrs. Dale through the ruse which separates Eugene and Suzanne—but Eugene has nevertheless been set free. In a denouement compounded out of literal autobiography and wish fulfillment, Eugene is fired from his job and Angela dies in childbirth. Freed from the restrictions of both marriage and a business career, Eugene—after a period of philosophical doubt and speculation—returns to his art contented and fulfilled. Dreiser's revision, in 1914, of his 1911 "happy ending," in which Suzanne and Eugene are reunited after several years, to an ending in which Eugene discovers that he no longer needs her is thus of little thematic significance. In the first version Dreiser was expressing a hope, in the second the reality and some sour grapes. But in both versions his stress was upon imagination and taste restored.

The "Genius" expresses several nineteenth-century myths of the artist, with a few twentieth-century clichés thrown in. The artist as Byronic or Shelleyan Hero requires freedom from social convention but must not use his freedom to fall prey to the Vampire of feminine possessiveness. If he does fall, salvation awaits him, in his guise of Victorian Poet, through the spirituality of feminine beauty, a beauty which symbolizes Art itself. And as Modern Artist he must ensure that his ideal of feminine beauty is also his equal intellectually and that he does not betray his talent to the false goals of wealth and position.

Dreiser's portrait of the artist is not only hackneyed but inept. (The considerable popular success of *The "Genius"* can be attributed both to its confirmation of popular assumptions about the artist and to its relatively frank depiction of Eugene's love affairs, a characteristic which led to the suppression of the novel by John S. Sumner's Society for the Suppression of Vice in 1916. By 1923, when Boni and Liveright republished the novel, it had achieved some notoriety as an under-the-counter book.) The weaknesses of the novel are so numerous and extended that to record them fully would itself be tedious. Dreiser's most obvious error, and surely the cause of much that is irritating in the novel, is his failure to distinguish between autobiographical purgation and fictional selectivity and economy. We are told a great deal more about various events and problems in Eugene's life than is relevant to the central issues of the novel. The impulse behind this fullness was no doubt the same impulse present in much "witness" or "testimony" writing—to lend credibility to a self-justifying narrative by plenitude of detail. But unlike his success in *Dawn* and *A Book About Myself*, Dreiser fails in *The "Genius"* to impose unity upon the mass of details drawn from the disparate experiences and impressions that represent the artist's life. The reason for this difference probably lies in the different narrative voices of the two forms. Writing in the first person in his autobiographies, Dreiser infuses into his accounts both the intensity of a narrator attempting to dramatize his past emotions and the wry detachment of a narrator aware of the fatuousness of many of these emotions. His voice has both a lyric and an ironic force, and it is the pervasiveness of this voice which unites and lends interest to the otherwise diffuse material of the autobiographies. In *The "Genius,"* however, Dreiser's third-person narrative voice is usually slack and colorless, as if the device of writing about himself in the guise of a fictional character required that he suppress his "natural" autobiographical tone. The diffuse and irrelevant in *The "Genius"* thus affect us as diffuse and irrelevant.

The second major reason for the failure of *The "Genius"* is its almost total collapse as fiction in Book III. The weakness can in part be attributed to Dreiser's indulgence in imitative form in the lengthy section of this book which follows the separation of Eugene and Suzanne. Eugene during this period seeks the consolations of various cosmic ideologies, and Dreiser tediously narrates Eugene's muddy speculations with a literal opacity. But a more significant cause of the fictional disaster in Book III is Dreiser's heavy emphasis on the character of Suzanne. Eugene's story, despite its diffuseness, had had considerable holding power up to the point of his infatuation with Suzanne. His early struggles as an artist, his nervous collapse, his domestic squabbles with Angela, his love affairs, and even his rise in advertising and publishing are credible if not compelling. With the introduction of Suzanne, however, the novel moves into fantasy. Suzanne is a giggling eighteen year old, yet Eugene—and Dreiser—endow her with the spiritual depth and artistic sensibility of the Muse of Art. Dreiser succeeds in capturing Suzanne's adolescent qualities—her enthusiasms, her inarticulateness, her revolt against family—but he fails completely to convince us that she has "the soul of an artist" (p. 531). Eugene is repeatedly amazed at the depth and breadth of her observations when in truth they are no more than the shallow responses of a bright adolescent to the leads supplied by a man of experience. Randolph Bourne once suggested that it is the permanently adolescent in Dreiser—for example, his "perpetual eagerness for life"—which attracts and moves us because most of us have long since passed into the unreflecting certainties of maturity.[30] But Dreiser could be seduced by his responsiveness to a youthful eagerness for life into the fatuousness of mistaking genuine adolescence for divine wisdom, as he seems to have done in his account of Eugene's love for Suzanne. Put another way, Dreiser's failure in portraying Suzanne was a failure of distance. He was still too close to his affair with Thelma Cudlipp to recognize the ludicrousness as well as the tragedy of the love of a forty-year-old married man for a girl of eighteen. Eugene's terms of endearment for Suzanne—Flower Face and Divine Fire—are those of Dreiser for Thelma.[31] They represent what John Cowper Powys called Dreiser's ability to capture "the drivel of ordinary conversation."[32] But to Dreiser in The "Genius" the terms are not drivel but rather the high poetry appropriate to a tragic romance. And in that failure of ironic self-perception lies the basis for much that is inadequate in the last third of the novel.

The principal value of The "Genius" is its dramatization of a disastrously bad marriage. Within this aspect of the novel, it is irrelevant that Eugene is an artist with ideas or that sexual excess symbolizes creative impotence. What is essential and what is powerfully conveyed is a gross mismating, in which both partners are at once innocent and guilty. Eugene is vain and egotistical, Angela moralistic and possessive. She wishes to "reform" him and he wishes to be free to pursue beauty. He views life as change, she as permanence. They are united only in their shared sensuality, yet they are locked into a seemingly unbreakable marriage—he by sorrow and guilt, and she by love and hate. Dreiser plays upon the emotional permutations in this dilemma with a literalness and fullness which communicate the pain and torment of their union. Theirs is a life of endless quarrels which begin in anger and recrimination and end in seeming reconciliation in bed; of alternation between silent anger and white-heat attack; of the growth in both partners of habits of stealth and deceit; and of descent into a desperate passivity which poses as a successful marriage. Much of the strength of this portrait of marriage stems from Dreiser's patent honesty; he does not indulge in a simple-minded "paying-off" of Sallie. Although Angela is a moralistic termagant, Dreiser captures in her both the pathos and the terror of a soul imprisoned by its own uncontrollable jealousy and emotionalism. And Eugene is by turns cruelly indifferent and ineptly griefstricken. At the end of one of their bitterest quarrels, Eugene breaks into tears. "He hardly knew why he cried, but the sadness of everything—life, the tangle of human emotions, the proximity of death to all, old age, Suzanne, Angela, all—touched him, and he shook as though he would rend his sides." When Angela tries to comfort him, he tells her, " 'No, no . . . it will pass. I can't help it. I'm sorry for you. I'm sorry for myself. I'm sorry for life' " (pp. 592–593). Dreiser is at his best at such moments. Whatever his personal bitterness over the failure of his marriage, that feeling was subsumed into a larger, more compassionate awareness of the tragic "tangle of human emotions" which ensnared not only himself and Sallie but all mankind.

The two abstract ideas which preoccupied Dreiser in his depiction of the bad marriage of an artist were those of the nature of art and the problem of marriage. Eugene's strength as an artist lies not merely in his natural talent and his choice of the city as a subject but in his romantic aesthetic. The beauty he finds in the city is essentially an Emersonian and Whitman-esque beauty: the artist discovers in the commonplace scenes of men at work or of machines in action or of city streets in rain and snow a personal vision of the vital, grandiose, and richly varied in life which affirms the beauty and wonder of all existence. Eugene's aesthetic, however, is a static and inconsequential theme in the novel as a whole. We hear of it almost entirely in Book I; it plays little role in the long history of Eugene's collapse, his business successes, or his affair with Suzanne. Marriage is a much more pervasive idea in The "*Genius*." One of Dreiser's alternative titles for the novel was "This Matter of Marriage, Now,"[33] and the published work begins with an epigraph from the marriage service. The problem of marriage is introduced early in the novel through Christina, a singer with whom Eugene has a happy affair shortly before marrying Angela. Christina points out to Eugene that marriage is dangerous to the artist because it drains his energy and limits his freedom. As an alternative, she advocates and practices discreet temporary alliances. Eugene is shocked by her views but his years of marriage to Angela convince him of their validity. When Eugene and Suzanne fall in love, the "matter of marriage" theme broadens and deepens. Eugene and Suzanne, one soul in bodies twain, are opposed by Angela and Mrs. Dale, who represent not merely propriety but a faith in the necessary role of social institutions in all ranges of life. And the problem of marriage now involves not merely Eugene's special needs as an artist but the validity of the institution for all men, since Eugene opposes marriage from the philosophical vantage point of an evolutionary Platonism which holds that all social forms are transient and superficial.

All the organized modes and methods of life were a joke to him. He saw through to something that was not material life at all, but spiritual, or say immaterial, of which all material things were a shadow. What did the great forces of life care whether this system which was maintained here with so much show and fuss was really maintained at all or not? (p. 681)

Yet despite Dreiser's greater attention to the marriage problem, this theme is also weakly rendered. The vital link between Eugene's personal amorous needs and his philosophical view of the inadequacies of marriage is poorly forged because the stimulus for Eugene's broader view, Suzanne, is an unbelievable character. So for both Eugene's romantic aesthetic and his philosophical objection to marriage Dreiser was unable to make Eugene's ideas function successfully within character and plot. We can sense Dreiser's strong endorsement of these ideas, but we do not come away from the novel either absorbed or troubled by them, as we do with the best novels of ideas.

The most important ideological element in *The "Genius"* is not Dreiser's introduction of ideas about art and marriage but his dramatization of an attempt by a particular kind of temperament to find a satisfactory philosophy of life and to translate that philosophy into action. Early in his career, during his Chicago years, Eugene encounters a full range of modern thinkers and begins to question and doubt conventional belief. After several years in New York and much further reading, Eugene's "philosophy of life" is fully formed. He believes that nature is indifferent to man and that all life is transient and inconsequential. "He came to the conclusion that he was nothing, a mere shell, a sound, a leaf which had no general significance. . . . Then came Darwin, Huxley, Tyndall, Lubbock—a whole string of British thinkers who fortified the original conclusions of the others, but showed him a beauty, a formality, a lavishness of form and idea in nature's methods which fairly transfixed him" (p. 157). In short, Eugene reaches the basic Dreiserian position that the world is governed by a process of mechanistic change which is both terrifying and beautiful.

This philosophy should have armed Eugene for the battle of life by supplying him with an operative contempt for the confining institutions of society and a complementary faith in his instinctive longing for beauty in the form of women and art. But the same speculative, introspective, and emotional temperament which encouraged Eugene to reach this amoral aestheticism prevents him from putting it into practice. Constantly examining all sides of a question and constantly responding sympathetically to the dilemmas of others, he has difficulty in translating a conviction into action. His major test, of course, occurs when he must make a decision about marrying Angela. Fully aware that he has grown beyond her, sensing as well that her principal appeal to him has been her unavailable sensuality, he nevertheless succumbs to her pressure and his own conscience. He had promised marriage; she had waited many years; and so he binds himself, as he knows he should not, with the cords of a false morality.

Dreiser's portrait of himself as Eugene is thus strongly self-critical. He characterizes himself as a man whose philosophy and whose love of beauty should firmly guide his life but who is nevertheless frequently led and defeated by such irrelevant forces as conscience, pity, introspection, and indecision. This self-criticism is clearly reflected in his decision to place Eugene's quality of genius within quotation marks. Throughout the novel, other characters recognize and acclaim Eugene's talent and insight as those of a genius, and Eugene himself accepts this designation.[34] But Dreiser also wishes us to understand that Eugene's genius is qualified by his inability to translate perception into action. He makes this limitation particularly clear through the irony of Eugene's own estimation of himself at a crucial point in his relations with Suzanne and Mrs. Dale. Eugene has tracked Suzanne to the Canadian retreat where Mrs. Dale has abducted her, and victory appears to be in his grasp. "Obviously, nature had intended this as the crowning event of his life. Life recognized him as a genius—the fates—it was heaping posies in his lap, laying a crown of victory upon his brow" (p. 654). But the posies of life, as Dreiser demonstrates through the events which follow, are for those who seize them, not for those who wait for the fates to distribute them among the worthy. Suzanne is lost as Eugene hesitates.

In his letter to Mencken in late 1914, in which he announced that he was placing quotation marks around *Genius* in the title of his novel, Dreiser explained that his intent was to avoid confusion with another current book called *The Genius* and "to convey the exact question which I mean to imply."[35] The question, I think, was not only "Is Eugene really a Genius?" but also "Is Genius enough?" Must it not be accompanied by strength even when the use of strength means pain for an Angela, a Mrs. Dale, and even a Suzanne?

But though Dreiser is self-critical in *The "Genius,"* his criticism is honorific in the sense that he elevates his weakness into a tragic inadequacy. When Eugene fails to act decisively in relation to Suzanne, Dreiser comments, "If he had but compelled her at once she would have been happy, but he was sadly in need of that desperate energy that acts first and thinks afterward. Like Hamlet, he was too fond of cogitating, too anxious to seek the less desperate way." (p. 602). Both the Hamlet allusion and Dreiser's only partially qualified designation of Eugene as a genius suggest that he wished to characterize Eugene not as a mere weakling but as a noble figure flawed by characteristics which in a lesser man would not be blameworthy.

While recovering from the collapse caused by his marriage, Eugene works as a laborer in a railway carpenter shop. There he observes in operation a natural hierarchy in which "almost animal intelligence" was directed by "greater, shrewder and at times it seemed to him possibly malicious intelligences . . . who were so strong that the weaker ones must obey them." He begins to think "that in a rough way life might possibly be ordered to the best advantage even under this system" (p. 326). He thus enters the cutthroat world of advertizing and of magazine publishing with the determination to be "strong, defiant, commanding" (p. 418). His talent and his apparent hardness bring him success, and it is at the height of this success that he meets Suzanne. In the triangle which emerges from this relationship, he decides that he must use the same ruthlessness which had gained him business success, and in his defiance of Angela he is cold and hard. Angela herself reflects that Eugene "had become stronger, more urgent, more defiant, during all these years in which he had been going upward" (p. 572). But in truth Eugene's hard shrewdness is only a facade. At the United Magazines Corporation he has been bested by a more determined man, his co-worker Florence White, who has operated behind Eugene's back to undermine his position. And in the key struggle with

Mrs. Dale over Suzanne, he permits her combination of deception and decisive action to win the day. "He was not truly ruthless ever," Dreiser notes, "but good natured and easy going. He was no subtle schemer and planner, but rather an easy natured soul, who drifted here and there with all the tides and favorable or unfavorable winds of circumstance" (p. 602). As Dreiser's Carrie-like sea imagery suggests, Eugene is still the nebulous, dreamy, impractical artist. He underestimates his opponents, overestimates his allies, and loses the initiative at crucial moments because of his compassion and sense of fair play.

Having lost both his job and Suzanne, and racked with guilt over Angela's impending difficult childbirth, Eugene again faces a nervous collapse. The restoration of his mental health differs from his earlier recovery in two significant ways. He immerses himself in the life-giving waters of philosophical affirmation rather than of physical labor. And he emerges from his period of despair with a cosmic overview which resembles his initial philosophical beliefs rather than his later and personally inapplicable Social Darwinistic concepts of power.

After the loss of Suzanne, Eugene becomes interested in Christian Science. He is moved less by the possible practical benefits of a belief in Christian Science—though it was physical and mental illness which led him to consult a healer—than by the philosophical base of the faith in a concept of the spiritual nature and oneness of all existence.[36] He then finds in the writings of Alfred Wallace a "scientific" confirmation of this truth, since Wallace deduces from the complexity, variety, utility, and beauty of life as revealed by evolutionary science the presence in the universe of "some vast intelligence, some pervading spirit" (p. 698).[37] Both Christian Science and Wallace's evolutionary theism are "consoling" philosophies; one views evil as a temporary "mental" aberration, the other as part of the divine order. Both affirm the presence of a controlling cosmic power which makes for good.

Eugene does not so much accept these beliefs intellectually as use them emotionally to restore his mental health and shattered nerves. In the years following Angela's death, Eugene continues his philosophical exploration. He returns at last to a state neither of belief nor of unbelief "but of philosophic open-mindedness or agnosticism" (p. 726) and achieves as well "his kind of normality—the artistic normality of which he was capable" (p. 724). In the closing scene of the novel, at peace with himself and the world, he reads an essay by Spencer on the Unknowable and concludes that

Spencer's belief in the mystery of "ultimate questions" is "the sanest interpretation of the limitations of human thought I have ever read" (p. 736).[38] And as he views the night sky immediately after this observation, he comments, " 'What a sweet welter life is—how rich, how tender, how grim, how like a colorful symphony' " (p. 736). In his evocation of a world of mystery and terror and beauty, Eugene reveals his return to the view of life which he held before his marriage to Angela. It is the view which is most congenial to his artistic temperament, since it permits him—now that he has passed through the misadventures of his marriage and business career—to resume his life as an observer and portrayer of the "sweet welter" and "colorful symphony" of existence.

This "solution" to Eugene's philosophical wandering and speculations may have satisfied Dreiser but it is unsatisfactory to any careful reader of the novel. Dreiser attributes to Eugene a Sturm und Drang period from which he emerges a whole man because of the depth and intensity of his struggle. But it is really Dreiser who, as deus ex machina novelist, has solved Eugene's major source of worry and despair by killing off Angela. And Eugene's final philosophical position does not really solve the problem presented by his temperamental love of feminine beauty. Though Dreiser comments briefly at the conclusion that Eugene is now "master" of his response to beauty in women, and though he depicts Eugene at this point as a stoical observer of the turmoil of life, it is difficult to believe that a figure who has been an uncontrollable and frenzied pursuer of young girls for some thirty years and 700-odd pages will now retire, "hardened intellectually and emotionally" (p. 734), into an asceticism in which he devotes himself, aside from a few casual affairs, to his art, his daughter, and the stars. In asking us to accept that Eugene's resolution of his philosophical difficulties also represents a solution of the practical problems of life created by his character, Dreiser has failed to distinguish between his own optimism as an autobiographical novelist looking forward and the doubts of any reader who has just experienced almost 350,000 words devoted in large part to Eugene's mistakes and limitations.

Yet despite these weaknesses in Dreiser's portrait of Eugene's career and philosophy, the character as a whole adequately reflects the complex and often irreconcilable beliefs of Dreiser the novelist. Eugene as a dreamy, seeking artist represents that side of Dreiser which could give shape to Carrie, Jennie, and Clyde, while Eugene's attempt to play the role of a ruthless man of affairs suggests the attraction of Cowperwood for

Dreiser. And Eugene as a compassionate and perceptive observer of the beauty and terror of life anticipates Solon Barnes and the Berenice of *The Stoic*.

Because Dreiser undertook his trilogy of desire almost immediately after completing *The "Genius"* in early 1911, it is perhaps Eugene's relation to Cowperwood which is of greatest comparative interest. In a sense, Eugene is an inept Cowperwood. Like Cowperwood, he realizes the transience, amorality, and beauty of existence. Indeed, his final view of life resembles both Dreiser and Cowperwood's belief that existence is an "equation inevitable." "All apparently was permitted," Eugene reflects, "nothing fixed. Perhaps life loved only change, equation, drama, laughter" (p. 726). But Eugene has achieved this recognition without acquiring the ability to pursue successfully the "all" that is permitted in an unfixed universe. The final scene of the novel, in which he sits by the fire in his comfortable suburban home, accompanied only by his daughter and the stars outside, pictures the artist as a figure who has withdrawn from the tumult of life the better to depict life. But a counter image which attracted Dreiser with equal force was that of the man of cool, conscienceless, and irresistible strength who plunges into the fray of life and takes what he wants. Dreiser longed, in short, to be, as he had not been, a man who had successfully resisted the intrigues against him within the Butterick organization, who had held Sallie completely in check, and who had won Thelma Cudlipp.

As the close of *The "Genius"* suggests, Dreiser felt that with the crises in his domestic and business affairs resolved he could renew his artistic career with full energy. And what better challenge to his abilities than an epic novel in which he attempted to sum up a whole phase of American civilization by a full study of a great tycoon. Moreover, he found in the configuration of Yerkes's career a means of fulfilling in fiction, as he had not in life, that part of his nature which viewed strength and shrewdness as the only means by which beauty could be won in the face of a restrictive social morality. No wonder, then, that Cowperwood not only shares Eugene's beliefs and desires but also some of his personal mannerisms—his wooing technique, for example.[39] And no wonder that Aileen and Angela have in common the fighting jealousy of the deeply passionate woman who has been scorned, and that Berenice has much of Suzanne's intuitive wisdom, aesthetic sensibility, and moral unconventionality.

But the Dreiser who no doubt vicariously shared the triumphs of

Cowperwood's career also imposed a pervasive irony upon that career. Despite Cowperwood's efforts to create an indestructible fortune and other lasting monuments, he is eventually defeated by the force of balance or equation present in all life. The Dreiser who wrote the first two volumes of the Cowperwood trilogy thus brought to bear on his characterization of Cowperwood both of the major qualities of the Dreiser depicted as Eugene in the last book of *The "Genius."* Dreiser may have longed to be a Cowperwood, but he knew that in truth he was an observer of the "welter" of life. Out of this mingled attachment and detachment there emerges the distinctive authorial tone of *The Financier* and *The Titan*.

The
Cowperwood Trilogy

A S T H E M A S T H E A D of O. S. Marden's magazine *Success* proclaimed in 1898, the way to wealth was Work, Sagacity, Honesty, Truth, Courage, and Energy. And as the journal's many stories and interviews revealed, wealth as a goal in itself was far subservient both to the joy of labor and to the social beneficence which wealth made possible. Marden had united the Calvinistic and Horatio Alger ideals of the spiritual value of work with the late nineteenth-century emphasis upon mental strength and self-help and had achieved a potent restatement of the American myth of success.[1] The image advanced by *Success*, however, of the American businessman as but another laborer in the vineyard of the Lord was opposed by the view of business life current in much fiction and in the rising school of muckraking journalism. In the novels of Frank Norris, Robert Herrick, and David Graham Phillips, and in the books and articles of Henry Demarest Lloyd, Ida Tarbell, and Lincoln Steffens, the businessman was a rapacious and brutal warrior who climbed to power over the dead bodies of both his enemies and the innocent public. Nevertheless, the underlying assumptions of those who exposed the realities of American business life were not very different from those who purveyed the myth of success. Both groups accepted as an ideal against which experience was to be judged the notion that honesty and concern for others—the traditional moral values, in short—should prevail in social life as they were presumed to prevail in personal relations.

Dreiser's career as editor, magazine contributor, and novelist up to early 1911 had called upon him to adopt various attitudes toward both the myth of success and its seemingly debunking counterpart of muckraking exposure. As "The Prophet" he had been predictably flexible. In his role as Social Darwinist, he viewed business and political struggle and corruption as inseparable from the American scene.[2] In his role as moralist, he deplored the methods and goals of the politically and financially great.[3] Later, as a well-paid interviewer for Marden, his standard sequence of questions implicitly endorsed the basic values of the myth of success. Such economic buccaneers as Philip Armour, Marshall Field, and Andrew Carnegie, who had clawed their way to the top of their empires, admitted, with the aid of Dreiser's leading questions, that hard work, frugality, and perseverance were the keys to their success and that their principal aim in acquiring great wealth was to aid their fellowmen.[4] It was no doubt Dreiser's sense of the discrepancy between the myth of success and the reality of American business life—the difference between what Armour said about his career and what Dreiser knew about it—which entered into his portrait of Robert Kane in *Jennie Gerhardt*. For Robert is a sanctimonious and rigid moralist in his personal affairs and is appropriately self-righteous in his estimation of himself, yet his business values and methods are those of the jungle. And it is Robert, not his more generous-spirited brother, who gains control of the family business and who builds it into a powerful trust.

Dreiser's portrait of Robert is fairly tame, however, for it was no news in 1911 (or indeed in 1901, when the character was first sketched) that there was a difference between the private and public morality of most successful Americans. Dreiser's basic social beliefs were indeed far more radical, as he began to reveal in *The "Genius."* For Eugene, with the author's endorsement, does not even profess a personal morality. Impelled during the period following his collapse by a powerful need to fulfill his desires and seemingly unhampered by moral values, he has a great advantage over those who permit themselves to be guided by ethical beliefs while playing the game of life. He fails in the long run because he has not completely purged himself of moral sentiments and because he lacks the strength to pursue his goals with a necessary single-mindedness. But his insight into the amorality of life nevertheless assaults the assumptions of both those who believe that the pursuit of success can occur within moral law and those who cry out at the violation of such law. In effect, Dreiser was saying that there is no law, that anything goes so long as it brings success.

In his many accounts of the origin of *An American Tragedy*, Dreiser always claimed that his interest in the situation of a man murdering his pregnant sweetheart in order to pursue a more socially desirable girl long preceded his choice of the Gillette case as a specific instance upon which to base his treatment of this situation. Although Dreiser left no account of the source of his interest in Charles T. Yerkes, this same sequence can be posited for the Cowperwood trilogy. It was not a desire to write a novel about Yerkes which prompted Dreiser to undertake the trilogy but a desire to write a novel about an American financier and the discovery that the career and personality of Yerkes were almost perfectly adaptable to his ends.[5]

Yerkes was a well-known figure in American life from approximately the mid-1880s, when he became prominent in Chicago gas and traction affairs, till his death in late 1905.[6] Dreiser had lived in Chicago for four years during the late 1880s and early 1890s and undoubtedly followed Yerkes's many financial battles as these were exhaustively chronicled in the local papers. And Yerkes's spectacular gift, in 1895, of a telescope to the University of Chicago was so widely noted that Dreiser himself commented on it in one of his *Ev'ry Month* columns.[7] Yerkes's full notoriety, however, occurred shortly after his death, when his fame was still great and when it was possible to write about him without fear of libel actions or other forms of retaliation. It was then revealed at great length and with much sensational detail that he had for many years neglected his wife for a young "protégé," Emily Grigsby. Moreover, Yerkes's widow, Mary, also created sensational news soon after his death when she married Wilson Mizner, who was some twenty years her junior. The marriage soon broke up in a scandal, with Mrs. Yerkes claiming that Mizner had married her by trickery while she was drunk, and Yerkes's life was again fully recounted. And this life, with its details of Yerkes's Philadelphia prison sentence, his divorce of his first wife, his dramatic rise in Chicago, his freebooting financial methods, his immense expenditures on his private art collection and his New York mansion, and his vast plans for a London traction system, was so inherently dramatic that a newspaper report of it just after his death was titled "The Materials of a Great Novel" and concluded with an appeal for an American Balzac to undertake the project.[8]

Yerkes's life continued to supply grist for various kinds of mills for five or six years after his death. The Sunday press found it an apt subject for elaborate spreads which emphasized his amours and his expensive tastes.[9]

Muckraking magazines found in his career in Philadelphia, Chicago, and London much which illustrated the evils of uncontrolled financial speculation. One such account, by Charles E. Russell, appeared originally in *Everybody's* magazine in September 1907 and then, in 1908, as two chapters in Russell's *Lawless Wealth*, published by B. W. Dodge, a firm in which Dreiser had a financial interest. Another, Edwin Lefèvre's "What Availeth It?" was published in *Everybody's* in June 1911, when Dreiser was beginning his research into Yerkes's career.

Despite this notoriety, the American scene contained financiers both more famous and more wealthy than Yerkes whom Dreiser might have turned to as prototypes. But Yerkes had several major attractions as a model besides the obvious though necessary one that he was dead. His life had indeed been dramatic and could easily be shaped into exciting fiction. But more significantly, Yerkes's methods and expressed beliefs would permit Dreiser to introduce a radical concept of American experience into his narrative. As Lefèvre noted, Yerkes "was not worse than so many other captains of industry. He merely was less hypocritical than the rest."[10] In Yerkes's honest practice of dishonesty Dreiser had an immensely effective tool for an ironic examination of the hypocrisy governing all American social and moral life. And, finally, Yerkes's interest in art and women permitted Dreiser to deal once again with the theme present in so much of his fiction—the desire of the seeking temperament for beauty.

I shall examine the specific nature of Dreiser's use of the circumstances of Yerkes's life in my discussion of each of the three novels of the trilogy. But it would be useful to note at this point that his research took three general directions: Yerkes's career, including the more elusive details of his personal life; American economic history from the early 1860s to Yerkes's death; and Philadelphia, Chicago, and London social and political history for the periods of Yerkes's activities in these cities. From the very first, even before he began to write *The Financier*, Dreiser planned that his study of an American tycoon would have an epic breadth. He would not merely tell the story of a particular "captain of industry" but would attempt to represent as well a whole phase of American social, economic, and moral life.

It was no doubt this epic impulse which Dreiser referred to in a 1912 interview when he commented that "In 'The Financier' I have not taken a man so much as I have a condition. . . ." He went on in the same interview to note that "It has always struck me that America since the civil war in its financial and constructive tendencies has represented more the natural action of the human mind when it is stripped of convention, theory, prejudice and belief of any kind than almost any period in the world's history."[11] His novel was thus epic not only because it depicted a vital moment in American life, one in which the "condition" of economic piracy flourished, but because it caught in its portrayal of that condition a permanent social and psychological reality. Stated in terms of its origin, the concept of man and society which underlies the Cowperwood trilogy is closely related to Spencer's law of equation or balance.

I have already discussed Dreiser's endorsement of the idea of equation in his *Ev'ry Month* editorials and in his 1899 story "The Shining Slave Makers." By 1911 the idea was firmly rooted in Dreiser's thinking; it was to remain the cornerstone of his philosophy for the rest of his life. Both his only published work of philosophy, *Hey Rub-a-Dub-Dub* (1920), and his massive though incomplete "Notes on Life" rest upon it. The "natural action of the human mind" which Cowperwood illustrates within Dreiser's idea of equation is both obvious and complex. Cowperwood is a clear example of the man who realizes that life is a struggle in which the strong battle the weak and that morality is merely a metaphor of this conflict. On a more complex level, Cowperwood's responsiveness to the equation of life is also a responsiveness to the beauty pervading all life, a beauty whose most compelling forms are art and women. And, finally, though Cowperwood (unlike Eugene) succeeds in fulfilling his desires, he nevertheless succumbs on several occasions to the counterpress of the mass in the "equation inevitable."

The idea of equation was thus useful to Dreiser as a metaphor for many of his basic beliefs and feelings. He could use it to express his contempt for conventional morality while affirming through it an order independent of human volition; and he could use its mechanism to attack human pride while affirming the perceptive and feeling mind which could sense the beauty present in a mechanistic world. And always it was a flexible idea, one which could accommodate his otherwise contradictory philosophical "moods." Thus, for most of his career he used it to attack moralistic reform movements, but in the 1930s he could adapt it to sanction reform, including reform through communism, by arguing that the social balance had swung too far in the direction of absolute power by the strong and that reform was the mechanistic response of the social organism to this imbalance.

The idea of equation was not only flexible but amorphous and could absorb Dreiser's various enthusiasms at different moments of his career. The mechanism of Jacques Loeb, for example, which he seems to have encountered about 1914 or 1915 (after completing *The Titan*),[12] confirmed as a specific biological reality the mechanism which Dreiser's idea of equation posited for all life. And in his essay on "The American Financier" in *Hey Rub-a-Dub-Dub* Dreiser offered the thought of Nietzsche and Marx as metaphoric statements of the two poles of individual and mass power within the idea of balance.[13]

Dreiser's use of Nietzsche in this essay as a metaphor of the ideal of individual power suggests the role of Nietzsche's thought during the composition of the first two volumes of the Cowperwood trilogy. Nietzsche had been well known as a "dangerous" philosopher since 1895, when Nordau had attacked him in his *Degeneration*, but his major impact upon English and American thought dates from 1908, when his ideas began to be seriously discussed and disputed. Mencken had been a Nietzsche enthusiast for some years, and in 1908 he published *The Philosophy of Friedrich Nietzsche*, a defense and exposition of Nietzsche's thought. He sent a copy to Dreiser, who replied favorably that he considered himself and Nietzsche as "hale fellows well met."[14] But in a letter to Mencken ten days later he qualified his earlier endorsement and referred to Nietzsche as "Schopenhauer confused and warmed over."[15] Both remarks suggest that Nietzsche's ideas, as explained by Mencken, served primarily to confirm views already held by Dreiser. He and Nietzsche were "hale fellows well met" because both rejected moral values which arose from supernatural sanctions and because both believed that life was essentially struggle. And Nietzsche appeared to be "warmed over" Schopenhauer because Mencken stated that Nietzsche's will to power was Schopenhauer's will to live and Dreiser himself had already deduced, from Spencerian Social Darwinism, that the struggle to live was principally a struggle for power.

Nietzsche's influence on Dreiser is perhaps clearest in the theme of contempt for the masses with their "slave morality" which runs through the first two Cowperwood novels and which made *The Titan* one of Mencken's favorite Dreiser novels. In all, however, Dreiser's encounter with Nietzsche's ideas (through Mencken) resembles his acceptance of many other "philosophies," several of them seemingly contradictory, for the remainder of his career. These beliefs, from socialism to technocracy and from Freudianism to Hindu mysticism, did not alter Dreiser's thought but rather were absorbed into his permanent and emotionally grounded cosmology of the equation inevitable.

The Financier

SOMETIME DURING the spring or early summer of 1911, after completing a first draft of The "Genius" and while revising Jennie Gerhardt for publication, Dreiser began his research for a long novel based on the life of Charles T. Yerkes.[1] Early in August, he wrote Mencken that "The data for book four—The Financier—is practically gathered. I shall begin writing in September."[2] Dreiser's newsy, straightforward remark to Mencken actually disguises an unresolved and perhaps unacknowledged dilemma. He wished to think of his novel as a single book, yet his research had so far included only general accounts of Yerkes's career as a whole and detailed material on his Philadelphia years. When he began writing in September, he had on hand very little precise information about Yerkes's complex financial activities in Chicago and London. His response to this situation was to entitle his holograph "The Financier: Part I" and to write in such detail about Yerkes's Philadelphia career that by November he had produced the equivalent of a full-length novel without having completed his account of this phase of Yerkes's life. Dreiser, in short, was faced with an insoluble problem. He wished to maintain the unity of his novel by considering it a single work with one title, yet his research and his writing were taking him in the direction of a multivolume novel with the implication that each volume would be complete in itself.

As the chapters of Part One piled up, he realized, of course, that the novel would have to be published in parts. But until July 1912, only three months before the appearance of The Financier, he still expected that the

160

three volumes would be called Part One, Part Two, and Part Three of *The Financier*.[3] Soon after, Harper's undoubtedly noted to Dreiser that a novel published as Part One of a longer work would be commercially handicapped and that the first volume should therefore be issued with a distinctive title and with no indication that it could not be read as an independent novel.[4] As a result of this late change in plans, the title page of the volume merely reads *The Financier: A Novel*, and nowhere in its front matter or dust jacket is there any indication that the novel is the first volume in a trilogy. Only in the second epilogue (pp. 779–80), which was added some time after the initial draft of the novel was completed in late July 1912, does Dreiser allude specifically to events in Cowperwood's life that are still to be narrated, presumably in additional novels. An allusion of this kind would not have been necessary if the novel had been called *The Financier: Part One*.

A novel published in three volumes is, in one sense, no different from exactly the same work issued as three novels which are designated as parts of a trilogy. However, in another sense there is a difference because readers tend to view individually named novels in a trilogy as distinctive works and to be less responsive to the overall effect and intent of the trilogy as a whole. Yet, ironically, this unintended loss of unitary impact in the trilogy as a whole is appropriate to the actual nature of the three volumes as published. Because Yerkes's Chicago career differed in several important ways from his Philadelphia years, *The Titan* is indeed quite different both thematically and structurally from *The Financier*. And because Dreiser brought to the completion of *The Stoic* in 1945 philosophical attitudes and ideas which preoccupied him during his later career, this volume is of greater interest as a distinctive novel of ideas than as the climactic work in a trilogy. So, in this instance, the seemingly disruptive needs of commercial publication actually reflect an emergent imaginative truth.

Dreiser's research during the summer of 1911 concentrated on biographies of prominent American financiers of the late nineteenth century, such as Jay Cooke and Daniel Drew, and on Yerkes's Philadelphia career.[5] In a newspaper interview of 1912, he noted that he had "spent some time in Philadelphia studying the location of the scenes and familiarizing myself with the machinery of local government." He also remarked that he had benefited greatly from "a private collection of newspaper clippings that was open to me and which covered many phases of the data I was seeking."[6] This collection, primarily from the *Philadelphia Public Ledger* and covering almost all of Yerkes's public activities, appears to have been made available to Dreiser through Joseph Coates, a Philadelphia publisher with whom Dreiser had become friendly during his stay in the city during late 1902. Coates also seems to have provided Dreiser with much detail about Yerkes's private life and, as his correspondence with Dreiser suggests, to have supplied background information whenever it was required.[7]

Faced with a great mass of detailed information about Yerkes and about the economic and political conditions in which he flourished, Dreiser adopted, for the first time in his career as a novelist, the technique of the research scholar. Using large yellow sheets, he took extensive notes on these matters, limiting each sheet to a particular event or historical moment. He noted at the top of each sheet the date of the event or condition which it chronicled, and when he had completed his note-taking, he arranged the sheets in chronological order.[8] He thus had available for immediate use at any point in his narrative a large body of detailed information about Yerkes's financial operations and about economic and political events related to those operations. These notes, however, contain very little about Yerkes's personal life in Philadelphia. This is not to say that Dreiser was completely in the dark about the private events of Yerkes's early life. From the magazine articles of Russell and Lefèvre, from newspaper stories surveying Yerkes's entire career, and from Coates he derived many anecdotes and details of his boyhood and rise to financial prominence as well as the vital facts of his marriage at twenty to the widowed Susanna Guttridge Gamble, of the faithful attentions during his imprisonment of Miss Mary Adelaide Moore (the daughter of a Philadelphia chemist), and of his subsequent divorce from his first wife and his marriage to Miss Moore.

As is suggested by the difference between this bare outline of Yerkes's private life in Philadelphia and the mass of information available for the depiction of his financial career, Dreiser's account of Yerkes's public life is for the most part literally correct while his portrait of his private life is largely imaginative. Scholars have identified the prototypes of almost all the political and financial figures in *The Financier*,[9] and both the general outline and the details of Cowperwood's financial activities derive from Yerkes's career. Dreiser's heavy reliance on the details of Yerkes's career, though of interest, is of less concern than his recreation of Yerkes's private life. By the time of Yerkes's death, the first Mrs. Yerkes was a shadowy figure. Though Dreiser may have relied on local recollections of her for some of the details of his characterization, his portrait of Lillian Semple Cowperwood appears to be shaped primarily by the role he wished her to play in Cowperwood's developing responsiveness to feminine beauty. The second Mrs. Yerkes, however, was very much alive in 1905, and her headstrong and often irrational behavior was much publicized in the press.

It was probably the known personality of Mary Moore Yerkes, as well as the circumstances of Yerkes leaving his first wife to marry her, which led Dreiser in the direction of his principal imaginative act in his transformation of Yerkes's life into that of Cowperwood. This act was the creation of the Butler family and the use of Edward Butler's conservative family morality and corrupt public morality as the pivot on which to turn both the personal and public plots of the novel. Dreiser's thinking, I believe, was roughly along the following lines. The second Mrs. Yerkes had been in her youth a robust, full-spirited girl who had become involved with an older man. Dreiser could thus conceive of her at that point in her career not as a jealous termagant resembling Sallie White, as she was to become in *The Titan* and *The Stoic*, but as another of his sisters. As a girl of this nature in the 1870s, she was no doubt in rebellion against her family. And if her father were himself prominent in political and financial affairs, and if he were deeply offended by his daughter's relationship with an older married man, would he not attempt to cause the downfall of that man? Either as a factor in this line of thinking or as a result of it, Dreiser recalled a Colonel Edward Butler whom he had known in St. Louis during the early 1890s. Butler was an Irish immigrant with a thick brogue who had begun life in America as a blacksmith. Early in his career he had entered city politics as a garbage contractor; by the time Dreiser knew him he had risen to be Democratic boss of St. Louis and was widely attacked as the source of political corruption in the city.[10] Dreiser, when he was sent to interview Butler by the Republican paper for which he was working, liked him and found in him an "innate gentility of manner and speech" despite his origins and activities.[11] By 1911, Butler had long since been removed from power, but Dreiser still remembered the circumstances of his life and his striking blend of personal grace, political immorality, and "earnest" Catholicism.[12] The effect upon *The Financier* of Dreiser's recasting of Colonel Edward Butler of St. Louis into Edward Butler of Philadelphia cannot be exaggerated, since it is Dreiser's dramatization of the Cowperwood-Ai-leen-Butler triangle which transforms what might have been a chronicle into effective fiction.

Dreiser began to write *The Financier* in early September 1911. By the second week in November he had completed thirty-eight chapters—that is, up to the point at which Cowperwood is about to announce the failure of his firm, or approximately three-fifths of the published novel.[13] At this point he departed for Europe, leaving behind the holograph with Harper's for typing. On his return in mid-April, he immediately began writing again and expected to complete the novel by the end of May or early June.[14] But his efforts were complicated by several changes which he decided to make in the structure of the novel and his work dragged on through July.[15]

Dreiser's two major structural revisions in *The Financier* involve the thematic and narrative center of the novel—the period between the Chicago fire and Cowperwood's imprisonment.[16] First, he carefully and extensively revised his account of Cowperwood's frenetic activities in the two days following the fire. His intent in this revision was twofold—to dramatize rather than summarize Cowperwood's attempts to save his firm and to interweave the various strands of narrative during these two days in order to stress the ironic relationship between Cowperwood's brilliant and heroic efforts and the powerful, inexorable forces opposing these efforts. Dreiser's second revision was to reorder the chronology of one of the principal "private" events of the novel, Butler's use of a detective to trap Cowperwood and Aileen in a house of assignation. Dreiser had originally placed this lengthy "discovery" incident between Cowperwood's trial and his imprisonment, apparently in response to a hint from his sources that Yerkes's attachment to Miss Moore reached a crisis during this period, since he did not live with his wife after his release. On second thought, however, Dreiser decided that the incident should occur earlier, between Cowperwood's financial failure and trial. In this new position it contributed to the strengthening of Butler's determination that Cowperwood should not only be convicted but should also be sent to prison. And it enlivened a portion of the novel otherwise devoted to a tedious recounting of Cowperwood's postcollapse financial affairs.[17]

When these and many other less important changes were completed, the novel was quickly typed and set up in galley.[18] Reviewing the book in this form, Dreiser recognized that it required careful and extensive editing.

Yet both he and Harper's wanted the volume to appear in the fall, Harper's because the firm had scheduled a fall publication, Dreiser for financial reasons. He wrote anxiously to Mencken in mid-September that the book would make up to over 800 pages.[19] And though he worked extensively on the proofs, he managed to cut only seventy-odd pages before page proof was set in late September. Mencken received a copy of page proofs with an urgent request for further omissions, but by the time he replied in early October the novel was in press and Dreiser was able to adopt only a few of his suggestions.[20] Dreiser's cuts during this hectic period were almost all from material written after his return from Europe. They involve primarily passages dealing with Cowperwood's financial dilemma and activities after his failure and much trial reportage, including a paragraph describing Thomas, the court cat, and lengthy speeches by the various lawyers and the judge.

Soon after the publication of *The Financier*, Dreiser began to be apologetic about its length and frequently commented that the book would benefit from further cutting.[21] He anticipated revising the novel upon the completion of the trilogy, when the three books would be reissued as a set.[22] But as the years went by and *The Stoic* remained unfinished, the possibility of the republication of *The Financier* as part of a set became more and more remote. Finally, in early 1926, with *An American Tragedy* out of the way and with *The Bulwark* once again at a dead end, Dreiser decided to revise and republish *The Financier* despite not having finished *The Stoic*. He chose as his collaborator in this enterprise Mrs. Louise Campbell, who had been aiding him as an editor since 1917. The revised edition of *The Financier*, cut by approximately one-third, was published in April 1927.

Who was responsible for what in the editing of *The Financier* in early 1926 is not clear. Dreiser's letters to Mrs. Campbell during this period are inconclusive,[23] but Mrs. Campbell's recollection in 1963 suggests that the process was the usual one of Dreiser initially asking for a complete revision by a trusted editor and then himself selecting what to accept or reject in this revision. "I rewrote it and made suggestions for a great part of it," Miss Campbell recalled. "But Dreiser . . . revised my revision, you might say, combining chapters, cutting and elaborating, etc."[24]

A good case can be made for the primary interest of either edition. The 1927 version is in some senses a better novel; its fictional pace is swifter and its characterizations sharper.[25] But the 1912 version, despite its occasional repetitiousness and tediousness, captures more fully and strongly the epic and cosmological themes which Dreiser wished to render through his narrative of Cowperwood's life. I have therefore chosen to discuss the 1912 edition because its acknowledged defects are nevertheless the typically Dreiserian defects of overelaboration of authorial commentary and expository detail and because these "defects" in fact often contribute to much that is vital and suggestive in the novel.

ꞓꞓꞓꞓꞓꞓꞓꞓꞓꞓꞓꞓꞓꞓꞓꞓꞓꞓꞓꞓꞓꞓꞓꞓꞓꞓꞓꞓ

Dreiser narrates the youth of Frank Cowperwood in the loose chronicle and anecdotal form of the Franklinesque American success story. A clever, vigorous, and industrious boy, Frank reveals an aptitude early in life for business affairs. He succeeds in his boyish enterprises, and when he leaves school for business he quickly makes his abilities felt and rises rapidly in the firms he is connected with. His is no rags-to-riches rise, since the Cowperwoods are a mildly prosperous middle-class family. But Frank's thrift, energy, and intelligence are nevertheless in the classic mold of the American myth of success.

Beneath his affability, however, Frank has a view of life at odds with the moral cast of the myth of success which he is apparently fulfilling so completely. Casual readers of the Cowperwood trilogy have often believed that Frank derives this view from his interpretation of what is perhaps the best known incident in all of Dreiser, that of the lobster devouring the squid. The incident, which is loosely based on an article called "A Lesson from the Aquarium" that Dreiser had published in 1906,[26] affirms that deceit, surprise, and strength are the sources of power and thus of survival in every range of life, from the struggle in the fishmonger's tank to the conflicts of men. The parable of the fish tank, however, in fact merely confirms in striking fashion a truth which Frank has already discovered in his own experience. Earlier in his boyhood, a young tough had attempted to bully him on his way home from school. Frank does not parley but rather,

Like a flash, though naturally calm, he dropped his books and went for his opponent. He wore a silver ring on his right hand which his mother had given him, and curiously it flashed into his mind in a lightning calculation to take it off, but he did not. Instead, he planted his right fist swift and straight on young McGlathery's jaw. . . . It was a terrific onslaught, quick and ugly. (p. 6).

The difference between emphasizing as the source of Frank's view of life his battle with McGlathery and his observation of the struggle in the fish tank is the difference between conceiving of Frank as a moral pragmatist or as a Social Darwinist. As the remainder of the novel makes clear, Dreiser characterizes Cowperwood not as someone who generalizes from animal life to social life but as someone who generalizes from his own experience to all experience.

Initially, of course, despite such incidents as his fight with McGlathery and the struggle in the fish tank, Frank has little opportunity to develop or refine his ideas about man and society. But gradually he realizes the full implications of the fact that life is essentially a battle between the strong and the weak. He begins to sense that strength in human affairs is principally quickness of wit, foresight, coolness under stress, and above all "subtlety"—the ability to mask one's true nature and intentions. It is this last quality rather than ferociousness which is the key to Cowperwood's success in *The Financier*. Dreiser repeatedly associates Cowperwood's activities and state of mind with an imagery of deceit derived from animal life, and he provides him with inscrutable eyes and an inscrutable smile. This theme reaches a climax in the first epilogue of the novel, in which Dreiser offers the Black Grouper as an illustration of the principle of "simulation" governing survival and power in all life. For Cowperwood, "subtlety," "inscrutability," and "simulation" involve two kinds of disguise. He adopts, particularly during his Philadelphia career, a pose of "regularity" in his personal and business affairs so as not to arouse suspicion in the world at large. And in the midst of a shady transaction, he carefully masks his underlying intentions.

Early in his career, Frank's goal is primarily the acquisition of money. But soon, as "a money-genius in embryo," he goes beyond a "sense of wealth as it is ordinarily understood. His total perception is of power" (p. 235). And power is the ability to answer the deepest call within him, that aspect of his nature which declares more openly and strongly than most men, "I satisfy myself." Thus, by his early twenties Cowperwood is able to express a code of life still related to the lobster eating the squid but more directly applicable to his own nature and goals. "The thing for him to do," he reflects, "was to get rich and hold his own—to build up a seeming of virtue and dignity which would pass muster for the genuine thing. Force would do that. Quickness of wit. And he had these. Let the world wag. 'I satisfy myself,' was his motto." (p. 244).[27]

Cowperwood also comes to realize that morality is irrelevant to the struggle between the weak and the strong which pervades all life. Men, he finds, are strong or weak because of temperament and the circumstances of their lives. Morality may be a refuge of the weak or a weapon of the strong, but it has no existence independent of power. Cowperwood's discovery of this truth colors his response to human failings. He is contemptuous of those who believe in moral responsibility and who judge others in accord with this belief. He himself detaches moral blame from the "guilty." Although Stener is morally corrupt in the eyes of the world, to Cowperwood he is merely weak. At a crucial moment after the panic caused by the Chicago fire, Stener fearfully refuses to aid Cowperwood, though his aid is necessary to save them both. "In his very crumpling, jelly-like weakness Cowperwood read his own fate. . . . And with a gesture of infinite understanding, disgust, noble indifference, he threw up his hands and started to walk out" (p. 395). Cowperwood's strength derives in part from this moral aloofness. He wastes little physical or psychic energy on such morally conditioned attitudes as condemnation or a desire for vengeance.

Despite his ability to formulate his understanding of experience, Cowperwood is not a speculative thinker in *The Financier*. He is a doer rather than a thinker. He does not reach his conception of force by studying "the subtleties of evolution" (p. 243) but by observing life. And he cares "nothing for books" but is drawn rather to "life, pictures, physical contact, trees" (p. 115). Yet Cowperwood's antiintellectualism does not prevent him from being a man of great rational powers and of "sensibilities of the highest order" (p. 633). Dreiser explains: "Back of that solid, corrective brain, which stood like a mailed knight at the drawbridge of his fortune, was a vague, cloudy realm of beauty as sensuous as a summer landscape, as alluring as a tinted sea" (pp. 235–36). The image is instructive because it suggests that the "brain" which protects the fortress of fortune is really protecting and aiding the fulfillment of the vital "realm of beauty" at the very center of Cowperwood's being. As Aileen alone senses in *The Financier*, "There was . . . in him, in some nebulous, unrecognizable form, a great artistic reality" (p. 289).

Dreiser's association of power and beauty in Cowperwood underlies the entire trilogy and requires several different kinds of interpretation. At its most autobiographical, the theme represents Dreiser's translation of Yerkes's penchant for young girls and expensive art into an amoral quest for beauty which Dreiser himself had fulfilled much less successfully. Dreiser was also expressing a basic romantic faith in somewhat new terms. His characterization of Cowperwood contains a belief that life is permeated with beauty and that it is men of insight and power—men of imagination, in short—who recognize and possess this underlying reality. Although Dreiser gave his depiction of power a Darwinian cast, he was nevertheless responding primarily to the evocative Keatsian premise that the first in beauty shall be the first in might. Moreover, for Cowperwood beauty is present in the mode as well as the goal of power. Dreiser wished to suggest, as he had in "The Shining Slave Makers," that for a man of Cowperwood's temperament the struggle for power is a process which in its drama and excitement partakes of the aesthetic.[28]

A final way of discussing Dreiser's association of power and beauty in Cowperwood is in relation to the fictional success of this theme. Dreiser's task was to make acceptable the notion that Cowperwood could be equally responsive to the distinctive natures of financial intrigue, feminine beauty, and art. He took considerable pains to establish a number of obvious connections among these pursuits, particularly in Cowperwood's application of a similar theory of amoral force to business and love and in the underlying aestheticism of his sexual desires. "Cowperwood was a financier," Dreiser stated, but he went on to claim that for Cowperwood this activity was a means toward an aesthetic appreciation of life rather than an obstacle to such an appreciation. "Instead of dwelling on the works of nature, its beauty and subtlety, to his material disadvantage, he found a happy mean, owing to the swiftness of his intellectual operations, whereby he could intellectually and emotionally rejoice in the beauty of life without interfering with his perpetual material and financial calculations" (p. 242).

So far so good. Dreiser had created in Cowperwood a paragon of amoral force and aesthetic sensibility, but paragons are not inappropriate to epic novels and their adventures among ordinary humans can be of much interest. Dreiser's difficulty was less with his abstract idea of Cowperwood than with the dramatic expression of that idea. He was committed to a full representation of the world of finance in which Cowperwood flourished, but he did not realize that this world, because of its weight of mundane detail and its pervasive emotions of greed, fear, and hate, was incongruous in relation to what Dreiser would have called Cowperwood's more "refined" interests. Henry James, whether consciously or not, sensed the difficulty of combining "high" and "low" matters in a single character. His American businessmen have a Cowperwood air about them because of their wealth and vigor, but James only hints vaguely at the nature of their business affairs and devotes himself to an account of their pursuit of a higher life. Dreiser, however, asks us to move suddenly and frequently from the dollars-and-cents, morally squalid stock exchange to the Palace of Art and Love, and we make this move both reluctantly and unbelievingly.

To put the problem another way, many critics have noted that the Cowperwood trilogy breaks down awkwardly into the subject matters of finance and love, and they have attributed this failing to Dreiser's frequent practice of devoting alternative chapters or parts of chapters exclusively to each of these subjects. Another cause of this awkwardness, however, may be that the subjects themselves are incompatible whatever their order of presentation—not intrinsically incompatible but incompatible given Dreiser's intent. He wishes us to believe that Cowperwood has two lives, that of the world and that of the spirit—that of "the mailed knight" and that of "the cloudy realm of beauty"—but Cowperwood carries away from his financial activities an aura of the worldly which adheres to him whatever his ostensible goals elsewhere. We are thus placed in the uncomfortable position of having to reject Dreiser's explanation of Cowperwood's nature because the fictional reality of his character in his financial dealings has led us to assume that his sexual activities and art collecting are not a quest for beauty but are rather further examples of his desire for possession and power.

But to maintain that the trilogy as a whole fails to make convincing the character of Cowperwood is not to suggest that Dreiser is not more successful in one novel than in another. Indeed, in *The Financier*—to my mind easily the best novel of the trilogy—he almost succeeds in making Cowperwood a believable and sympathetic as well as a compelling figure. Dreiser's comparative success in this novel is largely attributable to his dramatization of Cowperwood's life as an expression of "human" weaknesses and strengths rather than of "superhuman" values. In the two principal activities of the novel, business and love, Cowperwood's actions—whatever his beliefs—are those of any capable and forceful young man who is intent on making his way in the world. He succeeds initially in business because he is energetic and clever, and he later adopts the techniques of deception and bribery because he finds that these are almost universally practiced in the upper reaches of political and economic life and are required if one is to reach that level. Indeed, Dreiser even makes use of a conventional muckraking theme to exonerate Cowperwood, for he explains that we, the public, are to blame for political corruption because our failure to protest loudly enough permits it to flourish (p. 164). Although Cowperwood's financial collapse is attributable to the Chicago fire, the underlying reasons are his failure to keep sufficient money in reserve and his placing himself in a position where a weak and stupid man, Stener, can control his fate. And though the imprisoned Cowperwood maintains for the most part his stoic calm and courage, he also breaks down when Aileen's visit suddenly vivifies his realization of how lonely and miserable he is.

Cowperwood's love life has this same quality of the ordinary and believable. His first marriage combines the conventional elements of honorable intent and error in effect, and his love for Aileen—the only other romance in the novel—is one of high passion and spiritual communion. And in this instance he is "honorable" also, despite his adultery, for he promises to marry Aileen and indeed does so. In short there is little of the ruthless and lecherous titan in the Cowperwood of *The Financier*. He is primarily an exceptional young man who is having his ups and downs, and we tend to wish him success in his ventures and to sympathize with him in his failures, particularly since his opponents, with the exception of Butler, are either fools or villains. It is worth noting that the bulk of the novel, from the panic following the Chicago fire to Cowperwood's release from prison, is devoted not to his triumphs but to his difficulties and defeats. Only in the closing section of the novel, when his imprisonment has hardened and deepened his contempt for the masses and when, during the panic following the failure of Jay Cooke, he glories in his victories over his opponents, do we approach the Cowperwood of *The Titan*.

‹‹‹‹‹‹‹‹‹‹‹‹‹‹‹‹‹‹‹‹‹‹‹‹‹‹‹‹‹‹‹‹‹‹‹

One of the major themes in the Cowperwood trilogy as a whole is Cowperwood's love of feminine beauty. The theme involves a general idea which receives distinctive expression in each of the novels, though the impression which many readers have of the theme is heavily colored by the impact of Cowperwood's "varietistic" career in *The Titan*. Dreiser's conception of Cowperwood's responsiveness to women resembles his depiction of Carrie's association with men. Like Carrie, Cowperwood's relationships are hierarchal in a rising scale of the intrinsic worth of the partner and the "spirituality" of the union. In *The Titan* and *The Stoic*, Cowperwood's progress up this rising scale is on the one hand frenetic because of his restless seeking of feminine beauty and on the other overschematized because of his discovery of ideal beauty in Berenice. But Cowperwood's love affairs in *The Financier*, though still closely related to Dreiser's general hierarchal idea, have the naturalness and probability of Carrie's affairs with Drouet and Hurstwood.

The story of Cowperwood's personal life in *The Financier* is that of a young man of force and intelligence who is attracted by a somewhat older and more experienced woman. They marry and have several children, but he increasingly finds her limited in intelligence and vitality. He meets a vibrant young girl some ten years his junior who is flattered by his attention and is moved by the strength of his personality. They have an affair and are discovered, whereupon he leaves his family for a new life in a new city with the girl. Within this conventional plot—so conventional, indeed, that Dreiser had already used it for Hurstwood and Carrie—Dreiser expressed a highly idealistic notion of romantic love.

Dreiser's idea of love at its highest—that is, the kind of love which Eugene Witla and Cowperwood desire—involves a conception of woman as an art object and love as the physical possession of and spiritual communion with that object. To Cowperwood, Dreiser wrote in a cut portion of *The Financier*, "beautiful women were delicious. They were like wondrous objects of art, but to get the full value of their artistry he had to be in close individual relationship with them and that could only be achieved through the affections."[29] Since Cowperwood sees women "from the artistic side only," sexual possession alone is unsatisfactory. "He wanted personal reaction of thought and feelings, a certain kinship of soul or understanding in any woman he drew near to, and if he could not have that he was not interested" (p. 72). His early sexual experiences with "cheap women" repel him because such women have an "inartistic absence of refinement" (pp. 69–70). The great appeal of Lillian Semple to the youthful Cowperwood is therefore an indefinable quality of the "artistic" which he finds in her appearance[30] and in her "unconscious placidity of soul" (p. 67). A large woman, she is not only "peaceful and statuesque" (p. 67) but also seems to possess an emotional reserve which piques and fascinates the vigorous Cowperwood. She is like an inanimate object that he wishes to stimulate into life. Dreiser's frequently repeated statue imagery in connection with Mrs. Semple, however, suggests both her appeal and her limitations. For as Cowperwood eventually discovers, her limpid beauty reflects a heart that is cold and shallow and her placidity in truth is a phlegmatic emptiness.

Cowperwood and Aileen fall in love when he is twenty-nine and she is nineteen. Dreiser's characterization of Aileen is pervaded by an imagery of animal strength and beauty. She loves to ride and drive, and she herself has the "clean, clicking strength of a blooded horse" (p. 236) and the beauty of a young colt in springtime. She thus possesses the sensuality lacking in Lillian and a grace and strength of body and spirit which are essentially aesthetic. She is in effect a living rather than an inanimate art object, and Cowperwood finds in her not only a powerful sexuality but a "charm of soul or temperament" (p. 434). "They ran together temperamentally from the first like two leopards" (p. 289).

With Dreiser's introduction of Aileen, the nature and structure of his sexual theme in the trilogy as a whole begins to emerge. Cowperwood, as Dreiser tells us at great length, has by this time rejected conventional beliefs in the sanctity of marriage and the innate virtue of women. Women to him are objects of sexual and aesthetic pleasure, and the only guides to the relationship between men and women are self-satisfaction and freedom. Yet as Dreiser is at pains both to explain and to dramatize, Cowperwood's affair with Aileen has a morality of its own. Theirs is a relationship of similar temperaments, of "affinities," and their love is a celebration of the god of nature who draws men and women together in this fashion. As David Weimer has noted, Dreiser's novels frequently contain the symbol of "a secret room" where a man and woman worship a pagan god of love in opposition to the false god of marriage to which most men pay lip service.[31] This symbol, which is present throughout the Cowperwood trilogy, occurs for the first time in the trysting places of Cowperwood and Aileen in *The Financier*.

The liaison between Cowperwood and Aileen not only has a "sanctity of its own" but also takes on a moral coloration in relation to the hierarchal nature of Cowperwood's three major loves—Lillian, Aileen, and Berenice. All three are beautiful women who are in different ways art objects, but they are so in an ascending order. Put crudely, Lillian's beauty is surface, Aileen vitalizes beauty with animal force, and Berenice spiritualizes it by a subtlety and depth of spirit and mind. Stated another way, all are equal in exterior beauty but Cowperwood comes increasingly to value "interior beauty" as a necessary corollary. As in Carrie's relationship with Drouet, Hurstwood, and Ames, the dramatic effect of representing Cowperwood's discovery of a "finer" nature first in Aileen and then in Berenice is to render this discovery a moral act even though in both instances his discovery involves undertaking an adulterous affair.

Dreiser's love theme in the trilogy thus differs little from the theme suggested in *Sister Carrie* and elaborated fully in *The "Genius"*—that the artistic spirit seeks communion and renewal through love in a rising scale of aesthetic responsiveness to his mate and does so increasingly outside convention. Dreiser's representation of love at its highest level—as in Eugene and Suzanne or in Cowperwood and Berenice—derives not only from the myth of the romantic artist but also from nineteenth-century sexual mysticism. In both Henry Adams and Dreiser, sexuality and spirituality merge in the woman as art object, and the feminine thus becomes both a principle of worship and a source of creative power. And out of desire either sublimated or consummated there emerges such vast enterprises as a Gothic cathedral or a financial empire. In such works as the Cowperwood trilogy, *Mont-St.-Michel and Chartres*, and Frank Norris's *The Octopus*, the nineteenth-century worship of sex as a universal creative force is expressed as a mystical faith at the very moment that faith was to receive new and paradoxically scientific confirmation in Freudian psychology.

As usual in Dreiser, however, the fictional strength of a novel does not lie in his working out of an abstract idea—one recalls Ames and Suzanne, for example, as weak illustrations of a general thesis—but rather in his depiction of human relationships and conflicts that may be only parenthetically related to that idea. In *The "Genius"* and *The Titan* it is Dreiser's portrayal of marital infighting which supplies this strength; in *The Financier* it is primarily his moving account of the role of Edward Butler in Aileen and Cowperwood's lives.

Butler is both of the old world and of the new. His family pride and loyalty are those of the Irish peasant; his business and political success is that of the urban American. As a peasant, he is a moral conservative who demands and practices religious piety, sexual virtue, and familial respect and obedience. As an American, he is deceptive and corrupt and relies without conscience on the covert illegality of nineteenth-century American political and business life. Unlike Cowperwood, who applies a single ethical guide of "I satisfy myself" to every sphere of life, Butler distinguishes between the world at large and the family. The conflict between Cowperwood and Butler is therefore not only the conventional struggle between an outraged parent and a seducer. It is also a conflict between two generations of ethical belief and practice—between an older and widely accepted double standard which acknowledged that a man's public morality could differ from his private, and a newer, more powerful ethical standard which affirmed a single code of amorality. Butler's vulnerability derives from his failure to realize this difference between himself and Cowperwood and from his having placed Cowperwood in a semifamilial relationship. He had been one of Cowperwood's earliest supporters and had taken pride in Cowperwood's shrewdness and rapid success. His discovery of the relationship between Aileen and Cowperwood thus contains two sources of shock and despair. He has been betrayed within the moral sanctuary of his home by both his "son" and his daughter.

Dreiser's characterization of Butler resembles his portraits of the moralistic parent from Butcher Rogaum and old Gerhardt to Mrs. Griffiths and Solon Barnes. He is openly critical of Butler's attempt to thwart the "chemistry" of life which has brought Aileen and Cowperwood together (p. 360). Nevertheless, he portrays Butler's pain and suffering with great sympathy. And he conveys powerfully Butler's insoluble and self-destructive conflict between a desire to hold the daughter he loves and a desire to punish and condemn her for her wrongs. Eventually, Butler is defeated in his attempts both to hold and to punish. Aileen shrewdly realizes that she can exploit her father's love, and Cowperwood, though Butler is instrumental in sending him to prison, maintains his control of Aileen. The anguish of a parent over a wayward child always moved Dreiser. His condemnation of the parent's blind moralism was usually transcended by his compassion for the pain and frustration of thwarted parental love.

≪≪≪≪≪≪≪≪≪≪≪≪≪≪≪≪≪≪≪≪≪≪≪

In *The Financier* Dreiser convincingly dramatized two of the three major postulates of his idea of balance. All of his characters, from Cowperwood to Stener and from Butler to Aileen, are motivated by "moods, emotions, needs, greeds" (p. 432), and it is the "subtle chemistry of things" (p. 549)—the strength of the individual—which determines success. "The world was full of jails and laws and maxims and theories, and some men were strong and some weak" (p. 660). So Mollenhauer and Simpson, who are far more corrupt than Cowperwood, are the victorious champions of civic virtue and Cowperwood is an imprisoned malefactor because at a crucial moment they were stronger—that is, more subtle and treacherous—than he was. But though Dreiser adequately portrayed in *The Financier* the reality of power and the illusion of morality, he only hinted at the third major characteristic of the idea of balance—that the weak can unite into a force which is capable of defeating the seemingly impregnable giants of the earth. This theme appears to a minor degree both in the slight role of the Municipal Reform League in Cowperwood's conviction and in the deliberations of the jury, when one of the jurymen convinces the others that Cowperwood is a bad influence in the community and should be punished on general rather than specific grounds. But on the whole the struggle in *The Financier* is among the strong themselves, and Cowperwood's financial collapse—as I noted earlier—is attributable primarily to his lack of foresight rather than to the operation of mechanistic social law.

The *Financier* is probably better for Dreiser's neglect of this third aspect of his concept of balance. The fall of a character because of his own weaknesses and a stroke of chance is the solid stuff of fiction, while "the mass" is an awkward fictional entity, as *The Titan* reveals. Nevertheless, on completing *The Financier* Dreiser appears to have been uneasy because of the absence of a strong element of equation in his depiction of Cowperwood's affairs. He therefore added the second epilogue, "The Magic Crystal," not only to forge a link between *The Financier* and the remaining novels of the trilogy but to anticipate Cowperwood's ultimate fall. He began by noting Cowperwood's future triumphs, but he went on to remark that these would be colored by Cowperwood's increasing satiation and world-weariness and that in his heart all would be "sorrow, sorrow, sorrow" (p. 780). As always, a Dreiser epilogue misrepresents his novel, though in this instance the novel to come rather than the novel just completed. For Cowperwood's principal opposing force in *The Titan* (though not *The Stoic*) was indeed to be the "mass" rather than his own nature.

Dreiser did not view American history as a series of political and military events dominated by great national leaders. The Civil War receives scarcely an allusion in *The Financier*, and Lincoln is mentioned only briefly. To Dreiser, the significant characteristics of a nation's history are economic, social, and moral. He believed that in the late nineteenth century these characteristics were closely linked to the uncontrolled expansionism of the period and that American society was therefore a vast hypocrisy in which most commercial and public officials professed both a private morality and a devotion to the public welfare while robbing the public blind. The epic truth of American life was its facade of righteousness, its underlying rapacious self-interest, and its bestowal of its greatest riches upon those who had perfected the art of combining hypocrisy with theft. Cowperwood is an apt epic hero not only because his activities incorporate these broad movements in American social life but because his increasingly open acknowledgment of self-interest contrasts strikingly with the great number who profess a concern for the public good.

Many readers of the 1912 (and even the 1927) version of *The Financier* have found Dreiser's extended accounts of specific business practices and general economic and political conditions excessive and yet in some inexplicable way integral to the novel. Mencken's response to this aspect of *The Financier* is both characteristic and instructive. He complained in a letter to Dreiser that much of the detail in the novel appeared to be irrelevant when the reader first encountered it. But, he went on, "the irrelevant, in the long run, becomes, in a dim and vasty way, relevant. As you laboriously set the stage, the proscenium arch disappears, the painted trees become real trees, the actors turn into authentic men and women."[32] Mencken's imagery suggests that much of the detail in *The Financier* is background material against which the characters move. In fact, the great bulk of detail is intrinsic both to character and to action. Its vital role is obvious in such matters as the operation of the city treasury or the floating of street railway companies, for we have to understand these subjects if we are going to understand the actions and motives of Cowperwood, Stener, Butler, Simpson, and Mollenhauer, and thus understand the themes of the novel. But Dreiser also presents us with much additional detail which initially does not seem to inform or to shape a response. We learn, for example, about the social and family background of Stener, Mollenhauer, and Simpson, and of the kinds of homes in which they live and of their activities other than business. Dreiser's intent is not merely to fulfill a naïve belief that all life is interesting but to meet the needs of his instinctive aesthetic belief that the feel of reality is created by a sense of knowing. What Mencken referred to as relevancy is thus indeed dim and vasty because it is that indefinable quality of fictional density, of a living canvas, which is one of the great achievements of the nineteenth-century novel and of Dreiser at his best.

Despite this defense of detail in *The Financier*, there is no doubt that the novel would have benefited from the omission of two kinds of material—lengthy accounts of the characteristics of late nineteenth-century taste and full descriptions of the settings of particular dramatic moments. Most of the first kind of detail—on styles in architecture, interior decoration, and costumes and on vogues in art collecting—is intended by Dreiser both to document the taste of the period (as part of his epic purpose) and to illustrate the growth of Cowperwood's aesthetic sensibility. A great deal of this material, however, is morally colorless and thus lacks the thematic thrust of Dreiser's accounts of economic and political conditions. And Dreiser's depiction of setting often consists of an undisciplined accumulation of detail. For example, when he tells us, in preparing the stage for Cowperwood's trial, that the "oval-topped old-fashioned windows and doors" of Independence Hall "were set with those many paned sashes so much admired by those who love what is now known as Colonial" (pp. 547–48), both the tone and nature of the detail move us in the direction of the trivial.

««««««««««««««««««««««««««««

Brief general accounts of the Cowperwood trilogy tend to suggest that each of the novels is constructed in the form of a loose chronicle of Cowperwood's activities with alternate sections on his love life and business affairs—a huge club sandwich, in Stuart P. Sherman's undying phrase.[33] In addition, discussions of *The Financier* often imply that it is dominated by an imagery and symbolism of animal ferocity deriving from the notorious lobster-squid passage. The novel does indeed exhibit the usual catalog of Dreiserian flaws. It is occasionally melodramatically plotted (principally in the timing of the anonymous letters which denounce Cowperwood and Aileen), repetitious in its authorial commentary, and inept in its imagery and diction of love and art (Cowperwood is Aileen's "darling boy," and aesthetic sensibility is characterized variously as "re-fined," "dainty," "nice," and "artistic"). Nevertheless, on the whole the novel is carefully and successfully constructed, its narrative technique is frequently both powerful and sophisticated, and its imagery of animal strength is unobtrusive. True, there are some jungle metaphors, particu-larly when the fallen Cowperwood is at the mercy of his opponents. But Dreiser's imagery on such occasions is not excessive in relation either to the dramatic situation or to what Frank Norris, for example, produced in *The Pit*, where the fictional landscape is alive with snarling bears and stamped-ing bulls. Somewhat as in *Sister Carrie*, Dreiser used in *The Financier* a flashy "external" imagery (in this instance that of animal struggle rather than of the sea) and a less evident yet evocative "internal" symbolism derived from the concrete realities of his characters' lives—the clothes they wear, the houses they live in, the rooms in which they meet. Cowper-wood's rise and fall, for example, occurs not only in the fighting arena of the stock exchange but in the physical and emotional reality of his increasingly impressive homes, his new bank building, his "secret room" where he and Aileen meet, and his prison cell. And though some chapters of *The Financier* do indeed break into sections on Cowperwood's personal life and business affairs, this impression of the form of the novels in the trilogy derives largely from *The Titan*. *The Financier* is characterized primarily by long, unbroken sections devoted to one subject or the other—almost 60 pages on the wooing of Aileen, for example, and over 100 on Cowperwood's failure.

The Financier is thus not a novel constructed on the principle of thin, alternating slices of experience spiced with animal imagery but is rather shaped by a series of interlocking structures which are themselves threaded by the pervasive narrative technique of indirect discourse. In both its structure and its narrative voice *The Financier* represents Dreiser's most elaborate and successful venture in large-scale fictional architectonics during his early career and looks forward to his even more elaborate and successful experiments, along precisely the same lines, in *An American Tragedy*.

The most obvious characteristic of the form of *The Financier* is that the novel is divided into Cowperwood's rise, fall, and second rise. The first division occupies half of the novel, the second a third, and the last a sixth. I base this estimation of length on the assumption that Cowperwood's imprisonment is the beginning of his second rise to wealth and power. In prison he maintains his poise and self-confidence and even continues to conduct his business affairs. The brief section at the close of the novel, some twenty pages or so, which Dreiser devotes to Cowperwood's successful exploitation of the failure of Jay Cooke to regain his own fortune, is primarily a confirmation of the themes of continuing strength and anticipated renewal present in the prison section.

The Financier thus has the form of a progress through evershortening divisions of Cowperwood's life toward the climax of his victory despite his downfall. Within this forward movement, there are several carefully conceived and elaborately dramatized sets of ironically balanced events. For example, the novel contains two financial panics, that of 1871, in which Cowperwood loses his fortune, and that of 1873, in which he regains it. In 1871 Cowperwood is trapped by his extensive holdings, which decline in value as the market declines. In 1873, with little capital but a shrewd understanding of the opportunities offered by a panic, he profits from the rapid fall of the market by selling short and then waiting for stocks to decline before purchasing for delivery. Another, and perhaps the major, instance of structural balance in *The Financier* is the close relationship between the two most fully dramatized events in the novel, the single day of the house party and ball in celebration of the completion of the adjoining homes of the Cowperwood families, and the two days following the Chicago fire which conclude with Cowperwood's financial collapse.

The first occasion marks the height of Cowperwood's success. His banking career has brought him wealth and prominence, both of which are represented by his fine new house. And at the ball he and Aileen tentatively explore and then confirm their deep interest in each other. The hectic two days which follow the Chicago fire are the ebb stage of Cowperwood's career. His fortune disappears, he commits a technically illegal act, and his affair with Aileen is exposed to Butler and Mrs. Cowperwood. Dreiser narrates these dramatic high points of the novel with great skill. His technique is that of a gradually forward-moving chronology in which he constantly shifts the focus of his point of view, with much reliance on indirect discourse to render the ironic themes that are central to his depiction of Cowperwood's Philadelphia career. At the ball, for example, Dreiser's authorial representation of Cowperwood's thoughts establishes the disparity between the public gentility of the occasion—a gentility which symbolizes the voiced ethic of the leaders of Philadelphia life—and those qualities of human nature which are necessary to reach and maintain a genteel level of financial success and social prominence. "God, what a struggle," Cowperwood reflects. "The fights! The cries of the sinking! Strength was the thing. A strong, tactful man could do anything if he could scheme it out well enough beforehand; but one had to plan subtly, very subtly" (p. 230). And during the extensive negotiations between Cowperwood and those controlling his fate in the two days after the fire, it is indirect discourse which reveals the difference between the bland statements of the various figures and their underlying rapaciousness. As in *An American Tragedy*, Dreiser hones this technique into a biting ironic tool in the trial portion of the novel. It was always the institutionalized expression of morality which moved Dreiser to dramatize fully the difference between what men think they believe and what they truly believe, and between what men say and what they seldom acknowledge.

Another of Dreiser's major structural devices was a series of foils to Cowperwood which serves to express through dramatic repetition the permanent and essential in Cowperwood's character. These foils are of two kinds, financial and sexual. Cowperwood Senior is an example of the first, for he illustrates the danger of a financial career based upon the traditional virtues but lacking guile and strength. A careful, punctilious, and honest man who had inched his way forward over a lifetime, he is destroyed by the panic of 1871 and retreats into a painful obscurity. Stener reveals the futility of mere dishonesty without strength. Perhaps the most success-fully represented figure in the novel aside from Butler, he is characterized again and again as essentially gaseous, as a man without a center. Small-minded and cowardly, he is an absolute foil to Cowperwood, and from the panic of '71 to the close of the novel their careers are ironically parallel. Though both are guilty of the same crime, Stener begs on his knees before Mollenhauer while Cowperwood remains coolly aloof, and Stener col-lapses completely in jail while Cowperwood maintains and reasserts his strength. Cowperwood Senior and Stener thus confirm Cowperwood's assertion that morality is inoperative in the struggle of life. Although one is honest and the other dishonest, both are weak, and it is their weakness which shapes their fates.

Cowperwood's sexual life also contains a series of significant foils. Lillian illustrates a conventional disinclination to acknowledge her sexual nature, a quality of mind which eventually hardens into moral conserva-tism, and Butler also fails to accept the role of sexual attraction in determining the course of a life. Both, in other words, think of life in terms of social roles—those of faithful husband and pure daughter—which disregard the emotional (or in Dreiser's terms, the chemical) reality of the individuals involved.

Cowperwood's love of Aileen and his decision to marry her occur in relation to almost all the figures who are foils to his character and values. She is not only temperamentally and physically attractive to him, but also, under his tutelage, has fully accepted his philosophy of "I satisfy myself." She alone in Cowperwood's Philadelphia world both lives this philosophy and acknowledges it as a justifiable guide to life. Their departure from Philadelphia at the close of the novel thus represents not only a rejection of its closed social world but also of its confining moralism. They have, in effect, translated indirect discourse into motion, and—in fulfillment of a basic American myth—are going West for greater freedom of action and thought.

The Titan

D R E I S E R ' S O R I G I N A L S C H E D U L E for the Cowperwood trilogy, as outlined in a letter to Mencken in May 1912, called for publication of volume one in August 1912, volume two in March 1913, and volume three in August 1913.[1] His delay in completing volume one disrupted this plan, and it was not until November 1912, shortly after the appearance of *The Financier*, that he began the extensive research necessary for volume two, *The Titan*. He began in New York by gathering information about Yerkes's New York mansion and art collection.[2] In mid-December he left for Chicago and spent almost two months making detailed notes on Yerkes's Chicago financial operations and personal life.

Information about Yerkes's private and public career in Chicago was readily available to an active researcher. He had not left the city until 1898, and many of its prominent citizens still recalled him both in fact and legend. And from the early 1880s his financial buccaneering had been sufficiently large-scale and notorious for the Chicago newspapers to maintain a constant stream of articles and editorials about his exploits. Dreiser consulted various Chicago newspaper files at the Newberry Library,[3] while letters of introduction and the energetic efforts of Edgar Lee Masters (a Chicago lawyer as well as a poet) gained him interviews with many of Yerkes's contemporaries.[4] The initial product of this research was over 700 sheets of detailed notes on Yerkes's Chicago career and on many aspects of Chicago life of the 1880s and 90s. He also heard (but did not note) much about the shadier side of Yerkes's financial activities and sexual life.

In his depiction of Cowperwood's financial and political affairs in Chicago, Dreiser was almost completely faithful to the substance and chronology of this phase of Yerkes's life.[5] Like Yerkes, Cowperwood first gains a foothold in Chicago by his success in forming a gas trust, and then moves into street railroads. And like Yerkes, his Chicago career includes a great victory in the American Match battle but ends, in late 1897, with a failure to control the state legislature and the Chicago City Council in the crucial matter of extending his street railway franchises.

Most of the major characters in Cowperwood's public life are drawn from actual figures of the time, ranging from such giants as Philip Armour, Marshall Field, and Levi Leiter (Arneel, Merrill, and Schyhart) to such notoriously corrupt city councilmen as John Powers, Bathhouse John Coughlin, and Hinky Dink Kenna (McKenty, Tiernan, and Kerrigan). Almost all the major events which constitute the "story" of Cowperwood's financial and political activities—for example, his struggle to gain control of the Chicago River tunnels, his visit to Arneel's home during the American Match crisis, his donation of a telescope to the University of Chicago in order to bolster his financial image, and in particular his battle during 1896 and 1897 to gain a lengthy extension of his franchises—are present in detailed form in Dreiser's documentary sources and in his notes from these sources. Even such illegal activities as Yerkes's attempted bribery of Governor Altgeld and his financial arrangements with various state and city officials were widely reported and duly noted and recounted by Dreiser.

Yerkes's personal life during his Chicago years was also far more available in semidocumentary form than had been true of his Philadelphia career, for many of the extensive newspaper articles on him shortly after his death contained material bearing on his private life during this period. For example, reporters frequently noted two aspects of Yerkes's personal affairs which Dreiser developed into the principal motifs of Cowperwood's Chicago life—that Yerkes and his wife failed to gain a place in Chicago society, and that Yerkes's "influence over young women on sight was tremendous."[6] For the many minor affairs which Dreiser attributed to Cowperwood in Chicago, he seems to have drawn upon Yerkes's reputation and upon instances recalled by his contemporaries. Cowperwood's three major love affairs in *The Titan*, however, have specific sources, two of which received newspaper commentary. Cowperwood's first important affair, with Rita Sohlberg, reflects Yerkes's well-known and extended relationship (over three years in the early 1890s) with Anna Hyllsted, the wife of a Danish artist.[7] His second, with the young actress Stephanie Platow, represents a startling anomaly in the documentary accuracy of Dreiser's depiction of Yerkes's career. There is no evidence of Yerkes's interest in a half-Jewish actress who was active in an avant-garde Chicago little theatre company, but there is ample evidence of Dreiser's intense involvement with Kirah Markham, who is the exact prototype of Stephanie Platow, during the two months he spent in Chicago working on *The Titan*.[8] The Cowperwood-Stephanie section of *The Titan* is therefore an autobiographical rather than a historical *roman à clef*. The Garrick Players are the Chicago Little Theatre, Stephanie is Kirah, Lane Cross is Maurice Browne (the founder of the group), and Gardner Knowles is Floyd Dell. (Dell was Kirah's lover before Dreiser appeared on the scene.) Dreiser not only transposed his Chicago experience of 1912–13 into Yerkes's life of the mid-1880s but also playfully depicted himself in a double role. He is of course Cowperwood himself, the magnetic older man who is responsive to youthful beauty and who is capable of winning a young, sensual, and artistic girl away from his younger rivals. But he is also in part Forbes Gurney, a dreamy, moody poet and installment collector who competes successfully with Cowperwood for Stephanie's favors.[9] In what was perhaps a private joke between Dreiser and Kirah (who was to remain his mistress for almost three years), Stephanie is torn between her love for the young poet and for the man of power, with the implication that for Kirah, though not for Stephanie, the problem was solved by the uniting of the two figures in Dreiser.

Cowperwood's third and most important love affair in *The Titan* is with Berenice, who, as I have already noted, derived from Emily Grigsby and Thelma Cudlipp. As Philip Gerber in particular has demonstrated, Dreiser made use of a number of lengthy anecdotal newspaper stories about Yerkes and Emily Grigsby.[10] Emily's physical appearance and background, her sponsorship from adolescence by Yerkes, her exposure in the incident involving the drunken racehorse owner at the Waldorf-Astoria, and her acceptance of a large Park Avenue mansion which Yerkes had built for her—all were duly noted by Dreiser and used in *The Titan*. In his account of Cowperwood's later sex life, however, Dreiser suppressed the information that Yerkes had more than one "protégé," to adopt the term frequently used by contemporary newspapers when referring to Miss Grigsby. During the years he was "protecting" Miss Grigsby, Yerkes was also caring for a Miss Gladys Unger, a young American girl who was studying art in Paris and whom he first met in 1896, when he was fifty-nine and she thirteen. Dreiser took many notes on this relationship but decided to omit it, no doubt because two such relationships would suggest Cowperwood's pedophilia rather than his enshrinement of feminine beauty.

For his account of Aileen in Chicago, Dreiser had ample suggestion in post-1905 newspaper stories of Mrs. Yerkes's life that her social failure and Yerkes's many affairs had resulted in frequent scenes of drunken rage. But for his detailed rendering of Aileen's violent jealousy and self-pity, Dreiser drew upon the same memories of his twelve years with Sallie which had already been reflected in *The "Genius."* Aileen's one major affair in *The Titan*, with the Cowperwoodlike Polk Lynde, probably had its source in Chicago gossip. Since Dreiser included in both *The Titan* and *The Stoic* Aileen's use of a pretended interest in young men as a means of revenging herself against Cowperwood, it can be assumed that he had some private information on this subject.

On his return from Chicago in early February, Dreiser set to work writing *The Titan*. In a letter to Major F. T. Leigh of Harper's soon after his return, he estimated that he would finish the book in five to seven months.[11] Nine months later, however, in October 1913, the novel was still incomplete[12] and indeed was not to be finished until early December. One reason for this delay was that Dreiser was much occupied during 1913 with completing old projects and responding to new enthusiasms. But the major reason was that as usual Dreiser had too much material on hand and that much effort was required to shape it into the work of reasonable length that both internal and external pressures demanded. Both he and Harper's had been displeased by the massiveness of *The Financier*, and Dreiser had been asked expressly to submit a more "concise" second volume[13] in order to avoid the expensive and not always possible task of cutting a novel in proof. Dreiser's response to this need was to write, as always, an initial holograph draft in which he disregarded any consideration of length. But he then undertook an extensive exercise in cutting, first of the holograph and then of the typescript.[14] As a result of these labors, the published version of *The Titan* is half the length of the holograph.

Dreiser's cutting concentrated on no one portion and no one aspect of the novel. His primary intent was to reduce wordage by removing

anything which was not essential to the themes and the narrative movement of the work. Thus, for example, the first twenty holograph chapters
were reduced to ten in the published novel by removing chapters on
Cowperwood's financial activities in Fargo, on Addison's Chicago home,
on Chicago society, on the early married life of Cowperwood and Aileen,
and so on. In addition to cutting whole chapters, Dreiser also summarized
large segments of material and then condensed these summaries into a
single chapter. He cut uniformly only chapter-opening passages of philos-
ophizing and explicit sexual descriptions, such as Cowperwood's lovemaking with Antoinette and Lynde's attack on Aileen.

Dreiser also rearranged much of his material during this revision
process. One kind of reorganization involved creating longer sequences of a
particular narrative than had existed in the original. For example, Cowperwood's affair with Stephanie, which occurs in two long sections in the
published version of the novel, is much more widely dispersed in the
holograph among chapters containing Cowperwood's business activities.
Another kind of change was the relocation of various incidents either
forward or backward in time. Dreiser's ability to make basic narrative
changes of these kinds without radically reshaping the novel as a whole
reveals one of the principal characteristics of the form of *The Titan*. The
work is not a novel of plot in the usual sense of a tight causality between
incidents. It is more a picaresque novel, in which action flows from
disparate adventures of a central figure in a kind of timeless unity because
events draw their meaning and consistency primarily from his unchanging
nature rather than from a causal relationship to each other. For example,
aside from the thematic necessity that Cowperwood's love affairs with
Rita, Stephanie, and Berenice occur in that order, these affairs—and all the
others in the novel—could appear at any point in the narrative. And such a
major moment in Cowperwood's business life as his victory in the American Match collapse could also be placed almost anywhere.

Dreiser's cut and revised version of *The Titan* was set up by Harper's
in January 1914, and after some further revision in proof, final sheets were
run off in late February or early March. But at that point, for reasons that
are still not entirely clear, the firm decided that it could not publish the
novel. Harper's told Dreiser that it had concluded that the material of the
novel was too realistic. But trade gossip had it that the current owner of
Harper's had objected to Dreiser's depiction of American financial life and
that friends of Miss Grigsby, who was still prominent in English social life,

had brought pressure upon the firm.[15] As early as October 1911, Ripley Hitchcock of Harper's had warned Dreiser's literary agent that an account of Yerkes's later career might contain "inadvisable" material,[16] and this warning was now coming to fruition. To Dreiser, Harper's action was "Sister Carrie all over again."[17] But in this instance, the strenuous efforts of William Lengel soon produced another publisher for the novel, and *The Titan* was published by John Lane in May 1914, with Harper's sheets used unchanged.

𝕮𝕮𝕮𝕮𝕮𝕮𝕮𝕮𝕮𝕮𝕮𝕮𝕮𝕮𝕮𝕮𝕮𝕮𝕮𝕮𝕮𝕮𝕮𝕮𝕮𝕮𝕮

Early in *The Titan* Frank Cowperwood calls on the Chicago banker Judah Addison. As is true of many characters who are encountering Cowperwood for the first time, Addison is struck by his eyes. "They were wonderful eyes, soft and spring-like at times, glowing with a rich, human understanding which on the instant could harden and flash lightning. Deceptive eyes, unreadable, but alluring alike to men and women in all walks and conditions of life" (p. 7). The Cowperwood of *The Titan* is thus still "hard" and "deceptive." He is a man whose central creed is still "I satisfy myself" and whose Nietzschean ethics and Machiavellian deviousness are even more pronounced than in *The Financier* because of his greater power and the greater opportunity for the expression of these qualities in the expansive Chicago setting. But Dreiser also added a significant new element to his characterization of Cowperwood in *The Titan*. Cowperwood now possesses a "rich, human understanding." His actions are similar in both novels, but unlike the Cowperwood of *The Financier* who is preoccupied with his drive to fulfill his desires, the Cowperwood of *The Titan* is endowed with a speculative insight into human nature and experience. He now not only has the force which Eugene Witla lacked but has acquired in full Witla's philosophical awareness and depth.

One way of accounting for this important change in Dreiser's portrayal of Cowperwood is to attribute it primarily to the natural development of a character as he matures and presumably grows wiser. Another explanation lies in the close similarity between Yerkes's Chicago career and Dreiser's conception of his own life, a similarity which encouraged an even closer identification between Dreiser and his protagonist than had existed in *The Financier*. Yerkes in Chicago was an "outsider" who was struggling to fulfill himself despite the concerted opposition of established, conservative society. He was also saddled with a wife whom he no longer loved and who attempted to thwart the expression of his varietistic impulses as they sought fulfillment in the ideal of youthful beauty. Given this similarity between Yerkes in Chicago and Dreiser's interpretation of his own life since his marriage and the publication and "suppression" of *Sister Carrie*, it is not surprising that Dreiser attributed to Cowperwood a philosophical insight which he had already expressed as his own in the character of Eugene Witla.

Cowperwood in *The Titan* recognizes that life is governed not only by struggle but by change and that all experience is rendered both wonderful and terrible by the interaction of these two realities. He now senses for the first time "how comparatively unimportant in the great drift of life were his own affairs when about him was operative all this splendid will to existence" (p. 393). Yet his sense of insignificance is tempered by his realization of the "splendor" of the struggle, and he brings to experience an "appetite for the wonders of life" and an "appreciation of the dramas which produce either failure or success" (p. 347). He thus has the distinctively Dreiserian attitudes of compassion for the victims of life's inevitable destructiveness and of responsiveness to the beauty of the uncontrollable and destructive flux which is life. "It is too bad, but it was the only way" (p. 165), he says of his opponents after winning a battle. And his relationship with Aileen—the relationship which most clearly exposes his basic nature—is poised on the dilemma of his compassionate recognition that he is hurting someone because of the inevitable consequences of change and temperament. When Aileen tells him of her affair with Polk Lynde, an affair which she undertook in desperation because of his neglect of her, he is at first angry. But then, in an echo of the crucial scene between Eugene and Angela, "in a moment his mood changed to one of sorrow for Aileen, for himself, for life, indeed—its tangles of desire and necessity" (p. 317).

Cowperwood is also cast in a much more heroic role in *The Titan* than in *The Financier*. In the first novel, though we sympathize with Cowperwood's desire to succeed, we still sense that he is essentially a shark among sharks and that his success will benefit only himself. In *The Titan*, however, both Cowperwood and Dreiser stress that Cowperwood's business activities will also benefit mankind because an improved and extended city transportation system is a good thing even if it has been created by underhanded means and even if it brings great riches to one man. Moreover, Cowperwood's opponents in *The Titan* are now morally beneath him in two ironic ways. Their attempts to block his plans jeopardize progress, and their hypocritical moralism compares unfavorably with Cowperwood's open acknowledgment of his dishonesty. As Dreiser explains, "The humdrum conventional world could not brook his daring, his insouciance, his constant desire to call a spade a spade. His genial sufficiency was a taunt and a mockery to many. The hard implication of his eye was dreaded by the weaker as fire is feared by a burnt child. Dissembling enough, he was not sufficiently oily and make-believe" (p. 438). Dreiser's rhetoric in this passage—Cowperwood is "daring" while his opponents are "oily" and "make-believe"—and much similar rhetoric throughout the novel is that of Cowperwood as a heroic champion of an unfashionable truth who is defying the sham and pretense of his enemies. Cowperwood in *The Titan* discards hypocrisy for an open declaration of his nature, methods, and goals and thus achieves a kind of Satanic magnificence which to Dreiser is a heroic magnificence.

Dreiser's task in *The Titan* was therefore not merely to chronicle Cowperwood's activities in the new world of Chicago but to render as well his enlarged conception of Cowperwood's philosophical wisdom and heroic role. Though he conceived of both qualities as present in all of Cowperwood's activities, he dramatized the first primarily in relation to Cowperwood's love life, the second in relation to his business affairs.

Perhaps Dreiser's clearest account of Cowperwood's mature speculations on sex and beauty occurs in a lengthy passage which he cut from chapter 62 of the holograph:

Through many and promiscuous relations he was coming to see that what he had been seeking all this while and was still seeking was not so much one woman—or if so a paragon of beauty and ability—but that spirit of sex and temperament that lights up all women in fact, some possibly almost perfectly, although he had not encountered them. He was beginning to see that for him at least if not for other men, beauty spelled variability, that to satisfy the conception and the wonder of sex that was in him he should have to be permitted the privilege of browsing here and there. . . . He must have beauty in all forms, not the singular beauty of one woman but the braided beauty of many so that he could piece together in his own consciousness, the features of one, the hope of another . . . a spiritual and voiceless collection compounded in his own brain of thin air. It was like his gallery of masterpieces wherein were already gathered the streams and trees of Corot, the rocks and shepherds of Daubigny. . . . There were women and women, each representative in their way of some sweet mood, of an artifice of infinite variety. Why should he be satisfied with one example and could he be. Society said "thou must" and *Love*, to express itself properly, seemed to demand that one say "this is enough forever and ever. I will always be true." But alas, this was a shifty and changeful world in which only change was apparently important and only change wrought either perfection or pain.

In *The Titan* itself, the theme of "beauty spelled variability" initially takes the form of Cowperwood's growing discontent with Aileen; it ends, some fourteen women later, in his discovery of a "paragon of beauty and ability" in Berenice. Aileen's youthful energy and vibrancy had disguised her lack of subtlety and had also degenerated into a showy sensuality bordering on vulgarity. Once he has grown dissatisfied with Aileen, Cowperwood's "browsing" in the gallery of feminine beauty expresses itself in a series of brief affairs and in several more intense, more prolonged relationships.

Cowperwood has eleven minor affairs, from his initial unfaithfulness five or six years after he and Aileen arrive in Chicago until he meets Berenice approximately fifteen years later.[18] Dreiser presents some of these relationships by merely naming the woman concerned; others, such as those involving Antoinette Novak and Caroline Hand, he describes in a few pages. But all have two qualities in common. They are primarily sexual in nature, yet with the strong implication that varietism in sexual experience, with an attractive partner, is itself an aesthetic pursuit with an aesthetic goal. There is a suggestive verbal echo, for example, between Dreiser's comment that Cowperwood was seeking "not the singular beauty of one but the braided beauty of many" and his description of Cowperwood's interest in Antoinette, that "she figured in that braided symphony of mere sex attraction which somehow makes up that geometric formula of beauty which rules the world" (p. 130). And Cowperwood's affairs are with girls and women who unconsciously wish to be seduced. The women he wins by a magnetic glance are for the most part either spoiled girls eager for adventure or bored young wives of elderly husbands. Cowperwood's success as a seducer stems from his recognition that women of this kind are available and from his boldness in taking advantage of this recognition. These characteristics of Cowperwood's sexual life reveal that Dreiser was dramatizing in this aspect of the novel far more than the needs of a varietistic temperament. He was also suggesting both the now accepted but then radical idea that behind the late nineteenth-century facade of the

upper-class woman as a monument of purity was a core of sexual frustration and the still radical notion that sexual diversity is as much an aspect of
the "braided symphony" of life as any other pleasurable activity.

Cowperwood's second and more significant kind of love affair in *The
Titan* involves his extended and major relationships with Rita, Stephanie,
and Berenice. All are seeking, pagan spirits and are thus cast in the same
mold as many of Dreiser's portraits in *A Gallery of Women*. With each,
Cowperwood establishes a "secret room" which at first is a refuge from the
world but which is eventually violated by the world. Despite these
similarities, the three figures are also hierarchal in relation to each other,
most obviously in their relative age and "purity." When Cowperwood first
meets each character, Rita is twenty-seven and married, Stephanie is
eighteen but will have had two lovers before Cowperwood wins her two
years later, and Berenice is seventeen and a virgin. But the principal
difference among the three women is the degree to which their artistic
nature expresses itself not only as sexuality but as spirituality. Rita is far
more "refined" than Aileen in her tastes and activities, but her attraction is
primarily her soft and yielding sensuality. Stephanie, however, is not only
a "rank voluptuary" (p. 203) but is also completely the artist in temperament and ability, and Cowperwood finds her "a kind of artistic godsend in
this dull Western atmosphere" (p. 214). In Berenice, the balance of sexual
force and spirituality moves heavily toward soulfulness. "Delicately hag-
gard" (p. 351), with red hair and a fair skin, she is not pretty but rather has a
pre-Raphaelite beauty which Dreiser apparently associated with spiritual
depth and strength. It is thus above all her inner nature which moves
Cowperwood. Not only has she intelligence, breeding, poise, "unafraid"
eyes (p. 463), and a world-weary knowledge of life far beyond her years,
but also "the highest artistic tendencies"—tendencies which flower in a
"soul" eager for "romance and art and philosophy and life" (pp. 392, 394).
By the close of the novel, Cowperwood sees clearly, "as within a chalice-
like nimbus, that the ultimate end of fame, power, vigor was beauty, and
that beauty was a compound of the taste, the emotion, the innate culture,
passion, and dreams of a woman like Berenice Fleming" (p. 470). As
Dreiser went on to comment in a passage cut from this summary, "Now
Cowperwood was beginning to see and feel that the thing he was craving
was not flesh alone and not feeling alone and not beauty alone in its material
aspects but a certain selective artistry of spirit." And in Berenice he has
found a "perfect" embodiment of this quality. In a sense, Cowperwood has

also found in Berenice a youthful and idealized version of himself, and it is no wonder that he designates this narcissistic reflection absolute beauty and falls in love with it. But on the level of Dreiser's more immediate intent, Cowperwood has found an appropriate final objectification of his responsiveness to beauty, an objectification which has progressed upward through Lillian, Aileen, and Berenice in the trilogy as a whole and through Rita, Stephanie, and Berenice in *The Titan*.

Dreiser thus dramatized Cowperwood's fourteen love affairs in *The Titan* in relation to a central paradox in Cowperwood's sexuality—that his seemingly immoral "browsing" has at its goal an almost Platonic union with the spirit of absolute beauty. Yet though this theme has a perverse logic, Dreiser is unsuccessful in his attempt to embody it in moving or even interesting fiction. His offhand accounts of Cowperwood's many conquests create in the reader the effect of amused skepticism rather than an acceptance of the notion that Cowperwood is trying out the notes of the "braided symphony" of sexual variability. Of Cowperwood's major affairs, his relationship with Rita is the only one with any fictional credibility. She is persuasively characterized as a deeply sensual woman who is married to a weak, foolish man and who therefore seeks in Cowperwood an outlet for her feelings and her frustrations. Dreiser's depiction of Cowperwood's involvement with Stephanie, however, is badly warped by the autobiographical source of this portion of the novel. He devotes much of his lengthy account of the affair to Cowperwood's anxieties about her "varietistic" nature and her earlier lovers and to Cowperwood's attempts to entrap her with her new lover. Throughout the relationship Cowperwood is too much Dreiser himself and too little Cowperwood as we have come to know him. He is painfully and pettily jealous rather than coolly aloof, and the affair closes with an admonitory scene in which Dreiser (in the guise of Cowperwood), having discovered Kirah Markham (in the guise of Stephanie) in bed with another man, dismisses her from his life, while her pleading eyes unavailingly beg forgiveness. Many mistresses have had their charms immortalized in art, but few have been so fulsomely catechized and warned.

The principal weakness in Dreiser's depiction of Cowperwood's personal life lies, of course, in the unbelievability of Berenice. Dreiser attempted to make the love between Cowperwood and Berenice plausible despite the thirty-five years between them. She is attracted by his wealth and power and by a maturity which she finds lacking in the young men who have courted her. And he discovers in her not only the ideal beauty that age often finds in youth but one of the paradoxical responses of youth to age, "a large, kindly, mothering intelligence which could see, feel, and understand" (pp. 465–66). Yet from the moment that Cowperwood is attracted by a photograph of the youthful Berenice and sets out to win her, their relationship is conceived and portrayed on a level of Romance and Ideality which elicits from us a bemused wonder rather than a suspension of disbelief. In a novel which is basically "realistic" in the sense that it conveys a detailed social reality—the personal and business life of a late nineteenth-century American—Berenice is an abstraction of Ideal Beauty whose every act and speech appears contrived and unreal. It is a sad but true commentary both on the nature of fiction and on Dreiser's own special talent that Cowperwood fondling the softly compliant Rita is far more convincing (and compelling) than Cowperwood enthralled by the divine beauty of Berenice. As with Dreiser's characterization of Suzanne in *The "Genius,"* we do not find in Berenice what Cowperwood finds; she appears to be a clever and self-centered young woman, but neither her dabbling in various arts nor her pronouncements on life persuade us that she is the spirit of Beauty, Art, and Wisdom which Cowperwood (and Dreiser) believe her to be. In addition, the abstract idea that she is supposed to represent is unacceptable fictionally because such idealized conceptions, if they are to move us, must represent the essential tragedy of experience—that man can imagine the ideal but that he cannot achieve it. To have Cowperwood gain a concrete embodiment of an ideal and to end the novel on this note is to work against the grain of experience and to push the work in the direction of the sentimental romance.

On the whole, Dreiser is more successful in dramatizing Cowperwood's "heroic" nature in his business affairs. As in *The Financier*, Cowperwood's public life is also to a great measure the public life of late nineteenth-century America—in particular, the growth of great cities and the material progress and political corruption which accompanied this growth. In *The Titan*, Dreiser depicts the development of Chicago by focusing on Cowperwood's relations with three tightly interwoven but distinguishable groups: Financiers, Politicians, and the Public. Cowperwood's struggle initially is with the first group for control of the second in order to exploit the third. The broad and pervasive irony present in Dreiser's account of Cowperwood's battles with Arneel, Schryhart, Merrill, and Hand is that both Cowperwood and the Financiers wish to satisfy themselves but that the Financiers disguise this motive behind a veil of seeming concern for the Public. They too engage in deception, bribery, and coercion, but they use their control of the newspapers to maintain that Cowperwood is the real threat to the city. Yet despite their role as defenders of the common good, the Financiers share a deep distrust of the Public because of their fear that the "reform" which they call for might spill over into demands for public ownership of public franchises and even into a more broadly based socialism. Dreiser's depiction of Chicago political life of the 1880s and 1890s is thus an oblique attack on the 1912 Progressive ideal of an elite-led pursuit of social justice. In *The Titan*, reform is merely another weapon in the battle for power, and upper-class reformers seek above all, whether consciously or not, to maintain the status quo rather than to encourage a radical reconstitution of society.

Dreiser characterizes his Politicians with a greater sense of their distinctive social origins and roles than he does his Financiers. His cast ranges from good-natured, double-dealing Irish ward bosses to a figurehead reformist mayor to totally but ineptly corrupt rural nonentities who make up the state legislature. In striking relief to this rich canvas of genial dishonesty and self-serving moralism is Dreiser's portrait of Governor Swanson. Dreiser admires Swanson's idealism but he depicts it as almost totally ineffectual because of the opposition of Cowperwood and the Financiers (who distrust genuine idealism) and because almost every other Politician in the state can be bought, deceived, or controlled. Dreiser's tone in depicting Politicians thus ranged from compassion for Swanson, contempt for such a "moralistic ass" as Mayor Sluss (p. 326), and genial tolerance of the Irish ward bosses. Such men as McKenty and Gilgan are Cowperwood on a lower scale of brilliance and enterprise. They have found life to be a raw and brutal struggle and they fight the game of life with methods derived from experience rather than abstract values. " 'None o' that Christian con game goes around where I am' " (p. 338), says Kerrigan, as he rejects a proposal that having been paid to help elect a reform administration he should now refrain from asking for further payment to support it.

For the most part, the Public in *The Titan* is an entity to be manipulated in the struggle for power. Its beliefs and actions are shaped by those who control the newspapers, and its interests are sold out by whatever group has achieved power. The Public is a dupe, in short, as Dreiser both dramatizes and tells us directly. Cowperwood himself has little feeling toward the common man other than a sense of distance because of his own superior strength and tastes. Yet his actions, as both he and Dreiser note, put him in the paradoxical position of a man whose use of the Public for his own gain also eventually benefits the Public by raising the level of material life. Dreiser thus echoed the Social Darwinist apology for a totally free economic system. Although some men are harmed in the struggle for wealth and power, the consequences of struggle—a superior transportation system, new and more efficient manufacturing processes, etc.—in the long run aid the mass of men.

Toward the close of *The Titan*, the Public begins to play an active role in the struggle for power. In the course of the novel, Cowperwood has won a series of battles with the Financiers, culminating in his great victory in the American Match affair in the summer of 1896. He is now the principal financial figure in Chicago, and only the extension of his street railway franchises—due to expire in 1903—is necessary to place him in the forefront of American and even international money barons. Those opposing this extension are the usual array of a few sincere but weak reformers and a group of hypocritically moralistic Financiers. And the battle appears to take the usual form of a contest between rival groups seeking to buy Politicians and hoodwink the Public. But on this occasion, because Cowperwood's power is so great and so blatantly displayed, and because the Public has been whipped into a frenzy of anger and fear by the publicizing of his methods and motives, the battle alignment shifts. The Financiers withdraw because of their fear that public resentment toward great wealth and its perogatives may result in reforms which affect them as well as Cowperwood. And the Politicians now find that their choice of action has narrowed to the almost open acceptance of Cowperwood's bribes or to the adoption of a semblance of civic virtue. Intimidated by mass meetings and by threats of personal violence, the Politicians desert Cowperwood, and his franchise renewal bill is defeated in the Chicago City Council.

Dreiser is careful to distinguish between the victory of the Public in this battle and the triumph of right. He comments ironically on the simple-minded moralism of those who in the "destruction of Cowperwood . . . saw their duty to God, to humanity, and to democracy straight and clear" (p. 533). And his dramatization of the ward and council meetings reveals that Cowperwood is defeated not by sweet reason but by a crude approximation of his own methods as the Public pits the weight of its physical strength against his cunning and dollars. Cowperwood's defeat does not bring to an end either political corruption or the control of the city's resources for personal profit. His failure merely means that one man's rise to power has been temporarily checked; others will control and others will be corrupted. The basic theme which emerges out of Dreiser's detailed and convincing account of Cowperwood's struggle to extend his franchises is that the world is governed not by the "shoddy wares" of the moralist but by an "equation" (pp. 550–51) which ensures that the powerful do not become too powerful and the weak too weak.

Dreiser divides his epilogue, "In Retrospect," into two parts. In the first, he spells out his idea of equation; in the second he applies the idea to Cowperwood's Chicago experiences. "For the hour" Cowperwood had blazed aloft like a comet, "but for him also the eternal equation—the pathos of the discovery that even giants are but pygmies and that an ultimate balance must be struck" (p. 551). In the wake of his fall, both his supporters and opponents are left in stunned disarray, but he is only temporarily checked and will continue to pursue the destiny of his nature. "Each according to his temperament—that something which he has not made and cannot always subdue, and which may not always be subdued by others for him" (p. 552). The great temperament, rising mysteriously out of a "mulch of darkness," encounters the fixed law of balance, and from this clash there emerges the "splendid glories" and "dark, disdainful, contentious tragedies" (p. 552) of life, tragedies of a kind depicted by Homer, the Greek tragedians, and Shakespeare. Dreiser thus conceived of *The Titan* both as part of an epic trilogy and as a tragic work in its own right, one in which a vibrant, rebellious nature comes into conflict with the laws of the universe and thereby renews our sense of the mystery and terror and wonder of life.

Yet despite the overall coherence and suggestiveness of Dreiser's depiction of Cowperwood's financial career in Chicago, this segment of the novel is also not entirely satisfactory as fiction. Dreiser's weakness in this instance does not derive from inconsistency (as it did in Cowperwood's relationship with Stephanie) or from lack of credibility (as with Berenice) but from a dull similarity of material and tone. His secondary characters do not come to life, as had Butler and Stener, even though he introduces such parallel figures as Hand (a cuckolded husband who opposes Cowperwood) and Sluss (a weak politician who crumbles under pressure). Dreiser overpopulates *The Titan* and underdevelops the background of his minor characters—their homes, families, and actions—and the result is a bland sameness. His financiers blend into a group of straw men collectively gnashing their teeth over Cowperwood's latest success, and his newspaper editors and proprietors—though named again and again—are almost nonentities as individuals. Only his Irish political bosses achieve individuality, but they appear only briefly and even their distinctiveness is in part the stock equipment of the conventionally portrayed shrewd lower-class Irishman.

In addition, Cowperwood is involved in too many financial deals which create little impression of difference in their nature and outcome. Until the climactic American Match and franchise battles toward the end of the novel, all of Cowperwood's business activities represent a triumphant march forward as his magnetic force and "bland," "jaunty," and "trig" personality sweep all before him.

Another significant weakness of *The Titan* is that its two plots do not cohere fictionally. Their primary connection, of course, is that Cowperwood applies a similar ethic of "I satisfy myself" to love and business. But this connection fails to support the otherwise tenuous relationship between Cowperwood's two major interests. Dreiser tries to bring the two plots together at the close of the novel, when Berenice appears suddenly in Chicago on the evening of Cowperwood's great defeat and pledges herself to him. But though the climax of each plot arises out of Cowperwood's character—his pursuit of power and his pursuit of beauty—Dreiser has failed to interrelate these pursuits in the course of the novel. He has superficially intertwined them in his narrative (two chapters on a love affair followed by two chapters on a business complication, and so on), but insofar as one thread of action is related to the other thematically or causally we could just as well read one plot entire before beginning the other. There is nothing, for example, in Cowperwood's success in reorganizing the Chicago street railway system which is related to his concurrent affair with Stephanie, and his defeat because of the operation of the equation inevitable is independent of his recognition of ideal beauty in Berenice.

Yet *The Titan* cannot be dismissed merely as a bad novel in the sense that *The "Genius"* is a bad novel, despite such similarities in the two works as Dreiser's parallel failures in characterizing Suzanne and Berenice. Dreiser in *The Titan* appears to have been attempting to write a new kind of novel, as is suggested by several uncharacteristic qualities of his fictional technique in the work. For example, his chronology is frequently fuzzy and even inaccurate, and every event in the novel between the early 1880s and 1896 seems to be occurring in a timeless, static world. This temporal vagueness is matched by an equally uncharacteristic lack of substantiality in his depiction of setting. Except for a few paragraphs early in the novel on Chicago and some later descriptions of Cowperwood's mansions, *The Titan* lacks that sense of a character's deep involvement in the circumstances of his world which marks such works as *Sister Carrie*, *Jennie Gerhardt*, and *An American Tragedy*. Even the inevitable repetition present in any work of fiction by Dreiser is here not so much a powerful instrument of rhythmic structure as a form of absolute emphasis of Cowperwood's temperament and thus also a contribution to an effect of a timeless world in which only a cosmic law can momentarily check the successful expression of this temperament. It can therefore be suggested that Dreiser in *The Titan* was attempting to create a fictional equivalent of an epic in which the epic hero is a clearly outlined and looming force in the forefront of the narrative while the world around him, both as setting and event, shades into a cluttered but vague background whose principal function is to aid by contrast in the definition of the hero. But though this suggestion can be offered as a possible explanation of the form of *The Titan*, it cannot sustain a defense of the work as fiction for the apparently simple-minded but essentially profound reason that the novel fails to involve us deeply in its characters and events.

The principal exception to this criticism of *The Titan* as fiction, an exception noted by many readers, is Dreiser's depiction of Aileen. In the initial chapters of the novel she seems to be weakly characterized. Her love for Cowperwood is portrayed as a kind of adolescent enthusiasm on the level of " 'Frank . . . you're so wonderful' " (p. 31) and her all-consuming desire for social success suggests shallowness and trivial-mindedness. But gradually, as her hopes are destroyed and her world narrows, she deepens in nature and effect. She fails socially because of her innate lack of social grace and tact, and because society itself has an ideal of feminine "spirituality" which is affronted by her explicit sensuality. And she fails to hold Cowperwood not because she has changed but because of his "varie-tistic" temperament. As Aileen herself realizes, her social limitations and Cowperwood's seeking nature have now ironically placed her in the position occupied by Lillian when Cowperwood first met the youthful Aileen. But Aileen is far stronger and more passionate than Lillian, and for the remainder of the novel, as she discovers instance after instance of

Cowperwood's infidelity, she displays the full arsenal of emotional weaponry of the strong-willed and self-righteous woman who refuses to accept that the love for which she at one time sacrificed all is no longer desirable. Her tirades, her spying, her affairs, and her drunkenness are the outward signs not of mere jealousy but of a bankrupt spirit, as a woman whose only meaning in life is love finds that her love is valueless. Aileen thus not only reflects Sallie White (and Dreiser's earlier portrayal of Sallie as Angela Blue) but also Jennie Gerhardt. Like Angela and Eugene, Aileen and Cowperwood descend into a marriage in which indifference and rage alternate periodically, and in which self-pity and anger are met by deception, cajolery, and threats. And like Jennie, Aileen is a woman whose essential nature is that of loyalty and love but who discovers that these are insufficient to gain the happiness of a permanent union.

As in his depiction of Jennie and Angela, Dreiser's portrait of Aileen called forth some of his best and worst writing. He made powerfully evident the deep irony of Aileen's position, in which the despoiler of a home becomes the despoiled and the virtue of loyalty becomes the evil of self-torture. And he handles well Aileen's directness of attack when angry, in particular a verbal vigor which stems from her Irish immigrant roots. On other occasions, however, Aileen's pathetic situation drew Dreiser into the dangerous waters of the rhetoric of pathos. But despite some strikingly bad purple passages involving her self-torment, she lives as a character, and both we and the "bland" and "jaunty" Cowperwood cringe at the onset of another of her outbursts of animal fury. One successful character does not make a novel, however, and *The Titan* remains of interest primarily as a schematized dramatization of two of Dreiser's dominant ideas of the period—those of balance and beauty—and as an interpretation of American public morality.

PART THREE

An American Tragedy

FOR MORE THAN a decade after the publication of *An American Tragedy* in late 1925, Dreiser often explained in letters, articles, and interviews that his purpose in writing the novel had not been to exploit the fictional possibilities of a particular sensational crime but rather to express an archetypal American dilemma.[1] From youth, Dreiser recalled, he had been absorbed by magazine stories in which a working girl marries a wealthy young man or in which a poor young man marries well and thereby achieves prominence and luxury. In these versions of the American myth of success, marriage is a step upward socially and materially. Although youthful desire and effort might not gain immediate fulfillment, they would eventually be rewarded by a beneficent providence in one glorious act of recompense which combined love and success. By 1893, however, when Dreiser was a young reporter in St. Louis, he began to notice the prevalence of a crime which suggested the perniciousness of this myth, given the weaknesses of human nature. For in instance after instance, a young man resorted to murder when faced with the insoluble dilemma of a socially desirable match and an obstacle to that match. In the cases that Dreiser stressed—those of Carlyle Harris in 1893, Chester Gillette in 1906, and Clarence Richesen in 1911—this situation took a particularly evocative and "classic" shape.[2] An ambitious young man just beginning his career forms a secret attachment with a poor, socially unacceptable girl. He then meets and wins a girl from a prominent and well-to-do family, but at that point his first love, "Miss Poor," announces

203

her pregnancy and threatens to expose him to "Miss Rich."[3] Attempts at abortion fail, and in desperation the young man murders his pregnant sweetheart and is eventually apprehended and executed. The "tragedy" of this kind of crime, Dreiser felt, was that Harris, Gillette, and Richesen were impelled primarily by the irresistible pressure within American life to gain success—to gain it honorably if possible "but any old way" if necessary.[4] Gillette, Dreiser wrote, "*was really doing the kind of thing which Americans should and would have said was the wise and moral thing to do* [attempting to rise socially through the heart] *had he not committed a murder.*"[5] But because Gillette and the other two young men had not been resourceful or clever—because they did not know how to use contraceptives or how to get an abortion and because they did not have wealthy families to "handle the matter" for them—they had committed murder. They had thus been executed primarily for their inept attempts to fulfill the American dream by marrying "somebody with 'dough.' "[6]

Although Dreiser in these later accounts of the sources of *An American Tragedy* always emphasized that the appeal of the Gillette case derived from its full and dramatic exemplification of a pervasive social reality, much of the attraction of the case, and others like it, lay in its evocative echoing of some of the most compelling realities of Dreiser's own life. For Dreiser, too, as a youth had felt oppressed by his narrow and poverty-stricken background and, instructed by the popular weeklies, had projected his daydreams of a better life and of sexual fulfillment into the hope of marrying well. As a lonely and lowly young man in Chicago, he comforted himself with the dream of marriage to a beautiful and wealthy girl. "I could see myself in golden chambers, giving myself over to what luxuries and delights."[7] And a few years later, as an unemployed newspaperman, he gazed at the grandiose homes on Cleveland's Euclid Avenue, "envying the rich and wishing that I was famous or a member of a wealthy family, and that I might meet some one of the beautiful girls I imagined I saw there and have her fall in love with me."[8] Although Dreiser did not find a girl with golden chambers or a house on Euclid Avenue, he did experience several rough equivalents of the kind of dilemma faced by Harris, Gillette, and Richesen. In the early 1890s he had won first Nellie, a fellow worker in a Chicago laundry, and then Alice, a salesgirl in a store. But after reaching the "lofty position" of a reporter, he met a "little blonde" of far greater social position. "Because she was new to me," he recalled, "and comfortably stationed and better dressed than either Alice or N—— had ever been,

I esteemed her more highly, made invidious comparisons from a material point of view, and wished that I could marry some such well-placed girl without assuming all the stern obligations of matrimony."[9] From 1893, when he met Sallie White, to their separation in 1910, Dreiser's personal life had the configuration of a permanent triangle. Sallie was an unchanging base of drab and thwarting obligation, while in the green pastures of freedom were a seemingly unending chain of charming, clever, and wealthy women whom he was meeting through his work as reporter, magazine writer, and editor. No wonder that Dreiser indulged in the fantasy of killing off Angela-Sallie in The *"Genius"* and that his life with Helen Richardson, from their meeting in 1919 to their marriage in 1943, was marked by his constant efforts to limit severely the extent of his responsibility to her. In short, Dreiser's dramatization of the emotional reality of a wish to replace a "used up" woman with a more desirable one was as much a function of the memory as of the imagination.

Dreiser's novels before *An American Tragedy* can, in a limited but suggestive sense, be considered a search for an adequate form to represent his permanent preoccupation with the relationship between love and success. His interest in the myth of success took the form of studies of the variables in the basically unchanging pattern of "X" deserting "Miss/Mr. Poor" for "Mr./Miss Rich," a pattern in which wealth and position also implied a real or imagined "spiritual" superiority. So Carrie leaves Drouet for Hurstwood and then deserts Hurstwood with Ames in the back of her mind, while Lester leaves Jennie for Mrs. Gerald, Eugene seeks to leave Angela for Suzanne, and Cowperwood leaves Lillian for Aileen and Aileen for Berenice.

Dreiser also sought to express his interest in the myth of success in a number of studies in which the pursuit of Miss Rich leads to criminal acts. Of Dreiser's three such attempts before *An American Tragedy*, two survive in manuscript fragments and one is no longer extant. During the winter of 1914–15, Dreiser took extensive notes on the Roland Molineux case of 1899 and began writing a novel called "The Rake" based upon this well-known murder. A prologue and five chapters of this novel are in the Dreiser Collection.[10] Then, toward the end of the decade, Dreiser wrote six now-lost chapters of a novel based on the Richesen case and almost completed a long story called "Her Boy" about a Philadelphia criminal.[11]

Superficially, the Molineux case deviates from the pattern which most appealed to Dreiser, since it involved two men and a woman rather than a man and two women. Molineux had been courting a wealthy young girl. When a rival suitor appeared, Molineux's attempt to poison him resulted in the accidental death of an innocent woman. But Dreiser's depiction of Molineux as Ansley Bellinger is nevertheless closely related to his absorption in figures who commit criminal acts because of the irresistible pull of desire. Bellinger has an artistic temperament and is a lover of beauty, qualities which merge in his "keen passion for sex," but he is handicapped by a lack of money. He, too, therefore dreams of a romance with a beautiful well-born lady which will at once answer all his needs. When he encounters such a girl, he is sufficiently compelled by the demands of sex and ambition to attempt to kill the man who stands in his way.

"Her Boy" is about a young Irishman named Eddie Meagher who begins life with a weak and ineffectual mother and a brutish father. He drifts into petty crime and is at last shot while attempting to rob a bank. The source of the story was Dreiser's recollection of a Sullivan family and its bank-robber son. In recalling the background of the young man in *A Hoosier Holiday*, Dreiser remarked that he had "died a criminal in the chair owing to conditions over which he had no least control."[12] In "Her Boy," Dreiser, who at this point in his career was much taken with the mechanistic theories of Jacques Loeb, added a further note to this deterministic theme by citing Eddie's "chemistry" as a vital factor in his life. Yet Eddie is no mere cipher.

Intellectually he was destined never to be anything more than a clever artisan of some kind, though in the poorly combined substance of his chemistry, there were some registrations of beauty and possible phases of happiness which so early as thirteen and fourteen had begun to trouble his young soul—the beauty of girls, for one thing, the fine homes with their flowers and walks to be seen in other parts of the city—windows full of clothing, and musical instruments and interesting things, generally—things he had never known and was destined never to know in any satisfying and comforting way. For in spite of his poverty and all his need to bestir himself, Eddie's was still an errant mind, subject to dreams, vanities, illusions, which had nothing to do with practical affairs.

"The Rake" and "Her Boy" share an underlying theme whose presence in otherwise very different stories suggests its centrality in Dreiser's interest in the criminal as a fictional subject. Both Ansley Bellinger and Eddie respond to the beauty in life and both associate beauty not only with sex but with material possessions. Although one is intelligent, well-educated, and capable while the other is the opposite, both are dreamers who cannot brook the thwarting of their dreams. And out of this refusal there emerges a story of crime.

We do not know why Dreiser did not complete these various projects, but it is possible to speculate that each, in its way, failed to provide him with a satisfactory context for the representation of his basic theme. The Molineux case had a suitable protagonist but lacked the favored configuration of an old and new love. The action of "Her Boy" was too thin (Dreiser had only a sketchy awareness of the career of the Sullivan boy), and the background of the Richesen case no doubt centered too fully on the duties and world of a clergyman. (Richesen, a Massachusetts minister, had murdered his sweetheart in order to be free to marry a more suitable parishioner.) But in the Gillette case Dreiser had an almost ideal external shape for the expression of the themes which had preoccupied him in these tentative and abortive early efforts: a young man of limited background with an intense desire to advance himself; a triangle of a man and two women; and a fully reported crime of great dramatic potential.

Chester Gillette had murdered Grace Brown on July 11, 1906. His trial took place from November 13 to December 5, 1906, and he was executed on March 30, 1908. By late 1906, Dreiser had fully recovered from his breakdown of a few years earlier and was editing the *Broadway Magazine* in New York. He took considerable interest in the Gillette case as it was reported in the New York papers, though there is no conclusive evidence that he saved any clippings of these reports or that he planned at that time to use the case as the basis for a novel.[13]

The period between Dreiser's completion of *The Titan* in late 1913 and his early work on *An American Tragedy* in mid-1920 was one of intense literary productivity but little sustained work on any single novel. It was a period of many new literary interests—in drama, poetry, autobiography, and philosophical essays; of discouragement about the possibility of making a living as a novelist after the financial failure of *The Titan* in 1915 and the suppression of *The "Genius"* in 1916; and of an inability to proceed with such planned long works as "The Rake" and *The Bulwark*. In September 1919, Dreiser met Helen Richardson and in October moved with her to Los Angeles, where Dreiser hoped to complete *The Bulwark* for spring publication by his new publisher, Boni and Liveright. During the winter and spring of 1919–20, Dreiser continued to work sporadically on

The Bulwark as well as on the second volume of his autobiography and a new collection of short stories. We do not know precisely when he began work on *An American Tragedy*, but a rough date is the late summer of 1920. In a letter of August 13, 1920, to Mencken he outlined his literary activities in some detail but failed to mention a new project. Yet on the same day he also wrote the district attorney of Herkimer County, New York, to inquire about the availability of the verbatim record of the Gillette trial.[14] And on December 3, 1920, he wrote Liveright that he had begun work on a new novel "sometime ago" and that he hoped to finish it in April.[15] In fact, however, this project also faltered (for reasons I shall discuss later), and when Dreiser left Los Angeles for New York in November 1922, he had completed only twenty chapters of *An American Tragedy*.

Dreiser's notes for *An American Tragedy* have not survived, but he depended heavily and explicitly in the final version of the novel on the extensive coverage of the trial and its aftermath in the *New York World*. A file of the *World*, however, was not available to him in Los Angeles. And since the trial record of the Gillette case comprised three bulky volumes, it is extremely unlikely that his request for a copy was honored. He therefore relied in California either on clippings of the case sent to him from New York or on the lengthy accounts of the trial in the Los Angeles papers of 1906. From these sources, Dreiser learned that Gillette had been raised haphazardly by his missionary parents as they moved from one western town to another and that at the age of fourteen he had left his parents for a series of miscellaneous jobs. At eighteen he had attended Oberlin College for two years, supported both by his parents and an uncle who owned a skirt factory in Cortland, New York. He left college for a job as a brakeman, but in early 1905, at the age of twenty-two, moved to Cortland to work for his uncle. At the factory he had met Grace Brown, and there then occurred the events which led to her death a year and a half later.

The significance of Dreiser's reliance upon newspaper accounts of the Gillette trial both while in California and later in New York is that these journalistic sources, unlike the trial record, supplied a suggestive outline of Gillette's early life. Dreiser was immediately at home with this material in several important ways, and his decision to stop work on *The Bulwark* and undertake *An American Tragedy* can be attributed not only to the doldrums he was experiencing with the first but also to the excitement generated in him by the autobiographical potential of the second. For over five years Dreiser had been plumbing his memory for *A Hoosier Holiday* (1916) and for the unpublished but completed *Dawn* and *A Book About Myself*. He found, therefore, that the similarity of his own background to Gillette's provided not only an immediately available base of autobiographical detail and incident for fictional use but also a vital emotional identification with his protagonist which was a necessary stimulus for Dreiser in the undertaking of any lengthy project. He thus began *An American Tragedy* with an uncharacteristically full account of the early life of his central figure. All his other completed novels had begun either with their protagonists in their late teens (*Sister Carrie* and *Jennie Gerhardt*) or with brief sketches of their youth (*The "Genius"* and *The Financier*). Given this tendency and given the fact that the great bulk of Dreiser's available source material dealt with Gillette's Cortland activities, he would have been expected to have begun *An American Tragedy* with Clyde's arrival in Lycurgus (as he had begun *Sister Carrie* with Carrie's arrival in Chicago). Instead, Dreiser's twenty-chapter first draft of *An American Tragedy* has the autobiographical completeness of *Dawn*. It begins long before Clyde's birth with several chapters on his parents' background, and it concludes with Clyde still only in his midteens. Although Dreiser in later versions of the novel was to compress this chronology and to omit much explicit autobiographical incident, he was still to base the central themes of Book One of *An American Tragedy* on what can be called his autobiographical imagination.

The distinctive shape that Dreiser gave his identification with Gillette in *An American Tragedy* can best be described in connection with the prologuelike opening vignette in the novel, a vignette which is present in the first and all subsequent drafts of the work. The scene of the reluctant twelve year old accompanying his parents on a street-preaching mission while around him looms a desirable yet walled city expresses in one image of thwarted desire both the full range of Dreiser's youthful experience and his ability to project that experience into the circumstances of Gillette's life. As characterized in newspaper stories, Mr. Gillette was a nebulous and ineffectual figure, while Mrs. Gillette was the unworldly but resolute mainstay of the family.[16] Dreiser reinforced these accounts with his recollection of a fuzzy-minded real estate man named Asa Conklin and his strong-willed wife for whom he had worked in Chicago and his more recent impressions of a fanatically religious Los Angeles couple who were his landlords during the early portion of his stay in Los Angeles.[17] But underlying these sources was Dreiser's memory of the immense handicap imposed upon him by his own "peculiarly nebulous, emotional, unorganized and traditionless" family,[18] and in particular his memory of a father whose primitive religiosity made him incapable of fighting the battle of life and of a mother who was the stalwart emotional center of the family.

The Clyde who so hesitantly accompanies his parents in this opening scene derives loosely from Dreiser's knowledge that Gillette escaped from his parents' control at fourteen and that he was later attracted by socially prominent girls at Cortland. Gillette as one encounters him in all the sources available to Dreiser was a callous and shallow youth who undoubtedly murdered Grace Brown. The Clyde of the first draft of *An American Tragedy*, however, is primarily the "poetic" and "romantic" but ineffectual seeker of beauty who dominates Dreiser's self-characterization in *Dawn*. He is a youth "unduly responsive to the moods as well as the lures of life, speculative and meditative and yet with no great resources of either skill or subtlety in handling the material problems of life."[19] Like Dreiser's, his aspirations have been shaped by the American myth of success into a configuration in which sex and material splendor unite in the image of a beautiful and wealthy young girl. Clyde as a boy recalls stories in which "by reason of accidental contact with and marriage to some rich and beautiful girl, some youth no better than himself indeed had come into complete control of all her wealth. Verily. The papers said so." In his daydreams, "always he was some fabulously wealthy man's or woman's adopted son and heir, or the husband or lover of some marvellously beautiful and wealthy girl who was indulging him in every luxury."[20]

Thus, the two poles of Clyde's emotional life in the vignette—the limiting and embarrassing world of his family and the desirable and implicitly sexual and luxurious world of the city—are a distillation of the pain and frustration of Dreiser the outsider as depicted in *Dawn* and *A Hoosier Holiday*. More particularly, Dreiser later drew upon the specific circumstances which he associated with these emotional realities to create such major incidents in Book One as Esta's pregnancy and Clyde's work at the Green-Davidson. Gillette had in his background neither a pregnancy of this kind nor an association with a hotel. Dreiser, however, had been acutely troubled during his Warsaw years by the socially embarrassing affairs and pregnancies of his sisters. And as a young reporter in St. Louis he had delighted in the bustle and splendor of fashionable hotels and in the exciting freedom of bohemian restaurants.

But though the first draft of *An American Tragedy* which Dreiser wrote in California during 1920–21 begins with this powerfully evocative vignette, it is on the whole dull and formless. After the opening street scene, Dreiser goes back in time to recount at considerable length the early life of Asa and Elvira on New York farms, their engagement, marriage, and financial hardships, and their years in Chicago, Omaha, and Kansas City as evangelists. At Chapter VII he turns to Clyde, who is then seven. We learn of Clyde's difficulties at school because of his family and—for several chapters—of his experiences as an employee in a five and ten cent store. Chapters XII–XV continue to tell of Clyde's Kansas City life but also include accounts of Esta's seduction and pregnancy and of the decision of the Gillette family to move to Denver because of Esta. In Denver, Clyde gets a job as a stock clerk in a wholesale grocery, and the draft ends with an extended narrative of his duties and problems as a clerk.

One reason for the failure of this early version of Clyde's youth is Dreiser's paradoxical overdevelopment of the few specific details about Gillette's background which were at his disposal. For example, he knew from the newspaper accounts of the Gillettes not only that Mr. Gillette was fuzzy-minded and Mrs. Gillette a rough bulwark of strength, but that the family had been footloose during Chester's boyhood and that they had been followers for several years of the Reverend John Dowie, a faith healer who had established a community called the City of Zion near Chicago in the late 1890s. In the first draft, Dreiser dramatized these details literally and fully. As a result the draft has a static shapelessness, since Dreiser takes nineteen chapters to establish repetitiously themes implicit in the street-scene vignette of the opening chapter. To sense the prolixity and formlessness of the original version of *An American Tragedy*, one has only to contrast the splendid economy of Book One of the final version, in which we move swiftly from the opening vignette to the contrasting motifs of Esta's pregnancy and Clyde's job in the soda fountain.

Dreiser was also overcommitted in this first draft to specific autobiographical incidents as a means of expressing the themes he associated with his own youth. Although Dreiser no doubt intended in the long run to have Clyde work in a Green-Davidson kind of hotel in Denver, he nevertheless also thought it necessary to take him through a series of early jobs, each of which was loosely or explicitly based on an experience of Dreiser's own adolescence.

A final kind of literal-mindedness in the early version of *An American Tragedy* was Dreiser's overexplicit reliance on the Freudian and behavioristic ideas which had absorbed him during the half-decade or so before he began writing the novel. Freud's ideas had become known among American intellectuals and bohemians about 1910, and Dreiser almost immediately reflected this currency by a reference in *The Financier* to Cowperwood's "super-self" (p. 219). Dreiser himself, however, dated his full awareness of Freudian psychology from approximately mid-1914, when he settled in Greenwich Village.[21] By 1917 he had accepted many of Freud's ideas and was anxious to meet his foremost American disciple and translator, A. A. Brill. Freud, he wrote Brill in early 1919, after reading one of his translations, "is like a master with a key who unlocks subterranean cells and leads forth the hoary victims of injustice."[22] Dreiser was also an enthusiastic believer during these years in the theories of Jacques Loeb and in the behavioristic ideas of such followers of Loeb as George Crile. Loeb first came into national prominence in 1912 with his *The Mechanistic Conception of Life*. Dreiser became absorbed in his ideas a few years later at about the same time he was growing enthusiastic about Freudianism. "Mechanism plus behaviorism . . . had seized upon me," he recalled of his Village years before his departure for California.[23]

On the surface, it would seem that Freudianism and mechanism are antithetical, and indeed there was much hostility between followers of the two beliefs. While Freud viewed man as unique because of his repression of his instinctive emotions—a quality which results in the dark and impenetrable undergrowth of the unconscious—Loeb stressed that all life, including man, could be observed and explained as a tropistic response to external stimuli. One school sought complexity in the explanation of human nature, the other a reductive simplicity. Both, however, viewed human behavior as deterministically controlled. Man's actions, whether the product of the unconscious or of external stimuli, were conditioned by his biological makeup and his environment. It was thus not difficult for Dreiser to accept both theories and to combine their deterministic themes in the term "chemism"—a term which he began using in 1915 or 1916 and which, as Ellen Moers has shown, he derived from Freud but used principally with a mechanistic intent.[24] And it was inevitable, given Dreiser's penchant for intellectualizing his literary work, that these ideas should figure prominently in his writing of this period.

So Dreiser in *The Hand of the Potter* (1918), a play which he subtitled "A Tragedy," portrayed sympathetically a youthful sex maniac whose chemical makeup is the source of his behavior. So too the essays of *Hey*

Rub-a-Dub-Dub (1920) play alternately on the beliefs of Loeb and Freud in order to help establish the major theme of the book—that the "constant palaver"[25] about man's moral nature is indeed only talk and that the only "morality" in life is a mechanistic equation or balance.

Dreiser's twofold use of the ideas of Freud and Loeb—to defend those who are accused of "immorality" and to attack those who view life in moral terms—became increasingly strident during his last years in New York and his early stay in Los Angeles. For example, in his *Gallery of Women* sketches (written for the most part during the early 1920s), he analyzed such figures as Lucia, Emanuela, and Ernita as Freudian case studies. And in his story "Her Boy" he sharpened his earlier vague idea of "temperament" as the source of human motivation into an explicit Loebian behaviorism. "We think" he wrote in extenuation of Eddie Meagher, "that we act according to definite rules and judgments of our own or of others, but invariably, at each period we act only according to our internal chemical lures and attractions and compulsions and the outward pressures by which these same are surrounded."

The first draft of *An American Tragedy* has much of this doctrinaire quality. Esta is not only a "moony" and naïve adolescent but also the product of a particular chemical formulation. A minor figure, such as Clyde's Kansas City friend Teget (dropped entirely from later versions of the novel), is displayed as a mechanism. Teget is a boy with a wanderlust, but to Dreiser, "by reason of some tropism of his nature, [he] was all for travel."[26] It is Clyde above all who suffers the full burden of Dreiser's preoccupation with man as a biological formula. In an unpublished essay of 1918 or 1919 called "It"[27] ("it" is man's Freudian unconscious), Dreiser wrote: "The Freudians would have us believe . . . that even the so-called temperamental leanings which influence us to take up our various professions or labors are accidental, due to psychic wounds in infancy or youth, repressions or woes, which burst out later in retaliatory decision and works." In the first draft of *An American Tragedy*, Dreiser interpreted Clyde as a figure controlled by a psychic wound, and he apparently intended to make this interpretation central to his depiction of Clyde in the novel as a whole. While still attending school in Kansas City, Clyde lies to his classmates about his parents because he is embarrassed to admit that they are street preachers. His lies lead to a confrontation with several boys, one of whom strikes Clyde, who in his fear and chagrin does not fight back.

The incident, Dreiser tells us, was important because

a deep psychic wound had been delivered which was destined to fester and ramify in strange ways later on. It convinced him of the material, even the spiritual insignificance of that which his parents did. They seemed, if anything, more hopeless and incompetent than ever. It sickened him of this school, and this type of school work, as well as of the type of prosperous youth of better physique perhaps who could thus bluster and brag and insult and show off. At the same time, and by some psychic process of inversion, it gave him a greater awe of wealth and comfort, or at least a keener perception of the protective quality of a high social position in life.[28]

The final version of *An American Tragedy* still bears the marks of Dreiser's intense interest in mechanistic and Freudian ideas. Esta's adolescent mooniness is still a "chemism of dreams" (I, 16) and Mason, later in the novel, is briefly characterized in relation to a "psychic sex scar" (II, 92) which is the product of his boyhood experiences. But on the whole Dreiser was able to free the novel in later drafts from straitjacket formulistic characterizations by assimilating his Freudian and behavioristic beliefs into independently realized dramatic moments and psychological responses.

All signs indicate that Dreiser completed the twenty extant chapters of his first draft in early 1921 and that he then put aside the novel. Perhaps he felt the need to view the area in which most of the later action of the novel was to take place. But also, as is suggested by his having stopped work long before he reached the Lycurgus portion and by his later almost complete discarding of the draft, he was consciously or unconsciously dissatisfied with his overliteral, overpolemical technique and had therefore reached a temporary dead end. Dreiser returned to New York in October 1922. Although he may have done some additional research on the Gillette case during the next nine months, he did no writing. Liveright, however, was putting increasing pressure on him to deliver the novel which was to be the cornerstone of their new and elaborate publishing agreement. So in June 1923, Dreiser and Helen made a motor trip in which they visited Cortland, South Otselic (the Biltz of *An American Tragedy*), Herkimer (Bridgeburg), and Big Moose Lake (Big Bittern Lake). On their return, Dreiser began a new draft of *An American Tragedy*. He completed all work on the novel, some million words later, in late 1925.

❮❮❮❮❮❮❮❮❮❮❮❮❮❮❮❮❮❮❮❮❮❮❮❮❮❮❮❮❮

When Dreiser began work on his new version of *An American Tragedy* in the summer of 1923, he had available as documentary sources the extensive reports of the trial and execution of Gillette in the *New York World* and a small pamphlet called *Grace Brown's Love Letters* which contained the letters of Grace Brown to Gillette in the early summer of 1906, shortly before her death.[29] In addition, he had visited the towns and countryside which figure in the case, and he would soon make journeys to an upper New York state shirt factory and to Sing Sing prison.[30] The principal questions about Dreiser's use of his sources are: to what extent did he depend on the verbatim trial record of the case as well as the *World*, and to what extent does his account of the life of Clyde Griffiths after his arrival at Lycurgus differ from the account in his sources of Gillette at Cortland. Both matters are important, since the first bears on the shaping influence of a particular source and the second on the distinctive themes and form which Dreiser imposed upon his sources.[31]

Although Dreiser had asked to see the trial record of the Gillette case in August 1920, and though the record would have been available to him in New York City on his return in 1922, there is no evidence that he indeed ever did consult it.[32] Dreiser seldom discussed the explicit sources he used for the novel, and his fullest statement on this matter is ambiguous. He wrote in 1935 in "I Find the Real American Tragedy,"

Furthermore, in my examination of such data as I could find in 1924 relating to the Chester Gillette-Billy Brown case, I had become convinced that there was an entire misunderstanding, or perhaps I had better say non-apprehension, of the conditions or circumstances surrounding the victims of that murder *before* the murder was committed. From these circumstances, which I drew not only from the testimony introduced at the trial but from newspaper investigations and information which preceded and accompanied the trial . . .[33]

The key phrase in this recollection—"the testimony introduced at the trial"—would seem to refer to the trial record but for the fact that the *World* published much purportedly verbatim testimony and that a comparison of *An American Tragedy*, the *World*, and the Gillette trial record reveals that Dreiser depended exclusively on the *World* for his verbatim material and for almost all other explicit detail.

The *World* reporter did not take exact notes but rather paraphrased loosely and then placed this material in quotation marks as if he were quoting directly. All of Dreiser's verbatim use of material from the trial follows the *World*'s version rather than the trial record,[34] as can be seen from this comparison of the opening of the district attorney's speech to the jury at the beginning of the trial:

Trial Record	*New York World*	*An American Tragedy*
"You probably, those of you who are unfamiliar with the process of selecting a jury, have marvelled somewhat during the past week as the attorneys for the defense and the People have exercised those rights which the law gives to them in selecting a jury."[35]	"No doubt many of you have been puzzled during the past week by the care with which the lawyers in the case have passed upon the panels from which you twelve men have been drawn."[36]	"No doubt many of you have been wearied, as well as puzzled, at times during the past week," he began, "by the exceeding care with which the lawyers in this case have passed upon the panels from which you twelve men have been chosen." (II, 231)

Dreiser's dramatization of Clyde's life in Lycurgus, including the trip to the North Woods with Roberta, is equally conclusive in indicating the *World* as Dreiser's major source. He used a great mass of detail which is present only in the *World*, while conversely, with a few possible exceptions, he did not use any detail which is present only in the trial record.

The appeal of the *World* to Dreiser as the principal source of his knowledge of the Gillette case is readily explainable. The printed trial record comprises over 2000 pages of testimony, much of it involving the selection of a jury, extensive medical evidence, and the full examination and cross-examination of minor witnesses. The account in the *World* summarized such matters in favor of a full coverage of sensational evidence and emotional moments in the trial and much material on such vital concerns for a novelist as Gillette's background, his Cortland love affairs, the atmosphere in the court, the appearance and actions of participants in the trial, and the circumstances of Gillette's execution. Thus, for example, it was from the *World*'s emphasis on the formal addresses of the attorneys and on Gillette's testimony that Dreiser derived his own summary version of the trial, and it was from the *World* that he received the hint that Grace Brown had a single major rival for the affections of Gillette. The *World*, in short, supplied a good deal of grist for the novelist's mill not available elsewhere and gave this material, by means of emphasis and selection, a kind of preliminary fictional expression which Dreiser had the good sense to recognize as invaluable.

The nature and extent of Dreiser's use of the *World* reports of the Gillette trial are important because of the myth that *An American Tragedy* is merely a slightly fictionalized version of the case. In fact, Dreiser relied on the Gillette case but was not bound by it. His intent was not to retell a story but to recast Gillette's experience into an American tragedy—that is, into a story which would render the tragic reality at the center of the American dream. He therefore made a large number of changes from his sources, all of which are related to two basic impulses: to shift the unavoidable impression of the documentary evidence that Gillette was a shallow-minded murderer to the impression that Clyde might be any one of us caught in the insoluble conflict between our deepest needs and the unyielding nature of experience; and to transform the shapeless, repetitious, and superficial manifestation of life in an actual trial into the compelling revelation of human nature and experience present in fiction at its best. Dreiser's changes were therefore not so much those of addition or omission as of reinterpreting and reshaping what was available to him.[37]

The events of the Gillette case occurred in Cortland, Big Moose Lake, and Herkimer from early 1905 to the summer of 1906. Dreiser made two significant changes in this setting: he moved Clyde's Lycurgus experience forward into the post-World-War I period, and he changed the location of Cortland and Herkimer.

With some exceptions which I shall note later, Dreiser followed the chronology of his sources in his account of Clyde's arrival in Lycurgus in the early spring, his courting first of Roberta and then of Sondra that summer, fall, and winter, his expedition to the Adirondack lakes with Roberta the following summer, his trial that same fall, and his electrocution a year and a half after his trial. Yet he sets this sequence of events vaguely in the early 1920s rather than in 1905–8. Vaguely, because Dreiser does not mention a specific date or historical event in the entire novel. Rather, he depends on the prevalence and importance in the novel of automobiles, of references to movies and popular music, and of an ambience of dancing and prohibition style parties to establish a sense of the twenties. An indication of the specific period Dreiser had in mind is revealed by his statement both in the holograph and in an early typescript of Book Two that Clyde arrives in Lycurgus in 1919.

Dreiser moved the "present" of the novel forward into the contemporary because he wished to enforce the theme that America, for all its postwar "freedom" and even license, was still a nation in which the combination of the immense attraction of wealth and a pervasive moral hypocrisy could cause the destruction of a Clyde Griffiths. His intent, in other words, was to stress the continuity of American experience. When Dreiser read in the *World* that during a Sunday break in the Gillette trial, "the jury went in a body today to services at the Methodist church,"[38] he saw reflected the present of the 1920s as well as the past of 1906 and of his own boyhood. The "tragedy" of the Dreiser family in various small Indiana towns of the 1880s was still the American tragedy. Youthful desire and need were still fed the illusion of hope and were still blighted by the reality of blocked opportunities and a stifling moralism. As Dreiser wrote in an article of early 1921, "I can truthfully say that I can not detect, in the post-war activities or interests, social, intellectual or otherwise, of the younger or other generations of Americans, poor, rich, or middle class, any least indication of the breaking of hampering shackles of any kind—intellectual, social, monetary, or what you will."[39]

Dreiser was correct in his view of the twenties, for the myth of that decade as a period of freedom rests largely on Jazz Age writing of revolt and rebellion, of writing which is consciously opposed to such middle-class American beliefs and values as those expressed in the symbols of the Small Town, the Middle West, and Business. Acts of rebellion, whether in art or life, imply a powerful though sometimes inarticulate cultural base against which revolt takes shape and seeks expression. *An American Tragedy* is thus a novel of the twenties not so much in its external trappings as in the relationship of some of Dreiser's basic themes to the major fiction of revolt of the period. Like Hemingway, Lewis, and Fitzgerald, Dreiser depicts the falseness and destructiveness of such American illusions as the faith in moral abstractions, the implicit virtue of small-town or rural life, and the association of one's noblest dreams with a wealthy girl.

Dreiser's changes in the interior chronology of the Gillette case are of interest, but only two require discussion. He revised the date of Roberta's pregnancy from late March to early February in order to prolong and intensify the pressure on Clyde before the death trip and to make possible his several abortion attempts.[40] And he shifted the three-week-long trial backward from its opening date of November 13 to October 15. His purpose was to intensify a theme which had its origin in the Herkimer

County political scene at the time of the Gillette trial. Both A. M. Mills and Charles D. Thomas, Gillette's two court-appointed lawyers, were political enemies of George W. Ward, the prosecuting district attorney. On November 5, before the trial began, Ward had run for county judge on the Republican ticket and had won, while Thomas had run for state senator as a Democrat and had lost. This political rivalry then spilled over into the trial and was frequently commented upon by the *World*, including a remark that Ward had won in a closely fought contest primarily because of a campaign promise to prosecute Gillette vigorously.[41] In order to add strength to the theme that justice is often a contest in which the strong climb to success upon the backs of the weak, Dreiser moved the trial back almost a month and also made Belknap (one of Clyde's lawyers) and Mason (the district attorney) rivals for the same office. Thus, Mason is in a sense campaigning in court and the conviction of Clyde guarantees his victory.

Dreiser also changed the location of Cortland and Herkimer, the Lycurgus and Bridgeburg of *An American Tragedy*. Cortland, which is approximately thirty miles directly south of Syracuse, is in a comparatively poor and sparsely populated area of central New York. When Dreiser saw it in 1923, it had about 15,000 inhabitants. Dreiser's decision to increase its size and move it to a more prosperous and thickly settled area stemmed from his tendency in the use of his sources to widen the social and financial distance between Clyde and the Griffithses in order to strengthen the theme that Clyde's hopes are illusions. The Griffithses of Lycurgus are considerably more wealthy and socially prominent than were the Gillettes of Cortland, and Clyde is far more distant from their world initially than Chester Gillette had been from the Gillettes'. For many of these changes, as well as for the thematically important portrayal of the lively younger set of Lycurgus, with their exciting parties in neighboring cities, he needed a town which was larger than Cortland and which was located in a more prosperous and populous section. He therefore moved Cortland some 100 miles east into the area of large manufacturing cities at the confluence of the Mohawk and the Hudson, and he more than doubled its size.

Herkimer, the county seat where Gillette was tried, is near Utica on the southern edge of Herkimer County, which stretches about 100 miles from the far North Woods to the bustling Mohawk Valley. Dreiser moved Cataraqui County, his version of Herkimer County, further north and shortened its length to fifty miles. The effect of this change is to make

Bridgeburg, the county seat where Clyde is tried, a North Woods village and thereby to increase sharply the potential for portraying the narrowness and the pressures for conformity of village morality. Thus, Dreiser made Lycurgus more cosmopolitan than Cortland and Bridgeburg more rural than Herkimer.

Dreiser's most important changes, however, involve the participants and events of the Gillette case. His transformation of Gillette into Clyde was informed by two fundamental purposes. He wanted to give Clyde a powerful motive for the death of Roberta other than her pregnancy, and he wanted to cast doubt on the certainty that her death was a murder. Both of these desires led to considerable variation from his sources. In order to intensify and sharpen Clyde's motive, Dreiser lowered Gillette's social position, made his romance with Grace Brown a greater threat to his social aspirations, and supplied him with a second love who promised both wealth and position. Gillette had attended college, was readily accepted into "what passed for high society in Cortland" (Ellen Moers's phrase), and did not attempt to hide his affair with Grace Brown. In addition, though the *World* singled out Hattie Benedict, the daughter of a Cortland lawyer, as the most important of Gillette's interests among "the younger set" of the town, Gillette in fact played the field and had no single all-consuming passion similar to that of Clyde for Sondra. Given Gillette's circumstances in Lycurgus, it is no wonder that his murder of Grace Brown appears to be incredibly stupid and callous and that one of the principal defenses adopted by his attorneys was the lack of motive. Clyde, however, because he believes he can murder Roberta without detection and because of his overpowering desire to gain the kind of life represented by Sondra, is endowed with a motive which helps create the powerful psychological and narrative tension of Book Two.

The most damaging piece of circumstantial evidence against Gillette, in a case based entirely on such evidence since there were no eyewitnesses, was the tennis racket with which he supposedly struck Grace Brown. Gillette had left his suitcase and camera on shore while he and Grace Brown were on Big Moose together but had taken the racket with him. After her death, he had hidden the racket on shore. The battered and broken racket and Grace Brown's extensive head wounds strongly supported the contention of the state that Gillette, with premeditation, had first knocked Grace into the water with a blow to the face and had then struck her on the head with the racket until she sank. On his arrest, Gillette had explained that Grace fell into the water accidentally, though he offered at different times three varying versions of the accident. At the trial, however, his defense was that he told Grace while they were in the boat that her only recourse was to tell her parents about her pregnancy. She thereupon had stood up suddenly, had said "You don't know my father. . . . I'll end it all now," and had tipped over the boat.[42] She had already sunk, Gillette claimed, when he himself came to the surface.

Dreiser changed both the "facts" of Grace Brown's death and Gillette's "lie" about her death. He omitted entirely the tennis racket as a possible weapon and substituted for it a camera, an object which Clyde not only might legitimately take with him on the boat (thus making the case for the defense more plausible) but also one with which he could have struck Roberta accidentally (thus introducing the moral ambiguity of her death, a theme entirely lacking in the Gillette case). Dreiser's intent in this crucial change was to make Clyde much less obviously and conclusively guilty of murder both in our view, as "eyewitnesses" of Roberta's death, and in the view of the jury as it weighs the circumstantial evidence surrounding her death. So, too, he made Roberta's wounds much less severe than Grace's, and so, too, he omitted such clearly implausible testimony as Gillette's claim that he still loved Grace at the time of her death.

Dreiser's change of the "lie" about Roberta's death did not stem from his desire to make Clyde more sympathetic than Gillette in this particular instance. Both Gillette's account of Grace Brown's suicide and Clyde's change-of-heart story are patently false and self-serving. Rather he wished to substitute a thematically functional lie for one which was thematically inefficient. The lie which Clyde's lawyer Jephson prepares in order to explain the events in the boat is deeply and powerfully ironic in relation to Dreiser's reconstruction of Grace's death. For Clyde indeed did have a "change of heart," though of courage rather than of intent. And his recasting of that change into a "moral" decision for the benefit of the jury is so unconvincing that it in fact weakens rather than strengthens his case.

Of course, these and similar changes in the circumstances of Grace Brown's death and in Gillette's explanation of it are but the external signs of Dreiser's transformation of the superficial reality of the Gillette he knew into the psychological reality which is Clyde. It is a transformation which stems from the novelist's ability to take the faceless surface of experience—the testimony at a trial—and to create from it an inner life which, as Clyde sits transfixed in the boat while Roberta crawls toward him, we know fully and therefore compassionately. Dreiser's changes thus explain only the direction of his transformation; they do not explain the power of the novel.

Dreiser's knowledge of Grace Brown derived from testimony about her and from her love letters to Gillette, which were read in full at the trial by District Attorney Ward and then published in pamphlet form. Her letters are indeed moving, for they have the natural eloquence of a direct statement of need and heartbreak. The Grace Brown who emerges from the testimony, from her letters, and from Ward's constant reference to her as a "plucked flower" or its equivalent, is above all a pathetic figure. Dreiser was of course conscious of the pathos of the discarded woman and in particular the pathos of the pregnant lower-class girl who has nowhere to turn. Indeed, he created one of the most moving scenes in the novel—Roberta's interview with the doctor who refuses her an abortion—out of the experiences of his sisters Mame and Sylvia.[43] But he was also aware that a pathetic situation could arouse strength and resiliency in women, as in the strong-willed self-righteousness of Sallie and the intuitive selfishness of Mame at crises in their lives. He therefore maintained the pathos of Roberta's dilemma but also shaped her character into a far more complex and credible reality than the paragon of rural innocence who is the Grace Brown of the Gillette trial. Roberta's self-pity has both a soft and a hard edge during her later relations with Clyde; she not only begs but demands that Clyde "do right" by her. And her rural innocence is also a confining moralism which links sex irrevocably with marriage, a state of mind which Dreiser associated especially with Sallie.

District Attorney Ward referred both in his opening and closing speeches to Gillette's interest in socially prominent girls but was unable to prove a single dominant flirtation. The *World*, however, described Hattie Benedict as "the Cortland girl with whom Gillette is said to have fallen in love shortly before Grace Brown's death" and as the girl who "supplanted Grace Brown in Gillette's affections."[44] Miss Benedict testified briefly at the trial (the Gillette trial contained no "Miss X" agreement), as did a number of other girls of her set in whom Gillette had shown an interest. But she merely stated that she and Gillette had spent July 4 at York Lake, near Cortland, and that Gillette was only an acquaintance.

Dreiser seized upon the prominence given Miss Benedict in the *World* to create the figure of Sondra. Aside from Clyde's early and brief flirtation with Rita, his love affairs at Lycurgus are confined to Roberta and Sondra, unlike Gillette's wide-ranging activities. Dreiser's centering of all of Clyde's desires and dreams on the charismatic figure of Sondra was perhaps his most important imaginative act in his recasting of Gillette's life at Cortland, for the substitution of a single compelling interest for a general preference for socially prominent girls is the difference between the shapelessness of fact and the form of fiction. Dreiser followed broadly the outline suggested by the Gillette case in his account of Clyde's relationship to the Lycurgus Griffithses, to the factory, and to Roberta. But his account of Clyde's association with Sondra—her background and character, his courting of her, and the nature and intensity of his interest in her—was entirely "invented." And those facts of the case which conflicted with this "invented" material were suppressed or recast. For example, while Gillette and Grace Brown were traveling in separate railway cars on their way to Utica and then to the North Woods, Gillette met two upper-class Cortland girls whom he knew and made a date to go camping with them at Seventh Lake a few days later. After murdering Grace, he indeed did meet the two girls and go on a camping trip with them, and he was arrested at a Fourth Lake hotel three days after the murder. Dreiser substituted for this casual date with two Cortland girls Clyde's prearranged plan to join Sondra at Twelfth Lake. He thus changed Gillette's casual flirting to Clyde's tortured last days with Sondra, days in which his prize is near and yet is also receding rapidly as Mason approaches.

Almost all the action and minor characters of Clyde's life in Lycurgus are briefly sketched in Dreiser's sources or derive from the ability of the novelist to fill in vaguely introduced social realities, such as a family or a factory or a boardinghouse, with specific characters and events. Dreiser handles this thinly suggested material with great freedom in order to shape theme and form out of the flotsam and jetsam of experience. To cite an obvious example, Harold Gillette, Chester's cousin, is mentioned briefly in Dreiser's sources as a twenty-one-year-old superintendent in the factory who warned Chester that it was unwise to continue seeing Grace Brown. From these spare details, Dreiser created the major theme of Gilbert Griffiths as Clyde's double in physical appearance but his unreachable superior in class, wealth, and intellect. He spun out from this theme one thread of plot involving Gilbert's resentment against both Clyde and Sondra because they represent threats to his position at the factory and in local society and another thread involving Sondra's cultivation of Clyde in order to pique Gilbert. Another example is Gillette's two lawyers, Mills and Thomas. They are not sharply differentiated in Dreiser's sources except that Mills is considerably older than Thomas and is the senior counsel for the defense. But Dreiser, seizing upon the opportunity to create significant distinction where there are two of anything, shapes Belknap (Mills) into a worldly man of experience who sympathizes with Clyde, and Jephson (Thomas) into a brilliant young man who sees the case primarily as a challenge to his will and intellect.

Dreiser's use of the Gillette case also involved a recasting of his source from its form as evidence and commentary within a trial lasting three weeks into a narrative of a year and a half in Clyde's life. His basic method was to dramatize as a single sequence of action antedating the trial most of the repetitious detail presented in the trial which bears on Gillette's life in Lycurgus and to compress and reorganize the events of the trial itself in order to emphasize the thematically significant and the dramatic.

The Gillette trial, like most trials, was exceedingly tedious for the most part, even as reported in the *World* in condensed form and with the highlighting of sensational journalism. It took five days to select a jury, over a hundred witnesses were examined and cross-examined, and the largest single body of evidence involved technical medical details. By loosely following the *World's* pattern of summary and emphasis but by imposing on the material in the *World* a further selectivity and a fuller dramatization of key moments, Dreiser turned reportage into fiction. Thus, Dreiser devotes only a few sentences to the selection of a jury, and he summarizes briefly the medical testimony and the testimony of minor witnesses. (Indeed, he presents in testimony format only two witnesses other than Gillette.) On the other hand, he presents in great detail the courtroom atmosphere, the opening speeches of the prosecution and defense attorneys, and the examination and cross-examination of Clyde.

Dreiser begins his dramatization of the trial with a version of Ward's speech. By omitting most of Ward's lengthy account of the death trip and by introducing some of Ward's remarks from his closing summation speech, he underlined Mason's appeal to the sexual and moral prejudices of his audience. Dreiser then summarized the evidence offered by the state, stressing such sensational details emphasized by the *World* as the undeveloped pictures found in Gillette's camera and the "death scream" heard by a woman tourist on the lake. He concluded the state's case with Mason reading passages from Roberta's letters to Clyde. Clyde's defense, like Gillette's, consists almost entirely of his attorney's opening address and his own testimony. But Dreiser revised this material in several significant ways. He lengthened Belknap's opening speech, including in it material from Mills's closing speech in order to stress several themes that otherwise were weak or diffuse in the original defense—that Clyde was a "moral and mental coward," that he should not be convicted of murder merely because he wished to desert his pregnant sweetheart, and that the jury should weigh heavily the overpowering temptation provided by Miss X. Dreiser then expanded Clyde's direct examination to include much information on his youth and his relationship to Miss X which was not present in the direct examination of Gillette. The bulk of Clyde's direct examination is thus devoted to the most sympathetic side of his character—his boyhood deprivations and his intolerable position when he found himself caught between the demands of Roberta and the dream of Sondra. Unlike Gillette's direct examination, which was largely an implausible explanation of the events of the death trip, Clyde's is a moving plea for recognition of his dilemma.[45]

Clyde's cross-examination by Mason, lengthy as it is, is brief compared to the two days which Ward took to cross-examine Gillette. Dreiser preserved Ward's technique of moving rapidly from topic to topic (adopted, the *World* noted, to rattle Gillette) as well as Ward's attack on the contradictions and implausibilities in Gillette's story—the false names used on the trip, the suitcase left on shore, the failure to ask the price of the boat, the incriminating map of the Big Moose area, and so on. But he used verbatim very little of Ward's repetitious and often inept cross-examination (he had not used verbatim any of Mills's direct examination of Gillette), and he rearranged and made more emphatic the substance of Ward's attack on the credibility of Gillette's story. In short, he made Mason a more effective trial attorney than Ward.

Throughout the trial as recreated by Dreiser, the courtroom audience is a living presence. From hints in the *World* about the intense community antagonism against Gillette—at one time the judge was reported to be prepared to ask for state militia to prevent a lynching—and from a report on the nature of the jury's deliberations he created a felt presence of mass hate which colors Clyde's fate from the moment he walks for the first time through the hostile crowd on his way from the jail to the courtroom until the single juror holding out against conviction is cowed and threatened into submission by his angry fellow jurors.[46]

Dreiser's recasting of the trial was thus not only in the direction of compression and dramatic representation but also toward the theme that the complexities and needs of human nature are usually submerged and overcome by the certainties of group prejudice. He thus shifted our attention as observers of the trial from the "logic" of the mass of evidence against Gillette—in particular the medical evidence—to the principal extenuating circumstance in Clyde's actions, the meaning of Miss X in his life. We are moved to ponder not the blow on the head which was the immediate cause of Roberta's death, but the underlying cause—the emotional reality of Miss X.

Dreiser's use of Grace Brown's love letters offers the best single example of his shaping of documentary material into fictional reality and of his recasting of the trial as reported into the trial as depicted. Grace Brown wrote fourteen love letters, two in April during a brief visit to South Otselic and the remainder during June and July, while she waited in South Otselic for Gillette to take some action about her pregnancy. Ward arranged the state's presentation of evidence in strict chronological sequence. He therefore read all the letters to the jury early in the case—that is, before the extensive evidence concerning the death trip.

Dreiser's first major adaptation of this material was to move four of the longest and most crucial letters from the trial to the dramatic action of the period just before the trip to the North Woods. In these letters, Roberta's tone changes from loneliness and anxiety to threats as she begins to fear that Clyde will remain inactive if he can. In the trial itself, Dreiser rearranged the order of the state's case. Instead of reading the letters early in his presentation, Mason saves them until the close and then reads only six of the most pathetic passages in order to enforce emotionally his implied contention that Clyde deserves to die for mistreating and deserting his pregnant sweetheart whether or not he actually murdered her. Both in the letters used before the trial and in those read during the trial, Dreiser mixed verbatim quotation, loose paraphrase, and new material—yet maintained the emotional texture of alternating pleading and recrimination, and hope and fear, of the original letters.

The extent of Dreiser's verbatim use of Grace Brown's letters is exemplified by the four letters he worked into the narrative of Clyde's life in Lycurgus. Of these, one is almost entirely verbatim; one is heavily verbatim; one—the longest—is loosely paraphrased and adapted from a number of letters, with much new material as well; and one is completely new except for a single sentence.[47] Moreover, Dreiser sharpened Grace

Brown's threat to come to Cortland—presumably to plead directly with Gillette—into Roberta's explicit threat to expose Clyde to his relatives and upper-class girl friends. Dreiser therefore did rely heavily on Grace Brown's letters, often with a verbatim exactness. But he also rearranged the letters to permit them to play a more significant role both in his narrative of Clyde's life in Lycurgus and in his depiction of the trial, and he subtly intensified the heartbreak and the anger present in the originals into themes which bear directly on the characterization of Clyde and Roberta.

For Clyde in prison, Dreiser relied on the accounts in the *World* of Gillette's final days to shape a narrative in which Clyde alternated between the conflicting emotions of fear generated by the "death house," guilt arising from his lies to his mother, and hope because of the interest which the Reverend McMillan shows in his fate.[48] Mrs. Griffiths's activities in Book Three were based closely on those of Mrs. Gillette in the interval between Gillette's sentencing and his execution. McMillan has a distant source in the Reverend Henry MacIlravy who became Gillette's "spiritual adviser" in the weeks preceding his execution. With the aid of MacIlravy and the prison chaplain, Gillette released, just before his death, a penitent statement addressed to the youth of America that Dreiser used verbatim. And it was MacIlravy and the chaplain who stated to the press, immediately after Gillette's death, that in their view "no legal mistake was made in his electrocution."[49] Out of these slight leads involving MacIlravy, Dreiser created the powerful and significant figure of McMillan. He also shifted the thrust of the statement concerning "no legal mistake" forward to the crucial moment in the governor's office when McMillan, because he believes that Clyde is indeed guilty, refuses to intercede on his behalf. (In fact, though Mr. and Mrs. Gillette appeared before the governor, the Reverend MacIlravy was not present at this interview.)

ᴄᴄᴄᴄᴄᴄᴄᴄᴄᴄᴄᴄᴄᴄᴄᴄᴄᴄᴄᴄᴄᴄᴄᴄᴄᴄᴄᴄᴄ

The task of writing *An American Tragedy* was long and difficult, occupying almost all of Dreiser's efforts from July 1923, when he returned from his trip to upper New York state, to November 1925, when he revised proof for the last time. Dreiser's correspondence of 1923–25 reveals a rough chronology for the composition of *An American Tragedy*, though an exact chronology is almost impossible to establish because his steady progress in the preparation of a first draft was accompanied by constant backtracking to work on first, second, and third revisions of previously written material.

Dreiser's first job was to rewrite almost completely the twenty-chapter first draft dealing with Clyde's early life which he had prepared during 1920–21. In a letter to his secretary Sally Kusell in mid-August 1923, he stated that he had written six or seven chapters of the novel; he then went on to strike the note of labored effort characteristic of most of his comments on the composition of *An American Tragedy*:

I've been doing exceptionally well—writing almost every day—every other day anyhow. And that in the face of the damndest qualms and struggles in connection with the book. I have written and written—and at last I hope—and if I don't get cold feet on it and change it again, gotten a fair start. The trouble with me when I set out to write a novel is that I worry so over the sure even progress of it. I start and start and change and change. Have done so with nearly every one. What I really ought to have is some one who could decide for me—once and for all when I have gotten the right start—when I am really going ahead—or one who would take all the phases I pen down and piece them together into the true story as I see it. That is what I eventually do for myself—but all the struggles and the flounderings.[50]

Dreiser worked on his revision of Book One for almost six months, completing it in late December 1924.[51] In brief, he preserved almost unchanged his original opening chapter—the vignette of the Griffiths family on a street-preaching mission in Kansas City. He then summarized in Chapter II his earlier account of the Griffithses' background and of Clyde's boyhood. In Chapter III and in portions of later chapters he used much of his original material on Esta's elopement and pregnancy. But otherwise all of the earlier draft was discarded. And with a fuller awareness of the central themes of Books Two and Three, he incorporated into Book One much "invented" material which bears on those themes. For example, neither Gillette's nor Dreiser's background contains such activities as a job as a bellhop, a romance with a girl like Hortense, and a serious automobile accident involving the death of a little girl. Of course, this material is present in one way or another in Dreiser's experience. He and his brothers had been fascinated by luxury hotels both as boys and as young men; he had met in Los Angeles Helen's sister Myrtle who, like Hortense, was a bitchy flirt;[52] and he had already decided to use a fatal skylarking automobile excursion, derived from a newspaper story, as a crucial event in

The Bulwark. But in his adaptation of this material Dreiser was creating fiction out of his experience and awareness with imaginative freedom and power rather than limiting his imagination by subjecting it too fully to the control of his sources.

Dreiser began work on Book Two in early 1924 and spent almost a year on this portion of the novel, writing and rewriting.[53] His difficulty stemmed both from the technically complex narrative problem presented by Clyde's relations with Roberta and Sondra and from the highly charged emotional nature of the material itself. The novel "will be a terrible thing," he wrote to Louise Campbell on January 9, 1925, soon after completing Book Two.[54] And as he wrote to Helen on June 18, 1924,

I'm to where the factory girl and the rich girl in Clyde's life are enlarging and by degrees destroying him. . . . It seems simple. I know the story. The right procession and selection of incidents should be as nothing but it just chances to be everything. And so I write and rewrite. Sometimes I write enough to make two chapters or three in a day and yet 1/3 of one chapter that is eventually O.K.

Book Three, after some difficulty with its opening chapters, went much more swiftly, and Dreiser completed it in July 1925.

For each book of *An American Tragedy*, Dreiser wrote an initial holograph from which one or more revised typescripts were made. During the summer of 1925 a final independent typescript of the entire novel was prepared and revised, and in the late summer and fall the galley proof and then the page proof of this final version underwent extensive revision. Throughout this preparation and revision of the various stages of the three books and of the entire novel, Dreiser relied heavily on what can be called his editorial staff. After writing the holograph of a series of chapters, he would have this material put into typescript by Sally Kusell who also suggested changes and cuts. Dreiser reviewed her suggestions, accepting some and rejecting others. Beginning in early 1924, the revised manuscript would then go to Louise Campbell in Philadelphia for a second editing. Mrs. Campbell had been helping Dreiser edit his work since 1917, and he had great faith in her abilities. With Mrs. Campbell's proposed revisions to hand, Dreiser again reviewed the manuscript, again accepting some suggestions and rejecting others. Each book as it completed this process of revision was submitted to Boni and Liveright, where T. R. Smith (aided by Manuel Komroff) made a third series of suggestions, which Dreiser again reviewed. It is this elaborate process of revision which is reflected in Dreiser's notation on a late typescript of Book Two: "Finally revised and cut copy—with cuts by myself, S. K., L. C. and T. R. Smith. From this the final typed copy for the printer was made." Where Dreiser's composition had been comparatively swift and smooth, as in Book One, this process resulted in five integral writing states: a holograph, a typescript, a typescript of Book One which was part of a typescript of the entire novel, revised galley, and revised page proof. Where composition was much more difficult, as in Book Two, there were eight states: a holograph, four integral typescripts, a typescript of Book Two which was part of a typescript of the entire novel, revised galley, and revised page proof.

This immense bulk of extant material bearing on Dreiser's composition of *An American Tragedy*—some twenty manuscript boxes in the Dreiser Collection—reveals that once Dreiser recast his initial draft of 1920–21, his later revisions consisted principally of reorganization, compression, and omission. Although these later changes played a significant role in determining the final shape of the novel, very few resulted in fundamental shifts either in the basic themes or structure of the book. In general, most of the rearrangement of material occurred in the holograph and first typescript, as Dreiser struggled to weave his often complex pattern of incident and commentary into a satisfactory narrative. In particular, as his letter to Helen in mid-1924 suggests, he had great difficulty with the developing triangle in Book Two—not with the events themselves but with their sequential relation to each other. For example, in the holograph of Book Two, the scene in which Roberta is passionately jealous of Clyde's increasing interest in upper-class girls occurs after the Now and Then party in early December. In the first typescript, the scene occurs after the Griffithses' Christmas Day dinner. The difference represents Dreiser's indecision about when the emerging triangle begins to affect Roberta as well as Clyde, and his opting, finally, for a later date, probably to bring into closer ironic juxtaposition the onset of Roberta's pregnancy and her growing realization that Clyde is slipping away from her.

The major task of Dreiser and his "staff" was to compress and cut. It is difficult to estimate the length of the holograph, since Dreiser himself did not make a word count and since his holograph sheets are widely uneven in word length, but W. A. Swanberg has settled on the round number of a million words. The published novel contains about 400,000 words. The extent of the cutting can also be appreciated in relation to the reduction of chapters in the various books—in Book One from thirty-two in the holograph to nineteen in the published novel, in Book Two from seventy-one to forty-one. Much of this compression and cutting involves discursive background material on both major and minor characters. Other cuts were of lengthy passages of authorial analysis of the main characters' states of mind at crucial moments in their lives—almost two full chapters on Clyde and Roberta as he presses her to allow him to enter her room and she ponders the dilemma presented by his request, and a whole chapter on Clyde and Roberta in their Utica hotel. The general effect of these cuts was salutary. For example, in cutting Book One heavily, Dreiser stripped away material which did not bear directly either on the rival claims of Esta and Hortense upon Clyde or on the automobile excursion—a process of compression which sharpened the crucial similarity between Clyde's Kansas City and Lycurgus experiences.

Dreiser's two most important cuts occurred at the close of Book One and the close of Book Three. In his early version of Book One, the book concluded not with the accident but with an additional chapter on Clyde's departure from Kansas City in a freight car. In the version of Book One which he submitted to Boni and Liveright in June 1924, however, Dreiser cut this chapter entirely because, as he put it to Mrs. Campbell, "it adds pep so to do."[55] Less directly, the cut not only removed an anticlimactic chapter but also permitted Book One and Book Two to end on the striking parallel note of Clyde fleeing from a fatal accident in which he has played an ambiguous role.

Dreiser's most important cut did not occur until his revision of page proof in the late fall of 1925. In all his previous novels Dreiser had had difficulty with endings. In particular, he had tended to trail off into overblown and often tendentious and misleading epilogues. All the versions of *An American Tragedy* up to unrevised page proof contain a variation of a typically Dreiserian discursive and anticlimactic conclusion. Just after Clyde's death but before the "Souvenir" of Book Three, Dreiser placed a section of "documentary" material headed with an "N.B." The section consists of a statement by McMillan on Clyde's purported confession of guilt just before his death; a statement by Belknap and Jephson rejecting the possibility of any confession by Clyde; an interview with Jephson in which he attacked the conduct of the trial; a statement by Mason in which he repeated his belief in Clyde's guilt; and finally a news item on McMillan's suicide, eighteen months after Clyde's execution, because of mental turmoil caused by his "scruples in regard to his original decision as to Griffiths' complete guilt." All of this discursive material repeats themes that are already present in the dramatic action preceding Clyde's death. The long "N.B." thus adds a misleading note of "documentary" truth to the conclusion while interrupting the powerful movement from the emotional shock of Clyde's execution to the theme in the "Souvenir" that the matrix out of which Clyde came is soon to produce another Clyde in Esta's son. Fortunately, though this section got as far as page proof, Dreiser cut it at that point. Indeed, the final cutting and revision of galley and page proof, of which this major revision was a part, was so extensive that Dreiser had Louise Campbell come up from Philadelphia to aid in the work, and he later wrote to Mencken expressing regret that Mencken and Sinclair Lewis had received uncut and therefore weaker versions of the novel in galley for prepublication comment.[56]

In all, Dreiser's composition of *An American Tragedy* represents in full his mature method as a writer of fiction. Beginning with a documentary source, a powerful autobiographical confirmation of that source, and an elaborate "philosophical" explanation of his themes, he initially overdeveloped each of these interests. Having recognized the weakness of his early effort, he moved toward a more imaginative rendering that drew strength from documentary, autobiographical, and ideological roots but which was not confined by them. As always, Dreiser wrote diffusely at first. But aided by expert advisers and by his willingness to judge their advice on its merits, he produced a book which was not so much a combined effort as a distillation of his intent. There are many reasons for the eleven-year lapse between the completion of *The Titan* and the completion of *An American Tragedy* and for the twenty years between *An American Tragedy* and *The Bulwark*. But the record of the effort expended on *An American Tragedy* makes clear that one reason was the immense drain which the composition of a novel placed upon the energy and imaginative resources of the no-longer-youthful Dreiser.

ꞔꞔꞔꞔꞔꞔꞔꞔꞔꞔꞔꞔꞔꞔꞔꞔꞔꞔꞔꞔꞔꞔꞔꞔꞔꞔꞔꞔꞔ

Because *An American Tragedy* is a long and complex novel, it would be best to describe briefly some of its most important characteristics and the critical problems which emerge from them. Two significant passages in the novel will serve this purpose. The first occurs in Book Two, at a point when Clyde is faced with the dilemma of a pregnant Roberta and a successfully wooed Sondra:

[Roberta] was, as he saw it in connection with his very vital dream of Sondra, making a mountain—an immense terror—out of a state that when all was said and done, was not so different from Esta's. And Esta had not compelled anyone to marry her. And how much better were the Aldens to his own parents—poor farmers as compared to poor preachers. And why should he be so concerned as to what they would think when Esta had not troubled to think what her parents would feel? (II, 53)

The second passage occurs during the prison section of Book Three, after McMillan has failed to understand Clyde:

He had no one, who, in any of his troubled and tortured actions before that crime saw anything but the darkest guilt apparently. And yet . . . . he had a feeling in his heart that he was not as guilty as they all seemed to think. After all they had not been tortured as he had by Roberta with her determination that he marry her and thus ruin his whole life. They had not burned with that unquenchable passion for the Sondra of his beautiful dream as he had. They had not been harassed, tortured, mocked by the ill-fate of his early life and training, forced to sing and pray on the streets as he had in such a degrading way, when his whole heart and soul cried out for better things. How could they judge him, these people, all or any one of them, even his own mother, when they did not know what his own mental, physical and spiritual suffering had been? (II, 392)

Both passages reveal the importance of Book One in *An American Tragedy*—that the novel is not merely a story of crime and punishment but of how a young man's life is frozen by his nature and experience into an inflexible pattern and how society ignores this reality in judging him. The first passage in particular suggests the density of Dreiser's rendering of the complex interrelationship of the events of Clyde's life. Some of the key realities of Clyde's boyhood—his poverty, Esta's pregnancy, his "dream" of a better life and the various obstacles or "walls" barring him from fulfillment of his dream—are now the psychological and emotional imperatives of his response to the circumstances of his Lycurgus life: the "mountain" of Roberta, who represents both an obstacle to wealth and a return to poverty; the lesson of Esta that duty can and should be ignored; and the dream of Sondra. In Robert Penn Warren's phrasing, "a thousand strands run backward and forward in this documentation [of Clyde's life], converting what is a process in time into a logic outside of time," a logic which ultimately fuses the images of experience into "the poetry of destiny."[57] One of the principal tasks in the criticism of *An American Tragedy* is to unravel the major threads in this logic—to attempt to describe the ironic interweaving of character, event, and symbol which constitutes the novel's themes and form.

Although the second passage also introduces Clyde's past as a psychological reality in the present, the primary intent of the passage is to engage us in the emotional intensity of the present. Clyde's thoughts at this moment are a kind of soliloquy—a plea to an unknown and invisible presence for the understanding and compassion that he has not received from the known and visible in his life. The passage is closely related, in both form and content, to the important critical problem of the tragic theme in *An American Tragedy*. As Warren implies, this theme is inseparable from our compassionate involvement in the "logic" of Clyde's fate. Although we do not forget that he is weak and inept, we have also been made to understand and to share his "mental, physical, and spiritual suffering." And thus we are involved in one of the most moving of aesthetic experiences—to see and therefore to feel. We are moved, in other words, less by the abstract nature of Clyde and his dilemma than by their recreation in a form which involves us so closely and powerfully in his life that we cannot help but understand at a level of intensity that we associate with great tragic art.

The basic shape which Dreiser gave his recreation of Clyde's life was three divisions which are distinctive in form and theme and yet are tightly woven into the themes and structure of the novel as a whole. Each book has a different setting, a different supporting cast (aside from the reappearance in Book Three of Clyde's mother and some minor Lycurgus figures), and a different narrative form. Book One is primarily an ironic initiation story in which a youth does not learn from experience but rather is shaped by it. Book Two presents such a youth with an insoluble dilemma and its accompanying pressures and tensions. And Book Three dramatizes in three segments, each with its own climax, his capture, trial, and execution. All three books are also segments of the underlying ironic theme and form which is Clyde's life: his "education" by the world, his fall because of his nature and "education," and his punishment by a world which "educated" him but which has never taken responsibility for that instruction by understanding him.

Dreiser's intent in Book One was not only to anticipate almost every aspect of Clyde's character in Books Two and Three but to create that sense of inevitability in Clyde's later thoughts and actions which is one of the most powerful effects of the novel. Put simply, Dreiser's method in Book One was first to establish the impact upon Clyde of two irreconcilable worlds—one of dreary poverty and loneliness and a formalized religion of duty, the other of beauty, excitement, and wonder and therefore of a personal religious fulfillment. Dreiser then involved Clyde in a sexual triangle in which these two irreconcilable psychological and emotional poles received highly charged substantive forms which rendered Clyde almost completely ineffectual. Put even more simply, Book Two repeats the pattern of Book One but with more sharply defined and polarized social alternatives and sexual conflicts.

One of the "givens" of *An American Tragedy* therefore is that Clyde's character does not develop or deepen in the course of the novel except to a slight degree in the closing section of Book Three. Nor does the world to which he is exposed change in its basic characteristics. What Dreiser does vary in the novel, with great subtlety and effect, is the degree of destructiveness in this encounter between an unchanging weak temperament and an equally unchanging social and moral world—from the relative harmlessness of the engagement in Book One to the death of Clyde in the electric chair in Book Three. The underlying emotional effect of the novel, an effect which derives both from Dreiser's narrative voice and from Clyde's experiences, consists of our gradual move from a sense of superiority and even contempt toward Clyde to a sharing of the excruciating tension of his insoluble dilemma and of his unavoidable fate.

Dreiser's key term in establishing the character of Clyde in Book One is "sensitive." He uses it again and again in accounts of Clyde's basic nature, and it is the operative word in his description of Clyde's most distinctive physical characteristic, his "thin and sensitive and graceful" hands (I, 374), hands which Hortense, Rita, Roberta, and Sondra find attractive. Clyde's sensitivity links him with those Dreiser characters from Carrie through Eugene and Cowperwood whose finely tuned emotional natures make them responsive to the beauties of life. But though Clyde has "a more vivid and intelligent imagination" (I, 10) than his parents, he shares not only his father's "sensitive and therefore highly emotional" (I, 10) temperament but also his fuzziness and weakness of intellect and will. Dreiser frequently noted the "strain of refinement" (I, 70) in Clyde's character, as implied by the "graceful" in the description of his hands, but he joined to this quality the implication of weakness present in the "thin" which is also a part of that description.

There can be no successful flowering of Clyde's character on the barren soil provided by the Griffiths family. They are handicapped as parents both by their poverty and by their inability to comprehend anything of life unrelated to the "remote and cloudy romance" (I, 5) of their evangelical calling. Dreiser's depiction of the Griffithses contains the familiar but nonetheless effective ironic theme that those who seek the salvation of strangers often neglect the bodily and spiritual care of their own children. So Mr. and Mrs. Griffiths in their various missions provide a home and Christian counsel for the flotsam and jetsam of the city but do not prepare Clyde adequately for life because they neglect his education and limit his experience. Clyde's revolt against his family is thus predictably that of any sensitive imaginative boy who finds that his parents' life is constricting and irrelevant—in this instance, a life of dreary missions and a few "saved" drunks and derelicts in the face of an incredulous world. Clyde's rebellion, however, also is distinctively pathetic and ironic. The gospel which Mr. and Mrs. Griffiths preach is above all of God's love for man and of man's ability to make the spirit of God's love operative in his life. Yet Clyde at home is alone and loveless. God's love, in its human form of warmth, kindness, and understanding, is present as an abstraction in the Griffithses' sermons and as a superficial moralism in their mission activities but is absent from their family life. When Esta elopes with an actor, Mrs. Griffiths tells the family: " 'Our hearts must be kept open, soft, and tender.' She talked as though she were addressing a meeting, but with a hard, sad, frozen face and voice" (I, 22).

Although Clyde discards his parents' religious beliefs early in life, he cannot rid himself of a moralistic conscience. Throughout the novel he is emotionally crippled by a quality of mind which causes him to consider his sexual desires as evil and to denigrate any girl who succumbs to his desire. Thus, his sexual life is compounded of fear, guilt, and fantasy—fear and guilt when sex occurs, and fantasy when he believes he has found an ideal fulfillment of his desires and is therefore forced to assume the role of an asexual lover. One of the reasons Clyde cannot accept the idea of marrying

Roberta is that she has "fallen" and is therefore sullied, while his idealiza-
tion of Sondra requires that he divorce his love of her from sexual
desire.

Clyde's sexual nature owes yet another of its characteristics to his
boyhood. At one point in Clyde's pursuit of Hortense, Dreiser remarks
that she delighted in tormenting his "repressed" sexual desire—"a sadistic
trait which had for its soil Clyde's own masochistic yearning for her" (I,
108). Endowed with a weak father and a strong-willed mother, Clyde not
only searches for strength in masculine figures but also has a subconscious
yearning for his mother, which, because it causes guilt, expresses itself
primarily as a masochistic desire to be tormented by a dominant, teasing
woman. This Oedipal characteristic is the source of a major ironic motif in
Clyde's relationship with Hortense, Roberta, and Sondra—that a girl
whom he has persuaded to give herself to him for love is less desirable than
a girl who causes him pain.

These important weaknesses in Clyde's psychological makeup not
only justify the presence of Book One, in which their origin is dramatized,
but also suggest that Clyde is no mere superficial recasting of Gillette into
an ironic Alger hero. Although Clyde's desire to rise in the world leads him
to disaster, his significant qualities are finely fictional in the sense that they
arise out of a particularized and distinctive temperament and background.
It is the fictional validity of Clyde, not his archetypal quality, which is the
source of our involvement in his fate. That fate may and indeed does have
an archetypal resonance, but we are overabstracting what is initially
powerfully concrete if we fail to realize that fiction elicits a priority of
aesthetic responsiveness and that *An American Tragedy*, despite its title, is
first the tragedy of Clyde Griffiths and then an American tragedy.

Clyde's desire for "beauty and pleasure" (I, 5) is in direct conflict with
his parents' beliefs and activities, and thus Clyde's dominant impulse from
early boyhood is to escape. In the opening vignette, when Clyde is twelve,
the forms which beauty and pleasure are to take in his life are anticipated
by his covert interest in the "gay couples" and handsome automobiles of a
bustling Kansas City street. At fifteen he makes his first major break from
his parents and toward the life he desires when he gets a job as assistant
clerk at a drugstore soda fountain. This position, with its accompanying
"marvels" of girls, lively talk, and "snappy" dressing, offers a deeply
satisfying alternative to the drab religiosity of his boyhood. Clyde recognizes the appeal of this new world in "a revealing flash."

You bet he would get out of that now. He would work and save his money and be somebody. Decidedly this simple and yet idyllic compound of the commonplace had all the luster and wonder of a spiritual transfiguration, the true mirage of the lost and thirsting and seeking victim of the desert. (I, 26)

Dreiser's summary of Clyde's response to the lively worldliness of the soda fountain introduces a theme, and its imagery and tone, which pervades the entire novel. Clyde's need—his thirst—has the power to transform "spiritually" the tawdry and superficial into the wondrous and exalted. So frequent and compelling is Dreiser's use of "dream" in connection with Clyde's longing that we sometimes fail to realize that his desires also have a basically religious context in which his "dream" is a "paradise" of wealth and position ruled by a "goddess" of love. Clyde at this moment of insight at the soda fountain is truly converted. He has rejected the religion of his parents only to find a different kind of heaven to which he pledges his soul with all the fervor and completeness of his parents' belief. Yet, like their "cloudy romance" of a heaven above, Clyde's vision of a "paradise" below is a "true mirage"; it is a vision true to his spiritual needs but false to the objective reality of experience. Clyde has thus not really escaped from his parents, and his initiation into life at the soda fountain and the Green-Davidson is no real initiation, for he has merely shifted the nebulous and misdirected longings of his family from the unworldly to the worldly. He still has the naïveté, blindness, and absolute faith of his parents' enthusiasm and belief. And because he is, like them, a true believer, he does not learn from experience and does not change. Put in the context of the underlying religious force of Clyde's longings, his moment of stasis in the boat takes on added meaning. His inability to act is the product of a conflict not only between fear and desire but also between two religions—that of the old in Roberta which speaks with the voice of conscience, and that of the new in Sondra and the voice of an earthly paradise.

Dreiser's narrative style in this passage and elsewhere during Clyde's soda fountain experience is instructive. As with Carrie's desire for a "little tan jacket," his tone is one of identification with the longings of a character but distance from the intrinsic worth of the objects desired. He achieves this tone largely by a careful modulation of the technique of indirect discourse, a technique which represents the inner life of a character in language appropriate to the character's basic nature and which therefore combines psychological realism and irony. So when Clyde is described as conceiving of a job at the soda fountain as "this interesting position" (I, 25), we recognize both the author's ironic distance from Clyde's evaluation of the job and his sympathetic identification with the naïveté of a young man who is about to taste for the first time what he believes are the delights of life.

Clyde's job as a bellhop at the Green-Davidson is both an extension and an intensification of his conversion experience at the soda fountain. To Clyde, the hotel is "so glorious an institution" (I, 33), a response which at once reflects the religiosity of its sexual attractions and their embodiment in a powerful social form. The Green-Davidson has both an intrinsic and an extrinsic sexuality. So deep and powerful is Clyde's reaction to its beauty and pleasure—to its moral freedom, material splendor, and shower of tips—that he conceives of the hotel as a youth does his first love. The Green-Davidson to Clyde is softness, warmth, and richness; it has a luxuriousness which he associates with sensuality and position—that is, with all that is desirable in life. "The soft brown carpet under his feet; the soft, cream-tinted walls; the snow-white bowl lights set in the ceiling—all seemed to him parts of a perfection and a social superiority which was almost unbelievable" (I, 42). "And there was music always—from some-where" (I, 33). Clyde thus views the hotel both as "a realization of paradise" (I, 37) and as a miraculous gift from Aladdin's lamp, two images of fulfillment which, in their "spiritualizing" of his desires, appropriately constitute the center of his dream life.

But the hotel has a harsh and cruel sexuality in addition to its soft, warm, and "romantic" sensuality. Older women and homosexuals prey on the bellhops, who themselves frequent whores for their pleasure, and the hotel offers frequent instances of lascivious parties on the one hand and young girls deserted by their seducers on the other. Clyde, because of his repressed sexuality, cannot help responding to this aspect of sex with "fascination" despite his fears and anxieties. The sexual reality of the hotel is thus profoundly ambivalent. Clyde longs above all for the "romance" of sex and for warmth and a sense of union, but the overt sexuality which he in fact encounters is that of hardness, trickery, and deceit—of use and discarding. Both Clyde's unconscious need and his overt mode of fulfill-ment join in his response to Hortense. " 'Your eyes are just like soft, black velvet . . . ,' " he tells her. " 'They're wonderful.' He was thinking of an alcove in the Green-Davidson hung with black velvet" (I, 112). Clyde unconsciously desires "softness" and later finds it in Roberta, but he is also powerfully drawn by the "hardness" of wealth and sexual power which he finds in Hortense and Sondra and which he first encountered at the Green-Davidson. Thus, he endows Hortense with an image of warm softness which reflects his muddled awareness of his needs. For though Hortense is properly associated in his mind with the Green-Davidson because of their similar sexual "hardness," she is incorrectly associated with an image of softness and warmth.

Clyde's belief that the Green-Davidson is a "glorious . . . institution" also represents his acceptance of the hotel as a microcosm of social reality. So he quickly learns that to get ahead in the world—that is, to ingratiate himself with his superiors and to earn large tips—he must adopt various roles. So he accepts the hierarchy of power present in the elaborate system of sharing tips which functions in the hotel. So he realizes that he must deceive his parents about his earnings if he is to have free use of the large sums available to him as an eager novice in this institution. And because the world of the Green-Davidson—both within the hotel and as hotel life extends out into Clyde's relations with Ratterer, the other bellhops, and Hortense—also contains Clyde's introduction into sexual desire and sexual warfare, he assumes that the ethics of social advance and monetary gain are also those of love. Thus, when in Lycurgus he aspires to the grandeur of Sondra and her set, his actions are conditioned by an ethic derived from the Green-Davidson—that hypocrisy, dishonesty, role-playing, and sexual deceit and cruelty are the ways in which one gains what one desires. Dreiser's account of Clyde in the opening chapters of *An American Tragedy* is not a doctrinaire study in hereditary and environmental determinism. It is rather a subtle dramatization of the ways in which a distinctive temperament—eager, sensitive, and emotional, yet weak and directionless—interacts with a distinctive social reality which supplies that temperament with both its specific goals and its operative ethic.

One of the characteristics of Clyde's life which derives from his nature as a seeking but limited temperament is that with the exception of a few brief periods he is dissatisfied. His dissatisfaction frequently takes the shape of a sexual triangle in which the conflict between what he has or is and what he wishes to have or be involves both sexual possession and social position. There are four such triangles in Books One and Two, with the two in Book One prefiguring the two in Book Two, and with the last two sharpening and tightening the themes and pressures present in the first two.

The first triangle in Book One emerges out of Clyde's need to resolve the rival and irreconcilable claims made upon him by the pregnant and deserted Esta and by the desirable Hortense. Although Hortense, as Clyde soon realizes, is crude, coarse, and deceitful, her "small, sensuous mouth and bright hard eyes" (I, 73) image a sexual power which drives him wild with desire. A naturally shrewd girl from a working-class background, Hortense had learned early in life to "capitalize her looks and charm" (I, 102)—to be an entrepreneur of sex who sells promises of consummation to the highest bidder in a free market. She has a finely wrought ironic relationship to Roberta, who squanders her capital by accepting Clyde as a lover before marriage, and to Sondra, who, in a middle-class version of the same entrepreneurial spirit, holds herself dear for marriage rather than for gifts or a good time. Dreiser's characterization of Hortense is one of the minor triumphs of the novel. She is a superb portrait of the young girl as bitch. Confident of her charms and her power, she boldly plays off one suitor against the other and alternates threats of dismissal with promises of wonders to come. Yet she is no mere caricature. Her motives are under-standable—what else has she to capitalize but her sex?—and she has an occasional twinge of honest emotion.

Although Clyde is initially intrigued by Esta's seduction and deser-tion, he also senses from the first that her condition may impose obligations upon him and that it constitutes a social handicap and danger. "Here he was just getting a start, trying to be somebody and get along in the world and have a good time. And here was Esta . . . coming to such a finish as this. It made him a little sick and resentful" (I, 96). However, when he visits her for the first time after her return to Kansas City and finds her alone and tearful in a shabby rented room while awaiting the birth of her child, he is moved by her condition and dilemma. "Life was so strange, so hard at times" (I, 98), he thinks, and he is angry at her seducer. Dreiser then manipulates his plot so that these two poles of commitment—compas-sion and duty toward Esta, and desire for Hortense—come into direct conflict. Hortense tricks and cajoles Clyde into offering to buy her a fur coat, while Esta, as Mrs. Griffiths explains to Clyde, needs money to see her through her pregnancy. Faced with this conflict, Clyde now views seduction from a different perspective. He recalls the man who deserted the young girl at the Green-Davidson and reflects that he too wishes to play the role of a successful but irresponsible seducer of Hortense. But despite this significant shift from an ethic of compassion to one of desire, he cannot make a clear-cut decision about Esta. He lies to his mother and gives her some money while saving most for Hortense, hoping all the while that the problem of Esta will solve itself so that he can enjoy without hindrance the "paradise" and "unbelievable become real" (I, 116) of Hortense's total surrender.

Of course, there are several major differences between this triangle and that involving Roberta, Clyde, and Sondra in Book Two. Clyde is bound more strongly to Roberta than he had been to Esta, and his desire for Sondra sublimates the sexual within an all-encompassing paradise of fulfillment. Yet the two triangles have the same basic emotional configuration. An illicitly pregnant girl with whom he sympathizes deeply and to whom he feels a commitment is shunted aside because of the social handicap and retrogression which she represents and because fulfilling his obligation to her would blight his chances of winning a girl who represents the "stuff as dreams are made of" (I, 130). And in both instances the shunting aside is inept and crude, and it is events themselves which determine Clyde's actions and fate.

Book One contains a second triangle which bears heavily on Clyde's actions in Book Two. During the fully narrated automobile excursion that concludes Book One, a triangle develops among Sparser, Hortense, and Clyde. Sparser, a worldly youth who dances well and has access to a large Packard, is far more attractive to Hortense than the fawning and inexperienced Clyde. So despite Clyde's openly displayed jealousy and anger, she cultivates Sparser while still occasionally throwing in Clyde's direction some bones of contrition and of glories to come. And so Clyde alternates between fits of bitterness and despair and of supplication and hope. The relationship of this triangle to that of Sondra, Clyde, and Roberta in Book Two is that Clyde's role changes from a Robertalike figure in Book One to a Sparserlike figure in Book Two. From a naïve youth wracked by jealousy, anger, and fear, he becomes a worldly, upper-class personage who is the cause of these emotions. The tragic irony of the relationship between the two triangles is that though Clyde has himself suffered the agony and torment of jealousy and indeed can even make the identification between his earlier jealousy of Sparser and Roberta's of Sondra, he is unable to translate his experience and insight into compassionate action.

The principal burden of both triangles in Book One is that Clyde's sensitivity may lead him to recognize the emotional state and needs of others but it does not give him the capacity to subordinate his own intense desires to that recognition. He will fail to fulfill his commitment to Roberta as he had to Esta, though he has sympathized with both, and he will fail to recall as an operative force his own despair with Hortense when driven by the compelling dream of winning Sondra. The powerful effect of inevitability in Book Two thus arises from our awareness that Clyde not only lacks the native resources required to solve his dilemma but has already reacted in Book One to similar dilemmas in ways which now represent the grooved response of his character to the basic conflicts of experience.

The automobile outing of Book One differs obviously from the North Woods conclusion of Book Two in that Clyde does not undertake the first with murder in mind. Nevertheless, Clyde's thoughts and actions during the automobile excursion clearly anticipate his fatal journey with Roberta. Although he is doubtful and hesitant about the car expedition because he knows that Sparser is taking the Packard without the owner's permission, his desire to be with Hortense overcomes his scruples, much as he undertakes the death trip with the deepest fears yet overriding need. The automobile accident has much of the same moral ambiguity as the death of Roberta. Although Sparser is the one who is driving recklessly and though the little girl herself jumped in front of the car, all the bellhops, including Clyde, had urged Sparser to rush and all accepted his attempt to flee from the accident. Thus, the question of guilt is obscure, but all in the car, including Clyde, feel touched by guilt and all are considered guilty by the law. Finally, Clyde's actions when the car turns over prefigure his last anguished moments with Roberta in the boat. Clyde's initial thought, after the overturned automobile has come to rest, is that he "must get out of this [the situation] as quickly as possible" (I, 143) because a child has been injured or killed and because the police are in pursuit. At the same moment he realizes that several of their party are injured and that he should be helping Ratterer remove them from the overturned car. "But so confused were his thoughts that he would have stood there without helping any one had it not been for Ratterer, who had called out most irritably" (I, 144). Clyde's response to the conflicting demands of duty and desire—Esta versus a Hortense or a need to aid the injured versus a desire to flee—is to temporize into a stasis, to find himself caught between irreconcilable pulls and thus to be transfixed, to do nothing. In this instance, Ratterer's call moves him to action before he flees, but in the two crucial moments just before and just after the boat overturns he is locked in a stasis in which decision is frozen and all action is involuntary.

ꞒꞒꞒꞒꞒꞒꞒꞒꞒꞒꞒꞒꞒꞒꞒꞒꞒꞒꞒꞒꞒꞒꞒꞒꞒꞒꞒꞒꞒꞒ

When we first encounter Clyde in Chicago, some three years after the automobile accident which ends Book One, he appears more polished and assured. A series of miscellaneous jobs and life on his own have lent him a surface confidence and a strong desire to get ahead in the world. He believes, too, that he has profited from his Kansas City misadventure—that he can now recognize and resist temptation. Yet basically he is still the same Clyde. When Ratterer, his Kansas City mentor, arranges a job as a bellhop at an exclusive men's club, he accepts eagerly despite his earlier resolution that he would never again become involved in hotel work. And once installed in his new position, he again begins to dream. But now, because of the hardships of his life since leaving Kansas City and because of his continuing sense of guilt over "fleshy delights," his dream takes the form of an Alger myth heavily flavored by a strong dose of puritanism. If he works steadily and with sobriety at his post, he muses, some wealthy guest will take a fancy to him, offer him an important job in his firm, and so "lift him into a world such as he had never known" (I, 174). The fortuitous arrival of Clyde's wealthy uncle, Mr. Samuel Griffiths of Lycurgus, appears to confirm both the myth and its values, particularly after Clyde wins Mr. Griffiths's approval with his earnest statement that he wishes to "get in with some company where there was a real chance to work up and make something of myself" (I, 179).

Clyde's simple formula for success—to work himself up under the guidance of a generous patron while living a sober life—contains a number of insurmountable obstacles. Chief among these is the moral rigidity and blindness of the Lycurgus Griffithses and thus of Lycurgus in general. The preoccupations and values of the Griffiths family are firmly middle-class. Their beliefs about family dignity, acceptable marriages, and the nature and function of wealth are securely linked to an absolute moralism which derives not from religious faith, as with the western branch of the family, but from class assumptions about the immoral tendencies of the working class and the consequent need for moral leadership by the middle class.

They express this moralism in their lives and opinions, in the rules they impose upon their employees, and in the moral climate which they have established for the town as a whole.

At the core of the Griffithses' moralism is a puritan work ethic which views class differences as reflecting sharply defined moral differences. To acquire money and position and thus to rise in the world is principally a moral effort in the sense that it requires the virtues of devotion to work and freedom from vice. Workingmen should "become inured to a narrow and abstemious life. . . . It was good for their characters. It informed and strengthened the minds and spirits of those who were destined to rise. And those who were not should be kept right where they were" (I, 181). To rise in the world is therefore a desirable and worthy ambition, but it requires a form of monastic novitiate—a testing of one's spirit to determine if it is truly worthy of the paradise of wealth and position.

Dreiser's portrayal of the middle-class moralism of the Lycurgus Griffithses contains a number of ironic themes. Although the western and eastern branches of the family appear to be totally dissimilar—the one poor, ignorant, and unworldly, the other wealthy, well educated and well traveled—they share an unyielding moralism which endangers Clyde. His Kansas City home has driven him to seek life with a blind eagerness; his Lycurgus family places invisible barriers between him and his goals. Moreover, Clyde himself endorses the Griffithses' code. He does not realize how prejudicial it is to his basic nature and that its underlying effect is to close rather than open the door to advancement. For the work ethic of the Griffithses, beneath its apparent endorsement of an open society, serves principally to perpetuate a rigid social hierarchy. Dreiser dramatizes this theme by the similarity between the Green-Davidson and the Griffiths factory as social institutions. The hotel is morally free and licentious, the factory controlled and rigid. Yet the "rules" of both the hotel and the factory—that is, the conventions of social intercourse—serve primarily to aid those already in power to gain or maintain wealth. And because in the factory power is even more absolute and because deception and sexual laxness are forbidden rather than acknowledged and accepted, the factory in truth is a more dangerous world for Clyde than the hotel.

Although Clyde gladly accepts his role as novice, he finds himself under intolerable pressures within this role. On the one hand, he has an unpromising manual job in the basement shrinking room of the factory and a bleak boardinghouse existence. On the other, he admires the beauty and luxuriousness of the Wykeagy Avenue homes of the Lycurgus rich. He is particularly struck by the Griffithses' house, a structure which eventually becomes "the same as a shrine to him, nearly—the symbol of that height to which by some turn of fate he might . . . hope to attain" (I, 309). This second world appears available to him not only because it is so physically near in the small compass of Lycurgus but because Clyde's identity as a Griffiths suggests to the town that he is indeed a dweller in this world. Although the Griffithses themselves resolve to consider Clyde an ordinary employee until he proves himself, to the rest of the town he is a nephew of Samuel Griffiths and hence worthy of deference on the assumption that he will soon assume his birthright of wealth and position. Dreiser attempts to sharpen our awareness of Clyde's anomalous position by one of the few discordant melodramatic devices in the novel—the close physical resemblance between Clyde and Samuel's son Gilbert. Clyde envies Gilbert's wealth and assurance and begins to believe that he can readily acquire these qualities because he so closely resembles Gilbert and because others associate him with Gilbert. Yet though Gilbert shares Clyde's looks and vanity, the two young men are separated by an immense gulf of class and heredity. Gilbert is innately stronger than Clyde and he resents Clyde because Clyde is a potential usurper of his role and identity. Thus, as often occurs in Dreiser, melodrama moves in the direction of allegory—in this instance, an allegory of the psychological and social reality of the struggle and resentment underlying the platitudes of the Alger myth and a work ethic.

Clyde is particularly vulnerable as a novice because his dream of paradise includes the flesh of sex as well as the spirit of wealth and position. As he wanders around Lycurgus soon after his arrival, he muses about the wonders which might become his. "The beautiful Wykeagy Avenue! His uncle's great factory! The many pretty and eager girls he had seen hurrying to and fro!" (I, 196). But to the Griffithses, an aspirant to the world of the spirit must abstain from the delights of the flesh. As Gilbert explains to Clyde when Clyde assumes his post as foreman of the marking room, with its staff of young girls, " 'We can't have anything come up in connection with you at any time around here that won't be just right' " (I, 239). Indeed, Clyde has already reached a similar conclusion—that the road to "paradise" in Lycurgus is "Eveless" (I, 204) and that nothing should "come up" in his relations with Dillard, a boardinghouse acquaintance, and

Dillard's two friends, Rita and Zella, which might adversely affect his role as aspirant. Loneliness and sexual frustration had led Clyde to accept Dillard's eager proffer of friendship and to respond to Rita's soft sensuality. Although he had first been hesitant, he found it almost impossible to resist Rita's pliant charms and the promise of a quick victory. He continued to be plagued by doubts, however—"But this is not what I should be doing either, is it? This is Lycurgus. I am a Griffiths, here" (I, 213)—and is rescued by an invitation from the Griffithses to come to supper.

This initial Lycurgus triangle involving Clyde, Rita, and the Griffithses reveals how fully Clyde has accepted his role as novice. For unlike the two triangles in Kansas City, in which sex is the fulfillment of a dream, in this instance sex is an obstacle to that fulfillment. Clyde is suspicious of Dillard because he seems more interested in

the girls as girls—a certain freedom or concealed looseness that characterized them—than he was in the social phase of the world which they represented. And wasn't that what brought about his downfall in Kansas City? Here in Lycurgus, of all places, he was least likely to forget it—aspiring to something better as he now did (I, 206).

After he dismisses Rita and before Roberta appears in the marking room and before he is taken up by Sondra, Clyde in a sense is "free." Yet in another sense his future has been irrevocably shaped by his life in Kansas City and Lycurgus. For Roberta will combine the negative poles of Esta's claims upon him and Rita's lower-class compliant sexuality, while Sondra will unite the positive poles of the unattainable sexuality of Hortense and the high social plane of the Griffiths family.

Book Two has a distinctive and powerful narrative rhythm. The book begins with Clyde aspiring but lonely and therefore receptive to the temptation represented by Dillard, Rita, and Zella. The Griffithses' invitation moves Clyde to resist the temptation, but the Griffithses again neglect Clyde after this gesture and by early summer he is again lonely and depressed. Temptation thereupon reappears, in the form of Roberta, followed again by hope of advancement, in the form of Sondra. The book, in short, consists of a preliminary crisis which is resolved by a timely intervention and a parallel major crisis which Clyde is unable to resolve and which eventually crushes him under its weight.

When Clyde meets Roberta in early summer, he has been in Lycurgus for four or five months and has received from the Griffiths family only the token of a Sunday supper. He had had one glimpse of heaven, including a brief initial encounter with Sondra, and then blackness. And now, in langorous June, with Clyde the only man in a room full of young girls, "the chemistry of sex and the formula of beauty" (I, 244) have their effect on him and on Roberta. Clyde is initially interested in Roberta because he is lonely and because she is gay and good-looking and is obviously superior to the other girls in the room in grace, intelligence, and refinement. He is not aware, however, of a number of characteristics of her nature which will play vital roles in their relationship—her "self-reliant courage and determination" (I, 246), her vein of sensuality, and her moral conventionality. Though she appears to him to be "natural and unaffected" (I, 280) and "simple and confiding" (I, 281), her air of rural simplicity unconsciously disguises a powerful and complex temperament.

If Clyde views Roberta initially as a charming example of bucolic openness, she conceives of him even more mistakenly as an example of the wealth, prominence, and experience to be found in the city. From the first, she never forgets that he is a Griffiths and a supervisor, roles which make him attractive but also formidable and dangerous. Just as Clyde is to imagine Sondra as a gateway to a paradise of wealth, position, and comfort, so Roberta sees Clyde as a dream fulfilled, as an escape from the poverty, hardship, and bleakness of both her girlhood on her parents' farm and her factory hand's existence in Lycurgus. Clyde's superior position, however, constitutes a danger as well as a hope, for

the moment she heard that Clyde was so highly connected and might even have money, she was not so sure that he could have any legitimate interest in her. For was she not a poor working girl? And was he not a rich man's nephew? He would not marry her, of course. And what other legitimate thing would he want with her? She must be on her guard in regard to him. (I, 259–60)

Moreover, she also realizes, as does Clyde, that

there was a local taboo in regard to factory girls aspiring toward or allowing themselves to become interested in their official superiors. Religious, moral and reserved girls didn't do it. And again, as she soon discovered, the lines of demarcation and stratification between the rich and the poor in Lycurgus was as sharp as though cut by a knife or divided by a high wall. (I, 255)

From the moment that Clyde and Roberta begin to take an interest in each other in the warm, bright marking room, their relationship is colored and conditioned by the social roles in which they conceive each other within the divided town. Clyde views Roberta as a factory girl, as someone he might win and love and be happy with but as someone he would never marry, "for now his ambitions toward marriage had been firmly magnetized by the world to which the Griffiths belonged" (I, 264). And Roberta views Clyde as "a member of the Lycurgus upper crust and possessor of means and position" (I, 288), a role which Clyde readily adopts because it is one he aspires to achieve. Thus, early in their courtship she is the innocent working girl, wary of seduction but eager for marriage, disturbed by the reputed sexual licentiousness of his "set" but afraid of losing him if she resists too firmly, while he plays the sophisticated and knowing courtier who takes her to amusement parks called Dreamland and Starlight and teaches her to dance. After he has succeeded in sleeping with her, these roles harden and become permanent. He is proud of his conquest and conceives of himself as an upper-class Lothario, a view which confirms her position as a figure to be seduced but not wed. " 'After all,' " he thinks, " 'who was she. A factory girl'. . . . So it was that at moments and in his darker moods, and especially after she had abandoned herself to him, his thoughts ran. She was not of his station, really—at least not of that of the Griffiths to which still he most eagerly aspired" (I, 309). Roberta, however, once she has succumbed, falls instinctively into the role which her entire background had prepared her for, that of the submissive and dutiful wife who looks to her lord for support and direction. She is "dependent on his will and whim" and sets herself "to flatter him almost constantly, to be as obliging and convenient to him as possible. Indeed, according to her notion of the proper order of life, she was now his and his only, as much as any wife is ever to a husband, to do with as he wished" (I, 308).

The love between Roberta and Clyde is handicapped not only by Clyde's bitter identification of Roberta's initial reluctance with Hortense's tricks and stratagems but by the mythic roles which control its expression. Clyde's reference to his "station" and Roberta's to his "superior world" reveal that the two figures are living out the myth of the Nobleman and the Country Maiden of a typical Laura Jean Libbey or Bertha M. Clay popular romance. To Clyde, his role in the myth is that of a successful seducer of a girl of the lower orders; to Roberta, her role is that of "elevation" by her noble lord through marriage. In the myth itself, the seducer and his victim are at last permanently united, for the Nobleman is at heart generous and good; he thus recognizes the essential worth of the Maiden and marries her despite her low birth. But Clyde in fact is neither a Nobleman nor generous and good, and Roberta lacks the persuasive arts of the Maiden. So the two are locked in a relationship whose mythic role-playing will drive them further and further apart.

One of the most powerful ironic currents in the novel is that despite the barriers and suspicions and destructive roles which doom their relationship from the first, Clyde and Roberta have in their backgrounds and temperaments the basis for a deep and binding love. Roberta, too, has come from a deprived and emotionally closed world, one of rural rather than city poverty but one still shaped by the deprivations imposed upon the spirit in the name of "excellent" morals and religion. She has "a warm, imaginative, sensuous" (I, 250) nature which, like Clyde's during his mission youth, found no outlet for expression in her parents' bleak and drab farm or in neighboring villages. She has had a "conventional training" but possesses nevertheless a desire for "love, understanding, companionship" (I, 300). So Clyde finds in her not only a moving recollection of his own fumbling and exhilarating discovery of the wonders of the world—Lycurgus is her Green-Davidson—but a temperament as eager as his for the warmth of human companionship.

The early relationship of Roberta and Clyde contains three moments when the intense joy of their burgeoning love overcomes their fears and results in an epiphany. The first such moment occurs when they meet accidentally at Crum Lake not long after Roberta has begun working at the Griffiths factory. Her unexpected appearance, when Clyde has been thinking of her longingly, causes his face to be "lit by the radiance of one who had suddenly, and beyond his belief, realized a dream" (I, 265). And the entire occasion, despite their concern for secrecy, has the airiness, dreaminess, and beauty of the radiant, warm summer day on a lake. The second moment, when Clyde and Roberta meet on the edge of a cornfield, is also marked by fear and furtiveness. He declares his love, and as he kisses her again and again, she suddenly relaxes her body and rather than withholding herself stands "quite still and unresisting in his arms. He felt a wonder of something—he could not tell what. All of a sudden he felt tears upon her face, her head sunk to his shoulder, and he heard her say: 'Yes, yes, yes, I do love you' " (I, 282). "Touched by her honesty and simplicity" (I, 282), tears also spring to Clyde's eyes—tears of compassion and understanding and love. The third moment occurs after a tense period of sexual warfare in which he is haunted by fears that Roberta may be another Hortense and she by fears of seduction. Unable to risk the possibility of losing him, she surrenders and writes him a note while they are at work, in which she invites him to come to her room that night. He reads it, "and as instantly his body was suffused with a warm and yet very weakening ray" (I, 306). He looks at her, and

she as suddenly experienced a dizzying sensation, as though her hitherto constricted blood, detained by a constricted heart and constricted nerves, were as suddenly set free. And all the dry marshes and cracked and parched banks of her soul—the dry rivulets and streams and lakes of misery that seemed to dot her being—were as instantly flooded with this rich upwelling force of life and love. (I, 306)

So in one resonant image Dreiser renders the poignancy of their love. Their souls respond to love with a warmth and a flow of energy, but their relationship is also bound by a social reality which will eventually transform the life-giving waters of love to the death-enclosing waters of Big Bittern.

Clyde meets Roberta in June and sleeps with her for the first time in October. Their "honeymoon" lasts approximately a month and a half; in late November he is accidentally picked up by Sondra, and in early December he enters her world fully with the invitation to the Now and Then dinner dance. The motive force in Sondra's character is a powerful personal and social vanity. She is a "somewhat refined, . . . less savage, although scarcely less self-centered, Hortense Briggs" (I, 329), who wishes to demonstrate "the destroying power of her charm, while at the same time retaining her own personality and individuality free of any entangling alliance or compromise" (I, 329). Yet her vanity is rendered with a certain compassion and depth of implication by Dreiser. Because we see her so often through Clyde's eyes as a figure of great power and charm, we sometimes forget that she is very young and vulnerable. At seventeen, her vanity and coquetry are understandable and excusable. And when at the dinner dance she struggles to get Clyde "to sense how graceful and romantic and poetic was her attitude toward all things— what a flower of life she really was" (I, 334)—we realize that her role-playing is as pathetically inept as are Clyde's and Roberta's and that unlike Dreiser's earlier portraits of such upper-class young girls as Suzanne and Berenice, he himself is aware that her posing and self-centeredness are adolescent rather than "spiritual" attributes.

At first, Sondra cultivates Clyde because his adoration feeds her vanity and because she can use him in her battle with Gilbert for social supremacy in the town. But what is initially only the superficial gratification of vanity enlarges into love as her responsiveness to being loved intensely arouses the depths of her self-love. Thus, she is eventually trapped by her vanity and coquetry, and we should not let her adolescent baby talk or enthusiasms deter us from a recognition of the deep pain, compounded out of injured pride and the loss of first love, which Clyde's exposure causes her.

Nevertheless, it is primarily from Clyde's angle of vision that we experience Sondra, and from that angle she is above all the "ultimate triumph of the female" (I, 226) because of her youth and beauty and because she "materialized and magnified for him the meaning of the upper class itself" (I, 317). His attitude toward her is that of a "self-ingratiating and somewhat affectionate and wistful dog" (I, 313), for in the context of the Alger myth she is literally the master of his fate. "And what harm," he thinks to himself soon after their meeting in November, "was there in a poor youth like himself aspiring to such heights? Other youths as poor as himself had married girls as rich as Sondra" (I, 322).

There are thus for Clyde two roads to the paradise of Wykeagy Avenue—the long and arduous novitiate of the shrinking room, marking room, and so gradually upward, all while he lives in monastic isolation and deprivation; and the short, direct way of Sondra, which unites beauty and wealth. No wonder that Sondra has for Clyde a rarefied and almost disembodied meaning and that the imagery of his response to her is heavily religious. From their meeting in November, when he tells her that he had seen her in a flower parade during the summer and that " 'I certainly thought you looked beautiful, like an angel almost' " (I, 315), to his anguished appeal for a saviour because of his "crucifixion" (II, 66) by Roberta's pregnancy (" 'Oh Sondra, Sondra, if but now from your high estate you might bend down and aid me' " (II, 66)), the imagery of their relationship is of Sondra as a "goddess in her shrine" and a "saint" and of Clyde as a "devotee" (I, 323, 375). This imagery is far more prevalent in connection with Sondra than the frequently noted Arabian Nights imagery and is particularly significant in relation to Clyde's asexual attitude toward her. Although they kiss and fondle each other, Clyde does not wish to possess her sexually, as he had wished to possess Hortense, Rita, and Roberta. When he first thinks of kissing Sondra, "strangely, considering his first approaches toward Roberta, the thought was without lust, just the desire to constrain and fondle a perfect object" (I, 375). And as late as the trial, Clyde is indignant when Jephson suggests that he might have slept with Sondra.

One strain in Clyde's asexual response to Sondra is that to him she is indeed a "perfect object." To Clyde she is not a sexually desirable young girl but the fulfillment of a need so inclusive that only the language and emotion of religious devotion can suggest the depth and nature of that need. Sondra's upper-middle-class setting also has for Clyde a religious aura because it represents the objects and activities of delight and wonder in which his goddess flourishes. Her cars, imposing home, and servants and her swimming, boating, tennis, and riding are a kind of iconography—a pervasive imagery of wealth and leisure—which in their sum are his paradise. Above all, the image of a bright lake with beautiful homes and gay young people becomes in his mind's eye a vision of heaven on earth, just as the scraping poverty of Roberta's farm home suggests to him a living hell. As in *Sister Carrie*, Dreiser is at his best with imagery of this kind in which the physical setting of his characters' lives constitutes as well the emotional reality in which they seek and desire.

Another strain in Sondra's asexuality derives from her role in the Alger myth, in which courtship is pure because the eye of the pursuer is on the goal of marriage rather than on sexual gratification. Clyde's sexual relations with Roberta and his asexual attitude toward Sondra thus contain a not unusual but nevertheless effective irony. From a conventional point of view, the first relationship is immoral because of its illicit sexuality and the second is moral because it is not sexually consummated and because it looks toward marriage. Yet the first relationship is basically two figures drawn together by temperament and loneliness; the second is a boy and a girl exploiting each other for the gratification of vanity and the fulfillment of material gain. In Marxist terms, the first is a working-class love story, the second a bourgeois courtship, although such terms fail to capture either the biting irony or the psychological truth present in Dreiser's implicit comparison of the two affairs.

From Clyde's encounter with Sondra in late November until the death of Roberta in early July, the themes and the narrative structure of the novel appear to be self-evident. Tension heightens within a triangle as Clyde successfully woos Sondra, who agrees to marry him when she will come of age in October, and as he unsuccessfully attempts to overcome the obstacle of Roberta's pregnancy. Yet this movement in fact derives its strength and suggestiveness from the complex interaction of its parts and in particular from Dreiser's use of the inexorable pressure of time—a pressure inseparable from the chronology of a pregnancy—to structure basic changes both in his characters and in their situation.

For example, Clyde's attitude toward Roberta during the early winter, soon after he realizes that he has a chance to win Sondra, is far from the hate and fear of early July. Although he knows that he must eventually break with her—after all, "what had Roberta really to offer him" (I, 345)—he holds back because of his lingering affection for her and because of his unwillingness to undertake a difficult and unpleasant task. Faced with the dilemma of Roberta's hold and Sondra's attraction, he characteristically adopts the easiest way out and continues both relationships, lying to Roberta about the one, not revealing the other to Sondra.

On two occasions during this interim period from early December to Roberta's discovery of her pregnancy in mid-February, Clyde does have a chance to force a break. He had neglected Roberta during the Christmas season in order to fulfill his far more attractive social obligations to Sondra and her group, and in a meeting with Roberta just before she returns to Biltz for the holidays he senses her perplexed and incriminating disappointment. Despite his "fixed determination" (I, 346) to modify his relationship with her, he is moved by her pain and responds with a renewed expression of love rather than with a declaration of the source of his disaffection and a request for a separation. A parallel scene occurs on Christmas day. He has spent the day with the Griffithses, and she is intensely jealous both because he has broken his date with her to do so and because she suspects that his new social life includes attractive upper-class girls. She breaks into tears, and Clyde can see that

she was deeply hurt—terribly and painfully hurt—heartsore and jealous; and at once, although his first impulse was to grow angry and defiant again, his mood as suddenly softened. For it now pained him not a little to think that some one of whom he had once been so continuously fond up to this time should be made to suffer through jealousy of him, for he himself well knew the pangs of jealousy in connection with Hortense. He could for some reason almost see himself in Roberta's place. (I, 369)

He tries to placate her, and she cries, " 'But they've got everything. You know they have. And I haven't got anything, really. And it's so hard for me to keep up my end and against all of them, too, with all they have' " (I, 369).

Clyde is deeply moved by this outburst,

For obviously this was no trick or histrionic bit intended to influence him, but rather a sudden and overwhelming vision of herself, as he himself could sense, as a rather lorn and isolated girl without friends or prospects as opposed to those others in whom he was now so interested and who had so much more—everything in fact. For behind her in her vision lay all the lorn and detached years that had marred her youth. (I, 369–70)

For one moment Clyde's generalized sympathy for Roberta sharpens into a vivid and compelling emotional identification—Roberta as jealous as he was of Sparser, Roberta as poor and as longing as he had been in Kansas City and indeed still was. And though this moment, as Dreiser tells us, "was of brief duration" (I, 370), its force is sufficient to weaken again Clyde's resolve and to lead him again to declare his love and faithfulness.

Dreiser's intent in depicting Clyde's sympathetic identification with Roberta is not merely to dramatize once again Clyde's weakness and hesitation in the face of a difficult problem. He also wished to represent the tragic ambivalence of Clyde's nature. His sensitivity combines emotional insight and weakness of will; if he were either dull or heartless, he would dismiss Roberta at this point. But because he lacks the negative virtue of cruelty, his compassionate strain draws him into the vortex of Roberta's pregnancy. Although Clyde later becomes increasingly bitter and angry toward Roberta, he is never able to submerge entirely his responsiveness to her nature and dilemma. He is still moved by the open emotional appeal of her initial letter to him in June despite his resentment of her claim upon him. And both anger and compassion are present in the accidental blow with the camera in the boat. The force of the blow reflects Clyde's anger, yet he immediately and apologetically tries to aid her, an attempt which overturns the boat. When we seek to disentangle the various strands which make up Clyde's temperament and fate, we sometimes forget that one of his weaknesses—his inability to carry out an intention—contains a strain of emotional responsiveness, of sensitivity to others. Of course, Clyde is no Hamlet, though the difference between the two figures is more of intelligence, complexity of motivation, and sphere of action than of bedrock character. For both have the same fatal tendency to filter the need for action through an impeding moral and emotional consciousness, a process which is both admirable and self-defeating.

By the middle of February, Clyde has decided for the third time that he must attempt to dismiss Roberta. Her discovery of her pregnancy at this moment might be considered a forced exercise in irony. But like the pregnancy of Jennie after her one night with Brander, Roberta's pregnancy at this stage represents chiefly Dreiser's attempt to bring the underlying ironies of life to a dramatic point. It is thus bitterly ironic not only that Roberta should become pregnant just as she and Clyde are about to break up but that she should conceive at this moment after four months of inept contraceptive precautions and after their lovemaking has become "sporadic" (I, 382) and the product more of propinquity and habit than of love. It is also bitterly ironic that Roberta, who had earlier been subconsciously tempted by the possibility of using a pregnancy to insure her hold upon Clyde (I, 322–23, 359), now becomes pregnant despite her recognition that nothing she can do will hold him. And it is ironic, too, that Clyde, whose basic approach to any difficult problem is to temporize, should now be caught up in a dilemma in which time is an enemy rather than a friend.

To Roberta, the pregnancy is a complete disaster. She realizes that Clyde's weaknesses and his lack of permanent commitment to her make her pregnancy a terrible hazard rather than a possible salvation. Her increasing pressure on Clyde derives from two qualities of her nature—her faith, somewhat akin to that of Angela and Aileen when their loves strayed, that Clyde's affection if not love can be regained; and her fear of social exposure in Lycurgus and Biltz. The relationship between Clyde and Roberta now assumes a number of striking ironies. It is an ironic commentary on marriage, for example, that Roberta's insistence upon marriage as a solution to their dilemma increases in proportion to her awareness of Clyde's weakness, selfishness, and ineptness. And it is also ironic that Clyde and Roberta are now mirror images of each other's social hopes and fears. Now not only does she see Clyde as a step upward socially, as he sees Sondra, but both also view the exposure of their illicit relationship as the greatest danger facing their advance. So they are moved by similar sentiments to gain contrary aims—she to hold Clyde, he to escape.

Although he is dumbfounded by the pregnancy, Clyde's ignorance and inexperience lead him to believe that there must be an easy way out of this difficulty, and he readily agrees to help her. Yet even at this point he begins to form subconsciously an attitude toward Roberta which will eventually inform his acceptance of the "way of the lake." For his resolution to deny their relationship if he cannot help her without exposure is in essence an expression of a desire to remove her from his life 'at no cost to himself.

Clyde's reaction to the pregnancy is above all controlled by his dream of Sondra, a dream which prevents him from adopting either of the two most readily available solutions to the dilemma—to marry Roberta or to run away. To Clyde, however, neither is a solution since both would result in the loss of Sondra. And so, as winter advances into spring and as no way of achieving his primary end presents itself, he takes refuge in inertia while subconsciously pursuing with an increasing sense of pressure a solution which will not prejudice his chances with Sondra. For one moment, in mid-June, a fresh hope arises. Perhaps Sondra will elope with him and thus give him the power to deal with Roberta from a secure position. But it is another of the ironies of Clyde's dilemma that just as Roberta develops the hard and practical side of her nature because of her need, so Sondra, faced with the crisis of Clyde's elopement plans, reveals a "practical" and "material" streak (II, 34) and states firmly that they have everything to gain and nothing to lose by waiting a few more months until she is of age.

The events of mid-February to early July take place in a context of Clyde's increasing awareness of the opposing iconographies of wealth and poverty and of the social moralism which is preventing him from gaining his rightful place in paradise. Of the two Schenectady druggists whom he approaches out of a vague recollection that there are pills which can cause an abortion, one is a "confirmed religionist" (I, 388) who refuses aid while the other takes advantage of his ignorance to sell him a worthless remedy. And Dr. Glenn, though he has committed abortions, will not aid girls who are not of "good family" and are not "heavily sponsored by others" (I, 412) and therefore takes refuge in a self-righteous and self-protective moralism. When Clyde tells the haberdasher's assistant Orin Short an obviously false story about a colleague at the factory in order to gain information about a doctor who will perform an abortion, Orin realizes at once that Clyde is the man involved and for a moment wonders if the girl is Sondra. The irony is that if Clyde had indeed gotten Sondra pregnant, they would have had little difficulty in arranging an abortion.

Within this flux of alternating hope and ever-deepening fear—hope that the pills may work and then their failure, hope that the doctor will aid them and then his refusal—Clyde finds that the ever-present contrasting iconographies of wealth and poverty make his dilemma increasingly tormenting. A vacation at Twelfth Lake brings poignantly alive to him his dream world of dancing, riding, tennis, servants, beautiful homes, and a young and eager goddess to guide him among these delights. And an accidental visit to Roberta's farm home near Biltz dramatizes the bleakness, poverty, and dreariness of the life he associates with marriage to her. Early in June, Clyde receives letters from Roberta and Sondra which conjure up in his imagination these two worlds—"and it was the contrast presented by these two scenes which finally determined for him the fact that he would never marry Roberta—never" (II, 21).

As the pressure to solve their dilemma increases, the relationship between Clyde and Roberta changes. A "native shrewdness" (I, 424) and force emerge in Roberta. It is she who insists that Clyde act, who prepares for Dr. Glenn a far more effective story than the one Clyde had proposed, and who demands that they visit him a second time. And it is she who has the emotional integrity to point out to Clyde that he need not live with her after their marriage if he does not love her. But Clyde does not respond to this deepening of her nature, for he is engrossed in the one change in her behavior which has vitally affected him—her discarding of her ingratiating and pleasing role of pseudowife and her adoption of the terrifying demand that she be made a true wife.

Clyde's overt reaction to this demand is to simulate "interest and good-will and friendship" (II, 5) in order to placate Roberta and thus prevent her from exposing him. Ironically, he now acts with "tact and cunning" (I, 427) in deceiving Roberta, though he has not been able to bring these qualities to bear on their joint problem. Despite Clyde's remaining vestige of identification with Roberta, he has now also placed her in a significant new emotional context. Earlier, she had been a pathetic victim of the superior forces of life, as he had been a victim of poverty and of Hortense in Kansas City. But now he views her as someone to whom the world owes nothing, as both Esta's seducer and eventually he himself had viewed Esta despite her plight. In short, he has again moved from identifying himself with those who suffer to projecting himself into the roles of those who seek pleasure, from the reality that he is Esta's brother to the dream world of her seducer.

The long section of Book Two of *An American Tragedy* from Roberta's discovery of her pregnancy until her death is one of the most moving and harrowing in modern American fiction. It resembles the dramatic irony of *Othello* in its effect. In both works we experience the pain and frustration of observing a man and a woman go to their deaths despite their relative innocence—the innocence of ignorance, youth, poverty, and fear in Clyde's and Roberta's case—and despite the fact that a single ray of knowledge might save them. So we are fully aware of the destruction facing Clyde and Roberta while they themselves struggle and hope. Dreiser's introduction of a "doubling" structure in this portion of the novel increases our responsiveness to the fatalism inherent in the limited course of a pregnancy. As time begins to run out, Clyde's two earlier attempts to break off their relationship are matched by his two trips to the druggist for pills and by Roberta's two fruitless visits to Dr. Glenn. This repetitive emphasis of Clyde's ineffectualness combines with the increasing tension of the advancing months to produce an almost intolerable effect of two souls squirming in desperation as an inexorable fate draws near.

Dreiser modulates his narrative style in this section of the novel with great skill, moving from the drama of direct confrontation between Roberta and Clyde to the representation through indirect discourse of their thoughts and emotions to the "documentary" effect of Roberta's letters. His rendering through indirect discourse of Clyde's pain and frustration, his fear and indecision, tends to make Clyde's ineptness pathetic rather than contemptible. Everyone sees through his stories, all his attempts to solve his dilemma fail, and we begin to sense in his plight that nightmare quality of life in which before us is a high wall or a deep pit while behind us is something terrible and fearful pressing us forward. In particular, the scenes between Roberta and Clyde render one of the most poignant themes in the tragedy of love, that of the bitter recriminations and crosspurposes of two people attempting to share a burden when love has been replaced by fear and even hate. " 'To think that all our love for each other should have come to this' " (I, 431), cries Roberta at one point, and in that cry there is an echo of the Adam and Eve in us all, the Adam and Eve of Books IX and X of *Paradise Lost* who have suffered the fall but have not as yet gained the wonder of God's grace.

As spring advances into summer and Clyde has still not discovered a solution to his dilemma, his anxiety and fear become a psychological frenzy. Dreiser at first merely uses the language of mental derangement to describe Clyde's inner turmoil. For example, when Clyde's elopement plan fails, his face reveals "a nervous and almost deranged look—never so definite or powerful at any time before in his life—the border-line look between reason and unreason" (II, 35). But for the weeks preceding

Roberta's death, from the point when Clyde reads of the accidental tragedy at Pass Lake in which a girl drowns and her companion remains unfound, Dreiser adopts a more striking and significant means to suggest the violent struggle in Clyde between a native fear and hesitation and an overwhelming desire to solve his problem at all cost.

Influenced by Freudian ideas and by experimental movements in contemporary drama and fiction, Dreiser for some ten years before undertaking *An American Tragedy* had been writing plays and short stories in which he had attempted to represent dramatically the workings of the subconscious mind.[58] Thus, not only does Clyde have symbolic dreams which project the terrible danger represented by Roberta's pregnancy and the hope contained in the "way of the lake," but he also begins to live more and more within the internal reality of his terrible need to discard Roberta without exposure. His external surroundings become increasingly fuzzy and vague to him, while in the "enormous chamber" (II, 51) of his mind hope and fear engage in a kind of medieval debate on the feasibility of the "way of the lake," a debate in which Clyde's repressed desire to kill Roberta has created a straw man of caution whose ineffectual arguments are easily overcome. It is at this point, with Clyde on the edge of mental collapse and with his mind having already created "independent" moral voices, that Dreiser introduces a "supernatural" figure into Clyde's consciousness, an Efrit or genie who casuistically persuades him that the "way of the lake" is the only way and that it can be successfully accomplished.

Dreiser's use of a supernatural persuader may seem to be a fictional crutch because of his reliance on a conventional figure of Christian allegory and Arabian Nights fantasy to dramatize a complex psychological reality. In fact, however, the device is appropriate to Clyde. His imagination had been bred on evangelical Christianity and on a fantasy world in which dreams are magically fulfilled. The device also captures with considerable subtlety Clyde's state of mind at this moment of crisis. For by representing Clyde's destructive impulse as a supernatural entity, Dreiser suggests both the immense force of this impulse and its apartness from Clyde himself, the Clyde we have known. The Efrit who pleads the "way of the lake" arrives "in spite of himself" out "of some darker or primordial and unregenerate nature of his own" (II, 49). It arrives, in other words, from the subconscious as an atavistic fear and desire which is independent of Clyde's volition. So, when Clyde in early July, under the pressure of Roberta's explicit threat to expose him, speaks to her on the phone and begins to put the plan of the "way of the lake" into effect, "it seemed as though the Giant Efrit that had previously materialized in the silent halls of his brain, was once more here at his elbow—that he himself, cold and numb and fearsome, was being talked through—not actually talking himself" (II, 56).

Clyde's projection of his desire into a supernatural agent helps explain how a weak and fearful figure can attempt a murder and divorces the Clyde we have known from that attempt. To the "conscious" Clyde, his trip with Roberta to the North Woods is merely a means of pleading with her to release him, and her possible death during the trip would indeed be an accident. This separation of the conscious Clyde from the death of Roberta contributes to two important themes in the novel. It adds yet another strain of ambiguity to the problem of Clyde's guilt, since he was impelled by a kind of insanity during these last weeks before Roberta's death. (One of the ironies of the trial is that Clyde's lawyers initially believe that temporary insanity is their best defense but are dissuaded by the Lycurgus Griffithses because of the social stigma attached to this plea.) And it raises Clyde from his usual mediocrity of hesitation and fear to the momentary height of a man overcome and controlled by his darkest impulses. In short, out of the seemingly weak device of the Giant Efrit Dreiser creates moral complexity and a degree of tragic force.

Dreiser's depiction of Clyde as living in a kind of dream in which he is directed by his unregenerate nature reaches a climax during the death trip. On the train from Fonda to Utica Clyde's observation of the landscape is juxtaposed against a flow of his unrelated subconscious reflection to suggest his deep abstraction. Once at Big Bittern, all exterior action seems unreal to Clyde. He is "in a confused and turbulent state mentally, scarcely realizing the clarity or import of any particular thought or movement or act" (II, 70). He rents a boat and helps Roberta get in, "an almost nebulous figure, she now seemed, stepping down into an insubstantial rowboat upon a purely ideational lake" (II, 70). He is thus afloat with Roberta not only upon the lake but in a dream as the enormity of his plan forces him to divorce himself from its substantive reality. And it is upon this "ideational" lake that the Giant Efrit, at the crucial moment of Roberta's cry for help while drowning, makes his last and most important appearance and "advises" Clyde to let her drown.

Clyde and Roberta in the boat bring to a head not only the fictional tension of Book Two but also a number of vital themes. The moment contains several elaborate ironic threads. There is the obvious but nevertheless effective irony of Roberta's expectant joy and Clyde's turbulent fear and desire. There is also the ironic relation between this boat ride on a calm and beautiful day by a seemingly happy couple and a similar boat ride a year earlier on Crum Lake by the joyous Clyde and Roberta, with Clyde at that time assuring the apprehensive Roberta that the boat was "perfectly safe" (I, 267). There is the ironic nature of Roberta's death, since her death does indeed result from an accident, as Clyde had hoped it would. But since the external characteristics of a murder are present—Clyde's suspect behavior before and after the event and his powerful motive—he is to be convicted and executed for murder. And finally, there is the irony that Clyde had lied to himself that he wished to take Roberta to the North Woods in order to plead with her to release him but that his lawyers later adopt as his defense a version of this unconvincing lie.

Clyde's thoughts during the day on Big Bittern with Roberta touch constantly on the meaning of death. Throughout his preparation for the trip to the North Woods and during the trip itself, he has associated death with a dark destructive force. The Efrit is his "darker self" (II, 56); he feels a "dark and bitter resentment" (II, 57) toward Roberta; and his mood is "dark and tortured" (II, 58) as he broods on the "blackness" (II, 61) of his plan. At Big Bittern, this internal imagery of death is externalized into the stillness and darkness of the waters of the lake and the "cold" and "harsh" (II, 75) cry of the wier-wier bird.[59] But as the day advances, the negative imagery of death as an obliterating force, as a danger to oneself and others and as therefore an enemy, is paralleled by an imagery of death as a friend and comforter.

And as they glided into this [a small bay at the south end of the lake], this still dark water seemed to grip Clyde as nothing here or anywhere before this ever had—to change his mood. For once here he seemed to be fairly pulled or lured along into it, and having encircled its quiet banks, to be drifting, drifting—in endless space where was no end of anything—no plots—no plans—no practical problems to be solved—nothing. The insidious beauty of this place! Truly, it seemed to mock him—this strangeness—this dark pool, surrounded on all sides by those wonderful, soft, fir trees. (II, 74)

In this mood,

he now felt for the first time the grip of some seemingly strong, and yet friendly sympathetic hands laid firmly on his shoulders. The comfort of them! The warmth! The strength! For now they seemed to have a steadying effect on him and he liked them—their reassurance—their support. If only they would not be removed! If only they would remain always—the hands of this friend! For where had he ever known this comforting and almost tender sensation before in all his life? Not anywhere—and somehow this calmed him and he seemed to slip away from the reality of all things. (II, 74)

Clyde is thus "lured" into a sense that death is a solace and a guide. The imagery of death in this role—an imagery of softness and timelessness and yet also of a "firm hand" and strength—combines the qualities of a mother's warmth and protectiveness and a father's leadership and power, qualities which Clyde's parents had lacked and which he has always sought. Thus, for a brief moment death appears to be not dark and destructive but sweet and desirable. But then, as Clyde again gazes at the "magnetic, bluish, purple pool" (II, 75), it

seemed to change its form kaleidoscopically to a large crystalline ball. But what was that moving about in this crystal? A form! It came nearer—clearer—and as it did so, he recognized Roberta struggling and waving her thin white arms out of the water and reaching toward him! God! How terrible! The expression on her face! What in God's name was he thinking of anyway? Death! Murder! (II, 75)

Dreiser's intent in this powerful representation of Clyde's turbulent state of mind is not merely to depict the difference between an attractive illusion of death and its grim reality but to look forward significantly to the close of Book Three. For at that point Clyde again faces the problem of the meaning of death as his execution approaches. Again illusion and reality struggle for supremacy, and though he again wishes to accept illusion—this time the illusion provided by McMillan of a merciful God—the image of death which remains paramount in his mind is one analogous to that of Roberta struggling in the water—the image of the electric chair which awaits him at the end of the corridor.

Dreiser's narrative of Roberta's death combines high excitement and a thematic density which at once sums up many of the themes of Books One and Two and looks forward to those of Book Three. Alone with Roberta in a secluded reach of the lake, Clyde realizes that he must act.

All that he needed to do now was to turn swiftly and savagely to one side or the other—leap up—upon the left wale or right and upset the boat; or, failing that, rock it swiftly, and if Roberta protested too much, strike her with the camera in his hand, or one of the oars at his right. . . .

At this cataclysmic moment, and in the face of the utmost, the most urgent need of action, a sudden palsy of the will—of courage—of hate or rage sufficient; and with Roberta from her seat in the stern of the boat gazing at his troubled and then suddenly distorted and fulgurous, yet weak and even unbalanced face—a face of a sudden, instead of angry, ferocious, demoniac—confused and all but meaningless in its registration of a balanced combat between fear (a chemic revulsion against death or murderous brutality that would bring death) and a harried and restless and yet self-repressed desire to do—to do—to do—yet temporarily unbreakable here and now—a static between a powerful compulsion to do and yet not to do. (II, 76–77)

Roberta notices Clyde's strange and contorted appearance,

And suddenly rising, or rather leaning forward, and by crawling along the even keel, attempting to approach him, since he looked as though he was about to fall forward into the boat—or to one side and out into the water. And Clyde, as instantly sensing the profoundness of his own failure, his own cowardice or inadequateness for such an occasion, as instantly yielding to a tide of submerged hate, not only for himself, but Roberta—her power—or that of life to restrain him in this way. And yet fearing to act in any way . . . but angry and confused and glowering. And then, as she drew near him, seeking to take his hand in hers and the camera from him in order to put it in the boat, he flinging out at her, but not even then with any intention to do other than free himself of her—her touch—her pleading—consoling sympathy—her presence forever—God!

Yet (the camera still unconsciously held tight) pushing at her with so much vehemence as not only to strike her lips and nose and chin with it, but to throw her back sidewise toward the left wale which caused the boat to career to the very water's edge. And then he, stirred by her sharp scream . . . rising and reaching half to assist or recapture her and half to apologize for the unintended blow—yet in so doing completely capsizing the boat—himself and Roberta being as instantly thrown into the water. And the left wale of the boat as it turned, striking Roberta on the head as she sank and then rose for the first time, her frantic, contorted face turned to Clyde, who by now had righted himself. (II, 77–78)

She screams for help, "and then the voice at his ear":

"But this—this—is not this that which you have been thinking and wishing for this while—you in your great need? . . . An accident—an accident—an unintentional blow on your part is now saving you the labor of what you sought, and yet did not have the courage to do! . . . You might save her. But again you might not. . . . Behold. It is over. She is sinking now." (II, 78)

As at every crucial moment in his life, Clyde has been affected by a debilitating stasis. Roberta drowns, therefore, not because Clyde seeks to drown her but because he and she act at this moment with the same poignant combination of honesty and ineptness which characterized their early love for each other. Roberta senses Clyde's need and pain but in seeking to comfort him draws a blow, while Clyde in seeking to apologize and to aid capsizes the boat. Moreover, though the drowning is an accident in the senses that Clyde did not intend the blow and that the boat inadvertently overturned and struck Roberta, his suppressed anger had lent force to the blow and he had not come to Roberta's aid in the water. Until he confesses to McMillan, Clyde is the only one who knows the full circumstances of the drowning (he does not admit to Jephson and Belknap that he could have saved Roberta) and as he emerges from the water, it is with

the thought that, after all, he had not really killed her. . . . And yet . . . had he? Or had he not? For had he not refused to go to her rescue, and when he might have saved her, and when the fault for casting her in the water, however accidentally, was so truly his? And yet—and yet—. (II, 79)

But despite this complex moral reality, Clyde is a convicted murderer from the moment that Roberta's body is found and the complexities of experience begin to be translated into the absolutes necessary for the judgment and punishment of moral transgression.

《《《《《《《《《《《《《《《《《《《《《《《《《《《《

Book Three opens with a lengthy segment of double narrative involving the events from the death of Roberta on Thursday evening until Clyde's capture the following Tuesday. One narrative strand deals with the activities of the Cataraqui County coroner, district attorney, and sheriff's deputies as they quickly discover Clyde's identity and then run him down. The other follows Clyde himself from his trek from Big Bittern to nearby Twelfth Lake, where he joins Sondra and her set, until his capture while on a camping trip. The book begins, as did Book Two, at a point forward in time from the close of the previous book and with an entirely new cast of characters—the Cataraqui officials on the morning after Roberta's death. Then, six chapters later, with Clyde almost in their grasp, the narrative returns to him and presents his activities from the point of his departure from Big Bittern to the "present." The last portion of this escape-pursuit segment then alternates rapidly between Clyde and his pursuers until the two narratives join at his capture. On the surface, this opening section of Book Three might seem to be merely a successful exercise in suspense as a group of pursuers close in on their apprehensive yet hopeful victim. In fact, the section is not only excellent narrative but also an introduction to most of the central themes of Book Three.

One such theme is present in the swift capture of Clyde. Although the Giant Efrit had asked Clyde the seemingly unanswerable question " 'Where is the flaw?' " (II, 50) and though Clyde himself believes that he cannot be traced to Roberta's death, he has botched his planning. As we realize from the moment that Coroner Heit is suspicious of the circumstances of Roberta's death, Clyde will be quickly discovered and apprehended. The thematic thrust of the trail of clues which Clyde has left behind him, however, is less to enforce the certainty of his capture than of his conviction. The readily apparent details of his plan—his disguised identity, his preparations for an "accidental" drowning, his escape through the forest to Three Mile Bay and thence to Twelfth Lake—constitute such a coherent and self-evident pattern of intent and commission that they spell out immediately the "fact" that he is a murderer.

Moreover, many of the clues which lead to Clyde, such as Roberta's letter to her mother, her pregnancy, and most of all her letters to him, begin to shape and harden the community attitudes toward Clyde which will prevent the jury from entertaining any other "fact" than the circumstantiality of his plan. In the eyes of the countrified folk of Cataraqui County, Clyde is "a member of the well-known social group of the big central cities to the south" (II, 162). He is thus immediately cast in the role in which Roberta, herself a rural soul, had initially placed him, that of the city seducer of an innocent country maid. As the details of the crime unfold—Roberta's pathetic note to her parents, her "young and attractive" body (II, 87), her pregnancy, her simple, poor, and respectable parents—and as evidence of Clyde's appearance during his escape from Big Bittern is made known—"a smartishly and decidedly well dressed youth for these parts" (II, 89) and "more like a society man than anything else" (II, 95)—the myth of the city seducer takes firm hold in the minds of the people of Cataraqui County. So when Roberta's father learns of the circumstances of her death, at once, born for the most part of religion, convention and a general rural suspicion of all urban life and the mystery and involuteness of its ungodly ways, there sprang into his mind the thought of a city seducer and betrayer—some youth of means, probably, whom Roberta had met since going to Lycurgus and who had been able to seduce her by a promise of marriage which he was not willing to fulfill. And forthwith there flared up in his mind a terrible and quite uncontrollable desire for revenge upon any one who could plot so horrible a crime as this against his daughter. The scoundrel! The raper! The murderer! (II, 102)

The residents of Cataraqui County believe that because of Clyde's "desire to marry a rich girl he had most brutally assaulted and murdered a young and charming working-girl whose only fault had been that she loved him too well" (II, 160). In other words, Clyde's inability to fulfill successfully the role of an Alger hero has led to his condemnation as a city seducer. Moreover, this condemnation contains a third mythic element, for Clyde is also the rich nobleman of popular romance who should have honored the pledge of love and sacrifice of his rural sweetheart. Because he did not, he stands revealed as a villain and no doubt as a murderer. Clyde is therefore caught between the expectations raised by the absolute morality of these mythic roles; if he is not a genuine nobleman, he must be a city seducer. And so the mythic nature of American life comes full ironic circle in the career of Clyde. Aspiring to high estate but not achieving it, he nevertheless finds himself judged and condemned on the basis of the moral absolutes of the role of the sophisticated and wealthy nobleman which he had sought but not gained.

Cataraqui County reflects not only the moral prejudices of American life but also its political opportunism. Both of these social realities severely limit the possibility that justice can be rendered by the social and political institution which is the law. The only way to advance in America, Dreiser implies, is at the expense of one's fellows, and Clyde provides an excellent opportunity for anyone willing to exploit the popular interest in a sensational sex crime. He has been apprehended at a time when the political organizations of the county require a popular issue to revitalize their campaigns for various offices in the forthcoming election, and his trial therefore becomes an adjunct to the election.

The major themes which arise out of the nature of Cataraqui County—Clyde's role as a city seducer and his political usefulness—unite in the character of Mason, the district attorney of the county, who is also a candidate for county judge on the Republican ticket. Like McMillan later in Book Three, Mason shares Clyde's "romantic and emotional" (II, 91) temperament but not his weaknesses. Mason had been extremely poor during his boyhood and had also suffered a disfiguring broken nose, both of which had led to sexual repression and an intense competitiveness as well as to a bitter resentment toward those more favored in fortune and in sexual success. His envy of Clyde's seemingly well-to-do background and sexual adventurism combines with his desire to advance politically and socially to produce an immediate belief that Clyde is guilty and that he should be punished to the limit of the law. Mason's "victory" over Clyde during his cross-examination—a victory anticipated by his success in overawing and trapping Clyde from the moment of his capture—is therefore not merely that of the strong over the weak. It is more pointedly the victory of a man who, unlike Clyde, has successfully channeled his potentially destructive emotions into accepted modes of social action.

Clyde's final moments of freedom resemble two other climactic moments in the novel. As on the lake and as when he will have to choose between faith and doubt just before his execution, his response to a major dilemma is hesitation and stasis. During the camping trip, he senses that his capture is near. "Run, run, do not linger!" he admonishes himself, "yet lingering, and thinking *Sondra*, this wonderful life! Should he go so?" (II, 141). He makes a tentative effort to flee, but once outside the camp he reaches a state of complete immobility, neither returning to camp nor continuing to escape. And then at last, "out of the long, tall aisles of the trees before him" (II, 142) there appears one of Mason's undersheriffs. The setting of this moment of capture—"the tall shafts of the trees in the approaching dusk making solemn aisles through which they proceeded as might worshippers along the nave of a cathedral" (II, 144)—recalls the "tall and spearlike" trees of Big Bittern and the ambiguity of the lake as an image of death. But the cathedral metaphor also looks forward to the final stasis of Clyde's life when under McMillan's guidance he seeks the peace and comfort of expiation and life everlasting and yet secretly fears the terrible and absolute penance of death.

The longest segment of Book Three is concerned with the preparation for the trial and the trial itself. Like the other two parts of Book Three, it begins with a slow narrative pace as Mason, the Griffithses and their family lawyers, and Clyde's lawyers consider the details of the case. Then, again as in the other two parts, tension increases and reaches a climax—in this instance, the tension of the trial and the climax of Clyde's conviction. A trial, of course, often holds as narrative because of the opportunities it affords for bold characterization, open conflict, and suspense. But because a trial also casts into relief the differences in belief and temperament which divide men and the attempt by men to reconcile through law the conflicts which these differences occasion, the trial in *An American Tragedy* also brings into sharp focus most of the central themes of the novel.

Most of these themes make their reappearance during the three months between Clyde's capture and the trial. Clyde's ineffectual attempt to explain away the mass of incriminating circumstantial evidence convinces not only Mason but also all three of the Griffithses' family lawyers that he is guilty. The seemingly just yet inherently prejudiced actions of the Lycurgus Griffithses during this period suggest the difficulty which Clyde will have in getting a fair trial. Gilbert is predictably incensed, but Mr. Griffiths appears to be calm and sympathetic. He acknowledges that the family is partly to blame for Clyde's plight because of their failure to cultivate him initially and thereby prevent the loneliness which drove him into Roberta's arms. He therefore instructs his lawyers to determine if Clyde is guilty or innocent; if guilty, the family will offer only minimum support; if innocent, they will do all in their power to save him. Both the family and its lawyers are struck by the generosity of this decision—"the fairness of him in such a deadly crisis" (II, 178). But Samuel Griffiths, like the jury itself in a few months, is already convinced of Clyde's sexual guilt, of his "ungoverned and carnal desires" and the "uncontrollable brutality of seducing that girl" (II, 176), and is therefore predisposed to believe him guilty of murder as well. Easily persuaded by a succession of family lawyers that Clyde's story is unconvincing, Mr. Griffiths has little difficulty persuading his conscience that he owes Clyde only the minimum effort of hiring two local lawyers, despite his knowledge that a powerful outside firm might gain either a delay in the trial or a change in venue and thus aid Clyde's chances greatly. And as the case proceeds, Griffiths handicaps Clyde still further by refusing to permit his lawyers to plead temporary insanity and by refusing to permit Clyde's parents to appear on his behalf.

Clyde's attorneys, Belknap and Jephson, are well characterized by Dreiser in relation to the central irony of Clyde's life at this moment—that the truth of the events in the boat is neither convincing nor mitigating. Clyde confesses to his lawyers because he senses that they wish to understand and aid him. Yet both men, on hearing Clyde's story, have difficulty squaring his "change of heart" before the accident with the drowning of Roberta only a few feet from Clyde. Belknap in particular is responsive to Clyde. He is a worldly man who has a sympathetic awareness of the basic human impulses and the restrictive moral climate which contributed to Clyde's dilemma. Indeed, he himself as a youth had gotten pregnant a working-class girl but had had the good fortune to have well-to-do parents to rescue him. Jephson is a more complex and significant figure. Though younger than Belknap, he is stronger and more brilliant, with "a will and a determination of the tensile strength of steel" (II, 190). Clyde is immediately impressed by Jephson because he is "so shrewd and practical, so very direct and chill and indifferent, and yet confidence-inspiring, quite like an uncontrollable machine of a kind which generates power" (II, 198).

The two lawyers complement each other in their relationship to Clyde—the one responding with an underlying compassionate identification, the other having a "technical" rather than an "emotional" (II, 193) interest in Clyde's fate. Out of this "technical" interest, Jephson uses Clyde in two irreconcilable and eventually destructive ways—to construct a defense of symmetrical and logical beauty, and to shock and educate the "bumpkins" of Cataraqui County into a recognition of the "real facts" of life (II, 276). Although Jephson lacks faith both in Clyde and his story, he pretends to Clyde that he is convinced of his innocence. He cultivates Clyde's trust in him until his control is complete and he can undertake to recreate Clyde and the events of the death trip in order to win the case.[60]

In Jephson, Clyde once again is to find himself betrayed by a "father" who seeks to impose a foreign identity upon him. Paradoxically, Jephson is a "modern" thinker who expresses ideas which Dreiser usually endorses in his own polemic writing. Jephson's open contempt for the sentimental moralism of rural life and his adoption of a mechanistic determinism to defend Clyde—Clyde, he tells the jury, is "a moral and mental coward" who "didn't make" himself (II, 268)—are close to Dreiser's own beliefs. But Jephson is nevertheless a Hawthornelike villain in that his intellectual brilliance and coldness of heart lead him to manipulate Clyde's nature and fate without that sympathetic acceptance of the integrity of Clyde's essential being which is necessary if he is indeed to aid rather than destroy Clyde. Jephson's comment late in the trial, after Clyde has collapsed during cross-examination, " 'It musta been that he really did kill her' " (II,

325), reflects this basic coldness. His danger to Clyde is suggested most of all by "the windless, still pools" of his eyes (II, 205), eyes which provide Clyde a psychic strength during the trial but which represent as well an illusion of safety as dangerous as that of the waters of Big Bittern. Jephson and McMillan are the two major figures in Book Three to whom Clyde turns for understanding and aid. Although one is a modern thinker and the other a religionist, both attempt to reshape Clyde in conformity with their own vision of truth rather than accept the full complexity and ambiguity of his nature and acts. They thus construct ineffectual defenses of Clyde which in fact contribute to his death.

When Belknap hears Clyde's confession, he realizes that his story will not do, that what is needed is one which is "less cruel or legally murderous" (II, 189). The question of Clyde's "legal" guilt requires discussion because there has been much controversy over this problem since the publication of the novel.[61] Dreiser's key comment on the matter, derived no doubt from conversations with his lawyer friend Arthur Carter Hume during the composition of the novel,[62] is contained in Jephson's reaction when he hears Clyde's confession. " 'Of course you know,' " he tells Belknap, " 'constructively, in the eyes of the law, if we use his own story, he's just as guilty as though he had struck her, and the judge would have to so instruct' " (II, 190). The legal term "constructively" broadly means "by inference" or "by interpretation." More particularly, it means that if you intend to commit a crime and an act which can be construed as a crime occurs as a probable consequence of that intent, you have committed a crime in the eyes of the law even if there are no witnesses to that act. Thus, if Clyde admitted that he at one time intended to drown Roberta, and then—with no eyewitnesses other than Clyde—she does drown, the judge would have to instruct the jury that Clyde is legally guilty whether or not he admitted striking a murderous blow.

Dreiser's key irony in introducing the fact that Clyde is technically guilty of murder is that this fact is extraneous both to the moral complexity and ambiguity of the events in the boat and to the actualities of decision-reaching during a trial. Since Clyde never admits his intent during the trial, the burden of legal proof of guilt is circumstantial evidence of intent. As the judge carefully instructs at the close of the trial,

"If the jury finds that Roberta Alden accidentally or involuntarily fell out of the boat and that the defendant made no attempt to rescue her, that does not make the defendant guilty and the jury must find the defendant 'not guilty.' On the other hand, if the jury finds that the defendant in any way, intentionally, there and then brought about or contributed to that fatal accident, either by a blow or otherwise, it must find the defendant guilty." (II, 328)

But in fact the jury has already ignored this vital distinction and will continue to ignore it when reaching its formal decision. Prejudiced against Clyde from the first because of his sexual guilt, they have already found him guilty of murder precisely on the moral grounds that he did not attempt to save Roberta while she was drowning. As they hear the testimony dealing with Clyde and Roberta in the water, "after all, asked each juror of himself as he listened, why couldn't he have saved her if he was strong enough to swim to shore afterwards—or at least to have swum to and secured the boat and helped her to take hold of it?" (II, 305). And so each juror at this point in the trial finds in Clyde's manner and responses evidence that he is not only a "mental and moral coward" but "worse yet, really guilty of Roberta's death" (II, 305). McMillan is later to substantiate this basic tendency in the operation of justice. In the governor's office he tacitly confirms that Clyde is legally guilty because to McMillan, as to the jury, Clyde was morally and spiritually guilty in not coming to Roberta's rescue.

Dreiser's point in this dramatization of the law at work is first, that the truth seldom appears before the law because the truth is too complex to yield either the "exact justice" (II, 232) which Mason demands or the absolute distinction between intent and nonintent which the judge desires; and second, that what appears before the law for judgment in place of the truth is judged in any event on the basis of moral predispositions rather than legal distinctions. The jury does not know the truth of the events in the boat but does know the law; McMillan knows the truth but presumably is ignorant of the law. Yet both the jury and McMillan seize upon Clyde's clear-cut moral guilt to find him legally guilty, as one ignores the law and the other the truth. Clyde's legal guilt thus contains the major theme that the complexities of human desire and the ambiguities of moral responsibility cannot be adequately understood by a society which judges men on the basis of moral expectations and absolutes.

Belknap and Jephson realize that the law is primarily a means for the expression of moral and social prejudices and that in order to make Clyde's true story of the death trip "less cruel" they will have to overcome the myth of the city seducer embodied in that story. In order to fight fire with fire and to create sympathy for rather than resentment against Clyde, Jephson devises a "change of heart" story which casts Clyde in the role of the generous nobleman rather than the city seducer. According to Jephson's story, Clyde takes Roberta to the North Woods to plead with her to release him. If she will not, he plans to run away. At Grass Lake, however, where Clyde and Roberta spend their second night, he undergoes a change of heart and decides that he will marry her if she refuses to let him go. He tells her of his decision while they are on Big Bittern, and her shocked gratitude at his generosity leads to the accidental blow with the camera, the overturning of the boat, and her death. So Clyde is provided with a presumably unassailable moral story, one in which the events in the boat are close to their external truth but are made the product of a consciously noble and generous gesture rather than a stasis of indecision arising out of fear and desire. The story does indeed have a certain brilliance, as Mason later acknowledges, for when combined with an emphasis upon Clyde's "mental and moral cowardice," it accommodates both his secrecy before Roberta's death and flight afterward and turns the mass of circumstantial evidence bearing on the death trip in his favor rather than against him. As Jephson remarks, Clyde's nobility " 'ought to appeal to these fellows around here, these religious and moral people, ought'n it?' " (II, 201).

The trial is thus essentially a contest between rival sentimental myths—that of the city seducer versus that of the nobleman who had intended to expiate his seduction by marrying and elevating the poor and virtuous maiden because her qualities had at last impressed themselves upon his heart. Clyde's new mythic role of course requires that he assume a new identity, and coached by Belknap and Jephson he begins to attend church regularly and to adopt a pose of self-assured calm. But in truth Clyde has been given an impossible role to perform. Not only is his story full of loopholes and he himself a poor liar in any circumstances, but his own deeply ambiguous feelings about his innocence or guilt undermine the confidence necessary to play the role convincingly. Moreover, Clyde shares the mood of the courtroom; he believes that his sexual relations with Roberta were not only ill-advised but morally wrong for a young man aspiring to the world of the Griffithses and Sondra. So the change of heart device backfires, for once Clyde's sense of guilt and the weaknesses in his story become apparent, his lack of credibility in his new role weakens the credibility of his true account of the events in the boat.

Mason, of course, relies heavily on the city seducer myth throughout the trial. Roberta is a "poor little thing" (II, 238), and Clyde is a young man of social standing and advantages. The publication of Roberta's letters before the trial had unleashed "a wave of hatred for Clyde as well as a wave of pity for her—the poor, lonely, country girl" (II, 167), and Mason exploits this emotion throughout his presentation of the state's case. Belknap has a double rejoinder to Mason's moralism—that "unhallowed" relationships are not uncommon (II, 258), and that were it not for the unfortunate accident in the boat Clyde and Roberta would be safely married. Both sides, in short, base their case not on the reality of the events in the boat but upon the moral predispositions of their audience. And this audience, both the courtroom in general and the jury in particular, reflects in extreme form (because Cataraqui County is a backwoods community) the tendency of all men to believe what they wish to believe. The members of the jury, though professing to be open minded, are "with but one exception, all religious, if not moral, and all convinced of Clyde's guilt before they ever sat down" (II, 231). The irate woodsman who calls out at one point, " 'Why don't they kill the God-damned bastard and be done with him?' " (II, 313), is merely stating openly, and therefore unacceptably, a sentiment which receives more sophisticated and covert expression in the processes of the law.

The trial is not fictionally repetitious, even though it is devoted to recreating action which has already occurred, because that recreation is thematically alive. Such details of the death trip as Clyde's false hotel registrations and his camera, wet suit, suitcase, and straw hats occur in three contexts in the novel: their actuality during the trip and their roles in the opposing versions of the trip proposed by Mason and Jephson. The details therefore contribute to a sense of ironic density rather than to an effect of repetition. And the trial itself, as Dreiser boldly summarizes its evidence and concentrates on the long opening speeches of Belknap and Mason and the examination of Clyde, is good courtroom drama.

Our attitude toward Clyde during the trial is in one sense similar to our response to the criminal in any well-constructed detective novel. Despite the dexterity of Jephson's change-of-heart story, we sense from the first that it contains many loopholes. We thus participate in the excitement of Mason's exposure of these weaknesses during his cross-examination of Clyde. But though we may in part identify with Mason as the sharp-witted detective who relentlessly seeks to expose Clyde's lies, our fuller and deeper identification is with Clyde himself. For Clyde is no mere criminal but is rather someone who is attempting, albeit ineptly and weakly in the guise of his change-of-heart story, to preserve and present a truth of another kind—that of the intolerable pressures of his dilemma and of his confused, ambivalent beliefs about his guilt. We are like viewers of a tragic action who undergo a painful and irreconcilable identification both with the forces that make for order and clarity in life and with the reality which is the complexity and irrationality of human nature.

All of the last section of *An American Tragedy*, with the exception of a few scenes involving Clyde's mother and McMillan, deals with Clyde's prison life from his conviction to his death a year and a half later. A prison is a fitting symbol of the nature and direction of social reality in Clyde's life. From the relatively free world of the Green-Davidson to the more restrictive society of Lycurgus to the yet narrower setting of Bridgeburg and the courtroom, Clyde has reached the final expression of the basic irony in his life that the desirable is available only behind high walls of social and moral restriction and that the inept seeker is eventually not only barred but also imprisoned by these walls.

The death house is a microcosm of modern society. Its brute insensitivity derives from anonymous rules and regulations rather than individuals, and its seeming humane mingling of prisoners (in place of the earlier system of solitary confinement) in fact results in a soul-wearying sharing of terror. Dreiser supports this symbolism by a heavy reliance on the image of prison life as a machine pushing one on to the ultimate confinement of death:

There was a system—a horrible routine system—as long since he had come to feel it to be so. It was iron. It moved automatically like a machine without the aid or the hearts of men. These guards! They with their letters, their inquiries, their pleasant and yet really hollow words, their trips to do little favors, or to take the men in and out of the yard or to their baths—they were iron, too—mere machines, automatons, pushing and pushing and yet restraining and restraining one—within these walls, as ready to kill as to favor in case of opposition—but pushing, pushing, pushing—always toward that little door over there, from which there was no escape—no escape—just on and on—until at last they would push him through it never to return! (II, 401–402)

But though the prison is a narrowing down and an intensification of the restrictions imposed upon Clyde during his life (with the door of the mission and the door of the electrocution chamber bitterly and ironically similar to each other), the prison also contains a "dream" of a better life beyond its walls. Initially, Clyde dreams of freedom, but as that dream fades, he begins to hope for a heaven of peace and comfort. And as in Kansas City, Clyde is betrayed by a "father" who substitutes a belief in salvation for the need to solve an immediate practical problem. In this instance, the need is to save life itself.

Given the powerful symbolic role of the prison, the significant figure of McMillan, and the firm thematic connection between this portion of the novel and the work as a whole, it is surprising that the closing section of *An American Tragedy* is the weakest in the novel. Unlike the remainder of the work, which is Dreiserian in form and technique but in which Dreiserian virtues are to the fore and excesses under tight control, the prison section reveals an unregenerate Dreiser. Here, the technique of narrative irony which dominates the rest of the novel has to compete with Dreiser's openly expressed contempt for the injustices and cruelty of prison life and for the hypocrisy of organized religion. Moreover, as in Dreiser's worst fiction, the section is too long, primarily because of repetitious detail, and its prose is involuted and turgid. Perhaps Dreiser failed to revise and cut this section sufficiently, since comparatively little time elapsed between its completion and the submission of the entire novel. Or perhaps the material itself was intractable because it required a lengthy representation of Clyde's external inaction and internal turbulence. In any event, the prison section of *An American Tragedy* is the one major portion which seems to call out for further work.

With Jephson and Belknap no longer on the scene, Clyde's two greatest needs in prison are for help and understanding. When he sees his mother after the trial for the first time since Kansas City, it is with a "troubled" soul seeking to find in her "sanctuary, sympathy, help, per-haps—and that without criticism" (II, 341). For a brief period she and Nicholson, a refined and kindly prisoner who takes an interest in Clyde, seem to supply this need. But Nicholson is executed and Mrs. Griffiths is separated from Clyde by her basic nature. Although her strength and maternal sympathy are precisely what he needs, they come to him filtered through an evangelical Christianity which prevents her from reaching Clyde. Clyde senses this failure throughout their relationship in prison, and at the time of his greatest need, in the days before his execution, is able to express it fully.

It was as though there was an insurmountable wall or impenetrable barrier between them, built by the lack of understanding—for it was just that. She would never understand his craving for ease and luxury, for beauty, for love—his particular kind of love that went with show, pleasure, wealth, position, his eager and immutable aspirations and desires. (II, 401)

Dreiser's use of a wall image in this passage is particularly suggestive. The image implies that Clyde's life is tragic not only because of the wall of conventional moralism between his dreams and their fulfillment but because of a similar wall between his fundamental nature and the compassionate understanding of his deepest desires which he and all men require.

McMillan, however, appears to have an understanding and sympathetic temperament, as Clyde immediately senses. Like Clyde, he has a "poetic and emotional . . . sex nature" (II, 370), but he has sublimated his sexuality, Dreiser tells us, into a fervent evangelicalism. Moreover, he has the native strength and vitality which Clyde has always lacked and has therefore sought in others. He is "a strange, strong, tense, confused, merciful, and too, after his fashion beautiful soul; sorrowing with misery, yearning toward an impossible justice" (II, 371). Dreiser's initial characterization of McMillan is of a compelling figure who may indeed help Clyde at this desperate moment in his life. But the characterization is qualified by the ominous similarity between McMillan's craving for "an impossible justice" and Mason's call for "exact justice."

The relationship between Clyde and McMillan has some of the qualities of a love affair. Clyde is the feminine nature who seeks strength and guidance, McMillan the masculine nature who seeks not physical but spiritual possession of the beloved. " 'I bring you, Clyde,' " McMillan says at their first meeting, " 'the mercy and the salvation of your God. . . . ' He paused and stared at Clyde tenderly. A warm, youthful, half smile, half romantic, played about his lips" (II, 373). Clyde finds McMillan "arresting" and "attractive"—his "vital, confident and kindly manner—so different to the tense, fearful, and yet lonely life here" (II, 375, 377). So, while still maintaining his old doubts about the efficacy of belief, Clyde permits himself to be wooed and won by McMillan's deep interest and strength.

The newspaper reports of the trial had convinced McMillan of Clyde's guilt, but after meeting Mrs. Griffiths he wonders if indeed "a legal mistake had been made" (II, 371). He therefore approaches Clyde with a seemingly open mind about his legal guilt and with a desire to cleanse Clyde above all of the acknowledged spiritual guilt of his carnal relations with Roberta. As their relationship progresses and as Clyde gains confidence in McMillan's sympathetic nature, Clyde is moved both by his own need and by McMillan's encouragement to confess himself fully to McMillan. Although Clyde explains to McMillan that he wishes to know whether he is guilty in God's eyes of murdering Roberta, in truth it is McMillan's understanding of his dilemma that he wishes. When McMillan hears from Clyde the full story of the events in the boat and during Roberta's drowning, he selects from this body of complex motivation and action the single fact, one which he listens to with lips "tightly and sadly compressed" (II, 390), that Clyde did not swim to Roberta's aid because he was thinking that her death would permit him to marry Miss X. Then " 'in your heart was murder' " (II, 390), he tells Clyde. And after two weeks of brooding on the problem, he returns to inform Clyde that he believes him guilty of Roberta's death. Thus, as I noted earlier, McMillan's conviction that Clyde is "guilty before God and the law" is similar to the jury's belief that Clyde's sexual crime against Roberta was equivalent to murdering her. As Dreiser succinctly stated in the "N. B." section which he cut just before publication of the novel, McMillan believed "that spiritually *and hence* legally Clyde was guilty" of the crime attributed to him (my italics).

There are several ironies attached to McMillan's role in Clyde's life, most of which come to a head in the scene in the governor's office when McMillan's refusal to comment on Clyde's guilt convinces the governor that he does indeed believe Clyde guilty. Seeking human warmth and compassion, Clyde has placed his faith in a man whose genuine warmth is overlaid with the same narrowness and blindness which had condemned him. Moreover, though Clyde has professed a belief in the primary value of his immortal soul, it is life itself that he wants. And he has placed his life in the hands of a man whose scruples about the "validity" of his "spiritual" worth to Clyde (II, 398) prevent him from telling a "lie" which might save that life. Finally, Clyde's mother, with a mother's love, had crushed her doubts about his innocence and had willed herself to believe in him, even though he had not confessed to her. But McMillan, the last of the fathers in Clyde's life who betray him by their weakness or by their failure to understand his dreams, has on the basis of a "spiritual" love for Clyde doomed him to death despite his full knowledge of the events in the boat and of Clyde's need. It was audacious of Dreiser to introduce a new major figure into a very long novel some forty pages before its close. But despite McMillan's late and relatively brief role, he effectively summarizes in his character and in his impact upon Clyde's life the important theme that a blinding moralism can warp and misdirect essentially worthwhile qualities of human nature.

Clyde's interest in religious faith while in prison had been colored in part by his desire to please McMillan and in part by his need to gain an even more powerful and comforting Father than McMillan. Yet opposing this great need is Clyde's realization of the past and present failure of religious belief, and of the earthly agents of that belief, to aid him. So as Clyde's death nears, he expresses for the last time the stasis which is central to his character. He acknowledges to McMillan an acceptance of his guilt and a successful achievement of faith, yet in his heart he has doubts about both. His "victory" is complete (II, 403), he writes in his letter to the youth of America. But after his death McMillan recalls his final moments while he is being strapped into the electric chair—"his eyes fixed nervously and, as he thought, appealingly and dazedly upon him and the group surrounding him" (II, 406)—eyes which suggest that Clyde is still seeking aid and understanding, that he is still uncertain of both the past and the future at the very moment he is being propelled into his fate.

Dreiser seeks to raise the stature of Clyde throughout the closing prison section of the novel. Although we are used to thinking of Clyde as weak and though he does have moments of terror while in prison, his behavior on the whole is calm and almost stoical, particularly in comparison to the animal fear of the other prisoners. Moreover, his self-honesty—never a major characteristic of his nature—now becomes a significant force. He wants to explore as fully and honestly as possible the truth of his guilt and innocence, and his dreams are now not of an iconography of cars and boating but of the aid and compassion which might follow from this self-scrutiny. There is both dignity and passion in his pleas for understanding—the dignity of a being conscious of a pattern and a meaning in his life, and the anger of someone who finds himself judged by those who have not experienced or realized the "mental, physical, and spiritual suffering" of his life. Clyde's "appealing" eyes at the moment before his death represent one of the most poignant of human tragedies—the realization that we have been judged but not understood.

The "Souvenir" which closes *An American Tragedy* brings us forward a few years to a scene in which Clyde's parents are again, as in the opening chapter of the novel, on a street-preaching mission. Approximately ten years have passed since the initial scene and the city is San Francisco rather than Kansas City, but the vignette still dramatizes primarily an encounter between an ineffectual unworldliness and a mocking world. Dreiser enforces this similarity by repeating much of the language and detail of the first vignette. But now, instead of Clyde, the Griffithses are assisted by Esta's illegitimate child Russell, a boy of seven or eight who resembles Clyde and who has been "instructed in those fundamental verities which had irritated Clyde in his childhood" (II, 213). In a brief exchange between Mrs. Griffiths and Russell which is the only significant variation between the two vignettes, Russell asks for a dime to buy an ice cream cone. Mrs. Griffiths gives him the money, thinking, "She must be kind to him, more liberal with him, not restrain him too much, as maybe, maybe, she had—She looked affectionately and yet a little vacantly after him as he ran" (II, 409). And so with Mrs. Griffiths's uncomprehending and ineffectual gesture toward narrowing the immense gap between reality and desire, a gap which had appalled Clyde and which has begun to move Russell, the Griffithses enter, as they had ten years earlier, the "yellow, unprepossessing door" (II, 409) of mission life. As in an equally famous American novel of the 1920s, Dreiser could have appropriately included as epigraphs to *An American Tragedy* the statements that though a generation may be lost, the "earth abideth forever" and "the sun also riseth." But for Dreiser the epigraphs would have been ironic rather than affirmative. For *An American Tragedy* is a novel of man in society rather than in nature, and its earth and sun are not agents of renewal but rather that unchanging destructive social matrix out of which come not one but many lost generations, so long as wealth, class, desire, and weakness and strength are part of our lives.

ccccccccccccccccccccccccccccc

There are two almost insurmountable difficulties in any attempt to describe the tragic element in *An American Tragedy*. The first is that tragedy means different things to different people. When Irving Babbitt, the New Humanist critic of the 1920s, attacked *An American Tragedy* because it lacked "the final relief and enlargement of spirit" of true tragedy,[63] he was referring to a concept of tragedy very different from that which Dreiser expressed in a 1916 letter to Mencken when he wrote, "What has a tragedy ever illuminated—unless it is the inscrutability of life and its forces and its accidents?"[64] The second obstacle is our tendency to isolate in a complex work of art a dominant theme or aesthetic effect and to designate it as the source of the tragic quality we sense in the work. In so doing we often oversimplify the work and thus find that our use of the honorific term "tragic" has in fact weakened rather than strengthened our case for the significance of the work.

The wisest critics of *An American Tragedy* have therefore approached the problem of the meaning of "tragedy" in its title with a certain wariness. F. O. Matthiessen, for example, after noting that the novel's themes and form are not those of traditional tragedy, states that the work nevertheless reveals a "profoundly tragic sense of man's fate."[65] I have attempted in my own discussion to specify some of the themes and effects which make up this "tragic sense"—the powerful thread of inevitability in Clyde's fate given his character and circumstances, the element of undeveloped and unconscious yet potentially compassionate sensitivity in Clyde's makeup, the quality of our shared involvement in the harrowing of a creature whose principal weakness is often ignorance and naïveté, and above all our sense of oneness with a figure who, though weak and ineffectual, desires with a deepening need to be understood. These themes and effects are not coherently related to any single describable tragic theme, either traditional or otherwise. But they and other characteristics of the novel do move us deeply because we sense in them a mature vision of the most poignant strains in the lives of any of us who have ever dreamed. It is significant, I think, that in recent years most of the attention focused on the themes of *An American Tragedy* has been directed toward the meaning of "tragedy" rather than "American" in its title. A work which had its origin in Dreiser's fascination with a distinctively American crime now speaks above all to the "mental, physical, and spiritual suffering" which all men have shared.

〰〰〰〰〰〰〰〰〰〰〰〰〰〰〰

In late 1923, while writing *An American Tragedy*, Dreiser told an interviewer that a major fault of contemporary American realism was that most of its adherents were attempting the impossible task of presenting life on a "ten-inch canvas."[66] *An American Tragedy* of course conjures up comparisons with a mural rather than a miniature, yet paradoxically most readers familiar with all of Dreiser's novels come away from it with a sense of its greater structural and technical control than any other work, with the possible exception of *Sister Carrie*. The reasons for this striking effect (striking for Dreiser, that is) of formalistic discipline within a full-bodied work lie partly in the great editorial labor expended on the novel and in Dreiser's growth in narrative skill after twenty-five years of work in fiction and such other narrative forms as travel accounts and autobiography. But the principal reason lies in Dreiser's successful use in *An American Tragedy* of the major structural characteristic of *Sister Carrie*—a division of the novel into parts based upon change of setting. In *Sister Carrie*, this device permitted Dreiser to divide the novel into two narrative segments while playing constantly upon the ironic relationship between the situations of Carrie and Hurstwood in Chicago on the one hand and in New York on the other. In *An American Tragedy* Dreiser carried this device a step further. Now there are three divisions (or books), each sharply divided from the other by abrupt shifts in time, place, and characters, each with its own "complete" narrative, yet each linked to the other by a series of underlying thematic and formalistic threads.

Thus, *An American Tragedy* is like all of Dreiser's novels in its distinctively Dreiserian narrative voices within a "conventional" third-person biographical form, its narrative irony, and its heavy reliance on the interplay between an explicit pattern of imagery (paradise and dreaming) and an implicit pattern of detail (girls, cars, homes) which is the emotional equivalent of that imagery. But unlike Dreiser's other novels from *Jennie Gerhardt* to *The Titan*, in which a loose biographical form results in a frequently flabby and uncontrolled expression of these characteristics, the form of three separate narrative divisions appears to have had the effect of encouraging both greater concentration and discipline within these relatively brief parts and greater density of ironic relationship among the parts.

Each book exists as an independent narrative unit because of its distinctive setting and personae and because each rises from a slow-paced opening to a major climax. Yet each is related to the others not merely in being a major sequence of events in Clyde's life but in the reappearance from book to book of thematic motifs and fictional structures which knit the whole together. These include such devices as the enclosing vignettes of the Griffithses as street preachers; the parallel endings of Book One and

Book Two and the parallel openings of Book Two and Three; the heavy reliance on sexual triangles in Books One and Two to structure the dilemmas which arise out of the conflict between Clyde's nature and his world; the use of opposing iconographies, often inseparable from these sexual triangles—a dream or paradise of acquisition and rise on the one hand and a wall of social and personal limitations on the other, with the two seemingly balanced in Book One, the dream predominating in Book Two, and the wall in Book Three; the focus upon a major physical structure—the Green-Davidson, the factory, and the prison—to reflect the social and moral reality of the setting of each book; and the motif of a search for a father of strength and guidance, from Ratterer to McMillan and God.

Perhaps I can illustrate the richness in the thematic and structural interplay between the various parts of the novel by concentrating on Dreiser's manipulation of the motifs of dancing and water sports. Throughout Books One and Two, dancing is an overt metaphor of sexual interest and a covert one of sexual activity. Yet its metaphoric function is almost always ironic in the sense that any one instance of dancing stands in ironic relation to a sequence of instances. So Clyde, when still a virgin, is asked to dance by a blonde prostitute on his first visit to a whorehouse, though he has not as yet learned how. Then Hortense teaches him to dance, but it is while Hortense dances with the much more proficient and experienced Sparser that Clyde's jealousy flames. In Book Two, Clyde senses while dancing with the sensual Rita that she could readily be his, but his retreat from this easy conquest eventually leads him to teach the innocent yet intuitively rhythmic and inherently sensual Roberta to dance. And finally, it is Clyde's prowess as a dancer—a prowess gained in part by frequent practice with Roberta—which initially attracts Sondra once she has used him for her own social purposes. So the motif sinews and weaves through these two books, constantly imaging both the sexuality of Clyde's involvement with various girls and the ironic relationship between a particular moment of sexuality and those past and forthcoming.

Dreiser's use of dancing as a motif stems from his recollection of its role as a sexual surrogate in his own youth[67] and from its importance as a youthful social activity in the 1920s. The motif of water sports in *An American Tragedy* has a similar dual source. The automobile and greater leisure had made the twenties more sports-conscious then any previous period in American history. And Dreiser also recalled the lakes just outside the town of Warsaw, where he had spent his adolescence. These lakes were the scene of frequent outings by the well-to-do youth of the town, but they also contributed to Dreiser's nightmares of drowning which are reflected in his fiction by dream passages involving death by water.[68] Water sports in *An American Tragedy* thus represent both an escape into the illusion of paradise, particularly the paradise of sexual possession, and the bitter frustration and danger of this illusion. In Book One, the bellhops and their girls frolic on the ice during their outing. Their games are basically those of sexual pursuit and capture, in which Clyde at last appears close to possessing Hortense and yet is faced with the frustration of her sudden interest in Sparser. The motif reappears in Books Two and Three, but in a characteristically more involuted and moving form. Clyde associates his acquisition of various water skills with a preparation for the paradise of Sondra and her world, yet it is Roberta whom he meets and wins on Crum Lake—a Roberta who is afraid of boats and cannot swim. Later, with the dream of Sondra so close after his glorious week with her at Twelfth Lake, Big Bittern appears to offer the possibility of assuring that fulfillment. But the "way of the lake" is an illusion and a mocking of Clyde's hopes, as he discovers both while fearfully awaiting his capture in the North Woods lake country and while reliving the incidents of Twelfth Lake and Big Bittern during the trial.

My principal interest at this point, however, is to discuss at length two important aspects of the form of *An American Tragedy* which I have as yet only mentioned in passing—Dreiser's narrative voice and his prose style. Dreiser's narrative voice differs little in its basic characteristics from his voice in his other novels. Here, as usual, is an author willing to hector his characters and to engage in general observations on the nature of life. Yet his voice does differ significantly from its earlier presence in degree if not in kind. For example, during the conflict which arises out of Clyde's desire to sleep with Roberta, Dreiser comments, "This contest which every primary union between the sexes, whether with or without marriage implies, was fought out the next day in the factory" (I, 304). And when Sondra's parents succeed in suppressing any mention of her name during the trial, he notes, "That is what a family with money could do for you" (II, 257). But whereas these observations on the universality of sexual warfare and the power of money are here expressed in an independent clause and a brief sentence, in earlier novels they would undoubtedly have extended to at least a paragraph. The impression of many readers that Dreiser is almost absent from *An American Tragedy* as a "philosophical" voice in comparison with his earlier novels derives not from the relative number of his comments but from their brevity. Despite its length, *An American Tragedy* thus has a swifter narrative pace than Dreiser's other novels, with the possible exception of the closing prison section when his general observations resume their familiar length and prominence.

In addition to maintaining in modified form his philosophical asides, Dreiser in *An American Tragedy* is also not reluctant to comment directly on his characters' inadequacies. Clyde, we are told, lacks "mental clarity and inner directing application" (I, 174), has an "immature and really psychically unilluminated mind" (I, 194), is "naturally selfish" (I, 304), has "a soul that was not destined to grow up" (I, 174), and is endowed with a temperament "as fluid and unstable as water" (I, 318). But these comments, though they would appear to prevent us from becoming deeply involved in Clyde's dilemmas and fate, in fact contribute to that involvement. They all occur in Book One and in the early portion of Book Two. With the tightening of the noose of Clyde's difficulties in Book Two, they are replaced by Dreiser's increasingly heavy reliance on indirect discourse as a means of rendering dramatically the pain and terror of Clyde's consciousness. We are thus led by the changes in Dreiser's voice, as well as by the events of Clyde's life which this voice records, from contempt toward compassion.

Dreiser uses the technique of indirect discourse in *An American Tragedy* more fully and with greater subtlety than in any other novel. We sense that *An American Tragedy* is more dramatic than his earlier novels not only because of his obvious preference for "scene" rather than "portrait"—that is, for dramatic action rather than authorial summary—but also because of his extensive use of indirect discourse as a means of seemingly "direct" presentation of a character's thoughts and emotions. I say "seemingly" because the technique of indirect discourse creates an illusion of directness. It is the narrator who is summarizing and expressing the character's inner life, but his shaping of that expression into a prose style and diction appropriate to the character's thoughts and feelings at that moment suggests that we are bypassing the narrator for a direct involvement in the character.

Dreiser's use of indirect discourse to render Clyde's inner life also plays a major role in an important shift in emotional tone in the novel as a whole, a shift which I have already commented upon in noting Dreiser's dropping of his hectoring of Clyde after the opening sections of Book Two.

Early in the novel Dreiser's representation through indirect discourse of Clyde's wondrous response to the Green-Davidson and to Hortense results in much distance between us and Clyde because of the naïveté of his desires. However, as Clyde becomes trapped in the consequences of his ineffectual attempts to fulfill his desires, the technique of indirect discourse results in a gradual narrowing of our sense of distance because our sharing of the immediacy of his pain and frustration is more compelling than our recollection of the superficiality of mind which contributed to his dilemma. For example, when Roberta becomes pregnant, Clyde's initial fear is that Roberta will use her condition to demand marriage. Dreiser represents Clyde's fear through indirect discourse: "But that would be wild of Roberta to expect him to do that. He would not do it. He could not do it. One thing was certain. He must get her out of this. He must! But how? How?" (I, 393). The response which this passage elicits from us, in part through its repetition and parallelism, is less contempt for Clyde, though on reflection we may wish to feel such contempt, than of compassion for a limited mind faced with an overwhelming and seemingly insoluble problem. During the major climactic portions of Book Two and Book Three—Clyde on Big Bittern and Clyde facing imminent death—this technique dominates the narrative mode, since it is ideally suited to capture the intensity of Clyde's feelings and to involve us deeply and sympathetically in those feelings.

Another reason for our sense of the greater presence of the dramatic in *An American Tragedy* arises from Dreiser's adaptation to fiction of various film and theatrical techniques.[69] He had been intensely interested in the theatre from approximately 1913 to 1917, an absorption reflected in his plays of the period and in the dramatic form of the closing political scenes in *The Titan*. And during his years in Los Angeles with Helen, who played in several films, he acquired considerable knowledge of this new form. The theatrical appears in *An American Tragedy* in two ways—a greater reliance upon dialogue than had characterized Dreiser's earlier fiction, and a tendency toward the structuring of scene as setting and action. As far as dialogue is concerned, one has only to compare the trial in *The Financier* with that in *An American Tragedy*. The first contains much authorial description and analysis, the second is principally dialogue. Dreiser's tendency to structure scenes as setting followed by action is present throughout the novel but is revealed most obviously in the opening of the chapter depicting the conference in the governor's office: "The scene was the executive chamber of the newly elected Governor of the State of New York" (II, 396). Dreiser's fictional approximation of camera techniques is present in several key moments in the novel. Clyde and Roberta in the boat are presented to us in a montage of edited "shots" of the two figures which alternates between "close ups" and distant views from a vantage point above the lake. And Clyde entering the courtroom for the first time presses through the crowd rapidly with the crowd depicted from his angle of vision as a blurred image of anonymous hostility.

Despite the extensive editing of *An American Tragedy*, Dreiser's prose is still occasionally hopelessly muddled. Moreover, his dialogue sometimes reveals the same poor ear which led him to a fulsome use of clichés earlier in his career, particularly when he attempts to catch the flavor of collegiate slang of the twenties. But on the whole Dreiser's stylistic solecisms play a minor role in *An American Tragedy* compared to their heavy impact upon the sensitive ear and eye in his earlier novels. The most distinctive feature of Dreiser's prose in *An American Tragedy* is therefore not his clichéd diction or his overuse of a favorite adjective. Rather, it is his successful experimentation with the prose form of the sentence which is incomplete because it lacks a finite verb or complete subject but which is in parallel structure to similarly incomplete adjacent sentences.

It is difficult to determine a specific source for this striking technique, striking not so much in itself but in the extent and variation of its appearance in a very long novel. Dreiser had begun using it in fiction as early as 1919 in stories such as "Chains" in which he depended heavily on indirect discourse to render the consciousness of his central figure, and he also used it about the same time in a series of unpublished poems in which he was experimenting with themes and free verse techniques heavily influenced by Masters's *Spoon River Anthology*. He appears to have associated the technique, as did Virginia Woolf, with an uninterrupted stream of thought and emotion, in which the absence of finite forms and the constant repetition of structure suggest the swift, uncontrolled flow of interior reality. Of course, Dreiser varied both the intensity of the technique and the frequency of its appearance, reserving its most striking appearances for moments of high emotional tension which he was rendering through indirect discourse. The following characteristic example, in which Dreiser describes the brief period of emotional fulfillment and excitement after Clyde has succeeded in sleeping with Roberta, suggests the possible modulations and yet the distinctive rhythm and effect of the technique:

The wonder and delight of a new and more intimate form of contact, of protest gainsaid, of scruples overcome! Days, when both, having struggled in vain against the greater intimacy which each knew that the other was desirous of yielding to, and eventually so yielding, looked forward to the approaching night with an eagerness which was as a fever embodying a fear. For with what qualms—what protests on the part of Roberta; what determination, yet not without a sense of evil—seduction—betrayal, on the part of Clyde. Yet the thing once done, a wild convulsive pleasure motivating both. Yet, not without, before all this, an exaction on the part of Roberta to the effect that never—come what might (the natural consequences of so wild an intimacy strong in her thoughts) would he desert her, since without his aid she would be helpless. Yet, with no direct statement as to marriage. And he, so completely overcome and swayed by his desire, thoughtlessly protesting that he never would—never. She might depend on that, at least, although even then there was no thought in his mind of marriage. He would not do that. Yet nights and nights—all scruples for the time being abandoned, and however much by day Roberta might brood and condemn herself—when each yielded to the other completely. And dreamed thereafter, recklessly and wildly, of the joy of it—wishing from day to day for the time being that the long day might end—that the concealing, rewarding feverish night were at hand. (I, 307)

But Dreiser also used the technique for other purposes. One such use, perhaps borrowed from Whitman, was to suggest the separateness yet underlying unity of items in a descriptive list, as in the third paragraph of the novel:

And up the broad street, now comparatively hushed, a little band of six,—a man of about fifty, short, stout, with bushy hair protruding from under a round black felt hat, a most unimportant-looking person, who carried a small portable organ such as is customarily used by street preachers and singers. And with him a woman perhaps five years his junior, taller, not so broad, but solid of frame and vigorous, very plain in face and dress, and yet not homely, leading with one hand a small boy of seven and in the other carrying a Bible and several hymn books. With these three, but walking independently behind, was a girl of fifteen, a boy of twelve and another girl of nine, all following obediently, but not too enthusiastically, in the wake of the others. (I, 3)

Another was to suggest the swiftness and chaotic intensity of action by beginning a series of paragraphs with the same forward-pushing conjunction, usually an "and," as in the seven pages describing the opening of Clyde's trial (II, 224–30). And occasionally Dreiser will offer a series of parallel short sentence-paragraphs to imply the starkness and violence of the emotions these paragraphs are rendering, as during Clyde's preparations for the death trip and during much of the trip itself. Indeed, the prose of the chapters involving Clyde and Roberta on the lake, with its rich symbolism and its heightened use of parallel sentences to dramatize both the intensity of inner experience and the swiftness of external events, often has a powerful poetic effect.

Dreiser found in this technique not only a flexible and evocative means of rendering emotions and events but also, for the first time in his career, a prose form which imposed a certain discipline and order—that of parallel structure—upon his otherwise muddy prose sense. The form of the novel as a whole exhibits a similar happy combination of control and innovation—that of weaknesses curbed, strengths exploited, and a few successful experimental techniques buoying up the whole. One of the myths about modern American novelists is that they seldom develop. The myth may hold true for many figures, but not for Dreiser. Like Hawthorne's and James's, his career had its climax in the relatively late union of a life-long preoccupation in a compelling theme and a maturing technical capacity to express that theme in all its depth and power—a union which produced a masterpiece.

PART FOUR

The Years Between

TWENTY-ONE YEARS elapsed between the publication of *An American Tragedy* and the appearance of *The Bulwark*. During this period Dreiser was deeply involved in the preparation of a vast philosophical work and in various movements devoted to the achievement of greater social justice. Although it is not my task to describe fully his writing and activities of this phase of his career,[1] it is necessary to summarize the direction of his thought, since both *The Bulwark* and *The Stoic* were heavily influenced by the cast of his ideas during these two decades. It might be best to begin by noting that the great bugbear for many critics of Dreiser has been his intellectual inconsistency, both between his early and later beliefs and between his social and religious ideas during his final years. To many commentators, the Dreiser who believed that life was both a meaningless welter of struggle and a wondrous design of beauty, and the Dreiser who joined the Communist Party while celebrating the spirit of Brahma within every man, was hopelessly muddled as a thinker whatever his "power" as a novelist. But Dreiser's thought is consistent if one accepts the premise that what appears inconsistent in his beliefs is in fact the result of his emphasis, at different times and for different purposes, of ideas which are complementary rather than contradictory.

The basic paradoxes and shifting emphases in Dreiser's thought have their permanent center in his belief that life is a mechanistic equation or balance. Within this opposition of forces—good and evil, strength and weakness, riches and poverty—there is constant flux in which the individual counts for nought as opposites seek, but never achieve, balance. But though this never-ending struggle may terrify and crush the individual, it benefits the race and has as well a symmetry and beauty of design which suggests the presence of a vast underlying spirit both as its source and as its essential nature. Dreiser's basic shift in the course of his career was from a stress on the destructiveness, turmoil, and impersonality of the "formula" which is life to an emphasis on its wonder, beauty, and beneficence. Put metaphorically, he moved from a stress upon man as a blind figure chained to a huge, relentless engine to man as a figure who, while still chained to the engine, can nevertheless admire its intricate beauty and stand in awe at the power of its maker. Put in terms of Dreiser's characters, he shifted from Carrie's pathetic discovery that we are never satisfied in our pursuit of beauty to Solon's and Berenice's triumphant discovery of the still center of beauty in the underlying design and order of the processes of life of which we are a part. And finally, in social terms, he moved from a stress upon the impossibility of changing the qualities of human nature which are the source of struggle and flux to an emphasis upon the possibility and need of changing the social organism which can control the expression of human nature and thus lessen the extremes of variation with the equation.

Dreiser's central ideas resemble those of many late nineteenth-century thinkers—Spencer, Haeckel, and Wallace, for example[2]—whose cosmologies were informed initially by a desire to destroy a conception of the universe and man as supernaturally sanctioned and who therefore posited a world of natural law in which man is but an insignificant tool in the hands of vast impersonal forces. But these very laws, because of qualities of symmetry and purposeful direction attributed to them, became—by implication in Spencer and more directly in Haeckel and Wallace—metaphoric equivalents of the pantheism of romantic philosophy, in which God is immanent in the laws and substance of nature. In the writings of Spencer, Haeckel, and Wallace, Dreiser encountered early in his career both an attack on the old teleology and an affirmation of a "new" universe of order, purpose, and spiritual unity. The chronology of Dreiser's response to this dual emphasis in the cosmologies he absorbed in his youth was first to echo the attack but then, later in life, to stress the affirmation. Born and bred a Catholic in a secular age, his rejection of religion in his young manhood led him to accept naturalistic philosophies without diminishing the powerful will to believe at the center of his being.

From as early as the mid-1890s, Dreiser's notion of the world as struggle also contained a thread of wonder at the underlying design of nature, a thread which ultimately became the dominant strand in his thought. For example, he wrote in one of his *Ev'ry Month* columns of 1896:

A system which involves the regulation of countless sidereal systems and which shapes at the same time the material form of a mustard seed is to be trusted. Where countless forms are everywhere evident, each organized after a fashion wondrously adapted to surrounding conditions and each so admirable in the details of its economy, an over-ruling and kindly direction is implied. If the evident force in everything is not so directed, then why should it assume such multifarious forms, and why should each form resolve itself into such admirably arranged details? Force is but force, and if not regulated for a purpose, why need it bloom as a rose yonder, drift as a cloud there, flow as a brook through the grassy meadows or walk as a human in all the charm and radiance of manhood. . . .

Therefore, in the face of the countless calamities that assail mankind without let or hindrance, it must reasonably be contended, that while some men like some mustard seeds and some stars, may not be especially preserved from the destroying onslaught of superior forces, yet all such contending forms, both great and small, must conform to the laws of growth, form and duration, and this, if nothing more, would indicate that over all rules a Being, and that in His wondrous superiority, He is not unmindful of the least of His creatures.[3]

During most of Dreiser's career as a novelist, these two qualities of mind—the desire to destroy the old supernaturalism and its accompanying system of morality, and the desire to affirm a new supernaturalism and a morality of beauty—coexist in his thought as alternative but not mutually exclusive responses to experience. By the late 1920s, however, Dreiser's "reverence before the beauty and wisdom of creative energy"[4] began to be the dominant force in his thought. Loeb's mechanism, for all its usefulness as a confirmation of some of Dreiser's own mechanistic ideas, had proved incomplete because it failed to acknowledge the presence of a "constructive or commanding force" behind and within the laws of life.[5] So for over fifteen years, from the late 1920s to the early 1940s, Dreiser devoted much of his time and energy to gathering a mass of scientific and pseudoscientific data which supported his beliefs and to organizing this material into a large-scale philosophical work which would demonstrate both the insignificance of man and the wonder and beauty of the process of which he was a part.

Dreiser at various times called his book of philosophy "The Formula

Called Life," "The Illusion Called Life," "The Mechanism Called Man," and "Notes on Life." It occupies thirty-six manuscript boxes (many of which contain primarily notes and clippings) and remained incomplete at his death, though he did publish a number of its essays in various magazines during the 1930s and a selection from his manuscripts has also recently been published.[6] In some ways the book was to be an extension of *Hey Rub-a-Dub-Dub*, as is suggested by Dreiser's intent to open with "The Essential Tragedy of Life" and close with "Equation Inevitable," two essays which had appeared in *Hey Rub-a-Dub-Dub*.[7] But the principal direction of the book was to be an affirmation rather than a questioning of life. This shift is perhaps best noted not in the diffuse and involuted prose of the essays themselves, but in some of Dreiser's more concise statements in letters and in brief published remarks about his state of mind during this period. For example, in 1929 he wrote in "What I Believe" that "in spite of all this mechanistic response which disposes of the soul or entity, and in spite of obvious cruelty, brutality, envy, hatred, murder, deceit, and what not else, I still rise to testify to the aesthetic perfection of this thing that I see here and which we call Life."[8] Life to Dreiser had become perfect in its underlying design, and this vision contained as well a belief in the unity, worth, and purpose of experience which is the corollary of a mystic awareness of cosmic perfection. By the early 1940s, Dreiser frequently expressed this vision of life in its full quasireligious form. God, in the guise of creative energy, pervaded all life but was manifest most clearly to those, like the Quakers or Hindus or like Dreiser himself when admiring a flower or conversing with a snake, who faced life with the searching but intuitive faith of a mystic.[9]

Dreiser's social ideas underwent an analogous broad reorientation. For most of his career until the late 1920s, he was contemptuous—when not tied down by the obligatory do-goodism of popular journalism—of efforts at reform which ignored the irredeemable Adam in man's evolutionary nature. "Don't forget," he wrote to Upton Sinclair in 1924, "that the brotherhood of man . . . is mere moonshine to me. I see the individual large or small, weak or strong, as predatory and nothing less."[10] Yet coexistent with Dreiser's ready willingness to attack those he considered starry-eyed reformers was a broadly based sympathy with the aspiration and needs of the mass of men despite their weaknesses and limitations. He was no doubt also characterizing himself when he wrote of Cowperwood in *The Titan* that "individualistic and even anarchistic in character, and without a shred of true democracy, yet temperamentally he was in sympathy with the mass of men more than he was with the class, and he understood the mass better" (p. 27).

By the late 1920s, this predisposition united with Dreiser's increasing responsiveness to specific instances of social injustice to lead him to concern himself less with the impossibility of changing human nature and more with the possibility of ameliorating the effects of unrestrained greed and power. As early as *A Hoosier Holiday*, he had written, "I know the strong must rule the weak, the big brain the little one, but why not some small approximation toward equilibrium, just a slightly less heavily loaded table for Dives and a few more crumbs for Lazarus?"[11] This "approximation toward equilibrium," Dreiser began to argue in the 1930s, could be achieved by recognizing that society was not merely a static reflection of the permanent in human nature but was also an evolving organism. In a key article on "Individualism and the Jungle," which emerged out of his participation in the Harlan County coal strike of 1931, he wrote that society really

cannot be a jungle. It should be and is, if it is a social organism worthy of the name, an escape from this drastic individualism which, for some, means all, and for the many, little or nothing. And consciously or unconsciously, it is by Nature and evolution intended as such, for certainly the thousands-of-years-old growth of organized society augurs desire on the part of Nature to avoid the extreme and bloody individualism of the jungle.[12]

Dreiser argued in his social writing of this phase of his career that though life was indeed a struggle, the social context of this conflict had evolved to a point at which greater "equity"—that is, less extreme instances of imbalance in the equation inevitable—could and should be achieved. And to those who attacked Dreiser's desire for modification of the "natural" as inconsistent with his own mechanism, he replied that the desire for reform and social justice was itself a mechanistic response by the mass of men to the excessive power and wealth of the few.[13]

Both Dreiser's philosophical and his social ideas thus underwent a parallel movement from a stress on the limitations of man's understanding and volition because of the mechanistic nature of life to an emphasis on the opportunities for insight and action within a mechanistic universe. So at the end of his career Dreiser was able to endorse Quaker and Hindu belief on the one hand and to join the Communist Party on the other without a sense of contradiction either between these acts or between them and his earlier beliefs. His completion of *The Bulwark* and *The Stoic* during the last years of his life, decades after he had written the bulk of these novels, causes them to be anomalous yet intriguing metaphors of his intellectual history. For in his depiction of the beliefs of Solon and Berenice at the close of each novel he represented not the inevitable development of their own characters as they had originally been conceived and still in large part were but rather his own final beliefs, beliefs which he projected into his dramatic figures as a last testament in lieu of his incomplete philosophical study.

The Bulwark

DREISER BEGAN WORK on *The Bulwark* in the fall of 1914 and completed the novel in May 1945.[1] Because the history of the composition of *The Bulwark* extends over thirty years and comprises some fifteen boxes of manuscript, it might be best to begin with two general observations about the genesis of the book before pursuing the subject in greater detail. First, Dreiser's work on the novel divides into two distinct phases, from 1914 to 1920 and from 1942 to 1945, though there were also many stops and starts within these phases. Second, his conception of the setting, plot, and characters of the novel remained for the most part unchanged from 1914 to 1945, but his idea of its themes and form underwent considerable modification, principally because of a basic shift in his beliefs and interests between the 1914–20 period and the early 1940s.

The novel has a Jamesian origin in the sense that its principal source was an anecdotal account of a family told to Dreiser by a friend. In November 1911, just before leaving for Europe, Dreiser had received an enthusiastic letter about *Jennie Gerhardt* from Anna Tatum, a young girl of Pennsylvania Quaker background. A correspondence followed, but Miss Tatum and Dreiser did not meet until the fall of 1912. It must have been soon after this initial meeting that she told Dreiser the story of her father's life, for by January 1913, Dreiser was telling Edgar Lee Masters in Chicago of his plan for a novel based on the personal and business disasters of a Quaker who attempts to preserve a rigid faith in the face of a rising tide of modernism in his children and in his business affairs.[2]

Miss Tatum's story appealed strongly to Dreiser for several reasons. One obvious attraction was that her father's life strikingly complemented the life of Yerkes which Dreiser was at that time busily interpreting in *The Titan.* In one story, a conservative Philadelphia Quaker ineffectually attempts to hold back change, while in the other a Philadelphian of conservative background (indeed, Yerkes himself—though not Cowperwood—had been of Quaker stock) adapts to the amorality of life and of his own desires and rises to great power. Masters, who was himself a religious iconoclast, recalled that Dreiser had intended for "ironic portrayal" his story of "the good man who loved God and kept his commandments, and for a time prospered and then went into disaster."[3] But though Dreiser from the first intended to show Solon crushed and defeated despite the bulwark of his faith, he in fact wished to leaven irony with compassion. He wanted to render the tragedy of a good and feeling man who is trapped by his outmoded and blinding beliefs—the kind of tragedy he had already depicted in the comparatively minor figures of old Gerhardt and Edward Butler. Kirah Markham comes closer to suggesting the emotional tone of Dreiser's interest in the story when she recalled that Dreiser was profoundly moved and absorbed in late 1914 as he was "pouring out to me the soul agony of this Quaker."[4]

The underlying source of Dreiser's compassionate involvement in Gerhardt, Butler, and now Solon was, of course, his deeply ambivalent attitude toward his father. Like his father, Solon was to be someone who "must stick to his belief and yet be utterly crushed and defeated by the disasters which overtake him, because of his refusal to accept life 'realistically.' "[5] During Dreiser's boyhood and youth, he had bitterly resented his father's arbitrary and blind attempts to control his life. But as a young newspaperman in St. Louis, his attitude softened as he began to sense the disappointment and despair which were the products of his father's failure to shape and direct the lives of his errant children. He saw John Dreiser now as "a warm, generous, and yet bigoted and ignorant soul, led captive in his childhood to a brainless theory and having no power within himself to break the chain." On a trip to Chicago during the summer of 1893, he found his father old and lonely. As the two sat and talked, the one a "broken old man whose hopes and ambitions had come to nothing," the other a young man full of hopes and ambitions, the tragedy of life struck them fully and they began to cry.[6] Dreiser told Mrs. Marguerite Tjader Harris in 1944 that he had had in his mind from his earliest conception of the novel Etta's famous reply at its close, "I am crying for *life*," a claim borne out by his 1914 synopsis.[7] The line has echoes in other passages in Dreiser—in *The "Genius"* (p. 593) and in his play "The Spring Recital"[8]—but its principal source is undoubtedly that 1893 meeting when Dreiser and his father had wept over the universal tragedy of life contained in the misdirected love and thwarted hopes of a parent.

Another major reason for the appeal of Miss Tatum's story was that Dreiser saw in Miss Tatum herself a further example of the kind of seeking temperament he had already portrayed in Carrie and Jennie. She and Dreiser lived together intermittently for about a year and a half, from late 1912 to early 1914, when Kirah Markham took preeminence in Dreiser's personal life. As depicted by Dreiser in the figure of "Elizabeth" in a long 1929 sketch[9] as well as in Etta in *The Bulwark* itself, Miss Tatum was a woman of courage and sensibility. And in the character of Stewart, Dreiser found the equally moving figure of a youth whose deeply sensual nature leads him to rebel with tragic consequences against his parents' blind resistance to his needs. Indeed, the Barnes family as a whole is a semi-idealized version of Dreiser's own family—the strict religiosity of the father, the warmth of the mother, the children seeking the world in a spectrum ranging from the aesthetic and sexual to the social and material. The similarity which many readers have noticed between members of the Barnes family and Dreiser's fictional characters elsewhere derives not from his borrowing from his own work but from the common source of his characterizations in himself and his family. No wonder, then, that Dreiser was so moved by Miss Tatum's story and that he labored so long to write a novel based upon it. For its major theme of the irresistible tragic tensions which arise within a family as parents and children ally themselves with the past and present and as they seek as well both to affirm their basic natures and to maintain their love for each other was the deeply resonant paradigm of that which had been most compelling in his own experience.

The themes, characters, and basic plot of the novel were therefore well in hand from the first.[10] In addition, Dreiser's research into Yerkes's career had left him with a firm sense of the Philadelphia setting and of late nineteenth-century financial life.[11] What he needed was information to fill in the Quaker background of the Barneses and time to write the book. He began work on the first in early 1914, acquiring books on Quakerism and making several trips to the Philadelphia area.[12] The second became available in the fall of 1914, with *The Titan* published and *The "Genius"* requiring only minor revision before publication.

Dreiser worked sporadically on *The Bulwark* for the next six years but failed to complete the novel. The underlying reason for this failure was perhaps best stated by Dreiser himself in a letter to William Lengel in 1942, in which he explained his slow progress on the work at that time, an explanation which is applicable as well to Dreiser's thirty-year effort to write the novel. The book "is a very intimate and touchy problem in connection with religious family life," he wrote, "and . . . I find it difficult."[13] But during the 1914–20 period there were also a series of more immediate reasons, ranging from Dreiser's need to produce quickly more salable work to his frequent spells of gloominess over the prospect of achieving a popular success in the novel after the failure of *The Financier* and *The Titan* and the suppression of *The "Genius."* So, after a start during the winter of 1914–15, Dreiser put aside *The Bulwark* to work on short stories, plays, autobiographies, and *A Hoosier Holiday*. He fully expected, however, to complete the novel during the winter of 1915–16, and in response to this expectation John Lane prepared a salesman's dummy of the book which specified a 1916 publication.[14] But the winter was preempted by pressing personal affairs—illness and romance—and in the summer of 1916 there occurred the crushing and time-consuming suppression of *The "Genius."* Dreiser returned to *The Bulwark* in December 1916, and once again John Lane announced its publication, this time for the spring of 1917.[15] A full effort by Dreiser during the summer of 1917, in concert with his secretary Estelle Kubitz, still failed to produce the work. And with the collapse shortly thereafter of Dreiser's relationship with John Lane because of *The "Genius"* controversy, he again put the novel aside to work on sketches, plays, and short stories. In 1919, his new publisher Horace Liveright began to prod him to complete *The Bulwark*. Armed with an advance, Dreiser worked on the novel during 1920 while in California with Helen before putting it aside late in the year to undertake his first version of *An American Tragedy*.

Dreiser's work on *The Bulwark* during this six-year period survives in four forms: a plot synopsis, prepared before he began to write the novel; fragments of the holograph version of 1914–16; a twenty-seven-chapter carbon of the typescript version of late 1916–summer 1917;[16] and miscellaneous fragments of his 1920 efforts. The synopsis of the novel, typed on yellow half sheets, is of considerable interest. As planned initially by

Dreiser, the novel was to be forty-five chapters long. It would open with Solon's wedding and then shift immediately, in Chapter II, to the births of Solon's children. By Chapter V the various conflicts between Solon and his children have emerged. Each child is summarized much as he or she appears in the published novel, though there are some minor variations. Solon's business affairs are also somewhat more melodramatic in the synopsis and involve a transaction in which he unwittingly becomes a front man for unscrupulous western financiers. But the principal difference between the synopsis and the published novel is that the synopsis lacks any provision for accounts either of Solon's early life or of his final renewal of religious faith. Put simply, much of Dreiser's work on *The Bulwark* between his initial conception of the novel in 1914 and his completion of it in 1945 involved his attempts to shape satisfactory versions of Solon's early experience and final months around the comparatively permanent center of his family and business disappointments.

This process began with the draft Dreiser worked on intermittently between 1914 and 1916. The novel, as revealed by the surviving holograph fragments from this period, still begins with the wedding and is still devoted primarily to Solon's business and family life. But it now also contains a number of chapters immediately after the wedding in which Dreiser goes back in time to describe Solon's young manhood in Pennsylvania. In particular, Dreiser depicts at some length Solon's home life, his initial business experiences, and his courtship of Benecia. (In this and other early versions Benecia is called Cornelia.) Dreiser's interest in expanding his narrative of Solon's youth is revealed even more clearly in the twenty-seven chapters of the novel he completed in the summer of 1917. In this version, the wedding is postponed to Chapter XII, and the first eleven chapters are devoted to a detailed representation of Solon's Pennsylvania boyhood from the age of twelve to his marriage some ten years later. As in his later dramatization of a tragic event in *An American Tragedy*, Dreiser's initial interest had been in the event itself—in *The Bulwark* the revolt of Solon's children, in *An American Tragedy* the love triangle and murder. But in both instances he was soon moved to reconstruct imaginatively the moral and psychological setting out of which emerged a tragic figure—the Kansas City of Clyde's boyhood, the semirural closed religious and social world of Solon's youth which had conditioned and hardened a basically conservative temperament.

Dreiser's work on *The Bulwark* during 1920 is difficult to describe because his manuscripts of this period are widely dispersed in fragmentary form both among later drafts and among synthetic gatherings dealing with specific characters or events which he and Mrs. Marguerite Tjader Harris prepared when they worked on the novel in 1944. But as far as can be determined from these fragments and other earlier and later manuscript evidence, Dreiser's efforts during 1920 centered on returning the novel to its original structure of beginning with Solon's wedding, on cutting much of the excessive financial detail of the 1917 version, and on bringing forward the narrative to the point at which Solon is about to suffer the major blows of Etta's defection, Stewart's crime, and the collapse of his banking career.

As characterized in Dreiser's 1914–20 drafts of *The Bulwark*, Solon Barnes is a true believer who has unthinkingly accepted the absolutes of formal religion. Dreiser's tone toward Solon is often as biting as that which he had used to describe old Gerhardt's rigid religious beliefs in the opening sections of *Jennie Gerhardt*. Solon in the 1917 draft is "your true religionistic or philosophically speculative mind, without, however, any definite power of clarifying what he saw."[17] It is Solon's wont, Dreiser tells us, "to turn away from the hard cruel facts of life, viewing them more through the pale staining colors of religion and morality or fancy."[18] Perhaps Dreiser's tone in these early drafts is caught most clearly in his characterization of Justus Wallin. Wallin in the 1917 version is not the generous-spirited figure of the published novel who struggles with some honesty to reconcile his wealth and his Quaker belief. He is rather "just a mediocre brain invested with considerable commercial ability, and interested to fit all life into the moral groove which he personally was capable of understanding."[19]

When Dreiser completed *An American Tragedy* in late 1925, he had in mind three enterprises: revision of *The Financier* and completion of *The Bulwark* and *The Stoic*. Of these, it was initially *The Bulwark* which had priority, for he sent Louise Campbell a new plot outline to copy in November 1925.[20] But by January 1926 he was alternating between plans to revise *The Financier* and to complete *The Stoic*. And though he provided Mrs. Campbell in March with two old manuscript versions of *The Bulwark* to look over—apparently the 1914–16 and 1917 versions, according to her later recollections—and then questioned her about the structure of the novel, *The Financier* and then a number of other projects did indeed take precedence, until both Mrs. Campbell and Dreiser forgot that the manuscripts were in her possession.[21] By the late 1920s, *The Bulwark* took its place among those works which Dreiser hoped to complete whenever time and interest coincided.

Dreiser did not work on *The Bulwark* for over twenty years after his efforts of 1920. When he did return to the novel in early 1942, it was with a very different attitude toward the "true religionistic or philosophically speculative mind," one which led him to reshape both the opening and the close of the novel and to reject almost entirely his earlier authorial tone. I have already discussed briefly the broad shift in Dreiser's philosophical and social views between *An American Tragedy* and *The Bulwark*. But it is also necessary to comment on several specific events of the late 1930s which influenced the revision of *The Bulwark*.

The most significant of these events occurred in September 1938, when Dreiser met Rufus Jones, the eminent Quaker historian.[22] During the 1930s Dreiser had been increasingly impressed by the ability of many Quakers to unite an active social conscience and a mystical religiosity free of dogma.[23] In Jones, who was a leader of the Hicksite schism within the Society of Friends and whom he was seeing on matters connected with Spanish War relief, he encountered a stimulating embodiment of this ability and was immediately moved to learn more about Jones and his ideas. Within two months, he had acquired and read the second volume of Jones's *The Later Periods of Quakerism* (1921) and two of Jones's autobiographies, *Finding the Trail of Life* (1926) and *The Trail of Life in the Middle Years* (1934).[24] Jones's accounts of the Quakers and of his own spiritual history were closely allied to the direction which Dreiser now wished to give *The Bulwark*. For Jones had devoted much of his life to attacking the spiritually limited and tradition-bound Quakerism which characterized Solon and to calling for a return to a primitive Quakerism which affirmed man's capacity to discover intuitively his oneness with God, a return which Dreiser now wished Solon to make as well. Dreiser saw, in other words, that Jones's account of the history of Quakerism could be Solon's own history—its origins in the powerful intuitive faith of a simple and humble people, its decline in the nineteenth century to a dependence on regulation of dress and behavior accompanied by an increasing acceptance of worldly success, and its need to return to a faith which was rooted in the individual's sense of Godhead within himself and immanent in all other life.

Dreiser was particularly attracted by passages in Jones's books which stressed the presence of a creative force in all life which man could grasp and know. In *The Trail of Life in the Middle Years*, for example, he marked

Jones's recollection that "I had thoroughly outgrown the sky-god conception, the absentee deity of the eighteenth century, which ought to have died with Ptolemaic astronomy, and I was captivated with the idea of a resident, permeative divine Spirit working within the world and within the life of man."[25] Dreiser also read in January 1939 the *Journal* of John Woolman, the eighteenth-century American Quaker abolitionist and mystic, in an edition with an introduction by John Greenleaf Whittier. In both the *Journal* and Whittier's introduction, he found an appealing emphasis on Woolman's intuitive faith in a creed of love which was at one with the divine spirit pervading all life and which should be translated into social action. Although neither Jones nor Woolman was a pantheistic mechanist, Dreiser was moved by their faith in man's ability to intuit and make operative the spiritual meaning of life in a context of undogmatic humanitarianism. He thus had little difficulty viewing Jones's symbol of the divine spirit, God, as similar to his own, Nature. When Jones wrote, "I was convinced that this inner spirit of simplicity springs out of a unique fellowship with God," Dreiser circled "God" and wrote "Nature" in the margin.[26]

Whittier, in his introduction, had pointed out that both Woolman and Thoreau believed that man's spiritual integrity often required that he actively resist the pressures of the world. By a coincidence, Dreiser himself had had the opportunity only a few months earlier to discover other similarities between Thoreau's transcendentalism and Quaker faith. Commissioned to prepare a volume on Thoreau in *The Living Thoughts* series, he read some of Thoreau's most vital work in the fall of 1938, and, at about the same time he was reading Jones's books, wrote a long introduction for his volume of selections.[27] Thoreau, like Jones, confirmed the direction of Dreiser's thought during the previous decade. In particular, Dreiser was attracted by what he called Thoreau's affirmation of a "universal, artistic, constructive genius" beneath the apparent harshness and cruelty of natural life.[28] In Thoreau, Dreiser found Jones's faith in man's transcendental power stated in a context which most moved him—that of a "scientific" student of the laws of nature who discovers the underlying beauty and benevolence of these laws and who therefore intuits a divine spirit inherent in them and in nature. Indeed, during the 1930s Dreiser had not only studied nature scientifically, as had Thoreau, but had also had several transcendental encounters with particular natural objects. In the summer of 1936, he had spoken in kindness to a puff adder at Iroki (his Mt. Kisco home) and had felt that he had been understood.[29] And the following summer, while staying at the Cold Springs Harbor Marine Biological Laboratory, he had, in a moment of insight, sensed in a common flower "the same *design*, the same beautiful detail that he had been observing in the tiny forms under the glass [of the microscope]. What care, what love—had created these things. Not only some great intelligence, but a careful, loving Artist."[30]

When Dreiser revised and completed *The Bulwark* in the 1940s, he adapted these events of the late 1930s into the fictional expression of his new attitude toward religious faith. He introduced a section on Solon's Maine boyhood in which he drew heavily on Jones's autobiography for such details as the axe wound infection and the portrayal of Solon's parents, and he borrowed from Woolman's *Journal* the incident of Solon killing a bird. He attempted to capture in this new material the primitive but pure faith which Jones had depicted both in his own Quaker youth in Maine and in the early period of Quakerism. In writing the close of the novel, though he introduced the importance of Woolman's *Journal* in strengthening Solon's realization of the intuitive source of Quaker belief, he nevertheless made Solon's renewal of faith more Dreiserian than Quaker. In incidents similar to those of Dreiser at Iroki and Cold Springs Harbor, Solon regains his Quaker belief in a spirit of love pervading all life. But his faith is basically the distinctively Dreiserian one of awe and wonder at the design of beauty and utility beneath the apparent cruelty and tragedy of nature and of all life.

≪≪≪≪≪≪≪≪≪≪≪≪≪≪≪≪≪≪≪≪≪≪≪≪≪≪≪≪≪≪≪

There were a number of reasons why Dreiser, after a lapse of over twenty years, decided in 1941 to complete *The Bulwark*. He was growing doubtful that he would ever finish his massive philosophical study. He had a sense of economic well-being because of the sale of the film rights of *Sister Carrie*. His interest in Quakerism had been stimulated by his reading of Jones's books and his work on Thoreau. And after many years of disagreement with Simon and Schuster, he was being urged by his friend William Lengel to begin his relationship with his new publisher, Putnam's, with a long-awaited novel after over fifteen years' silence in fiction since *An American Tragedy*. In March 1941, Dreiser signed a contract with Putnam's which called for delivery of the manuscript of *The Bulwark* in June 1942, though illness and the outbreak of the war led him to postpone work on the novel until March 1942. He worked intermittently on *The Bulwark* until March 1943, when he once again put it aside after having completed a new draft of most of Part One.[31] Drawing heavily and explicitly on Jones's recollections, he included in this draft a number of introductory chapters in which he portrayed Solon's Maine boyhood.[32] He then began yet again his narrative of Solon's early life in Dukla and had reached Chapter XXXV (Chapter 18 of the published work), when he began to despair of ever completing the novel. Over seventy-one and in poor health, he felt that he could not continue without expert and full-time editorial aid and encouragement.

Fortunately, Dreiser found such an editor in Mrs. Marguerite Tjader Harris, whom he met again in May 1944, while visiting New York to receive an award from the American Academy of Arts and Letters, and whom he persuaded to join him in Los Angeles in order to complete *The Bulwark*. He had met Mrs. Harris in 1928, when she aided him in the editorial preparation of his *Gallery of Women* sketches. They had remained friends throughout the 1930s; Mrs. Harris worked for Dreiser on occasion, and he contributed articles to her left-wing magazine *Direction*. In 1944, Mrs. Harris had three invaluable attributes insofar as completion of *The Bulwark* was concerned. She was a professional editor; she had her own means of support and was free; and she shared Dreiser's beliefs in the mystical foundation of religion and in the need for social reform. With Mrs. Harris, Dreiser's career as a novelist comes full circle, for her expertise, encouragement, and congenial temperament recapitulated his relationship with Arthur Henry forty-five years earlier.

Dreiser's work with Mrs. Harris on *The Bulwark*, from her arrival in Los Angeles in August 1944 to the completion of the novel in early May 1945, comprised four stages. They began by editing and revising all of Dreiser's previously written material.[33] This first stage was perhaps the most difficult, and in order to aid their efforts they arranged much of Dreiser's earlier work in packets, with each collection of manuscript devoted to a particular character or narrative sequence. From these packets either a new version was distilled or a particular earlier version was chosen for revision and inclusion. With this task completed, and with Dreiser fully in touch with the novel again, he dictated its concluding portions on Etta's departure for Wisconsin and her Greenwich Village affair with Willard

Kane, on Stewart's crime and suicide, and on Solon's decline, "conversion," and death. Dreiser then cut drastically his 1942–43 work on Part
One and completed this portion of the novel. Finally, both Mrs. Harris and
Dreiser revised the full rough draft of the novel before a final typescript
was prepared.[34] This clean typescript of the draft consisted of 577 pages.
Dreiser lightly revised the original and Mrs. Harris entered his revisions on
the two carbons.

Although Dreiser and Mrs. Harris had edited *The Bulwark* in both its
rough and final typescript forms, Dreiser felt that it would profit from
further editing by Mrs. Campbell, with whom he had worked so closely
during the twenties on *An American Tragedy* and the shortened version of
The Financier. Of the three typescripts of the novel, Dreiser in early May
sent the original to his Doubleday editor, Donald Elder (Doubleday had in
1945 become the fourth publisher to contract for *The Bulwark*), and a
carbon to Mrs. Campbell, keeping the second carbon for himself. There
then followed, until Dreiser finally returned galley proof to Elder in
December 1945, a complicated long-distance debate over the novel involving Dreiser, Mrs. Harris, Mrs. Campbell, Helen, Donald Elder, and
James T. Farrell.[35] Mrs. Campbell, who knew nothing of Mrs. Harris's
participation in the book until after Dreiser's death, thought that the novel
was the work of a sick man and was "appalled at its stretches of banality"
and its structural and stylistic deficiencies.[36] Warned by Helen, however,
that Dreiser's spirits needed pumping up if he were to finish *The Stoic*, she
merely wrote him that she thought that the novel needed extensive revision
and asked whether he wished her to proceed. Dreiser replied that she
should send the novel to Farrell, who was a warm admirer of Dreiser's
work. He then wrote to Farrell, summarizing Mrs. Campbell's opinion and
asking for his own.[37] A worrisome delay of over a month followed until
Farrell had a chance to read the manuscript in late June, and in the
meantime Elder himself had suggested to Dreiser the possibility of some
cutting. Farrell disagreed with Mrs. Campbell's estimation of *The Bulwark*
but felt that the novel would benefit from careful editing. After consulting
with Mrs. Campbell by telephone (he and Elder were in New York, Mrs.
Campbell in Philadelphia, and Dreiser, Helen, and Mrs. Harris in Los
Angeles), he returned the carbon to her and wrote Dreiser a twelve-page
typewritten letter in which he outlined his suggestions for revision.[38]
Dreiser was now deeply involved in his attempt to complete *The Stoic* and
was also in poor health. He therefore advised Mrs. Campbell to use her

own judgment in editing the novel and also sent her Farrell's long letter as a further guide. [39] Late in July she sent Dreiser sixty pages of edited text for approval, and when he found them satisfactory she continued her labors, completing her work in late August. [40]

Mrs. Campbell's revisions were principally of three kinds: much cutting of detail, simplification of Dreiser's prose style, and considerable cutting of entire incidents and of Dreiser's authorial commentary. In particular, she found objectionable Dreiser's religious and nature mysticism as well as his characterization of his women figures and did much rewriting and cutting of material of this kind. Her revision of the carbon was so extensive that she made a new typescript of the entire novel, and it was this new version—with the novel reduced from 577 to 415 pages—that she sent Dreiser for approval. After reading it and making scarcely any changes, Dreiser thanked her for her excellent work, sent the new version to Elder, and asked Elder for the return of the original typescript. [41]

Early in September 1945, Elder found himself with two different texts of the novel. He was now aware that Mrs. Harris had worked with Dreiser on the original version, that Mrs. Campbell was fully responsible for the second version, and that Dreiser's interests had turned from *The Bulwark* to *The Stoic*. After considering the two versions carefully, he wrote Dreiser on September 20 asking permission to edit the novel once again in order to include "such changes of Mrs. Campbell's as seem to me suitable, but putting back much that she has eliminated and restoring the pace of your style to its original tempo." [42] Dreiser granted this request, [43] and Elder—after conferring several times with Farrell (though Farrell himself never participated directly in the editing)—went ahead. He wrote Farrell on October 11, "I have put back the first four or five chapters almost exactly as Dreiser wrote them with only certain editing for style, and I am going over the two manuscripts page-by-page, putting back some very important material." [44] Elder's rejection of Mrs. Campbell's editing, however, was not as complete as this letter would suggest. As he recalled in a letter to Robert Elias in 1949, "I am not sure that it is accurate to say that I discarded Mrs. Campbell's alterations. As I remember it, what I did was to put back a great deal that she had cut out of Dreiser's version. . . . Mrs. Campbell's alterations were largely omissions. She made a great many very good alterations when she tried to clarify the narrative, and I didn't discard many of those." [45] In fact, Elder preserved intact almost two-thirds of Mrs. Campbell's typescript. He added to this, primarily at the opening and close of the novel, about 130 fair-copy pages containing his own revision of Mrs. Campbell's revision and about twenty-five pages of the original typescript submitted by Mrs. Harris and Dreiser. This pastiche manuscript struck a rough mean of 478 pages between the 577 of the original and the approximately 415 of Mrs. Campbell's version. Dreiser apparently did not see the Elder version of *The Bulwark* until he received it in galley-proof form in December 1945. He returned the galleys with only minor revisions and praised Elder for his work.[46]

As was not infrequent in Dreiser's career, the tensions and rivalries generated by his feminine attachments during this period played a role in the composition and editing of *The Bulwark*, though perhaps to a greater degree in this instance because of Dreiser's greater dependence on feminine aid during this last phase of his career. Helen had helped Dreiser with the novel during 1942–43 and was antagonistic toward Mrs. Harris, while Mrs. Harris felt that the novel drew its strength from the religious values which she and Dreiser shared and that an "outsider," such as Mrs. Campbell, would emasculate the book. After the publication of Elder's version, these resentments hardened into attitudes toward the quality of the novel. Mrs. Harris claimed that the editing subsequent to her work with Dreiser had weakened the book,[47] while Mrs. Campbell, backed by Helen, believed that her efforts were responsible for the narrative clarity and force of the novel.[48] In fact, the key figure in the editing of *The Bulwark* was Elder, for it was he who played the decisive role of adjudicator of suggested revisions, a role which Dreiser himself usually played. The Harris version was indeed flabby, as Dreiser, Farrell, and Elder agreed, but Mrs. Campbell had cut too much. With the two versions before him, Elder could distinguish between cut material which had been judiciously omitted and cut material which contributed significantly to the themes and pace of the novel. On the whole, Elder performed this task with taste and discrimination. For example, he wisely failed to restore such repetitive or insignificant material as Solon's initial concern over Wallin's wealth, Orville's killing of a cat, and Stewart's boyish misadventures and adolescent longings. Perhaps only in his preservation of Mrs. Campbell's omission of Dreiser's comments on Stewart's and Etta's rejection of Quakerism and on Solon's attitude toward his business career after Stewart's death could one quarrel with his decisions.

The Bulwark adversely reflects the history of its prolonged and complicated genesis in two important ways. First, because Dreiser in effect imposed his later beliefs on earlier material, the book breaks in two both thematically and structurally. The central portion of the novel, from Solon's early career in Dukla to the death of Stewart, is the narrative of a family gradually torn apart by the failure of the father to respond to the realities of change and of human nature because of his blind and rigid faith. This section no longer contains the bitterness and mockery of Dreiser's earlier tone, but it remains a chroniclelike account of Solon's business affairs and of the experiences of his five children. The sections of the novel that Dreiser wrote primarily in the 1940s—those involving Solon's early life in Maine and his final revitalized faith—not only focus primarily on Solon himself but on the permanent center of his religious belief: a profound emotional and spirit-renewing acceptance of the beauty and beneficence at the heart of the created design which is life. One tragic theme in the novel is that of time, of life moving past a man and leaving him with an inoperative and destructive code of belief. The other is the timeless duality of life, the essential delight of the design which is existence despite the pain and death inseparable from that design. These themes are of course related in that the passage of time is one of the major characteristics of the design which is life. But Dreiser does not permit them to function together as a powerful and unified tragic theme because the center of the novel is dominated by a family chronicle involving a dull-minded patriarch. This long central portion diffuses our interest in Solon and limits our responsiveness to Dreiser's attempt at the close to establish him as a fully tragic figure.

The second detrimental way in which *The Bulwark* reflects its genesis is in its inconsistent setting. Dreiser's date for Solon's wedding in all his pre-1942 drafts was 1875. The historical moment for most of the action of the novel in these early drafts was therefore the late nineteenth and early twentieth century. It is a period in which the environs of Philadelphia are peaceful and almost bucolic, in which financiers are concerned primarily with speculation in railroads and public utilities, and in which a youthful quest for life finds expression in a formal dance party or in reading such forbidden authors as Daudet and Flaubert. When Dreiser returned to *The Bulwark* in 1944, he moved the date of the wedding up to the "turn of the century." But on the advice of James T. Farrell, who believed that this date would require some reference to the first World War, he settled finally on "late in the nineteenth century."[49] Because of this arbitrary manipulation of specific chronology and because of Dreiser's late introduction of allusions to such distinctive phenomena of the twenties as the movies, the novel exists in three incongruous historical moments. The designated chronology of the novel is Solon's life-span, approximately 1865–1925, a chronology which sets most of the adult activities of Solon's children in a post-World-War period. But the flavor and tone of much of the detail involving the rebellion of the children are those of a prewar setting. And the least revised portions of the novel, the sections dealing with Solon's business and banking career, have a distinctly late nineteenth-century cast.

On the whole, the editing of *The Bulwark* after it left Dreiser's hands in May 1945 resulted in the emphasis of two tendencies already present in the novel. Much of the cut material which Elder did not restore involved the experiences of Solon's children. Thus, Dreiser's already thin account of the Barnes family in the central portion of the novel became even more spare and chroniclelike. Even more significantly, Elder for the most part maintained Mrs. Campbell's simplification of Dreiser's prose style. Dreiser's prose in the pre–1942 versions of *The Bulwark* is as involuted and awkward as in *The Financier* and *The "Genius."* His post–1942 drafts, however, reflect Dreiser's move, since the early 1920s, toward a more direct and smooth prose style when writing fiction. Influenced in addition, it seems, by Jones's limpid prose, which Dreiser associated with the candor and directness of Quaker belief, and also by Mrs. Harris's editorial eye, Dreiser's prose in his May 1945 version of *The Bulwark* resembles that of *An American Tragedy* in its comparative directness, as Farrell immediately noted when he read this version.[50] Mrs. Campbell took this tendency very much further. And though Elder believed that she had gone too far, and though he did return some passages to their original form, on the whole he accepted her revision of Dreiser's style. The difference between some of the most characteristically Dreiserian passages in the May 1945 version of the novel and the revision of these passages in the published book is often startling:

May 1945	Published Text
The reception by Solon and his parents of this invitation from Mr. and Mrs. Wallin, to say nothing of the small note addressed to Solon at his offices in Dukla in which Benecia ex-	To Hannah Barnes, the invitation to Solon was not so much of a surprise as it was a premonition of some social change in their affairs, for which, as she saw it, they were scarcely fitted. (p. 60)

plained that at last her parents were visiting her and that she wanted him to come too, was not so much a surprise or shock as it was a premonition of something—some social change in their affairs, perhaps, for which, as all saw it, seeing how simply they had lived before ever moving to Dukla, they scarcely felt fitted. (p. 115)

In addition to all this, as Solon observed, were suspended, from the very high ceiling above, five large and handsomely gilded gasoliers, each of which carried fifty gas jets, and the same which, when lighted, as was the case on cloudy or rainy days, flooded the great chamber, central cage, officers' rooms and all with light—so much so that Solon was over-awed and slightly confused. (p. 178)

Large, handsomely gilded gasoliers were suspended from the enormously high ceiling. Solon was overawed and slightly confused by the magnificence of it all. (p. 86)

It is difficult to judge whether such radical stylistic revision is defensible and whether it aids or harms the novel. On the one hand, the prose style of *The Bulwark* is distinctly non-Dreiserian, and most readers who are familiar with his other novels find it anomalous. On the other hand, Dreiser had been tending toward a simpler fictional prose style, he approved Mrs. Campbell's extension of this tendency, and it can be argued that there is a significant relationship between the directness of the prose in the novel and the simplicity of Quaker life and faith which the prose describes.

ᴄᴄᴄᴄᴄᴄᴄᴄᴄᴄᴄᴄᴄᴄᴄᴄᴄᴄᴄᴄᴄᴄᴄᴄᴄᴄᴄᴄ

Dreiser became fond of dividing his novels into three parts, and all his novels after *Sister Carrie* and *Jennie Gerhardt* use this form, the Cowperwood trilogy being the most extended example. Like *An American Tragedy*, *The Bulwark* is the story of a tragic life from the youth of the protagonist to his death, with the first part devoted to the origin and nature of his character, the second to the full expression of his weakness, and the last to his fall. Dreiser even used a similar framing device in the two novels, beginning in medias res with a family vignette and ending with a parallel vignette. (Solon's wedding and funeral in *The Bulwark*). Of course, the two works are very different in most other aspects of theme and form, but in their overall structure they represent Dreiser's mature conception of the shape of the tragic novel.[51]

Part One of *The Bulwark* is itself enclosed by chapters which describe the wedding of Solon Barnes and Benecia Wallin in the Dukla meeting house. Dreiser expresses directly in his depiction of the wedding the theme of change, of the coming of a spirit of worldliness and modernity into the timeless spirituality of Quaker belief. In the costumes and demeanor of the participants in the wedding,

one could perceive the lag of a great ideal. A formal man could sit here in the ordered dignity of the church, rise and make moving remarks upon that "light which leadeth to perfection," and still go forth into the ordinary ways of life, and there as a builder of ships, a keeper of stores, an officer of banks and corporations, or worker in any field, scarcely retain more than a thin formalistic trace of all that Fox had believed and dreamed. (p. vii)

Solon himself has undergone this transformation from a pure to a formalistic faith. His Maine boyhood had been dominated by his mother's adherence to the Quaker ideals of simplicity, love, and belief in God's immanence in every aspect of life. But in Dukla he has gradually though unconsciously become less deeply impelled by the Quaker spirit of love. His marriage to Benecia, the daughter of the wealthy and "formalistic" Wallin, is the symbolic climax of this transition and therefore appropriately opens and closes an account of his boyhood and young manhood.

The life of the Barnes family in Segookit, Maine, is one of material simplicity and moral purity. Rufus and Hannah have succeeded in instilling in their children a faith in "the truth of Divine Creative Presence in everyone, by reason of which all things lived and moved and had their being—the Guiding Inner Light" (p. 3). Solon is a religious boy both by training and temperament. In particular, he is deeply influenced by his love for his mother, a saintly figure whose every thought is shaped by kindness and warmth. Solon also reflects his father's practical self-sufficiency as a Maine farmer, and is thus "a boy of so peculiarly sturdy and yet sensitive a temperament" (p. 14)—a boy physically robust and outwardly dull yet inwardly emotional and sensitive.

The direction of Solon's life is suggested by the four incidents which dominate Dreiser's depiction of Solon's Maine boyhood. At the age of five or six he unthinkingly kills a bird and is then deeply troubled by his act. Some years later he injures himself with an axe and becomes seriously ill when an unskilled surgeon dresses the wound, but he is saved from death by his responsiveness to his mother's belief in the wonder and beneficence of God's will. Not long afterward, he successfully defends himself against the town bully. And in a final incident—narrated somewhat later by Dreiser—he is outraged by the licentious French Canadian mill workers of the town and condones the burning of their saloons. The four events illustrate the strengths and limitations of Solon's moral nature. He can be profoundly moved by the problem of evil, but he can also reflect his ignorance and prejudices in his reaction to specific instances of evil. He can respond to the misfortunes of life with a deeply felt recognition of the healing power of love, but he can also assert his strength to overcome that which he believes wrong. The bulk of the novel is structured in relation to Solon's twofold moral potential, and in particular to his loss of the spirit of simplicity, love, and beauty represented by his mother, his turn to a religion and life of authority and prohibitions, and his final return to a recognition of the redeeming power of love in man and the world.

The Barnes family is drawn to Dukla by the virtuous motive of a desire to aid Hannah's widowed sister, and in Dukla they continue to live a Quaker life. But they are also increasingly affected by the values and interests of a more prosperous and cultivated community. Rufus is successful in his business affairs and is also attracted by the elegance and beauty of their home at Thornbrough. He believes that they can have a more comfortable and aesthetically satisfying life and still serve God, that their recognition of the "practical" needs of their earthly existence does not preclude a commitment to the priority of spiritual values. But despite this conviction, the family, with the exception of Hannah, begins to change. They lose not their outer Quakerism—its customs and moralism—but the inner vibrancy of a life unencumbered by any concern except the love of God and man and the driving need to make that love operative in every aspect of life.

The association of Rufus and Solon with the worldly Quakerism of the Wallins aids and sanctions this crucial change. Rufus's simple business ethic—to aid others and to make a modest profit—has been elaborated and refined by the shrewder Wallin into a defense of his large fortune. He had "hit upon the—to him—logically acceptable truth that business or trade was a creation of the Lord and intended by Him for the maintenance, education, general welfare, and enlightenment of all of his people on earth" (p. 40). It is the function and duty of those capable of performing the Lord's will in this sphere to gain sufficient wealth and power to perform it well. The rich man is a "steward" or agent of God who gathers wealth to aid mankind both directly through beneficence and indirectly by contributing to material progress. Wallin has come to this belief only with the accumulation of his fortune and is still somewhat uncomfortable with its easy rationalization of the Quaker mistrust of wealth, while Rufus has just begun to sense the usefulness of the concept of stewardship. The attraction between the families thus has an allegorical simplicity. The Wallins are drawn by the greater spiritual cleanliness of the Barneses, while the Barneses are moved by the greater power and prominence of the Wallins. And so the past and the present feed upon each other and gradually reshape themselves into the future.

Solon initially remains a "backward" Maine Quaker. He keeps his room at Thornbrough bare and simple, and when he enters business at sixteen it is with the motive of benefiting those with whom he trades. But his love for Benecia Wallin eventually compromises his Quakerism in the same way that the beauty of Thornbrough had compromised his father's. Aspiring to be accepted as a suitor by the family of the beautiful and good but well-to-do Benecia, Solon moves to Philadelphia to learn the banking business. Thus he leaves Hannah's world and enters that of the Wallins' Philadelphia home and the Traders and Builders Bank. That is, he leaves the world of love, of giving without question, for that of a superficial moralism and the goal of taking and gaining under the cover of the stewardship principle.

Of course, Solon does not fall dramatically or even consciously. The Wallins are good people, and Solon lacks the experience to sense the hard and shrewd materialism beneath the conservative business ethics of the bank. Earlier, when furnishing his first business office in Dukla, he had acquired three books—the Bible, the Quaker *Book of Discipline*, and Woolman's *Journal*. The Bible represents the permanent core of religious faith and the *Book of Discipline* and Woolman the twofold potential of that faith—toward authority or love. By the close of Part One, Solon has unthinkingly moved in the direction of law rather than love, the direction of a religious formalism represented by the bank and the Wallins rather than the innate mystical faith of his mother. So it is to the *Book of Discipline* that Solon appeals for his moral authority in Part Two in his attempts to curb his wayward children (pp. 212, 242), and it is to Woolman that he returns in Part Three when he has rediscovered that the principle of love animates all life.

Part Two is devoted to the ironic theme that Solon becomes a bulwark of his faith because of the conservative solidity of his home and business life and yet fails completely in both spheres. This portion of *The Bulwark* contains six narrative strains—the experience of each of Solon's five children, and Solon's own life as a Philadelphia banker—each of which bears upon Solon's moral and intellectual rigidity and naïveté. The thematic restatement by each narrative of Solon's inadequacies is unfortunate because this emphasis tends to diminish our involvement in a character whose qualities of mind and temperament have already made him a less than compelling protagonist.

Solon's role in the imprisonment of Walter Briscoe, early in Part Two, foreshadows his lack of perceptiveness in his relations with his children. Since Walter is the son of a devout Quaker, Solon recommends him for employment at the bank and then is shocked when the young man, eager for the delights of the city and kept on a tight rein by his father, steals from his employers. He permits the bank to take legal action against Walter, and it is only with his imprisonment that Solon begins to sense that forgiveness and kindness would have been the more appropriate Quaker response to Walter's dereliction. The incident is a paradigm of Solon's deficiencies as a parent. His naïveté initially permits him to be taken in by Walter's seeming propriety, and his moralism causes him to react in a conventional fashion to his crime. Put in another context, the incident also reveals Solon's inability to understand the seeking spirit which leads the young to rebel against the confining roles in which their parents cast them.

Solon is both any parent who seeks to shape his children in his own image and a particularly fallible parent in that this image lacks substance and validity, since it is only a shell of admonition and prohibition rather than the vital heart of belief which it was in Solon's own youth. The home which Solon creates for his children is a fortress or sanctuary of the upright life. But though Solon sees this fortress as protective, to his children it is restrictive, and each seeks in his own way to break out, to find in the outside world that which answers the need of the spirit. So Solon's genuine love and kindness are viewed by his children as restraint and imperception, and the children respond to his misunderstanding of themselves and of life with resentment and deception. This response, though believable, is perhaps shaped by Dreiser into too neat a spectrum. The oldest child is almost crushed by the weight of the past, the next two children cynically accommodate themselves to their father's moralism and achieve their ends by deceit, and the two youngest openly rebel.

Isobel, Solon and Benecia's first born, reveals from the first that a good home and moral precepts are not enough to satisfy a young and eager spirit. Her life is blighted because Solon fails to realize that the set mold of marriage and child bearing is not for her, that she requires new worlds in which to discover and expand her inner life. But because she is the oldest and most family-dominated child, she is "too fearsome and restrained to affront convention" (p. 193) and permits herself to be shipped off to a marriage-oriented school where her unattractive appearance and subdued temperament doom her to a directionless spinsterhood. Solon himself is taken aback by the inexplicable evil which Isobel's unattractiveness represents. Unlike his earlier experience in Maine with the axe wound or his later observation of the fly eating a flower bud, he has at this point no true bulwark of mystical faith to provide the miracle of insight into the design of life which would make this evil tolerable both to Isobel and himself.

Orville and Dorothea are more superficial and more successful seekers than Isobel. Both wish to escape the chill plainness of their lives for the social prominence and material display which a good marriage and wealth would provide. Orville is a smug and priggish social climber, somewhat like Gilbert Griffiths in *An American Tragedy*. Dorothea, however, is more ingenuously acquisitive, and her delight at the splendor and excitement of her first ball, at "the magic world that had opened its gates to her" (p. 191), has the appeal of Carrie's response to the pleasure of life. Orville and Dorothea are for Solon the least discomforting thinning out of Quaker faith between his father's and his children's generations. For though their Quakerism is only a veneer of Sunday ceremoniousness and of moral conservatism, they are not openly sullen or rebellious and they carefully disguise from him their deep preoccupation with the material joys of society and wealth.

Of Solon's five children, Dreiser devotes most of his attention to the two youngest, Etta and Stewart, with Etta dominating Part Two and

Stewart Part Three. The pervasive irony which controls Dreiser's characterization of Etta and Stewart is that though their rebellion against Solon is more pronounced and more overt than that of the other children, they also most resemble him, most understand him, and most love him. Both have the same core of sensitivity which marked the youthful Solon and which they feel in him beneath the stolidity of his role as bulwark of the faith. Solon, however, lacks the moral imagination to realize that Etta and Stewart, in their responsiveness to art and sex, are expressing in the context of their temperaments and circumstances the same emotional depth which characterized his own boyish responses to life. So Solon and his two youngest children are separated by a wall of misunderstanding despite their basically similar natures.

Etta combines in one character the most distinctive qualities of both Carrie and Jennie. Hers is at once a dreaming, artistic, seeking temperament—indeed, Dreiser depicts her at one point as musing while in a rocking chair (p. 130)—and a nature which is fulfilled primarily by the giving of love. She is thus a more refined Carrie and a more intellectually sophisticated Jennie. And though her refinement and intellectuality in part lessen her vibrancy as a character in comparison to either Carrie or Jennie, she is still an appealing and effective figure.

From her childhood Etta has sought to beat an independent path—to go to a school of her own choosing and to make her own friends—not for the sake of rebellion itself but to find "the affection and understanding for which her whole nature cried out" (p. 203). Solon, though he loves her deeply, cannot understand her desire for self-development and self-fulfillment, and she is forced to run away, first to the University of Wisconsin and then to Greenwich Village. Dreiser's portrayal of the village period of Etta's life is unfortunately a tired reprise of several of his habitual themes. Etta becomes another figure in Dreiser's "gallery of women" who has escaped from middle-class restraints and who finds aesthetic awakening and sexual freedom in the form of an affair with an artist. And her lover and mentor, the painter Willard Kane, is both a more up-to-date Ames and a less sensual and philosophical Eugene Witla. He loves beauty in women and is anxious to introduce them into the wonders of the aesthetic life, but he is unwilling to sacrifice his freedom as an artist for love. Kane is a shadowy and idealized self-portrait of Dreiser, and Etta's Wisconsin and village friend Volida La Porte is also one-dimensional. But Dreiser's portrait of Etta herself is not unduly weakened by this Greenwich Village phase, and her characterization gathers new strength in Part Three.

Although Stewart is still in his teens at the close of Part Two and has not shaped the direction of his life as firmly as have the other children, his character has assumed a full outline. He is a high-spirited and mischievous rather than maliciously inclined boy, but his escapades have aroused fear and distrust in Solon. Like Clyde as a boy, Stewart desires the beauty and pleasure of life which he feels others are savoring, and his deeply sensual nature soon seizes upon sexual gratification as the chief goal of this desire. He is repelled by the "unreal" nature of Quaker belief and is drawn to the adventure and excitement which the city offers, while his father remains dumbfounded by his wayward sexuality.

Solon's career as a banker follows the same course as his relationships with his children. His naïve belief that men achieve wealth principally because of their sobriety and industry is parallel to his confidence that his children will be content with the same placid and simple life which has satisfied him. But as he rises in the hierarchy of the bank and comes to know more of its inner workings, he realizes that most of his colleagues and clients would gladly use sharp and even legally suspect practices to make money. His response to this realization is to take self-righteous refuge in his own honesty and limited ambitions.

During this long middle phase of his life, the "mingled wisdom and dullness" (p. 184) of Solon's basic nature express themselves primarily as dullness, as a lack of insight into events and people. So he admires Orville, accommodates to the speculative actions of the bank, does not realize what he must do to aid Isobel, and crudely misunderstands the fumbling efforts of Etta and Stewart to reach out for a wider life in the form of French novels and burlesque shows. He is thus a bulwark primarily in the ironic sense of representing all that is narrow and dim and therefore obstructive in the religious mind. He is of course not an aggressive tyrant; he is always a good and kind and easily moved man, and it is these qualities, as well as the power of change and of youthful desire, which make him an ineffective bulwark. He is disturbed by the inexplicable inefficacy of God's word and increasingly takes refuge in the routine of business and in Benecia's love. Yet both are in truth suspect retreats, for the first prolongs his involvement in the affairs of the bank and the second his moralism toward his children. Benecia's open endorsement of his actions and her implicit confirmation by her love of the rightness of their way of life reinforce Solon's belief that theirs is the only road to the good life. So their love sanctifies and makes even more rigid his adherence to the moral values of the past.

Part Three has much greater fictional cohesion than Part Two. The accounts of the children now center on the experiences of Etta and Stewart, and Solon is much more in the forefront of the action. Yet this portion of the novel still has major weaknesses. Stewart's story is almost an inset tale as we follow his sexual adventures for many chapters with little reference to any other aspect of the novel. And the business plot, because of its discordant ironic tone and vague chronology,[52] is poorly integrated into the remainder of the action.

Most of the opening half of Part Three is devoted to Stewart. Consumed by sexual desire, he is eager for any adventure which may lead to possession of a girl. But like Eugene and Clyde, Stewart's sexual desires are linked intrinsically with his desire for beauty—"the mystic formula which expresses itself in line and form and color" and particularly in "all things feminine" (p. 267). His sexuality, like Etta's, is the concrete and immediate expression of a deeper need—art and freedom for her, excitement and wonder for him, and beauty for both. And like Clyde, the restrictions placed upon him force him into rebellion and into covert, illicit, and eventually tragic sexual liaisons. But though Clyde and Stewart are remarkably similar, they also differ in a number of significant ways. We never feel that Stewart is as weak or unperceptive as Clyde. His derelictions are "cubbish" (p. 244), the product of adolescence rather than inadequacy, and he senses the tenderness at the base of his father's "hard rock of duty and morality." When the girl whom he and his companions have drugged becomes ill, he alone wishes to risk detection by going for aid. And when she dies, his deep remorse—as well as his fear that he can never make his father understand—leads to his suicide.

The difference in characterization between Clyde and Stewart arises primarily from a difference of roles in their respective novels. Dreiser's emphasis in *The Bulwark* was less on the inability of the world to judge the tragic complexity of a particular kind of seeking nature than on the tragic inability of a father to recognize the worth of his son beneath the appearance of evil. Stewart is therefore a more superficial and conventional figure than Clyde, since he is the prodigal son who would have returned but for an unfortunate accident. Like Etta at the close of the novel, he too would no doubt have shared in and confirmed Solon's new faith. His rediscovery of the Inner Light in the brief period between his imprisonment and his suicide suggests that like Etta his revolt against Quakerism was against its surface moralism rather than its spiritual center.

Superficially, it appears that Solon's final activities at the bank represent the triumph of financial morality over immorality, since he grows more and more distrustful of the directors, informs the United States Treasury of their suspect actions, and at last resigns his post. But in fact Solon resigns with the same sense of failure which characterizes his deep dismay over the death of Stewart. In both instances, his role as a bulwark had prevented him from grasping the truth and from acting as a true Quaker. He had failed to see the perniciousness of Averard (the principal architect of the new spirit at the bank), he had failed to realize the needs and worth of Stewart, and thus he had sanctioned and protected the corrupt dealings of the first by his presence and had helped to destroy the second by his withdrawal of love. He had acted "correctly" in a worldly sense in both instances, but, as he finally realizes, he had not acted with love and simplicity as his basic guides and had therefore failed.

Solon's initial response, however, to the delinquency of Etta and Stewart and to affairs at the bank had been a protective self-righteousness. He had tried to bring up his children correctly and he had tried to act with honor as well as discretion as a banker. But with the overpowering emotional impact of Stewart's crime and death, he is overcome by deep personal and religious doubts. He begins, in other words, a religious conversion, in which the first step is the sweeping away of the rubble of protective but inadequate old beliefs so that the spirit lies bare and open to new truths. At the news of Stewart's imprisonment, Solon feels "as if this were some part of a tragedy almost too great for him to comprehend, which seemed to bring down into ashes every wall of the Barnes structure" (p. 291). With his wall or bulwark of moral assurance destroyed, Solon enters a period of "sudden and deep spiritual uncertainty" (p. 298). A virtuous man in pain because of his losses and his doubts, he feels himself deserted by his God and begins to associate himself with Job and Christ. "Almost, like Jesus on the Cross, he was ready to cry, 'My God, my God, why hast Thou forsaken me?' " (p. 299). God answers his unspoken plea in the form of three events which revitalize his faith. He discovers the spirit-renewing power of a forgiving parental love in his reconciliation with Etta; he perceives at last, by means of several transcendental encounters with natural objects, the role of evil within the beneficent and beautiful design which is life; and he finds a confirmation of the truths of love and design in the writings of John Woolman. These three sources of belief have been present in Solon's life from his youth in the forms of the lesson of his mother's love, the natural beauty of Thornbrough, and his possession of Woolman's *Journal*. But he had not taken advantage of their presence and had instead wandered in the spiritual desert of a conventional moralism. His is not the buoyant wonder of a youthful conversion but rather the tragic and poignant final triumph of a wayward believer whose return to faith also includes a realization of the harm and pain his blindness have caused himself and others.

Solon's spiritual renewal begins with his realization that his mother's way with an errant child would not have been, as was his way with Stewart, "to drive him, spy on him, irritate him with his constant queries," but to apply "the last measure of tenderness and liberality" and above all of "love" (p. 298). He finds confirmation of this way in the return of Etta and in the replacement of the enmity and misunderstanding which had existed between them by sympathy and love. Etta herself had recently suffered the loss of Kane and had felt that she "stood alone, rejected and forsaken" (p. 311). And it is with Etta's heightened sensitivity to life which is the result both of her New York experiences and of her fresh responsiveness to the beauty and peace of Thornbrough that she meets Solon not in bitterness but with "an all-embracing love, sympathy, and understanding" (p. 313) and thus embodies and revitalizes for Solon the spirit of Hannah. Etta and Solon are reconciled in a scene which recalls the reunion of Lear and Cordelia, as out of their rediscovery of the healing power of love and humility she asks forgiveness for the suffering she has caused him and he refuses to judge her while implicitly expressing his own need for forgiveness. " 'God and God alone can forgive,' " he tells her. " 'Pray to Him as I do now, every hour' " (p. 314).

The final four chapters of the novel deal with Etta and Solon's confirmation in nature and in Quaker belief of the philosophical truth contained in their rediscovery of the principle of love. After Benecia's death, Solon and Etta frequently walk along Lever Creek at Thornbrough. One day, "Solon was arrested by the various vegetative and insect forms obviously devised and energized by the Creative Force that created all things in apparently endless variety of designs and colors" (p. 316). He sees a large and translucent green fly eating a flower bud, and asks himself,

"Why was this beautiful creature, whose design so delighted him, com-pelled to feed upon another living creature, a beautiful flower?" (p. 317). After noting similar examples elsewhere in the garden, "he turned in a kind of religious awe and wonder. Surely there must be a Creative Divinity, and so a purpose, behind all of this variety and beauty and tragedy of life. For see how tragedy had descended upon him, and still he had faith, and would have" (p. 317). Not long afterward, Solon encounters a puff adder in the garden and senses that it understands him when he tells it that he intends it no harm. He says to Etta, " 'I thank God for this revelation of His universal presence and His good intent toward all things—all of His created world. For otherwise how would [the puff adder] understand me, and I it, if we were not both a part of Himself?' " (p. 319). Etta asks if he had always thought of nature in this way, and he replies that he had not. " 'God has taught me humility—and, in His loving charity, awakened me to many things that I had not seen before. One is the need of love toward all created things' " (p. 319).

In one sense, Solon's progress from humility to a love for all life has a persuasive emotional logic. Like Lear, he moves from a painful recognition of the falseness of his superiority to self-abasement and to sympathy for his fellow "poor naked wretches" of the world. But in another sense, we share Etta's surprise that Solon has suddenly made this transition in the context of nature—that social outcasts are the common varieties of garden life, that God is a Creative Force, and that His immanence is in the form of an "energized" presence. Dreiser's portrayal of Solon's renewal of faith as a discovery of a pantheistic truth is thus both fictionally inept and themati-cally appropriate. The language and specific philosophy of Solon's re-sponse to nature are more characteristic of Dreiser's 1943 essay on "My Creator" than of the banker-father figure we have encountered for most of the novel.[53] Yet Solon's response to nature does reaffirm the spiritual realities of his Maine boyhood: that God's presence in life involves pain and destruction and seeming evil as well as beauty and good; that all life is bound together by the spirit of love which emanates from its source; and that man can intuit and communicate with the spirit of God in life. Solon has moved, by this reaffirmation, from the ideals of stewardship and authority to those of simplicity and love, and from a vain attempt to impede or ignore change to a recognition of the still center of eternal truth. Although we in part stand aside from this conversion because of our sense that Dreiser has imposed its specific rhetoric upon Solon, we are also at one with the structural and thematic symmetry present in his return to the pure faith of his youth.

Solon becomes ill, and as he sinks toward death, he finds a third confirmation of his renewed faith in his rediscovery of the underlying truths of Quakerism expressed by John Woolman in his *Journal* and in his life. He is particularly moved by Woolman's belief that God announces his presence in the world by the love which men can feel for each other and that men everywhere, whatever their sect or station, can intuit this truth and order their lives in accord with it. Solon is deeply engaged by Etta's reading from Woolman, for he now perceives that his error as a Quaker was in failing to understand and apply the living heart of his religion. So the three events of Solon's decline—Etta's return, the recognition of nature, and the rereading of Woolman—are joined under the general rubric of pantheistic transcendentalism. God, or Creative Energy, is alive in every creature, binding all men and all living objects in an infinitely varied but interwoven design of beauty and tragedy, good and evil, and every man has the power to sense this design either in nature or in human relations themselves.

Etta, under the influence of her renewed love for her father and her sympathetic involvement in his responses to nature and to Woolman, also undergoes a significant spiritual transformation. She now finds a beauty and simplicity and truth in the doctrine of the Inner Light. "Here was no narrow morality, no religion limited by society or creed, but rather, in the words of Woolman, 'a principle placed in the human mind' " (p. 328). And she finds in the spirit of love, as expressed by Woolman and her father,

something beyond human passion and its selfish desires and ambitions—the love and peace involved in the consideration of others—her father first and foremost. And so through her service to him she could see what it might mean to serve others, not only for reasons of family bonds or personal desires, but to answer human need. What love, what beauty might not lie there? (p. 331)

Like Berenice at the close of *The Stoic*, she, too, as a survivor and interpreter of a tragic life, articulates a religious creed which requires that men translate the beauty and love they find in life into a desire to aid all men. She reads in Whittier's introduction to Woolman's *Journal* that

"His religion was love. His whole existence and all of his passions were love," and this was a love that first turned toward God and thence spread out over all people and things—a love that extended to the poor, the weak, the slaves, the miners; whereas hers was a love that had extended to one man—Kane. It was this greater love which, as she now felt, was moving through her father and which had literally raised him out of the black shadow of grief that had all but removed him from life itself, and now caused his sympathy and interest to reach out again—to her and Isobel, to the flowers and insects and fish in Lever Creek, and even to the snake that had so miraculously and yet plainly understood his tenderness through his voice. Now she felt it moving through her, too, and she was ready to receive it. (p. 331)

Dreiser joins in Etta's final awareness, as well as in Berenice's, the major currents of his philosophical thought and his social activism during the 1930s and 40s. Etta's beliefs affirm both the mechanistic design which Solon had found in nature, in which life feeds upon life, and the conviction that we must translate our realization of the design of life into a desire to aid all men—that is, to aid "the poor, the weak, the slaves, the miners" who are the fed upon in the design of human society. The themes of the close of *The Bulwark* thus have a coherent relation to Dreiser's earlier thought, whatever the deficiencies of these themes as an accurate description of man, society, and nature. From a belief that the universe is a mechanistic equation of forces, Dreiser had moved to a faith that these forces are part of a divine, though still mechanistic, plan, and that the need to achieve a greater balance between such opposing forces as strength and weakness or wealth and poverty is sanctioned not only by the mechanism of equation but by the underlying spirit of love in all life. In short, he moved his earlier amoral cosmology up a kind of ethical slope, and at last found within that cosmology, at the height of the slope, an emotionally satisfying view of the universe as good and as potentially better.

The Bulwark is a story of a destructive failure to realize the great truths of life and of a triumphant final recognition of these truths. It is this tragic ambivalence in the nature of experience—that we see only after much pain—which is reflected in two significant comments on Solon's life after his death. The first is by Hosea Gorm, a stalwart Quaker who has long admired Solon and who tells Etta that " 'truly thy father was a bulwark of our faith, and his memory will strengthen us, wherever his name is known' " (p. 334). The second is by Etta herself. Orville has reproached her for crying, since she was " 'the one to start all the trouble in our family' " (pp. 336–37). She replies, " 'Oh, I am not crying for myself, or for Father—I am crying for *life*' " (p. 337). At three earlier points in the novel Solon had been called a bulwark by admirers, but this praise was in the ironic context of his conventional and conservative family and financial moralism.[54] Now the irony shifts direction, for Solon has indeed become a bulwark of his faith—not in the sense intended of a good and devout life but in the deeper sense of his perception, at last, of the underlying truths which are the vital core of Quaker belief and practice. Solon's triumphant renewal of faith is colored, however, by his earlier failures in understanding and sympathy. So Etta is crying not for any one individual but for the basic contour of life itself—for the fact that we come so slowly to a realization of the need for love and that we cause so much pain and destruction as we progress along the road to understanding.

ttttttttttttttttttttttttttttttttt

I have already discussed two of the most distinctive characteristics of the form of *The Bulwark*—its chroniclelike narrative and its prose style. It remains to discuss a third such quality, the tendency within the novel to move symbolism toward allegory. Of course, all of Dreiser's novels are symbolic to some degree, but *The Bulwark* both extends the degree and varies the kind. As I have noted on several occasions, Dreiser's symbolism emerges out of three kinds of fictional expression in his novels: imagery, which is often clichéd, forced, and muddy; incidents or objects which he consciously introduces for symbolic effect, such as Carrie rocking or the train at the close of *Jennie Gerhardt*; and the inarticulate response of a character to the physical circumstances of his life, a response which imparts symbolic value to these circumstances, such as Clyde in relation to the Green-Davidson and Carrie to the stage. *The Bulwark*, because it contains very little of the first or third kind of symbolism and much of the second, is a novel in which overt and readily grasped symbols assume allegorical patterns of meaning.

There are several reasons for this unusual emphasis in the symbolism of *The Bulwark*. The most obvious is that Dreiser's prose style has been so cleansed that it is almost free of simile and metaphor. Another is that the narrative frequently resembles a synopsis because of its brief vignettes and summarized action and thus takes on the quality of a parable in which every detail appears to be a symbolic thread in a clearly patterned cloth. The novel is also surprisingly free of Dreiser's characteristic narrative voice of indirect discourse. Instead, all is dramatic scene or "neutral" authorial summary—neutral in the sense that the narrative voice remains colorless and dispassionate when describing a character's state of mind rather than seeks to render through diction and prose rhythm the intensity of feeling or thought of the character involved. As a result, there is a curious flatness in the narrative voice of the novel—curious for Dreiser, whose narrative voice is usually heavily colored either by his own presence as commentator or by his efforts at indirect discourse. This flatness, in its seeming simplicity, artlessness, and directness, resembles the effect of Hemingway's narrative style. And as in Hemingway, a dispassionate and unanalytical style directs us away from the author and the characters' interior states and toward the events and objects of the novel and their possible schematic symbolic significance.

The primary effect of this tendency toward allegory in *The Bulwark* is that we respond to the distinctiveness of the events, characters, and setting of Solon's life as relatively insignificant in comparison to the allegorical implication that his career is a modern approximation of a saint's life. His life begins with his acceptance of the wonder of God's grace, descends into a period of dull practice rather than living faith, and rises at the close to a victorious rediscovery of the vital presence of God in every aspect of life. His children also represent a schematization of the nature of faith. Some fall off into a safe but essentially destructive conformity; others seemingly reject belief but nevertheless maintain that underlying spiritual strength and desire for faith which is the foundation of belief. Minor characters and events are almost entirely allegorical. Rhoda Kimber, for example, is a worldly tempter who lures first Dorothea and then Stewart into a need for the delights of life, and each of the family gatherings marks a significant phase in the evolution of belief within the Barnes family. The setting is also allegorical within the overall structure of a saint's life. Solon initially believes that Philadelphia is a godly city, and he even images the bank as a religious edifice, but he discovers at last that both are hells of temptation and worldliness. At first, Solon and his parents respond to the garden and Lever Creek at Thornbrough as merely physically beautiful. Solon and Benecia pledge their worldly love for each other at the edge of Lever Creek, but their union receives religious sanction in the meeting house. Solon and Etta at last discover, however, that it is in their garden rather than the meeting house that they can best find evidence of the beauty and love emanating from God and present in all life.

But to note the pervasiveness and consistency of the allegorical mode in *The Bulwark* is not to claim that the mode is successful. The novel does have some of the traditional strengths of allegory—a clarity and firmness of authorial intent, an economy of method, and an occasional scene of direct power. On the whole, however, these strengths are far outweighed by the limitations of a saint's life in fictional form. Because worldliness in a saint's life is largely a foil to immortal spirituality, Dreiser uncharacteristically fails to bring alive the pull of desire present in each of Solon's children. The narrative contains none of the rich fullness of detail which in his earlier novels creates for us the emotional reality of the desire which his characters feel. We therefore respond to Dorothea's delight in glitter, to Etta's need for love, and to Stewart's sexuality as weak echoes of Carrie, Jennie, and Clyde rather than as moving portraits in their own right. In addition, fiction is a poor vehicle for the representation of religious miracles unless the psychological characterization and emotional texure of the work have prepared us to accept the reality of the supernatural. Dreiser has not so prepared us in *The Bulwark*, and we are therefore not persuaded by Solon's sudden discovery of a transcendental faith at the close of the novel despite the allegorical logic of that discovery. And finally, and perhaps most damaging of all, the lives of saints are not as interesting as those of sinners. Solon is a good man who has lost his way, and we applaud his move from an unperceptive narrowness to a living faith. But his goodness and dullness do not make for compelling fiction. Our interest in *The Bulwark* is therefore akin to that in *The "Genius."* Both novels offer insights into Dreiser's life during a period of intellectual ferment, but Dreiser was not successful in adapting either autobiography or hagiography into successful fiction.

Because *The Bulwark* is so clearly an allegorical novel, there is a temptation to view its primary allegorical level of a saint's life as a means for the expression of less immediately evident but more probing cultural and personal themes. There is little to be gained, however, in attempting to interpret the novel as an allegory of American life or of the Quaker experience. *The Financier* and *The Titan* express Dreiser's permanent view that the central reality of American life is struggle. And Solon's loss of innocence in Philadelphia cannot be considered a mythic theme in the same sense that Jay Gatsby's is, for to Dreiser the green shores of pure faith are not receding for us here in America but are still available in the garden of life which exists for all men. Nor is the novel an allegory of the history of Quakerism, except perhaps in its first two parts. Dreiser's depiction of

Solon's return to a primitive Quaker mysticism at the close of the novel represents more the state of his own belief and the hopes of Rufus Jones than the contemporary state of the Society of Friends.

If there is a secondary allegorical meaning in *The Bulwark*, it is that of Dreiser's own spiritual history. Although he was never a bulwark of any faith, Dreiser's interior life roughly resembles that of Solon. Like Solon, he had been raised in a moralistic, sectarian religion but had found that his emotional and spiritual life centered primarily on the love emanating from his mother. Both Solon and Dreiser had devoted their adulthood to worldly concerns, those of a prosperous middle-class existence for Solon and those of struggle and desire for Dreiser. And both in old age had turned to a belief which transcended the superficiality of the worldly and the sectarian and which affirmed the timeless, universal truths underlying all faith. Other more specific similarities between Dreiser's spiritual history and Solon's might be cited, such as the confirmation in Solon's experience of Dreiser's belief that the flame of spirituality is best kept alive in a woman capable of giving love, and the implicit modification in the fly-bud incident of the lobster-squid theme of an earlier phase of Dreiser's belief. But the similarity cannot be pressed too far, and no doubt it was the larger configuration of Solon's spiritual life with which Dreiser identified himself. Solon is any man who has moved from the narrow and the personally tragic in experience to a deep and compensatory sense of the wonder and beauty of life, and he is Dreiser himself as he undergoes the same change—not the Dreiser of "actuality," of course, but rather the Dreiser of the early 1940s as he reviewed and interpreted his life and in part recreated it in Solon.

The Stoic

A L T H O U G H D R E I S E R' S P L A N in early 1912 was to write and publish the three volumes of the Cowperwood trilogy at six-month intervals,[1] by the time *The Titan* appeared in early 1914 he had grown disheartened with the project. The preparation and writing of the first two volumes had taken more time than he had expected. He was anxious to pursue such new and more compelling interests as *The Bulwark*, his autobiographies, and a series of plays. In addition, the financial failure of the first two volumes and his difficulties with Harper's over publication of *The Titan* had tempered his earlier desire to complete the trilogy in one prolonged effort. So despite having done much research on Yerkes's activities for the period between late 1897 (the close of *The Titan*) and Yerkes's death in 1905, Dreiser put *The Stoic* aside as a project without having written a word of it. He would complete the trilogy, he thought, when time and circumstance permitted.

Time and circumstance seemed to permit in 1926. Dreiser had just published *An American Tragedy* and was free to undertake three long-delayed plans—revision of *The Financier* and completion of *The Bulwark* and *The Stoic*. He chose to begin with *The Financier*, and by the time he finished its revision he had begun that deep absorption in social causes and in philosophical and scientific study which engaged so much of his energy for over fifteen years. *The Stoic*, however, remained constantly on his mind during the opening phase of this long period between *An American Tragedy* and his return to fiction in the early 1940s. He did some additional research on Yerkes during his trip to London and the continent in late 1926, and he made tentative gestures in 1928 and 1931 toward beginning the book.[2] And finally, in early 1932, he made a major effort, working on the novel intensively for six months and completing approximately two-thirds of it.

Since almost two decades had elapsed since Dreiser had done the bulk of his research on the final years of Yerkes's career, his first step in his work on *The Stoic* in early 1932 was to have a secretary prepare a number of summaries of his old notes. One such summary was a year-by-year account of events; another dealt with the experiences of the major figures in the novel; and a third concentrated on Yerkes's intricate maneuvering to gain control of the London underground and on the equally intricate suits and countersuits which followed his death. From this material, Dreiser prepared a short plot synopsis,[3] and in April 1932 he began to write at great speed.

Dreiser's 1932 summaries and plot synopsis reveal that he intended to complete the trilogy with the same combination of fidelity to Yerkes's public career and imaginative recasting of his private life which had characterized the earlier two volumes. If anything, he was to be even more faithful to his sources in *The Stoic*, for he had available much more detailed information about Yerkes's personal affairs than he had had for the periods covered by *The Financier* and *The Titan*. So Cowperwood's financial career in England was to follow Yerkes's closely, both in the details and in the spirit of Yerkes's activities. Dreiser had noted the frequently made comment of the time that Yerkes had adapted his buccaneering American style to the relatively uncorrupt and less raucous British manner of conducting large-scale financial transactions.[4] So, too, Cowperwood's private life was to be based on the triangle of Yerkes, Mrs. Yerkes, and Emily Grigsby, with the added spice of Yerkes's affairs with Gladys Unger, a young London playwright, and with his niece Ethel Yerkes, a dancer. Much was to be made, of course, of the melodramatic death of Yerkes in a New York hotel while Mrs. Yerkes and Miss Grigsby fought over who was to nurse him during his final illness. And much also was to be made of the events between Yerkes's death and that of Mrs. Yerkes in April 1911. In particular, Dreiser apparently planned to describe in some detail the disastrous marriage of Mrs. Yerkes, a month after Yerkes's death, to the young playwright Wilson Mizner (she claimed that she was the victim of a confidence game), the dissipation of Yerkes's fortune in the many suits and claims which followed his death, and the failure of his plans for lasting fame as his art collection was sold at auction in 1910 and as his provision for a charity hospital remained unfulfilled. In short, Dreiser's theme and structure in *The Stoic* were to be the same as in the first two novels in the trilogy. Cowperwood's initial success in love and business—his successful foray into English public transit financing, and his happiness with Berenice—were to be followed by a fall as the "equation inevitable" shaped his destiny. But in this instance his fall was to be the permanent one of death and of the complete collapse of his financial empire and of his dream of immortality.

When Dreiser began to shape this abundance of material into fiction in 1932, he made a number of changes in plot and dramatis personae, though not in theme or structure. He invented two major characters—the gigolo Tollifer, whom Cowperwood hires to amuse and occupy Aileen, and Lord Stane (called Lord Ripplebrook in the 1932 draft), who unsuccessfully challenges Cowperwood for Berenice's love. In addition, he cut entirely the role of Gladys Unger, despite the large amount of information he had gathered about her. These changes had the same general intent as Dreiser's earlier variations and inventions in his handling of Yerkes's private life—to cast the facts available to him into a coherent and convincing interpretation of Cowperwood's temperament. In *The Stoic*, this attempt included a desire to render the poignancy of Cowperwood's relations with Aileen and the strength and depth of his love for Berenice.

Dreiser traveled a good deal between April and August 1932, but he nevertheless succeeded in completing fifty-five chapters of *The Stoic* during this period.[5] This work, which represents forty-nine chapters of the published novel, brought him to the point at which Cowperwood returns to England after his brief affair with Lorna Maris (Ethel Yerkes) and is reconciled with Berenice. As Dreiser finished a group of chapters, he sent them to his secretary, Evelyn Light, who prepared a typescript in three copies as well as a running plot summary for his use as he continued to write.[6] After revising a batch of typescript, Dreiser sent it to Louise Campbell for further editing.[7] And in August William Lengel read the entire completed portion of the novel and also made suggestions.[8]

Then, sometime in August, Dreiser abruptly stopped work on *The Stoic*. No doubt the failure of Liveright in July had a depressing effect. But also Dreiser had become deeply engaged that summer in the time-consuming project of launching the *American Spectator* and in the election campaign of 1932. And then, in the fall, came a new fictional interest—to write a novel about the revolt of a group of Kentucky tobacco farmers against the Duke tobacco trust. Early in 1933 Miss Anna Tatum reappeared in Dreiser's life. She had aided him while he was writing *The Titan* in 1913, and he now gave her both a clean copy and an already partly edited copy of *The Stoic* to edit still further. She performed her task boldly and capably, cutting large sections from Dreiser's extremely detailed account of Cowperwood's London financial maneuvering and reshaping the order of narrative between segments of his private and public life.[9] But despite this aid, and despite a contract which he signed with Simon and Schuster in 1934 which called for delivery of *The Stoic* by the close of 1935, he did no further work on the novel during the 1930s except to edit and have retyped the version which Miss Tatum had prepared of the completed portion of the book.

««««««««««««««««««««««««««««««««

With *The Bulwark* at last finished in May 1945, Dreiser turned with some eagerness to *The Stoic*. After he and Mrs. Harris looked over his summaries and drafts of the early 1930s, they prepared a brief outline of the portion of the novel which Dreiser had still to write. But he soon grew dispirited about *The Stoic*. Its financial emphasis and details now seemed very distant from his interests, and Miss Tatum's editing too severe.[10] So he put the novel aside for a few months. When he returned to it in July, it was with an enthusiasm which saw him through to its completion in December. For he had decided that he would introduce into the closing portion of the novel the new theme of Berenice's discovery in Eastern philosophy of a moving spiritual and social idealism.[11] He would thus close the trilogy on a rising as well as a falling note, much as he had introduced into the tragedy of Solon's fall the triumph of Solon's and Etta's renewed faith.

The closing third of *The Stoic* which Dreiser wrote in 1945 therefore departs in several ways from his 1932 plan. Rather detached at this point from the financial themes and narrative of the novel, he dealt only perfunctorily in this final section with two subjects which he had originally intended to develop at great length—Cowperwood's conflict with Stanford Drake (J. P. Morgan) for control of the London underground system, and the complex legal tangle which occurred after Cowperwood's death and which contributed to the loss of his fortune and the death of Aileen. In addition, he decided to eliminate the role of Wilson Mizner in Mrs. Yerkes's life. As a result of these and similar changes, there is a sharp and discordant shift in the published work from the explicit detail and chronology of the events between 1898 and 1901 (the 1932 portion) and the loose, fuzzy plotting and time scheme of the events between Cowperwood's return to Berenice in 1901 and the end of the novel in 1911 with Aileen's death and Berenice's return from India. And of course there is the even greater anomaly of Dreiser's shift from a novel centered on the financial and amorous adventures of Cowperwood to one involving the spiritual and philanthropic experiences of Berenice.

Dreiser had some slight justification in his sources for sending Berenice to India to study Yoga. Among his clippings for *The Stoic* is one from the *New York American* of January 13, 1913, headed "Emilie Grigsby Goes to India for Health." The story noted that Miss Grigsby had been ill and was also losing her beauty. It went on to comment:

For several years, since the fiasco of her social aspirations in England at the time of King George's coronation, she has taken a great interest in the Yogi philosophers of Hindustan. Her trip to India will take her into the extreme interior, where ancient philosophy may bring ease to her mind and take the place of her waning beauty.[12]

In his 1932 character summary of Berenice, Dreiser had noted that in late 1911 she "goes to India for health." But it seems certain that Dreiser's plan in 1932 was merely to comment at the close of the novel that Berenice had departed for the East. He had no knowledge of Miss Grigsby's experiences in India, and there is no evidence that she became a convert to Hindu mysticism or that she occupied herself with social work after her return. Indeed, it was Mrs. Yerkes, rather than Miss Grigsby, who fought for a Yerkes memorial hospital, a hospital which in fact was never built.

Dreiser's intent in developing the hint of Miss Grigsby's trip to India into the major thread of Berenice's conversion was to introduce the theme that life has beauty and meaning despite its tragedies so long as man has the power to perceive the spiritual unity at the heart of life and to translate this perception into inner peace and social action. In reshaping *The Bulwark* during the 1940s in order to introduce this theme, Dreiser had found a vehicle in the already present material of Solon's Quakerism and the beauty of Thornbrough. Thus, his central figure could discover the basic truths of life within the context of his Quakerism and—less convincingly—his natural world. Cowperwood, however, was an unlikely subject for a discovery of this kind, given the facts of Yerkes's life and Dreiser's characterization of Cowperwood as a man whose will to satisfy himself had never wavered. So Cowperwood, in effect, was permitted to die undisturbed, while Berenice—who was presumably more spiritual from the start—was sent off to India to discover, in the form of Hindu belief, the truths which Dreiser himself had found during his fifteen-year search for the meaning of existence.

Dreiser had had some awareness of Eastern philosophy from the beginning of his career, since nineteenth-century evolutionary theists were fond of noting the similarity between their own pantheism and that of Hindu mysticism. During the late 1920s he came into close contact with Hindu and Buddhist belief through Helen, whose wide-ranging interest in the occult and mystical had taken her to these areas of thought.[13] And of course during the thirties he began to see certain similarities between his own basic ideas and those of Hindu and Quaker belief. Indeed, Dreiser often approvingly noted in his books on Eastern thought the closeness of Eastern philosophy to Quaker beliefs in transcendence and immanence.[14]

When Dreiser in 1945 decided to conclude *The Stoic* with a section on Berenice's acceptance of Hindu mysticism, he turned to the *Bhagavadgita* as his major source. He wished to suggest the poetic appeal of mysticism to the feeling mind, and the intense lyricism of the *Bhagavadgita* was far superior for this purpose than any discursive discussion of Hindu thought. Helen had been interested for some time in the teachings of the Los Angeles guru Swami Prabhavananda.[15] In 1944, the Swami collaborated with Christopher Isherwood in a translation of the *Bhagavadgita*, and it was this edition which Dreiser relied upon for his quotations and summaries of Hindu thought in the Indian chapters of *The Stoic*.[16] Dreiser of course chose selectively from the *Bhagavadgita* and from such other explanations of Eastern thought available to him as Harendranath Maitra's *Hinduism*.[17] He was moved most of all by the beliefs that the world was an expression of the divine and that man could intuit the divine both in nature and in himself. To this core of Hindu transcendental pantheism, Dreiser added in *The Stoic* his own particular emphasis on the role of science in confirming the reality of the indestructible creative energy at the heart of existence and the need of the individual to translate his sense of oneness with all men into social action.

Aided by Helen (Mrs. Harris had returned to New York), Dreiser completed *The Stoic* in mid-October 1945.[18] The rough draft of the novel consisted of fifty-five chapters of Dreiser's 1932–33 work, thirty-four additional chapters, and a characteristic Dreiserian epilogue, "Concerning Good and Evil."[19] After a fresh typescript was prepared, Dreiser sent a copy of it to James T. Farrell in early December, requesting his opinion and suggestions.[20] He apparently had deep reservations about the conclusion of the novel; even before hearing from Farrell he wrote him on December 14 and inquired, "Would you prefer, personally, to see the chapters on Yoga come out of the book? If so, what would be your idea of a logical ending? I thought once of ending the book with Aileen's death, but later felt that I had to go farther with it."[21] Farrell's reply, on December 19, resembled his response to *The Bulwark* in length (twelve typed pages) and thoroughness. After making several criticisms echoed by almost all readers of the novel (that Cowperwood's sincere interest in the benefits to society of his business enterprises was out of character, and that it was anomalous for the trilogy to end with Berenice), he suggested that the epilogue (or postscript, as Dreiser called it in this novel) should be eliminated and that Dreiser should rewrite the conclusion to include a Carrielike reverie by Berenice on the irony of the immensity of the world's misery in relation to her efforts to alleviate that misery.[22] Dreiser immediately accepted Farrell's suggestion that he recast the conclusion. He wrote Donald Elder that the manuscript which Farrell was to deliver to him was incomplete, since he intended "to write another chapter and a half about Berenice—a psychological study of her at the end of the book."[23] He got as far in this project as to write two chapters dealing with Berenice's activities after her return from India and to revise the first of these—chapter 90 of the typescript and 79 of the published novel—before his death on December 28.

Helen's initial response to the problem presented by Dreiser's failure to revise fully the conclusion of *The Stoic* before his death was to believe that she herself could reconstruct the last chapter, since she and Dreiser had gone over his projected revision together. And of course she regretted deeply that Dreiser had not had a chance to write the final "soliloquy" of Berenice which he had planned.[24]

As the months went by after Dreiser's death, a course of action for the editing of the manuscript of *The Stoic* developed which closely resembled the editing process of *The Bulwark*. Late in March, Mrs. Campbell received a typescript of the novel for editing with firm instructions directly from Helen and indirectly from Elder that she was not to cut as much as she had in preparing *The Bulwark*.[25] While she was working on the novel, Elder suggested to Helen in late April that the best solution to the problem of the conclusion would be for Helen to sketch, in the form of an appendix, Dreiser's plan for the revised last chapter and for the unwritten soliloquy.[26] Early in July, Helen received Mrs. Campbell's version. Despite the admonitions of Elder and Helen, Mrs. Campbell had indeed cut the novel heavily, reducing it from 90 chapters and 921 pages to 78 chapters and 510 pages. Nevertheless, Helen found Mrs. Campbell's version excellent and sent it to Elder unchanged.

The appendix which Helen prepared for Elder consisted of a compressed version of Dreiser's original final chapter (Chapter 91 of his typescript) and four additional paragraphs (pp. 309–310). The four paragraphs are of considerable interest, since they reveal the direction of Dreiser's ideas about the conclusion of the novel after he had received Farrell's criticism. According to Helen, Berenice in her final reverie would have reflected on the insignificance of her efforts to aid the poor and weak in comparison with the needs of the world, on the irony of Cowperwood's struggle for power and wealth in relation to his loss of both, and on her resolution to continue her effort to "acquire, if possible, a real and deep understanding of the meaning of life and its spiritual import" (p. 310). Dreiser had apparently been attracted by Farrell's idea of introducing a Carrielike irony in Berenice's final position and state of mind, an irony which would counter the effect of artificiality and superficiality in her religious conversion and social beneficence. Like Carrie, Berenice would have attained awareness and success, but she would also have begun to know how little she knew and how little she had achieved. The soliloquy remained unwritten, and the four brief concluding paragraphs do not prevent the conclusion of *The Stoic* from having the anomalous effect which Farrell feared it would have. And even the full soliloquy, had Dreiser written it, would probably not have precluded this effect.

As with *The Bulwark*, Elder had before him both Dreiser's uncut version and Mrs. Campbell's fresh typescript of her version. He found in this instance that Mrs. Campbell's cuts, which were mostly of financial detail, were judicious and that her editing in general improved the novel.

He therefore edited Mrs. Campbell's typescript only slightly, primarily restoring some passages dealing with "the poetic and spiritual side of [Berenice's] nature,"[27] and used it as printer's copy.[28] This choice meant that Mrs. Campbell's simplification of Dreiser's prose style, as in her editing of *The Bulwark*, was the principal consequence of her work on the novel. Helen's appendix he accepted almost as written, adding only the brief editorial note which precedes it, a note which Helen approved.[29] All parties seem to have agreed that Dreiser's epilogue, the essay "Concerning Good and Evil," should not appear, and it did not.

ɛɛɛɛɛɛɛɛɛɛɛɛɛɛɛɛɛɛɛɛɛɛɛɛɛɛɛɛɛɛɛ

The Stoic, like *The Titan*, begins at an ambivalent moment in Cowperwood's life. He has again suffered a temporary setback in his drive toward great wealth and power, but again his defeat is accompanied by the possession of a beautiful and fascinating young girl. And again he and his love are to seek in a new setting, this time London, both the social success and the financial power which are appropriate to a man of Cowperwood's energy, strength, and vision.

Much in the themes and structure of *The Stoic* up to the death of Cowperwood continues this parallelism between the second and third volumes of the trilogy. Although Cowperwood had pledged to Berenice that he would operate on a "higher plane" (p. 130) in London, he soon discovers that as an outsider he must use the same device of "subtlety"—that is, of secrecy and deception, though not in this instance of illegality—which had characterized his Chicago career. As in *The Titan*, Cowperwood's personal life centers on his deception of Aileen in order to keep her occupied and unsuspecting while he pursues his own love affairs. And again he is at first successful in both his financial and personal activities. By the time he becomes seriously ill, he has, with the aid of Lord Stane, gained almost complete control over the vast and complicated enterprise of financing and constructing the London underground, and he and Berenice have had a happy and socially successful life in London.

Dreiser's title for the third volume of his trilogy suggests that a fresh theme in this novel will be Cowperwood's conscious withdrawal from the battles and turbulent emotions of life because of a new-found philosophical awareness of the inefficacy and harmfulness of struggle and emotion. In fact, however, Cowperwood does not so much acquire a new philosophy as reflect the tiredness and world-weariness of an overworked and aging man. This theme is introduced early in the novel, as he muses on the collapse of his vast Chicago plans, and it increases as his labors in connection with the London underground begin to exhaust him. The serious illness of Caroline Hand, a younger woman whom he had once loved, encourages thoughts about "the tenuousness of human existence" (p. 184), which in turn lead to speculations about the worth of his accomplishments. Observing the simple lives and apparent happiness of the poor farmers and fishermen of Norway, he wonders if they are not happier than he is. And among the tombs of the great artists in the Père-Lachaise cemetery, he is saddened by thoughts of how much of his own life he has devoted to the grind of finance rather than to the beauty of life and art. But the habits and structured will of a lifetime are not easily overcome, and Cowperwood remains in harness up to and even through his fatal illness. Thus he dies not only with his labors incomplete—the underground is just in the opening stages of construction and he has still not achieved his goal of world-wide fame—but also "a little bored and spiritually dubious of the import of life itself" (p. 262).

To the reader who comes to *The Stoic* immediately after completing *The Titan*, this new theme appears anomalous. There is no lapse of time between the two novels, yet in the first Cowperwood is a still youthful and vigorous man of affairs while in the second he quickly becomes "stoical" in Dreiser's sense of weariness and doubt. But of course the most significant gap between the two novels is not in Cowperwood's age but in Dreiser's. The vibrantly active writer who had finished *The Titan* in 1914 in his midforties had returned to *The Stoic* in his early sixties and had completed it at the age of seventy-four. Yet despite the incongruity between the Cowperwood of *The Titan* and the Cowperwood of *The Stoic*, the self-questioning and the final enervation of the latter figure play an appropriate role in the basic theme of *The Stoic*. For in Cowperwood's doubts about a life devoted to worldliness, Dreiser was sketching not so much an inevitable development in his protagonist as the final moment in his own intellectual history, a moment which received full representation in the complementary themes of Cowperwood's questioning of the value of a life pledged to acquisition and of Berenice's discovery of the beauty and satisfaction of a life pledged to giving.

Cowperwood has several other characteristics which are more closely related to his new "stoicism" than to his earlier depiction. The Cowperwood of *The Financier* and *The Titan* had increasingly desired women in whom a vaguely defined aestheticism was a major attribute, but he had also found that even an entirely sensual relationship with an attractive woman contained elements of beauty. In *The Stoic*, however, Cowperwood recoils with disgust from his primarily sexual affair with Lorna Maris, and he returns to Berenice, whom he now loves above all for her aesthetic qualities, in penitential abjectness. In addition, Cowperwood now desires to aid others through his financial activities, not merely to gain favorable publicity but with a genuine regard for the well-being of the London poor who will gain cheap and swift transportation as a result of his labors. And his plans to leave his fortune to maintain his New York mansion as a public art gallery and to build a charity hospital reflect this same basic shift from an ethic whose sole aim is "I satisfy myself" to one of responsiveness to the feelings and needs of others.

Dreiser's overall scheme for *The Stoic*—to continue to portray Cowperwood's titanlike activities in business and love while introducing his new doubts and interests—fails completely in execution. The old themes involving Cowperwood are indeed old, in the sense that they are both repetitious and lifeless. Cowperwood's financial activities, though often recounted in full detail, lack the fictional vitality of Dreiser's earlier account of similar enterprises. In *The Financier*, Cowperwood's financial and personal affairs had drawn energy and focus from each other through their intertwined presence in the Butler family. And in *The Titan*, Cowperwood's business life often had a bright sparkle because of Dreiser's delight in the cupidity of human nature revealed by the close link between politics and business. But in *The Stoic*, Cowperwood's financial affairs are a colorless and directionless body of activity; their principal fictional interest is the rather shallow one of the romance of high finance. Moreover, because of the history of the composition of *The Stoic*, this material is grossly ill-proportioned. Early in the novel, relatively minor figures and events are fully described, while in the later sections major transactions are only briefly and fuzzily summarized.

Cowperwood's personal life is also both familiar and dully rendered. Aileen is still vulgar, destructive, and clinging, and Berenice is beautiful, charming, aesthetic, and infinitely variable. The drawn-out subplot involving Tollifer's paid courtship of Aileen is one-dimensional and goes nowhere once its central motif has been established.

The plotting of both the business and personal segments of the novel creaks and groans with awkward transitions and with obvious and overcontrived foreshadowing and parallelism. For example, Cowperwood becomes jealous of the interest of the comparatively youthful Lord Stane in Berenice while he himself has arranged for the youthful Tollifer to entertain Aileen, who is herself jealous of the youthful Berenice. And Cowperwood becomes seriously ill at Lord Stane's house party, an event which joins the apogee of his success in love, finance, and society with the beginning of his fall, as the equation of life (in the form of time) begins its downward swing.

Finally, the solidity of setting so important in *The Financier* is here absent. The novel is comparatively brief yet encompasses three plots—Berenice and Cowperwood at Pryor's Cove, Aileen and Tollifer in Paris, and Cowperwood in London, New York, and Chicago—which results in a thin realization of the social and physical substance of place, unlike the representation of Philadelphia in the earlier novel. London is merely the name of a metropolis with various potential underground routes, and Paris—the Paris of Dreiser's 1911 tourist impressions—is a city devoted to the exotic entertainment of the idle rich, as in a cheap popular romance. Both the thinness and triteness of Dreiser's rendering of setting in *The Stoic* have the unfortunate effect of placing in sharp relief the banality and triteness of some of his dialogue and themes—in particular the dialogue between Berenice and Cowperwood and the theme of the sexual attractiveness of a dynamic man no matter what his age.

All of which is to say that the frequent comment that *The Stoic* is a failure because of its concluding section on Berenice's religious conversion is beside the point. The conclusion in fact comprises only a tenth of the novel, and though it is a structural and thematic botch, it merely puts the final seal of failure on an already seriously flawed work. Whatever the reason—whether because of the long lapse between his completion of *The Titan* and his work on *The Stoic*, or whether because of his loss of interest in a Cowperwoodlike protagonist—Dreiser was unable to create successful fiction out of his material, and *The Stoic* is a failure both as the final volume in a trilogy and as an independent novel. Within the trilogy, it brings Cowperwood's life to a predictable and hackneyed end. As a novel in its own right, it is dull and wooden.

This is not to say that the concluding section of the novel, after Cowperwood's death, lacks a rough logic both in relation to *The Stoic* as a whole and within itself. Cowperwood's gradual loss of interest in worldly gain and in himself is carried to its conclusion by Berenice's renunciation of materialism and of self. And Dreiser carefully balances in these final chapters the ironically parallel careers of Aileen and Berenice during the six years between Cowperwood's death and the end of the novel. Aileen, seeking to preserve Cowperwood's fortune in order to carry out his philanthropic plans, is defeated by the same worldly trickery and deceit which Cowperwood had both used and fought against, and at last dies crushed and embittered. Berenice, abjuring worldliness while studying under a guru in India, gains spiritual insight and uses her new power—as well as the fortune Cowperwood had given her before his death—to found the hospital which he had desired.

Despite this appearance of an acceptable theme and structure, the conclusion is very bad fiction. Most obviously, it throws the entire novel out of balance. From a work centering on Cowperwood, we move to one in which he is completely absent and in which Berenice in her new role is largely a new character. And from a fictional mode in which verisimilitude is achieved through detail, the narrative changes radically to that of scenario both for Berenice's India experiences and for the dissipation of Cowperwood's estate. Indeed, these concluding chapters more often resemble notes for further development than fiction itself. As a result, Berenice's India adventure in particular has a fatuous ring, as Dreiser crowds into one brief chapter four years of study and much Hindu philosophy. Berenice's conversion, moreover, is out of character. Her inherent spirituality, one assumes, has been represented earlier by her aestheticism. But Dreiser had also told us earlier that "mentally and philosophically, Berenice was more of a cold, realistic turn than otherwise" (p. 219). And it has been her "cold, realistic" desire for wealth and power in order to support her aesthetic tastes which has been the major element in her character. Now, at Cowperwood's death, she is struck by a sudden need for spiritual solace and peace, even though she had earlier shown much interest in social prominence and in the beauty of life independent of Cowperwood's presence. In short, we do not accept that her rejection of worldliness has a believable base either in her character or her condition, and we thus view her conversion as a gross manipulation of character and event. And Dreiser does not enhance his portrait of Berenice in these closing chapters when he shows her standing in wide-eyed, gaping wonder before the wisdom of the East or returning to the luxury of the Plaza after five years' contemplation of India's starving masses.

In truth, the conclusion of *The Stoic* is not conventional fictional narrative but rather an overblown and semidramatized example of Dreiser's predeliction for Balzacian epilogues. Considered as an epilogue, it is a philosophical summary not only of *The Stoic* but also of the trilogy as a whole. It is a poor epilogue to both *The Stoic* and the trilogy. A novel and a trilogy which have been devoted largely to Cowperwood and the principle of equation should have come to an end with his death and the subsequent dissolution of his wealth.

The conclusion of *The Stoic* can most profitably be viewed as an epilogue to Dreiser's own life and thought. In form, it represents his loss of interest in fiction during the last twenty years of his life, since only a writer more concerned with his philosophical pronouncements than with fictional effect could append such a narrative monstrosity to a novel. In theme, its Hindu mysticism is principally a metaphor of Dreiser's own ideas of the previous two decades rather than an accurate reflection of Hinduism.[30] Although he drew heavily on the *Bhagavadgita*, he reshaped its pantheism—particularly in the speeches of the guru—into his own vision of a universe in which science is a guide to the beauty of the mechanistic design of reality and in which social action is the inevitable product of a realization of the unity of all life.

The conclusions of both *The Bulwark* and *The Stoic* thus have a basic similarity not only in theme but in symbolic method, as Quakerism and Thornbrough become Hinduism and India. At the end of both novels, Dreiser shaped religion and setting into symbols of his own deepest beliefs, though he imposed symbolic meaning at this point by authorial main force rather than generated it from within by the fictional dynamics of the entire novel. Berenice's final view of life is therefore almost exactly the same as Solon's and Etta's. Responding to the divinity present in all nature, she realizes both her own insignificance and the insignificance of the tragedy and turmoil of all life in relation to the underlying beauty of experience. Indeed, just as Solon can find the beauty of spiritual design in a fly eating a bud, so she can now find in Cowperwood's frenetic pursuit of women "a constant search for beauty" which was "nothing more than a search for the Divine design behind all forms—the face of Brahman shining through" (p. 305). And like Etta, she translates her awareness of the unity and beauty of life into a desire to devote herself to aiding mankind.

So Dreiser had at last solved the problem implied by the conclusion of

Sister Carrie. Carrie had also realized the narrowness and insignificance of her earlier endeavors and had determined to devote herself, through her art, to the betterment of all men. But Dreiser had written in 1900 that hers was to be an unending quest—that when she fulfilled a particular vision of the good life, she would recognize its limitations and thus lose the happiness she had temporarily gained, and that this cycle is never-ending. The guru, however, told Berenice that by setting aside "this apparent, illusive world, and by seeing God in everything one can find real happiness" (p. 299). When Berenice puts this philosophy into practice through her work with blind children at the hospital she has helped found, she indeed does find happiness, and it is in this seemingly permanent state that we leave her.

Whatever the element of sentimentality in Dreiser's final evocation of Carrie rocking in her chair and dreaming of a happiness she shall never gain, his portrait derives its strength from his vision of life as a forever seeking and a never finding, as a constant flux of momentary delight and prolonged dissatisfaction. His portrait of Berenice, content in her modest room as she happily devotes her life to her children's hospital, constitutes a deeper and more vitiating sentimentality, for in this instance the artist has shaped his vision of life to represent what we should be and should do rather than what we are. Although we can value the conclusion of *The Stoic* as an apt statement of Dreiser's resolution of the problem of happiness, we can appreciate as well that resolutions of this kind are not the stuff of successful fiction.

NOTES

ABBREVIATIONS

Book—*A Book About Myself* (New York, 1922).
Dawn—*Dawn* (New York, 1931).
Dudley—Dorothy Dudley, *Forgotten Frontiers: Dreiser and the Land of the Free* (New York, 1932).
Elias—Robert H. Elias, *Theodore Dreiser: Apostle of Nature* (New York, 1949; rev. ed., Ithaca, N.Y., 1970).
Helen Dreiser—Helen Dreiser, *My Life with Dreiser* (Cleveland, 1951).
Hey—*Hey Rub-a-Dub-Dub* (New York, 1920).
Lehan—Richard Lehan, *Theodore Dreiser: His World and His Novels* (Carbondale, Ill., 1969).
Letters—*Letters of Theodore Dreiser*, 3 vols., ed. Robert H. Elias (Philadelphia, 1959).
Matthiessen—F. O. Matthiessen, *Theodore Dreiser* (New York, 1951).
Moers—Ellen Moers, *Two Dreisers* (New York, 1969).
Pizer—*Sister Carrie*, ed. Donald Pizer (A Norton Critical Edition) (New York, 1970).
Swanberg—W. A. Swanberg, *Dreiser* (New York, 1965).
Tjader—Marguerite Tjader, *Theodore Dreiser: A New Dimension* (Norwalk, Conn., 1965).

All citations from Dreiser's novels are from the following editions:
Sister Carrie (New York: Doubleday, Page, 1900; republished in facsimile by Charles E. Merrill Pub. Co., 1970).
Jennie Gerhardt (New York: Harper, 1911).
The Financier (New York: Harper, 1912).
The Titan (New York: John Lane, 1914).
The "Genius" (New York: John Lane, 1915).
An American Tragedy, 2 vols. (New York: Boni and Liveright, 1925).
The Bulwark (New York: Doubleday, 1946).
The Stoic (New York: Doubleday, 1947).

Notes

Unless otherwise noted, all unpublished material cited in the text and notes is in the Dreiser Collection of the University of Pennsylvania Library. I have not distinguished in my notes between those letters to or by Dreiser in the Collection which are originals and those which are carbon or photoduplicated copies.

Since the publication of Robert H. Elias's pioneer biography in 1949 and F. O. Matthiessen's important critical study in 1951, there have been a number of significant books and articles about Dreiser and his work, particularly in the last decade. Of these, I am particularly indebted to Elias's edition of Dreiser's letters and to W. A. Swanberg's *Dreiser*, Ellen Moers's *Two Dreisers*, and Richard Lehan's *Theodore Dreiser: His World and His Novels*. My notes inadequately reflect the extent to which I have depended on the findings of these and other scholars, since in order to avoid excessive documentation of secondary material I have confined myself to the citation of instances of specific indebtedness or dispute and of major discussions elsewhere of a major topic. An interpretive survey of Dreiser scholarship can be found in Robert H. Elias's "Theodore Dreiser," *Sixteen Modern American Authors*, ed. Jackson R. Bryer (Durham, N.C., 1973). For a checklist of writings by and about Dreiser, see Donald Pizer, Richard W. Dowell, and Frederic Rusch, *Theodore Dreiser: A Primary and Secondary Bibliography* (Boston, 1975).

Introduction: A Summer at Maumee

1. Dreiser to Mencken, May 13, 1916; *Letters*, I, 211.

2. For the first phrase, see *Book*, p. 106. The second phrase occurs in a letter to Emma Rector, March 1, 1894; Richard W. Dowell, ed., " 'You Will Not Like Me, I m Sure': Dreiser to Miss Emma Rector . . . ," *American Literary Realism*, III (Summer, 1970), 268.

3. For Dreiser and *Ev'ry Month*, see in particular Moers, pp. 32–43, and Joseph Katz, "Theodore Dreiser's *Ev'ry Month*," *Library Chronicle* of the University of Pennsylvania, XXXVIII (Winter, 1972), 46–66.

4. Dreiser to Mencken, May 13, 1916; *Letters*, I, 212–13.

5. See *Book*, pp. 490–91, and Elias, p. 88.

6. "Forgotten," *Ev'ry Month*, II (August, 1896), 16–17. Dreiser may have contributed still other fictional sketches to *Every Month* under a pseudonym.

7. Swanberg, p. 84.

8. Arthur Henry to Dreiser, [August, 1900].

9. When Dreiser collected these stories in *Free and Other Stories* (1918), he changed the titles of "The Shining Slave Makers" and "Butcher Rogaum's Door" and extensively revised the text of all the stories except "When the Old Century Was New." All quotations from the four stories in this chapter are from the text of their original publication. Since none of the stories is more than nine printed pages, I have not thought it necessary to supply a reference for each quotation.

10. *Demorest's*, XXXV (April, 1899), 123–25, and *Demorest's*, XXXV (January, 1899), 38–39.

11. Dreiser to R. U. Johnson, January 9, 1900; *Letters*, I, 45–46.

12. *Book*, p. 325. The newspaper account appears to be "A Negro Lynched. Taken from Jail at Rich Hill, Mo., and Hanged—His Crime the Usual One," *St. Louis Republic*, September 17, 1893, p. 2.

13. "Reflections," *Ev'ry Month*, III (February, 1897), 4.

14. "Reflections," *Ev'ry Month*, III (March, 1897), 3.

15. *Book*, p. 457.

16. The discrepancy also results from the fact that Dreiser's *A Book About Myself* ends in late 1894, soon after his first encounter with Spencer's thought. In *The "Genius,"* which deals fictionally with Dreiser's years in New York between 1894 and 1910, he reveals his modification of his earlier despairing response to Spencer's philosophy, a modification also apparent in his *Ev'ry Month* editorials of 1895–97. See *The "Genius,"* pp. 156–57.

17. For Spencer's concept of rhythm, see his chapter on "The Rhythm of Motion," *First Principles* (New York, 1886), pp. 250–71. For Dreiser's association of the term "equation" with Spencer, see "Equation Inevitable," *Hey*, pp. 168–69.

18. *First Principles* (New York, 1886), p. 192c.

19. Dreiser's allusions to specific contemporary scientific discoveries place the composition of the essay roughly in this period. Many of the essays of *Hey Rub-a-Dub-Dub* (1920) contain similar allusions. *Hey Rub-a-Dub-Dub* itself is essentially an application of the idea of equation to various ethical, social, and literary problems. See, in particular, "Equation Inevitable," pp. 157–81, and also pp. 17, 21, 90, 207. During the 1930s, Dreiser planned that "Equation Inevitable," in expanded form, would be the keystone essay in his major philosophical work, a book variously titled "Notes on Life," "The Mechanism Called Man," etc. The best brief discussions of Dreiser's philosophical thought are by Lehan, pp. 45–53, and by J. D. Thomas, "Epimetheus Bound: Theodore Dreiser and the Novel of Thought," *Southern Humanities Review*, III (Fall, 1969), 346–57.

20. *The Data of Ethics* (New York, 1882), pp. 25, 113.

21. In *Dawn*, p. 557, Dreiser recalled that "the things these men offered me were splendid intellectual suggestions, pro-moralistic at times, it is true, but also liberal, sympathetic, intelligent." In a letter to Richard Duffy, November 18, 1901 (in the Lilly Library, Indiana University), he noted that "Gunsaulus' sermons delivered Sunday evenings at Central Music Hall fired me immensely." He met Gunsaulus in late 1898 and wrote a commendatory article about him, "A Leader of Young Mankind, Frank W. Gunsaulus," *Success*, II (December 15, 1898), 23–24.

22. "Reflections," *Ev'ry Month*, II (June, 1896), 4. See also *Ev'ry Month*, IV (May, 1897), 21.

23. "Statements of Belief," *Bookman*, LXVIII (September, 1928), 25.

24. *Hey*, p. 180.

25. Otis Notman, "Talks with Four Novelists," *New York Times Saturday Review of Books*, June 15, 1907, p. 393.

26. "What I Believe," *Forum*, LXXXII (November, 1929), 280.

27. "Equation Inevitable," *Hey*, p. 166. See also Dreiser's essay "Change" in *Hey*.

28. Dreiser to Sergei Dinamov, January 5, 1927; *Letters*, II, 450.

29. *A Hoosier Holiday* (New York, 1916), p. 226.

30. *Dawn*, p. 159.

31. Dreiser's most well-known statement of his indebtedness to Balzac is in *Book*, pp.

411–12. A less familiar account is in a 1911 interview: "Just about then, in Pittsburgh, where I was working as a newspaper man, I came across Balzac and then I saw what life was—a rich, gorgeous, showy spectacle. It was beautiful, dramatic, sad, delightful, and epic—all these things combined." *Cleveland Leader*, November 12, 1911. See also Lars Ahnebrink, "Dreiser's *Sister Carrie* and Balzac," *Symposium*, VII (November, 1953), 306–22.

32. *Harper's Weekly*, XLVI (December 6, 1902), 53.

33. Helen Dreiser, p. 25.

34. "Theodore Dreiser's Transcendentalism," in *English Studies Today, Second Series*, ed. Georges A. Bonnard (Bern, 1961), p. 237.

35. *Dawn*, p. 210.

36. "The Lynching of Nigger Jeff"; Los Angeles Public Library (photocopy in the Dreiser Collection).

Part One: *Sister Carrie*

1. *Dawn*, p. 149.

2. My account of Emma and Hopkins in Chicago is drawn from contemporary newspaper reports of the theft and elopement. I reproduce five such reports, from the *Chicago Mail* and *Chicago Tribune* of February 15, 16, and 17, 1886, in my edition of *Sister Carrie*, pp. 374–79. These newspaper stories were first noted and discussed by George Steinbrecker, Jr., "Inaccurate Accounts of *Sister Carrie*," *American Lieterature*, XXIII (January, 1952), 490–93.

3. My account of Emma and Hopkins in New York derives from *A Book About Myself* and from Dreiser's fuller account of their experiences in the manuscript of this autobiography in the Dreiser Collection.

4. Lehan, pp. 11–12, is in error when he maintains that Emma was still living with Hopkins as late as 1911. The husband whom Emma refers to in the correspondence cited by Lehan is John Nelson, Emma's second husband, whom she married in 1898.

5. "A Dashing Blonde," *Chicago Mail*, February 17, 1886; Pizer, p. 378.

6. "He Cleaned Out the Safe," *Chicago Mail*, February 15, 1886; Pizer, p. 374.

7. *Book*, pp. 463–64.

8. See, for example, Dreiser's "Whence the Song," *Harper's Weekly*, XLIV (December 8, 1900), 1165–66a, which recounts the "real life" story of the daughter of a Chicago butcher who achieves success as a popular singer.

9. *A Traveler at Forty* (New York, 1913), p. 8.

10. See *Dawn*, p. 125.

11. See in particular his "Why Not Tell Europe about Bertha M. Clay," *New York Call*, October 24, 1921, p. 6.

12. Although the American sentimental novel of the late eighteenth century and the early nineteenth century has received considerable attention, the late nineteenth-century version of the form has been inadequately discussed. Leslie Fiedler, in his *Love and Death in the American Novel* (2nd ed., New York, 1966), pp. 247–55, maintains that Dreiser wrote completely in the spirit of the sentimental melodrama; Daryl C. Dance, in "Sentimentalism in Dreiser's Heroines Carrie and Jennie," *CLA Journal*, XIV (December, 1970), 127–42, argues that Dreiser relies on some conventions and devices of the form while parodying others.

13. In holograph chapter XLIX, these are the authors (along with F. Marion Crawford!) whom Carrie recalls having read at Ames's urging when they meet again at the end of the novel. Dreiser later revised this passage and only Balzac is mentioned in the published version (Chapter XLVI). See also pp. 45–47 below.

14. Dreiser to Mencken, May 14, 1916; *Letters*, I, 215.

15. Although the holograph of *Sister Carrie* is in the New York Public Library, a photocopy of it is in the Dreiser Collection. I will therefore consider the holograph as available in the Dreiser Collection and will not hereafter cite its location.

16. The article is reproduced in Pizer, pp. 416–23.

17. See the *New York Times*, January 15 and 16, 1895.
18. See, for example, his comments in his "Reflections" column of October, 1896; in Pizer, pp. 399–400.
19. *Letters*, I, 213.
20. Dudley, p. 160. Dreiser again confirmed the story in a letter to Robert H. Elias, January 28, 1945; in the Cornell University Library.
21. *Letters*, III, 794.
22. The holograph of *Sister Carrie* comprises Chapters I-L and an epilogue (there is no Chapter XXX, however; Dreiser apparently inadvertently skipped this number). The typescript and published volume comprise Chapters I–XLVII. When revising the typescript, Dreiser and Henry on two occasions telescoped heavily cut adjoining chapters into single chapters. In my references to chapters in *Sister Carrie*, I have cited both the holograph and published chapter numbers for specific quotations from the holograph when these numbers differ. Unless otherwise noted, all other references to chapter numbers refer to the chapters as numbered in the published volume.
23. Elias, pp. 106–109, and Moers, pp. 159–61, have authoritative accounts of the dating of the composition of *Sister Carrie*.
24. Dudley, p. 162.
25. *New York Herald*, July 7, 1907.
26. The notes, on the same paper used for the holograph, comprise thirteen unnumbered pages. They are bound in at the close of the holograph.
27. The order of this material in the holograph is of some interest. Chapter XLIX (pp. 1–49) contains the long Ames-Carrie interviews. It is followed by a seventeen-page fragment which picks up the narrative at p. 20 of Chapter XLIX but which both summarizes the Ames-Carrie exchanges and includes new material on Hurstwood. (The first twenty pages of XLIX and this fragment constitute Chapter XLVI of the published novel.) The fragment is followed by Chapter L, which concludes with Hurstwood's death and Dreiser's note "The End." There then follows a version of the epilogue in Dreiser's hand, a fair copy in Henry's, and Dreiser's and Henry's notes for the epilogue.
28. Ellen Moers, pp. 67n, 130–31, discusses two comparatively minor revisions by Dreiser in the holograph: his late borrowing from George Ade's "The Fable of the Two Mandolin Players and the Willing Performer" and his efforts to work into the narrative his vignettes of New York life published in late 1899 as "Curious Shifts of the Poor."
29. An exception to this general observation is the cut toward the close of Chapter XVIII of the holograph (Chapter XVII of the published novel) of a brief but significant passage in which Hurstwood presses $100 upon Carrie to be used for new clothes for her Avery Hall appearance.
30. Dreiser to Louis Filler, December 16, 1937. See also Dudley, p. 162. Both Elias (*Letters*, I, 52n) and Swanberg (p. 85) mention that Miss Mary Annabel Fanton, an editor of *Demorest's Magazine* with whom Dreiser had become friendly in 1898, helped edit *Sister Carrie*. Although Miss Fanton may have read the holograph or typescript of the novel, neither of these versions exhibits evidence of editorial work other than by Henry and Dreiser. Miss Fanton appears as Miriam Finch in *The "Genius,"* a figure who is a cultural mentor of Eugene Witla (Dreiser) rather than a critic of his work.
31. For a different view of Dreiser's intent in the cutting of *Sister Carrie*, see Lehan, pp. 60–66. Lehan believes that Dreiser consciously set out in his deletions to make Carrie and Hurstwood less treacherous and lustful and more innocent and victimized than they are in the full draft of the novel. Lehan ignores, however, the strong possibility that much of the cutting of the typescript was by Henry. He also fails to consider that the omissions which he cites—including a key passage on Hurstwood's indecision before the safe—are all obviously repetitious or digressive and that the primary intent of Henry and Dreiser in omitting these passages was to shorten the novel by eliminating material of this kind.
32. A comparatively minor though intriguing crux in the revision of the various versions of *Sister Carrie* involves the date of Carrie's arrival in Chicago. The date in the holograph was

originally 1894, but it has been erased and 1884 written over it. In the typescript, 1894 is the typed date, but it has been written over in pencil with the date 1889. This date, 1889, appears in the published version. As has often been noted, 1889 is the only specific date in the entire novel and is therefore the "key" to the documentation of social detail in the work.

Dreiser's revision of the date of Carrie's arrival probably took the following form. He initially used 1894 but soon decided that 1884 would be a more appropriate date because it is close both to his own first impressions of Chicago and to Emma's affair with her architect lover. (In the holograph, there are a series of questions at the close of Chapter III, not in Dreiser's hand, quizzing Dreiser on the validity of his Chicago details. All of these questions refer to the date 1884.) As Ellen Moers suggests, however (pp. 118–19), Dreiser settled upon 1889 as his working date when he wrote the New York portion of the novel because this date permitted him to synchronize Carrie and Hurstwood's New York experiences with his own knowledge of New York life of the midnineties. In preparing the typescript, Miss Mallon misread 1884 for 1894, but in revising the typescript Dreiser recognized both her error and his own need to have a later date than 1884 and corrected 1894 to 1889.

The principal effect of Dreiser's lack of certainty about the date of Carrie's arrival is that though the novel gives the impression of detailed accuracy in its rendering of social history, this impression is in fact "true" only for the New York material. Dreiser's Chicago in *Sister Carrie*, with its horsecars, newly developed department stores, specific theatrical performances, etc., is Chicago of the mid-1880s rather than 1889–90.

33. Pizer, pp. 434–54, reproduces the correspondence of the summer of 1900 which bears on the controversy.

34. The contract is in the Dreiser Collection.

35. A characteristic passage noted by a question mark in the margin and cut by Dreiser in the typescript was Dreiser's comment in Chapter V that Hurstwood occasionally visited "those more unmentionable resorts of vice—the gilded chambers of shame with which Chicago was then so liberally cursed."

36. Some of this inconsistency is apparently attributable to changes in the galley. For example, Dreiser crossed out all references to Sherry's in the typescript and penciled in Delmonico's, but in the published work most—though not all—of these references have been changed back to Sherry's.

37. See Philip Williams, "The Chapter Titles of *Sister Carrie*," *American Literature*, XXXVI (November, 1964), 359–65.

38. Dreiser to Frederick A. Duneka, February 20, 1912; *Letters*, I, 135.

39. In addition to the excellent discussions of *Sister Carrie* by Matthiessen, pp. 55–92, and Lehan, pp. 67–79, see Kenneth S. Lynn, "Introduction," *Sister Carrie* (Rinehart Edition) (New York, 1957), Claude M. Simpson, Jr., "*Sister Carrie* Reconsidered," *Southwest Review*, XLIV (Winter, 1959), 44–53, and Mary A. Burgan, "*Sister Carrie* and the Pathos of Naturalism," *Criticism*, XV (Fall, 1973), 336–49.

40. Many critics have written perceptively on the role of the city in *Sister Carrie*, but I am particularly indebted to David R. Weimer's discussion in *The City as Metaphor* (New York, 1966), pp. 65–77.

41. Dreiser's own paraphrase of this philosophical position can be found in his "Reflections" column in *Ev'ry Month*, II (September, 1896), 6–7.

42. The Ames-Carrie interviews occur in Chapter XLIX of the holograph and Chapter XLVI of the typescript and published volume.

43. For Dreiser's own low opinion of musical comedy, see "Reflections," *Ev'ry Month*, III (January, 1897), 5–6.

44. Dreiser's original draft of the epilogue stresses this "quest for beauty" theme even more fully than does the published version. The final two sentences of his draft are: "In your rocking chair, by your window, dreaming, shall you long for beauty. In your rocking chair, by your window, shall you still know such happiness as you may ever feel." Henry, in his fair copy of the epilogue, omitted the "for beauty" in the first sentence, and it was Henry's version which served as copy for the typescript and thus for the published novel.

45. See, in particular, Dreiser's interviews with Philip D. Armour, Chauncey Depew, and Marshall Field; *Success*, I (October, 1898), 3–4; I (November, 1898), 3–4; II (December 8, 1898), 7–8. In the Field interview, Dreiser quoted Field as saying, "There is no happiness in mere dollars. . . . It is only in the wider public affairs, where money is a moving force toward the general welfare, that the possessor of it can possibly find pleasure, and that only in doing constantly more."

46. See Ellen Moers, pp. 43–56, for Tolstoy's vogue in America during the 1890s and on the interest of Howells and Dreiser in his social ideas. By concentrating on Tolstoy's *What to Do?*, however, Miss Moers neglects the impact of *What Is Art?* on Howells and Dreiser. *What Is Art?* was published in English in mid-1898 and by the fall had been widely reviewed and discussed. Tolstoy held that art was essentially the communication of emotion and that the only worthwhile art communicated emotions which created a sense of universal unity among men. He noted in particular as among such emotions "the simple feelings of common life accessible to every one without exception—such as feelings of merriment, of pity, of cheerfulness, of tranquility, and so forth"; *What Is Art?* (London, 1942), p. 240.

47. "How [William Dean Howells] Climbed Fame's Ladder," *Success*, I (April, 1898), 5–6 and "The Real Howells," *Ainslee's*, V (March, 1900), 137–42. Miss Moers notes (p. 326n3) that the *Ainslee's* article, which contains a full discussion of Howells's devotion to Tolstoy's ideals, was written between March and October, 1899—that is, before Dreiser began *Sister Carrie*. In an extraordinarily effusive letter to Howells on May 14, 1902 (Moers, pp. 175–76), Dreiser described Hardy, Tolstoy, and Howells as his three principal spiritual mentors.

48. *Cleveland Leader*, November 12, 1911.

49. *My Literary Passions* (New York, 1895), p. 251.

50. See Sheila H. Jurnak, "Popular Art Forms in *Sister Carrie*," *Texas Studies in Literature and Language*, XIII (Summer, 1971), 313–20.

51. See William A. Freedman, "A Look at Dreiser as Artist: The Motif of Circularity in *Sister Carrie*," *Modern Fiction Studies*, VIII (Winter, 1962–63), 384–92.

52. See Dreiser's comment as reported in the *Bookman*, XV (March, 1902), 13.

53. For a somewhat different but perceptive analysis of Hurstwood's indecision before the safe, see Gordon O. Taylor, *The Passages of Thought: Psychological Representation in the American Novel, 1870–1900* (New York, 1969), pp. 151–57.

54. Dreiser to Walter H. Page, August 6, 1900; *Letters*, I, 62.

55. Otis Notman, "Talks with Four Novelists," *New York Times Saturday Review of Books*, June 15, 1907, p. 393.

56. "The Saddest Story," *New Republic*, III (June 12, 1915), 155.

57. Mencken to Dreiser, April 23, 1911; *Letters*, I, 115.

58. Julian Markels has discussed this aspect of Dreiser's technique with great perception in his "Dreiser and the Plotting of Inarticulate Experience," *Massachusetts Review*, II (Spring, 1963), 431–48, as has Ellen Moers in her "The Finesse of Dreiser," *American Scholar*, XXXIII (Winter, 1963–64), 109–114.

59. *Book*, p. 412.

60. The phrase is William J. Handy's in his "A Re-Examination of Dreiser's *Sister Carrie*," *Texas Studies in Literature and Language*, I (Autumn, 1959), 385.

61. Dreiser's imagery in *Sister Carrie* and in his other novels receives excellent discussion in William L. Phillips, "The Imagery of Dreiser's Novels," *PMLA*, LXXVIII (December, 1963), 572–85.

62. Ellen Moers and Joseph Katz have written at length on Dreiser's debt to Stephen Crane's "The Men in the Storm" for the flophouse portion of *Sister Carrie*. See Moers, pp. 60–68, and Katz, "Theodore Dreiser and Stephen Crane: Studies in a Literary Relationship," in *Stephen Crane in Transition*, ed. Joseph Katz (Dekalb, Ill., 1972), pp. 174–204.

Part One: *Jennie Gerhardt*

1. Dreiser to Arthur Henry, July 23, 1900; *Letters*, I, 53.

2. My account of the composition of *Jennie Gerhardt* differs in several important details

from that found in Swanberg, pp. 96–100, and Lehan, pp. 81–82. In particular, Swanberg neglects entirely the holograph which Dreiser prepared in early 1901, and Lehan errs in dating a large portion of this holograph as 1904, an error which then leads him to misdate the composition of the second draft. Dreiser's letter to Brett on April 16, 1901 (see below) establishes that he had completed by that date as much of the first draft as he was to write.

3. Dreiser to George P. Brett, April 16, 1901; in the Macmillan Collection, New York Public Library.

4. This typescript, of which thirteen much revised chapters are extant, can be identified as Miss Mallon's work because she used her letterhead stationery as cover sheets for each chapter.

5. My account of Mame's life is based on Dreiser recollections in *Dawn* and *A Book About Myself*, on his fuller and more explicit narrative in the manuscript of *Dawn*, and on Swanberg's scattered references to her and to Austin Brennan. The holograph of *Dawn* is in the Lilly Library, Indiana University; the Dreiser Collection contains a microfilm copy of this draft.

6. Dreiser disguised this consequence of Mame's relationship with Colonel Silsby in *Dawn* (pp. 73–75) by assigning it to a friend of Mame's, one Kitty Costigan. In the typescript of *Dawn* the event is assigned to Mame.

7. When in *Dawn* (p. 356) Dreiser recalled Mame's report in 1889 of a visit to the Brennans, he noted as well his own visit to the Brennans' Rochester home "years later." A probable date for Dreiser's visit is late December 1900, when John Dreiser died in Rochester at the home of Mame and Austin Brennan.

8. Dreiser to Mencken, May 14, 1916; *Letters*, I, 215.

9. Dreiser to Richard Duffy, February 2, 1902; William White, "Dreiser on Hardy, Henley, and Whitman: An Unpublished Letter," *English Language Notes*, VI (December, 1968), 122.

10. See Dreiser's tribute to Hardy in the Harper promotion brochure *Thomas Hardy: Notes on His Life and Work* (New York, [1925]), p. 15.

11. Dreiser refers specifically to *Tess* in the holograph of *Sister Carrie*. Ames had recommended Hardy to Carrie, and when Mrs. Vance comments that she had found *Tess* too sad, Ames replies (Chapter XLIX, p. 30) that one has to "feel the pathetic side of life" to respond properly to the novel.

12. See in particular Dreiser's characterization of Mame in *Dawn*, p. 356, and *Book*, pp. 27–29.

13. Though *Tess* was undoubtedly the principal literary influence on Dreiser's portrait of Jennie, George Moore's *Esther Waters* (1894) also seems to have played a role. In particular, Moore's seduced servant girl—unlike either Mame or Tess but like Jennie—not only bears an illegitimate child but also devotes much of her life, at great personal sacrifice, to its upbringing.

14. My quotations from the first draft of *Jennie* are cited from the fair-copy typescript of this draft, since they are more readily available in this version than in the heavily revised holograph.

15. Rutger B. Jewett to Dreiser, September 30, 1901, enclosing a contract for republication of *Sister Carrie*, and Rutger B. Jewett and Joseph F. Taylor to Dreiser, October 26, 1901, indicating a willingness to subsidize the completion of *Jennie Gerhardt*. Jewett was a member of the firm of J. F. Taylor and Company.

16. Dreiser to Joseph F. Taylor, November 25, 1901; *Letters*, I, 68–69.

17. Rutger B. Jewett to Dreiser, April 24, 1902. On April 9, before Jewett received this initial group of chapters, he suggested to Dreiser that he change the title of the novel to "some abstract word or combination of words," and on April 12 he asked for a few pages of manuscript from the opening of the novel in order to prepare a publisher's dummy, since Taylor and Company hoped to issue the novel during the fall or winter. Dreiser responded with a new title, *The Transgressor*, and with two or three pages of typescript. The firm then prepared a title page and two pages of printed text (in the Dreiser Collection), though a full dummy was apparently never produced.

18. Rutger B. Jewett to Dreiser, June 19, 1902. Dreiser sent a third and last installment to Jewett in July, though he continued to work on the novel until early 1903.

19. Dreiser's diary of the last phase of his Philadelphia sojourn, from October 22, 1902, to February 17, 1903, is in the Lilly Library, Indiana University. The diary contains frequent references to his attempts to work on *Jennie*.

20. Rutger B. Jewett to Dreiser, December 19, 1902.

21. Dreiser to Ripley Hitchcock, February 27, 1903; *Letters*, I, 70.

22. See particularly the two paragraphs on pp. 75–76 beginning "There are crises in men's lives. . . ."

23. Lester appears initially in Chapter XXI of the first draft and Chapter XIV of the second draft. In the first draft Jennie works in a Cleveland factory and is accosted by Lester on the street. He arranges to meet her at a hotel, where, in a long sequence based on an experience of Dreiser's sister Sylvia, he attempts to seduce her. Dreiser compressed this section of the novel by substituting Jennie's brief encounters with Lester at Mrs. Bracebridge's for the attempted seduction at a hotel.

24. The evidence in this matter is inconclusive. In 1907 Dreiser reported that his editorial labors prevented him from working on *Jennie* (Otis Notman, "Talks with Four Novelists," *New York Times Saturday Review of Books*, June 15, 1907, p. 393), and his letter to Edna Kenton on July 31, 1911 (in the Columbia University Library) strongly suggests that he did not work on the novel between 1902 and 1911. "You know," he wrote, "I abandoned trying to write Jennie Gerhardt in 1902 or 3 and took to editing. Last fall I took it up again." However, he permitted Grant Richards to see twenty chapters of the novel in March 1908, with an eye toward future publication of the novel by Richards (Richards to Dreiser, March 6, 1908), and he told Dorothy Dudley in 1930 that he had worked on the novel in 1908 (Dudley, p. 225). Dreiser's Butterick job, which he began in mid-1907, gave him the financial security which permitted him to think forward to the possibility of completing *Jennie*. I believe that it is this renewed interest in the novel (stimulated as well by the republication of *Sister Carrie* in 1907) rather than work itself which is reflected in Dreiser's overtures to Richards and in his later recollections.

25. Dreiser announced to Grant Richards on December 2, 1910 (University of Illinois Library), that "the successor to Carrie is being typewritten."

26. Lillian Rosenthal to Dreiser, January 25, 1911.

27. See Dreiser to Fremont Rider, January 24, 1911; *Letters*, I, 110.

28. Joseph H. Coates wrote Dreiser on January 11, 1911, "Is Mrs. Dreiser still abroad, and with your novel?" See also Swanberg, p. 143, and p. 356, n30 below.

29. Dreiser to Mencken, February 24, 1911; *Letters*, I, 111.

30. Dreiser to Fremont Rider, March 15, 1911. The carbon of *Jennie Gerhardt* in the Barrett Collection of the University of Virginia Library reveals much about the history of the novel during 1910–11. Until the middle of Chapter XXXIV (Chapter XXXVI of the published work), the carbon is of the original typescript of December 1910. From that point, the typescript consists of a new carbon with a few sections of the old carbon (dealing primarily with Lester's financial affairs) spliced in. The carbon bears on its cover the stamp of Curtis Brown and Massie, the London literary agent, and is therefore no doubt the copy which (in its original form) Sallie took to London in January. It also contains a packing slip addressed from Mencken to Dreiser and is thus the copy which, in its revised but uncut form, Mencken read in April 1911.

31. Swanberg (p. 143) estimates that more than a dozen friends read the "unhappy ending" version in typescript.

32. This figure is a rough estimate. On July 31, 1911, Dreiser wrote Edna Kenton (in the Columbia University Library) that the novel was "nearly 200,000 words." On October 25, 1911, Mencken, who had read both the typescript submitted by Dreiser to Harper's and the published novel, wrote Harry Wilson that Harper's had cut 25,000 words from *Jennie* (Guy J. Forgue, ed., *Letters of H. L. Mencken*, [New York, 1961] p. 18). Since the published novel is approximately 150,000 words, it can be assumed that Dreiser's "nearly 200,000" was closer to

175,000 and that Mencken was correct in estimating that Dreiser and Harper's agreed on a 25,000 word cut. Not extant are the original typescript which Dreiser and Harper's cut and which served as printer's copy (perhaps the manuscript of *Jennie* sold by Dreiser in 1922; see Swanberg, pp. 267–68) and galley proof.

33. Dreiser to Mencken, September 4 and October 20, 1911, and Mencken to Dreiser, November 9, 1911; *Letters*, I, 119, 124.

34. Dreiser's quotation is from Jefferies's essay "Beauty in the Country," *The Open Air* (London, 1885), pp. 198–99.

35. "The Art of Theodore Dreiser," *Dial*, LXII (June 14, 1917), 508.

36. However, for a suggestive recent attempt to distinguish between the tragic and pathetic in *Jennie Gerhardt*, see Warwick Wadlington, "Pathos and Dreiser," *Southern Review*, VII (Spring, 1971), 411–29.

37. Huneker to Dreiser, June 4, 1911.

38. Harper's kept the novel in print until 1924, when A. L. Burt Company published it under agreement with Harper's. The Boni and Liveright edition appeared later in 1924. All three publishers used the original 1911 plates. The epilogue was dropped some time between 1911 and 1924, since there are copies of the Harper's edition both with and without the epilogue but all copies published by Burt and by Boni and Liveright omit it.

Part Two: *The "Genius"*

1. See Dreiser's letters to Mencken during the winter and spring of 1911; *Letters*, I, 111, 113, 114, 119.

2. Dreiser to Mencken, April 10, 1911; *Letters*, I, 113.

3. Dreiser's term, in a letter to William C. Lengel, October 15, 1911; *Letters*, I, 122.

4. *Letters*, I, 119; and Dreiser to Grant Richards, July 7, 1912.

5. Lengel to Dreiser, February 21, 1913.

6. Lengel to Dreiser, May 3 and May 15, 1913.

7. There is considerable confusion over how many typescripts of *The "Genius"* Dreiser lost and when the losses occurred. In July 1913, he wrote Mencken about his Chicago loss, announcing that "the second & only remaining copy (type) of *The Genius* was lost in the mails. Loss—$135. A recopying is necessary" (*Letters*, I, 155). On June 22, 1914, he wrote Mencken that "*The Genius* of which I lost two complete typewritten copies worth $175.00 all told is nearly recopied" (*Letters*, I, 169). Since the $175 Dreiser mentions in his second letter could not represent the $135 his earlier letter plus an additional complete recopying, it appears that Dreiser lost a typewritten copy of *The "Genius"* sometime before his trip to Chicago as well as shortly after the trip. An earlier loss would also clarify Dreiser's comment in his July 1913 letter to Mencken about a "second and only remaining copy (type)"; he means the first copy had been lost earlier and that the second and last copy had just been lost. It is not clear which of these copies was an original and which a carbon.

8. Dreiser to Major Leigh, February 24, 1913.

9. *Letters*, I, 164–65.

10. For a somewhat different account of both the chronology and the significance of Dreiser's revision of the conclusion of *The "Genius,"* see Robert H. Elias, "Bibliography and the Biographer," *Library Chronicle* of the University of Pennsylvania, XXXVIII (Winter, 1972) 25–44. Elias believes that Dreiser completed his revision of *The "Genius"* in late 1913 because he deposited a copy of the novel with the Century Company at that time. However, the manuscript left with the Century Company could have been the original holograph, and Dreiser's letters to Mencken of March 25, 1914 (*Letters*, I, 164–65) and June 22, 1914 (*Letters*, I, 169) appear to indicate revision in March and preparation of fresh typescripts in June 1914.

11. See Joseph Katz, "Dummy: *The "Genius,"* by Theodore Dreiser," *Proof*, I (1971), 330–38. Katz correctly posits that this copy of the typescript became the basis for the publisher's dummy issued by John Lane in mid-1915. Dreiser was unsuccessful in finding a

serial outlet for *The "Genius"* at this time, but the novel did appear in the *Metropolitan Magazine* in 1923.

12. Dreiser to Mencken, November 30 and December 8, 1914; *Letters*, I, 183, 184.

13. Dreiser to Mencken, November 10 and December 8, 1914; *Letters*, I, 182, 184. This carbon, which served as printer's copy, is extant in the Dreiser Collection in fragmentary form, from chapter XXXII (Chapter IV of Book Two) to the end of the novel.

14. *Letters*, I, 184.

15. See Swanberg, p. 187.

16. Floyd Dell, *Homecoming* (New York, 1933), p. 269. Louis J. Oldani, in "A Study of Theodore Dreiser's *The 'Genius'* " (Ph.D. dissertation, University of Pennsylvania, 1972), pp. 90–102, estimates that Chapman and Dell were jointly responsible for the cutting of approximately 20,000 words.

17. It is difficult to estimate the length of the original holograph, but Dreiser himself, in a letter to Mary Fanton Roberts on June 26, 1911, judged it to be 425,000 words. The published novel is approximately 350,000 words.

18. Dreiser to Mencken, November 30, 1914; *Letters*, I, 183.

19. Dreiser to Mencken, March 8, 1943; *Letters*, III, 977.

20. Robert H. Elias has discussed Dreiser's use of this early version of *The "Genius"* in *A Book About Myself* in his "Bibliography and the Biographer," pp. 41–44. Scholars have often confused this early version of *The "Genius"* with an early version of *An American Tragedy*; see p. 364 n. 10 below.

21. The letters appear on p. 104 of *The "Genius"* and p. 127 of *A Book About Myself*. Most commentators, noting the similarity between the letters, have assumed that Dreiser merely adapted the "real" letter to fiction and that the letter in *A Book About Myself* is indeed the "real" letter. In fact, if a "real" letter existed, Dreiser initially adapted it to fiction for his 1901–2 version of *The "Genius"* and then, except for the change of names, used this fictional version verbatim in *A Book About Myself*. (The passage containing the letter in the holograph of *A Book About Myself* is on small yellow sheets pasted on large white sheets.) In his 1910–11 draft of *The "Genius,"* Dreiser used a slightly revised version of the letter, probably recasting it from memory.

22. This incident appears in *The "Genius"* in the form of Eugene's infatuation with Frieda Roth. A much fuller account of the experience occurs in his sketch "Rella" in *A Gallery of Women* (1929). In both accounts Dreiser stresses the shock and the bitter frustration of his discovery of the limitations which marriage placed upon his love of youthful beauty.

23. Perhaps the major differences, aside from those involving the opening and close of the novel, are Dreiser's compression of his experiences as a reporter in Chicago, St. Louis, and Pittsburgh into Eugene's career as a Chicago newspaper illustrator, and Dreiser's omission of the worst phases of his nervous collapse.

24. This aspect of Dreiser's life has been examined by a number of critics, in particular by Joseph J. Kwiat in "Dreiser and the Graphic Artist," *American Quarterly*, III (Summer, 1951), 127–41 and Moers, passim. Dreiser's sketch of "Ellen Adams Wrynn" in *A Gallery of Women* reveals his close involvement in New York art life during his 1905–10 editorial years.

25. "The Color of To-day," *Harper's Weekly*, XLV (December 14, 1901), 1272–73; republished as "W. L. S." in *Twelve Men* (1919).

26. See Joseph J. Kwiat, "Dreiser's *The "Genius"* and Everett Shinn, the 'Ash-Can' Painter," *PMLA*, LXVII (March, 1952), 15–31.

27. The sketch was published in the magazine *1910*; the painting is briefly described on p. 110 of *The "Genius."* Dreiser's sketch may itself have been inspired by a Shinn painting.

28. This observation is in part confirmed by Dreiser's enthusiasm for the work of Alfred Stieglitz. In his photographs of New York street life, Stieglitz was attempting to achieve an effect closely related to the goals of The Eight. Indeed, as Philip L. Gerber points out in his *Theodore Dreiser* (New York, 1964), pp. 117, 196n.8, Dreiser used Stieglitz's famous photograph "Winter on Fifth Avenue" as the basis for a description of a painting by Eugene (*The "Genius,"* p. 227). See also Moers, pp. 10–13.

29. In the nineteenth century it was commonly held that sexual overactivity was a cause of "nervous disease." Dreiser cut from Chapter XL of the typescript a direct allusion to this belief. Eugene's "own feeling," Dreiser wrote, "was that over-indulgence in the sexual relationship was the deadly rival of whiskey and the destructive opiates."

30. Randolph Bourne, "Theodore Dreiser," *New Republic*, II (April 17, 1915), 8.

31. See Dreiser's letters to Thelma Cudlipp, October 3, 4, and 7, 1910; *Letters*, I, 104–109.

32. John Cowper Powys, "Theodore Dreiser," *Little Review*, II (November, 1915), 10.

33. The holograph of *The "Genius"* has on its second cover sheet the following note in Dreiser's hand: "Alternate Titles. Would those who read this manuscript kindly indicate here any other title which may occur to them as appropriate and forceful. Or check the one they prefer. This Matter of Marriage, Now. The Story of Eugene. Eugene Witla. The Hedonist. The Dreamer. The Sensualist."

34. Those who consider Eugene a genius are Miriam Finch (p. 153), Angela (pp. 199, 484), M. Charles (p. 232), Hiram Colfax (p. 663), and Suzanne (p. 671). Although none of these designations is intended ironically by the character involved, Dreiser himself never describes Eugene as a genius except in the qualified form of the title of the novel.

35. Dreiser to Mencken, November 30, 1914; *Letters*, I. 183.

36. Sallie had been interested in Christian Science for some years, and when Dreiser went through a period of depression shortly after leaving his Butterick position he consulted a practitioner. (Dreiser's untitled manuscript reminiscence of O. S. Marden, the proprietor of *Success*.) The Christian Science section in *The "Genius"* is so muddy that many readers have been at a loss to discern both Dreiser's attitude toward the faith and the role of the section in the novel. Dreiser explained his intent in a letter to Edward H. Smith on January 10, 1921; "I tried to show just how it was that he came to dabble with Christian Science, and why, in the long run it failed to hold him. Having recovered a part of his mental strength he shed it, as a snake does a skin" (*Letters*, I, 338).

37. The long quotation from Wallace on pp. 697–99 consists of miscellaneous passages from the concluding chapter of Wallace's *The World of Life: A Manifestation of Creative Power, Directive Mind, and Ultimate Purpose* (New York, 1911).

38. The passage from Spencer quoted on pp. 735–36 is from his essay "Ultimate Questions" in *Facts and Comments* (New York, 1902), pp. 303–304.

39. Both figures use the technique of a short, affirmative rhetorical question when they sense a degree of feminine responsivness—"You love me, don't you?" or the like. See, for example, *The "Genius,"* pp. 150, 341 and *The Titan*, p. 133.

Part Two: The Cowperwood Trilogy

1. There is a growing body of criticism on Alger and on other aspects of the success myth. I have profited in particular from Irvin G. Wyllie, *The Self-Made Man in America* (New Brunswick, N.J., 1954) and Richard Weiss, *The American Myth of Success* (New York, 1969).

2. See "Reflections," *Ev'ry Month*, I (January, 1896), 4–5 and III (March, 1897), 3.

3. See "Reflections," I (February, 1896), 6 and III (February, 1897), 2.

4. See Dreiser's "Life Stories of Successful Men—No. 10. Philip D. Armour," *Success*, I (October, 1898), 3–4; "Life Stories of Successful Men—No. 12. Marshall Field," *Success*, II (December 8, 1898), 7–8; and "A Monarch of Metal Workers" (Carnegie), *Success*, II (June 3, 1899), 453–54. See also Walter Blackstock, "Dreiser's Dramatization of American Success," *Florida State University Studies*, XIV (1954), 107–29.

5. Although Edgar Lee Masters's memory was not always reliable in his later years, he recalled in *Across Spoon River* (New York, 1936) that Dreiser told him in early 1913 that "he had looked into the careers of twenty American capitalists and that Yerkes was the most interesting of all of them" (p. 329).

6. Among studies of the relationship of Yerkes's career to Dreiser's portrait of Cowper-

wood, I have relied particularly on Lehan, 101–104; on Robert E. Wilkinson, "A Study of Theodore Dreiser's *The Financier*" (Ph.D. dissertation, University of Pennsylvania, 1965); and on Philip Gerber, "Dreiser's Financier: A Genesis," *Journal of Modern Literature*, I (March, 1971), 354–74, "The Alabaster Protégé: Dreiser and Berenice Fleming," *American Literature*, XLIII (May, 1971), 217–230, and "The Financier Himself: Dreiser and C. T. Yerkes," *PMLA*, LXXXVIII (January, 1973), 112–21. In a letter to Robert H. Elias on November 17, 1937 (in the Cornell University Library), Dreiser remarked that Cowperwood was pronounced Cooperwood.

7. "Review of the Month," *Ev'ry Month*, I (December, 1895), 10. In "An Address to Caliban," *Esquire*, II (September, 1934), 20, Dreiser claimed that he had met Yerkes. He supplies no date, but the context of his recollection suggests the summer of 1898 when he visited Chicago to prepare a series of articles and interviews. It should be noted, however, that Dreiser nowhere else recalls meeting Yerkes.

8. The article appeared in the *New York World* on February 4, 1906. Since a clipping of the article is among Dreiser's notes for the Cowperwood trilogy, Philip Gerber suggests—in his "Dreiser's Financier," pp. 372–74—that Dreiser preserved the article on its appearance because of his interest in writing a novel based on Yerkes's life. But though Dreiser may have seen the article on its appearance, the clipping itself probably derives from the collection of clippings on Yerkes's life which he acquired in 1911. See pp. 161–62 below.

9. There are many clippings of this kind among Dreiser's notes for the trilogy. See pp. 184–85, 333–34 below.

10. Edwin Lefèvre, "What Availeth It?" *Everybody's*, XXIV (June, 1911), 840. Dreiser mentions Lefèvre's article in *The Stoic*, p. 303.

11. "Theodore Dreiser Now Turns to High Finance," *New York Sun*, October, 19, 1912.

12. Dreiser later ranged from 1912 to 1919 in his recollection of when he first read Loeb. Ellen Moers (p. 246) believes that his knowledge of Loeb's ideas dates from 1915, a supposition confirmed in part by the frequent appearance of Loeb's name and ideas in Dreiser's unpublished essays from that point. In a letter to Loeb on May 29, 1919 (in the Library of Congress), Dreiser noted that he had read Loeb's "The Mechanistic Conception of Life" (1912) "several years ago."

13. *Hey*, p. 89.

14. Dreiser to Mencken, December 6, 1909; *Letters*, I, 97.

15. Dreiser to Mencken, December 16, 1909; *Letters*, I, 98.

Part Two: *The Financier*

1. The earliest record of Dreiser's research activity is a letter from Ripley Hitchcock of Harper's to Dreiser on June 30, 1911, concerning Dreiser's use of the files of the *New York World*.

2. Dreiser to Mencken, August 8, 1911; *Letters*, I, 119.

3. In letters of May 26, 1912, to Grant Richards (*Letters*, I, 143) and Mencken, Dreiser wrote that he planned to issue *The Financier* in three parts because of its length. On July 7, 1912, in a letter to Richards, he noted that "Parts II and III will carry separate titles as I see it now."

4. The nature and extent of Harper's pressure upon Dreiser are suggested by a letter of Ripley Hitchcock to Dreiser, June 6, 1912: "Sequel is an unhappy word, particularly at the outset. What seems to me essential is to get a cumulative effect. If we proclaim the whole cycle at the beginning it will be dangerous. You will hold readers with 'The Financier.' Then with that book launched let us adroitly pave the way for the second, and finally for the third, and then we will put three books on the altar and dance and clash the cymbals over the completion of the perfect work."

5. For Dreiser's extensive use of Ellis P. Oberholtzer's biography of Jay Cooke, see Philip

L. Gerber, "Dreiser's Debt to *Jay Cooke*," *Library Chronicle* of the University of Pennsylvania, XXXVIII (Winter, 1972), 67–77.

6. "Theodore Dreiser Now Turns to High Finance," *New York Sun*, October 19, 1912.

7. Coates's correspondence with Dreiser about details of the Philadelphia background of *The Financier* extends from August 1911 to September 1912. Since Coates was Dreiser's primary source of information about the Philadelphia of Yerkes's day, the clipping collection was probably acquired through his good offices.

8. The sheets are preserved in the Dreiser Collection in two sequences. The first, consisting of notes for *The Financier* and *The Titan*, contains over 900 numbered sheets, of which approximately the first 200 are in chronological order. The second consists of notes for *The Stoic*. Its sheets are numbered only by their location in the file folder in which each sheet has been placed. Dreiser apparently had at one time a single more or less chronologically arranged sequence of notes on Yerkes's career. But he also apparently rearranged portions of his notes when writing *The Titan* and then separated out all material on Yerkes's later career in 1932 when he began work on *The Stoic*.

9. See the studies listed on p. 359, n. 6. Of some interest are three variations from his sources which Dreiser introduced into his account of Yerkes's career: he depicted Yerkes as an independent financial operator while in fact Yerkes was closely associated with several Philadelphia financial giants; he reversed the order of the Philadelphia city election and the political scandal attached to Yerkes's failure, placing the scandal before the election; and he radically foreshortened the period Yerkes remained in Philadelphia after his release from prison.

10. Butler appears frequently in the political news reports and editorial columns of the *St. Louis Globe-Democrat* and *St. Louis Republic* during the periods Dreiser worked for these papers. For a characteristic attack on his corrupt practices, see the *St. Louis Republic*, November 4, 1893. Butler is described at length in Lincoln Steffens, *The Shame of the Cities* (New York, 1904), pp. 56, 105–43.

11. *Book*, p. 109.

12. *Book*, p. 110.

13. Dreiser to Mencken, November 11, 1911; *Letters*, I, 127. Dreiser noted in his letter that he had completed thirty-nine chapters and that the novel was one-third finished. However, the typescript prepared from this manuscript is only thirty-eight chapters long (thirty-seven in the published version), and Dreiser's one-third refers to his original intention that *The Financier* would be a single novel covering all of Yerkes's career.

14. Dreiser to Grant Richards, May 26, 1912; *Letters*, I, 144.

15. Dreiser to Grant Richards, July 7, 1912.

16. Extant as a basis for the discussion which follows are Dreiser's complete holograph of the novel and the thirty-eight-chapter typescript prepared in late 1911.

17. My interpretation of the nature of this second revision is based on the facts that the original holograph does not contain this incident, that a large gap in the sequence of chapters in the holograph occurs during the narration of the events between Cowperwood's trial and imprisonment, and that there exists an independent manuscript fragment which is apparently a revision of this missing sequence and which is in a direct line of descent to the published version of the incident. In short, Dreiser cut the incident from its original position in the holograph and then revised it in a separate holograph fragment for inclusion at an earlier point in the novel.

18. Dreiser had not completed the novel by July 7 (Dreiser to Grant Richards) but by August 28 he was reading galley (Dreiser to Mencken; *Letters*, I, 145).

19. Dreiser to Mencken, September 14, 1912; *Letters*, I, 146.

20. See Mencken to Dreiser, October 6, 1912, and Dreiser's undated reply; *Letters*, I, 146–47.

21. Dreiser wrote Mencken on November 4, 1912, that "the book should have been cut 170 pages instead of 77." In a letter of December 2, 1912, to Willard Wright (in the Yale

University Library) he expressed his dismay at "the obvious defects of The Financier—defects which more time and means would have permitted me to correct."

22. Dreiser wrote Albert Mordell on September 25, 1913 (in the University of Virginia Library) that "The Financier lacks in drama and condensation in spots but I expect to go over it and re-issue it much improved for the final set."

23. See *Letters to Louise: Theodore Dreiser's Letters to Louise Campbell*, ed. Louise Campbell (Philadelphia, 1959), pp. 30–31, 34, 36.

24. Louise Campbell to Robert E. Wilkinson, November 11, 1963; Robert E. Wilkinson, "A Study of Theodore Dreiser's *The Financier*" (Ph.D. dissertation, University of Pennsylvania, 1965), p. 33.

25. The fullest study of the differences between the versions is by Robert E. Wilkinson in his 1965 University of Pennsylvania dissertation. See also Matthiessen, pp. 149–52. One anomaly noted by both Wilkinson and Matthiessen is that in 1912 Dreiser cut at the last moment, on Mencken's advice, the lengthy speeches by the district attorney and defense lawyer at Cowperwood's trial but that he restored these speeches—while cutting almost every other aspect of the novel—in the 1927 edition.

26. *Tom Watson's Magazine*, III (January, 1906), 306–308. Although Dreiser does not use the lobster-squid example in this article, he nevertheless finds exact parallels between the struggle for existence in marine and business life.

27. Dreiser derived this phrase from a long article on Yerkes, dated December 26, 1898, which he preserved as a clipping in his notes (folder 16, p. 16). The article, based largely on an interview with Yerkes, quotes him as saying, " 'Whatever I do, I do not from a sense of duty, but to satisfy myself.' "

28. Dreiser's clearest statement of this theme occurs in *The Titan*, when Stephanie, who is herself an artist, senses an aesthetic force in Cowperwood. "She conceived of him as a very great artist in his realm rather than as a business man, and he grasped this fact after a very little while and appreciated it" (pp. 215–16).

29. Chapter 62 of the holograph.

30. See pages 66–72 for Dreiser's almost obsessive use of this term in his description of Cowperwood's early response to Mrs. Semple.

31. David R. Weimer, *The City as Metaphor* (New York, 1966), pp. 71–72.

32. Mencken to Dreiser, October 6, 1912; *Letters of H. L. Mencken*, ed. Guy J. Forgue (New York, 1961), p. 24. In writing to others, however, Mencken was more severely critical of Dreiser's excessive detail in the novel.

33. "The Naturalism of Mr. Dreiser," *Nation*, CI (December 2, 1915), 650.

Part Two: *The Titan*

1. Dreiser to Mencken, May 26, 1912.

2. In a letter to Mary Fanton Roberts, November 4, 1912, Dreiser inquired about gaining permission to "look through Mr. J. P. Morgan's private art gallery or the residence of the late Charles T. Yerkes or both."

3. William Lengel, then living in Chicago, had arranged much earlier for Dreiser to have access to various Chicago newspaper morgues (Lengel to Dreiser, August 28, 1912). Dale Kramer, in his *Chicago Renaissance: The Literary Life in the Midwest 1900–1930* (New York, 1966), pp. 185–86, notes Dreiser's work at the Newberry Library.

4. Masters appears to have played much the same role in aiding Dreiser's research for this portion of the trilogy that Joseph Coates had played earlier for Yerkes's Philadelphia career. Besides writing letters of introduction to such figures as Carter H. Harrison (the Mayor Walden Lucas of *The Titan*), he apparently served as a mine of information about Yerkes's public and private affairs. When Dreiser required further details about Chicago matters while writing the novel during the summer of 1913, he corresponded with Masters. And on completing the book, he sent a copy of galley proof to Masters for checking (Masters to Dreiser, January 28, 1914).

5. In addition to the studies by Lehan and Gerber cited on p. 360, n. 6 above, see John T. Flanagan, "Theodore Dreiser's Chicago," *Revue des Langues Vivantes*, XXXII (1966), 131–44; Ray Ginger, *Altgeld's America* (New York, 1958); Walter T. K. Nugent, "Carter H. Harrison and Dreiser's 'Walden Lucas,' " *Newberry Library Bulletin*, VI (September, 1966), 222–30; Bessie L. Pierce, *A History of Chicago*, III (New York, 1957); and Lloyd Wendt and Herman Kogan, *Lords of the Levee: The Story of Bathhouse John and Hinky Dink* (Indianapolis, 1943).

6. Page 668, dated July 2, 1896, of Dreiser's notes for the Cowperwood trilogy.

7. Page 541, dated October 3, 1890, and page 542, dated January 8, 1890, of Dreiser's notes for the Cowperwood trilogy.

8. The fullest accounts of Dreiser's involvement with Kirah Markham and the Chicago Little Theatre group during the winter of 1912–13 are by Kramer, *Chicago Renaissance*, pp. 185–99, and by Dreiser himself in "This Madness—An Honest Novel about Love: Sidonie," *Hearst's International-Cosmopolitan*, LXXXVI (June, 1929), 84–87, 156–68 and LXXXVII (July, 1929), 86–87, 179–86, in which Kirah is Sidonie Platow and Dell is Webb Collins.

9. This identification of Dreiser with Forbes Gurney was first made by Kramer, *Chicago Renaissance*, p. 195. There is also a possibility that Dreiser modeled Gurney's poetry and perhaps some aspects of his "dreamy" character upon Vachel Lindsay. Lindsay's "General William Booth Enters Into Heaven" appeared in *Poetry* magazine in January 1913 and made a great stir. Lindsay, unlike Gurney, was notoriously shy with women, but Dreiser's quotation of two lines from a Gurney poem

"With eerie flute and rhythmic thrum
Of muted strings and beaten drum" (p. 227)

suggests a parody of Lindsay's style.

10. Gerber, "The Alabaster Protégé: Dreiser and Berenice Fleming," *American Literature*, XLIII (May, 1971), 217–30. Miss Grigsby's first name was variously spelled Emilie or Emily both in newspaper reports and by Dreiser in his notes.

11. Dreiser to Major Leigh, February 24, 1913.

12. Dreiser to Albert Mordell, October 21, 1913; in the University of Virginia Library.

13. Ripley Hitchcock to Dreiser, March 6, 1913.

14. Extant, besides many fragments, are the initial holograph in revised form complete through Chapter 103 (Chapter L of the sixty-two-chapter published novel), an additional five chapters of revised holograph and revised typescript (approximately Chapters LI to LVI of the published novel), and the first twenty-nine chapters of the initial typescript (Chapters I to XIX of the published novel). Dreiser may have had some aid in his editing from Anna Tatum, who was acting as his unofficial secretary, and from Kirah Markham, who joined him in New York in the early fall of 1913, as well as from Harper's editors. But he did not circulate the manuscript widely among friends with requests for changes and cuts, as he had done with both *Jennie Gerhardt* and *The "Genius."* One reason for this change may have been his anxiety to place the novel in Harper's hands in time for spring 1914 publication.

15. See Swanberg, pp. 172–73.

16. Ripley Hitchcock to Flora Mai Holly, October 17, 1911.

17. Dreiser to Albert Mordell, March 6, 1914; in the University of Virgina Library.

18. The eleven affairs are: three before he meets Rita (pp. 109–11); Antoinette (pp. 129 ff); four between Rita and Stephanie (p. 202); and three between Stephanie and Berenice (pp. 244–45, 264).

Part Three: *An American Tragedy*

1. Dreiser's interviews, not only on the novel but on its dramatic and film versions, are too numerous to cite. For a typical Dreiser explanation of the origin of the novel, see his letter to Jack Wilgus, April 20, 1927; *Letters*, II, 457–58. During Dreiser's quarrel with Paramount in 1931 over the film version of *An American Tragedy*, he wrote many letters to prospective supporters of his position in which he explained his intent in the novel. (For one such letter,

see *Letters*, II, 526–30.) The Robert Edwards murder case of 1934 prompted Dreiser to write two series of articles in which he compared the Edwards and Gillette cases and explained his interest in murders of this kind: "Theodore Dreiser Describes 'American Tragedy,' " *New York Post*, October 2–6, 1934 and "I Find the Real American Tragedy," *Mystery Magazine*, XI (February–June, 1935). The Newell P. Sherman case of 1935 called forth a similar article, "Crime Analyzed by Dreiser," *Los Angeles Examiner*, July 23, 1935. For the discussion which follows, I rely primarily on Dreiser's unpublished 1934 "American Tragedies" manuscripts and on the first installment of his "I Find the Real American Tragedy" series, *Mystery Magazine*, XI (February, 1935), 9–11, 88–90.

2. Other cases which Dreiser frequently mentioned were those of Roland Molineux in 1899, William Orpet in 1916, and Harry New in 1919, as well as several for which he did not remember the names of the principals.

3. "American Tragedies," manuscript A. (There are two typescripts of "American Tragedies." I designate as "A" the typescript beginning "The psychologic problem presented or developed in my novel . . . "and as "B" the typescript beginning "Back in the summer of 1905 at Big Moose Lake . . . . ")

4. "American Tragedies," manuscript B.

5. "I Find the Real American Tragedy," p. 88. Dreiser's italics.

6. "American Tragedies," manuscript B.

7. *Dawn*, p. 542.

8. *A Hoosier Holiday* (New York, 1916), p. 228. Dreiser used almost the same wording when recalling the incident in *Book*, p. 376.

9. *Book*, p. 72.

10. Dreiser's interest in the case was probably stimulated by the widely reported death of Molineux in late 1914. Dreiser began writing the Prologue on January 14, 1915, a date he noted on its first page. There has been some confusion among Dreiser scholars in their discussion of the nature and date of "The Rake" because Dreiser also used this title when referring to an incomplete autobiographical novel of 1901 or 1902. But it is clear that this reference is to an early version of *The "Genius"* (see pp. 137–38 above) and that his work on a fictional study of the Molineux case dates from 1914–15.

11. Dreiser noted in "American Tragedies," manuscript A, that he wrote six chapters of a novel based on the Richesen-Linnell case. Since he placed this attempt just before his turn to the Gillette case, a 1919–20 date is probable. Dreiser's letters to William Lengel on January 23, 1921, and August 23, 1922, reveal that he had been working sporadically on "Her Boy" since his arrival in California in late 1919.

12. *A Hoosier Holiday*, p. 418. See also *Twelve Men* (New York, 1919), pp. 82–83.

13. Swanberg (p. 254) states that in 1906 Dreiser saved clippings of the case and discussed it with Richard Duffy as a possible subject for a novel. Helen Dreiser, in a letter of February 15, 1945, to Robert H. Elias (in the Cornell University Library) enclosed a list of replies to a series of questions which Elias had asked Dreiser in a letter of February 4, 1945. In one such reply, Dreiser noted that he had been interested in the case in 1906 but that he did not think of it in connection with a novel "until four or five years" afterward. Dreiser's first recorded mention of the Gillette case occurs in his essay "Neurotic America and the Sex Impulse," written in 1918 and published in *Hey Rub-a-Dub-Dub*.

14. W. Earl Ward to Dreiser, September 7, 1920, in reply to Dreiser's inquiry of August 13.

15. *Letters*, I, 309. Dreiser's wildly optimistic date of completion no doubt reflects his need to placate Liveright, who believed that Dreiser was close to finishing and delivering *The Bulwark*.

16. Gillette's family background is described in the *New York World*, November 29, December 2, 6, and 11, 1906.

17. See *Dawn*, pp. 469–76, and Helen Dreiser, pp. 36–37. Although *Dawn* was completed by late 1919, it was not published until 1931. Dreiser was therefore able in the published version to note his use of the Conklins as a source for the Griffithses.

18. *Dawn*, p. 9

19. Chapter VII, p. 3. My quotations are from the carbon of the typescript which Estelle Kubitz ("Gloom") prepared for Dreiser. Miss Kubitz became Dreiser's secretary in 1916, and though she remained in New York on his departure for California in 1919, she continued to prepare typescripts for him for several years.

20. Chapter XIX, pp. 6–7.

21. In his sketch of Edith De Long Smith as "Olive Brand" in *A Gallery of Women* (New York, 1929), I, 82, Dreiser recalled that Miss De Long had introduced him to much avant-garde thought during his early years in the village, including Freud's *Three Contributions to the Theory of Sex* (translated by A. A. Brill in 1910). Floyd Dell, another early Freudian, appears to have also played a role in stimulating Dreiser's interest in psychoanalytical theory during this period. But Freudianism was "in the air" during 1914–19, and Dreiser required no specific mentor.

22. Dreiser to Brill, January 20, 1919.

23. *A Gallery of Women*, II, 769. Ellen Moers (pp. 240–70) discusses at length the influence of Freud and Loeb on Dreiser during his village period.

24. Moers, pp. 256–70.

25. *Hey*, p. 5.

26. Chapter XII, p. 1.

27. The essay can be dated by its cover address of 165 West 10th St. (Dreiser's 1914–19 address) and by Dreiser's reliance on Brill's "The Psychopathology of the Selection of Vocations," which appeared in the *Medical Record*, February, 1918.

28. Chapter VIII, p. 14.

29. The letters were published in pamphlet form a few days after they were read at the trial. Dreiser recalled his use of a pamphlet version of the letters in a letter to Donald Friede, August 23, 1930.

30. There is some confusion about which factory Dreiser visited. Correspondence in the Dreiser Collection indicates that Dreiser made arrangements in January 1923 to visit the Cluett and Peabody factory at Troy, New York. (See also Swanberg, pp. 286–87.) But Robert H. Elias (in his notes in the Cornell University Library) comments that the plan fell through and that Dreiser instead visited the Lion Collar and Shirt Company plant at Troy through the good offices of William Lengel. It is not known when Dreiser visited Sing Sing during 1923–24, but he mentioned such a visit to Manuel Komroff of Boni and Liveright (Swanberg, p. 296).

31. The only full-length study of Dreiser's use of his sources in *An American Tragedy* is John F. Castle's "The Making of *An American Tragedy*" (Ph.D. dissertation, University of Michigan, 1952). Castle's work is an excellent introduction to a complex subject. However, he often misleads because he invariably cites the trial record rather than the *World* when a specific item used by Dreiser appears in both the trial record and the *World*. This method of citation suggests that Dreiser relied heavily on the trial record when, as I demonstrate below, both internal and external evidence indicates that he used the *World* almost exclusively.

32. Since Gillette appealed his conviction, the verbatim trial record of the case was printed. According to general practice, a copy of the trial record would then have been deposited in the law libraries of the state, including the university law libraries of New York City.

33. "I Find the Real American Tragedy," *Mystery Magazine*, XI (February, 1935), 11, 88.

34. Other examples besides those noted below are the opening speech of Belknap (A. M. Mills), the testimony of Titus Alden and Mrs. Donahue (Frank Brown and Mrs. Carey), the charge to the jury by Judge Oberwaltzer (Judge Devendorf), Clyde's remarks on being sentenced, and his final letter to American youth. In addition, Dreiser used verbatim some of the *World*'s background material contained in interviews with Mrs. Gillette and in accounts of courtroom behavior during particularly sensational moments of the trial. Compare, for example, the reaction of Clyde and his attorneys to Mason's announcement that he has an

eyewitness to the crime (II, 239–40) and the description in the *World* of November 18 of a similar moment during the trial.

35. *State of New York/Court of Appeals/the People of the State of New York/vs/Chester Gillette*, I, 478.

36. *New York World*, November 18, 1906.

37. Dreiser's principal omissions were the state's use of the foetus as evidence of Grace Brown's pregnancy (a procedure objected to by Gillette's attorneys in their appeal but upheld by the appeals court on the grounds that the evidence was material and that the jar in which the foetus was introduced had been kept covered) and a purported confession made by Gillette in private to his attorneys and overheard by a deputy sheriff. His major additions were the attempts at abortion (see p. 366 n. 43 below), the newspaper story of a death by drowning at Pass Lake, and Clyde's enforced return, after his capture and imprisonment, to Big Bittern.

38. *New York World*, November 19, 1906.

39. "Americans Are Still Interested in Ten Commandments—For the Other Fellow," *New York Call Magazine*, March 13, 1921, p. 7.

40. The change, however, resulted in an anomaly later in the novel. Grace Brown was less than four months pregnant when she died but Roberta is closer to six months. Roberta would therefore have presumably begun to reveal her pregnancy sometime before her death given the mode of dress in the early 1920s. Dreiser ignores this probability aside from Roberta's comments (II, 7, 15) that she must do something soon or the girls in the factory will begin to notice her condition.

41. *New York World*, November 15, 1906.

42. *New York World*, November 29, 1906.

43. Ward knew of an abortion attempt by Gillette but was apparently unable to get the doctor involved to testify. He therefore questioned Gillette briefly on this matter and then dropped it (*New York World*, December 1, 1906). Dreiser developed this hint in two ways. Like Carlyle Harris and Clarence Richesen, Clyde seeks to find pills that will bring on an abortion. And like Mame and Sylvia, Roberta is unsuccessful in her attempt to persuade a moralistic doctor to perform an abortion. In particular, Dreiser adapted his recollection of Sylvia's account of being lectured by a Warsaw doctor (*Dawn*, pp. 261–62) into the scene between Roberta and Dr. Glenn.

44. *New York World*, November 13 and 14, 1906.

45. The extent of this "new" material can be estimated by the fact that it constitutes twenty pages of Clyde's twenty-nine page direct examination (II, 266–94).

46. Dreiser's account of the browbeating of a holdout juror derived directly from the version in the *New York World*, December 5, 1906.

47. The letters, in the order in which I note them, are June 14 (II, 38–39), based on Grace Brown's letter of June 20; undated (II, 37–38), based on Grace Brown's letter of June 19; June 10 (II, 19–21); and June 30 (II, 54).

48. See the *New York World*, March 28 to April 1, 1908. Dreiser ignored the new "evidence" which Gillette's attorneys presented to Governor Hughes—that Grace Brown was an epileptic and that she had been sleeping with another man at the time she became pregnant.

49. *New York World*, March 31, 1908. Dreiser used this key phrase verbatim in the "N.B." portion of the novel which he cut in page proof. (See pp. 231–32 below.) As reported by the *World*, the full statement issued by MacIlravy and the Reverend Cordelle Herrick (the prison chaplain) reads: "Because our relationship with Chester Gillette was privileged, we do not deem it wise to make a detailed statement and simply wish to say that no legal mistake was made in his electrocution."

50. Dreiser to Sally Kusell, August 16, 1923; University of Virginia Library.

51. Louise Campbell to Dreiser, December 16, 1923.

52. *A Hoosier Holiday* reveals Dreiser's fascination with hotels, both as a boy and as a man of forty-four. For Myrtle, see Dreiser's sketch "Reina" in *A Gallery of Women* and Helen Dreiser, p. 45.

53. Dreiser's letter to Louise Campbell, January 9, 1925, notes his completion of Book Two; *Letters*, II, 433.

54. *Letters*, II, 433.

55. Dreiser to Louise Campbell, June 30, 1924; *Letters*, II, 427.

56. Dreiser to Mencken, November 4, 1925.

57. Robert Penn Warren, "An American Tragedy," *Yale Review*, LII (October, 1962), 7. Other significant attempts to describe the complex, interwoven nature of the themes and form of the novel are by Lehan, pp. 164–69; Irving Howe, "The Stature of Theodore Dreiser," *New Republic*, CLI (July 25, 1964), 19–21; (August 22, 1964), 25–28; and Sheldon N. Grebstein, "*An American Tragedy:* Theme and Structure," in *The Twenties*, ed. Richard E. Langford and William E. Taylor (Deland, Fla., 1966), pp. 62–66.

58. See the final six plays in *Plays of the Natural and the Supernatural* (New York, 1916) and the stories "Chains" (1919), "Fulfillment" (1924) and "The Shadow" (1924) in *Chains* (New York. 1927).

59. As John T. Flanagan has noted—"Dreiser's Style in *An American Tragedy*," *Texas Studies in Literature and Language*, VII (Autumn, 1965), 288—there is no such bird as a wier-wier. Dreiser is playing either upon the Anglo-Saxon meaning of "wyrd" as fate (Lehan, p. 162) or upon the common use of "weird" as a synonym for "strange."

60. Dreiser's desire to stress Jephson's hold upon Clyde led him to vary his source and have Jephson (the Charles Thomas of the Gillette case) examine Clyde during the trial when in fact it had been A. M. Mills who had examined Gillette.

61. For example, the matter was discussed sufficiently for Boni and Liveright to conduct a publicity-seeking contest in 1926 on the topic "Was Clyde Griffiths Guilty of Murder in the First Degree?" The contest was won by Professor Albert H. Levitt of Washington and Lee University. See Vrest Orton, *Dreiserana* (New York, 1929), pp. 52–53. Robert Penn Warren examines the problem at length in his *Homage to Theodore Dreiser* (New York, 1971), pp. 159–66.

62. See Swanberg, p. 292.

63. Babbitt, "The Critic and American Life," *Forum*, LXXIX (February, 1928), 168.

64. Dreiser to Mencken, December 18, 1916; *Letters*, I, 241.

65. Matthiessen, p. 207.

66. Rose C. Feld, "Mr. Dreiser Passes Judgment on American Literature," *New York Times Book Review*, December 23, 1923, p. 7.

67. See the autobiographical passage in *The "Genius"* (p. 78) in which Ruby teaches Eugene to dance.

68. For the Warsaw lakes, see *Dawn*, pp. 185–86, 265–67. For a characteristic dream in Dreiser's fiction of death by water, see Jennie's dream in *Jennie Gerhardt* of Lester's forthcoming death (pp. 419–20).

69. Robert Penn Warren, in "*An American Tragedy*," p. 8, was the first to compare several of Dreiser's techniques in the novel to those of the film.

Part Four: The Years Between

1. The fullest and best discussion of Dreiser's social and philosophical thought between the late 1920s and his death is by Lehan, pp. 170–221.

2. I have already discussed Dreiser and Spencer (see pp. 10–14, 157–59 above). For Dreiser's response to Wallace's evolutionary theism, see *The "Genius*," pp. 697–99. Dreiser's heavily marked copy of Haeckel's *The Riddle of the Universe* (1901) is in the Dreiser Collection.

3. "Reflections," *Ev'ry Month*, II (September, 1896), 7.

4. Dreiser to Ruth E. Kennell, September 5, 1928; Ruth E. Kennell, *Theodore Dreiser and the Soviet Union* (New York, 1969), p. 222.

5. See Dreiser's story "The 'Mercy' of God," *Chains* (New York, 1927), p. 373. The story was initially published in August 1924.

6. Besides Lehan, pp. 209–221, see Neda Westlake, "Theodore Dreiser's *Notes on Life*," *Library Chronicle* of the University of Pennsylvania, XX (Summer, 1954), 69–75, and Marguerite Tjader and John J. McAleer, eds., *Notes on Life* (University, Ala., 1974).

7. Dreiser to George Douglas, January 26, 1935; *Letters*, II, 719–20.

8. "What I Believe," *Forum*, LXXXII (November, 1929), 320.

9. Dreiser's most succinct and clear statements of his later beliefs are his essay "I Believe," in *I Believe: The Personal Philosophies of Certain Eminent Men. . . .*, ed. Clifton Fadiman (New York, 1939), 355–62 and his testament of November 1943, "My Creator," *Notes on Life*, pp. 327–33.

10. Dreiser to Sinclair, December 18, 1924; Lilly Library, Indiana University.

11. *A Hoosier Holiday*, (New York, 1916), p. 60.

12. "Individualism and the Jungle," *New Masses*, VII (January, 1932), 1–2. Quoted from the revised and expanded version of the essay in Dreiser Introduction to *Harlan Miners Speak*, ed. Theodore Dreiser et al. (New York, 1932), pp. 15–16.

13. See "The Reformer" in *Hey Rub-a-Dub-Dub*.

Part Four: *The Bulwark*

1. Besides the invaluable references in Swanberg and in the *Letters* to Dreiser's work on *The Bulwark* during this thirty-year period, I have relied on the recollections of three women who were closely involved in the composition of the novel: *Letters to Louise*, ed. Louise Campbell (Philadelphia, 1959); Helen Dreiser, *My Life with Dreiser* (Cleveland, 1951); and Marguerite Tjader [Harris], "Dreiser's Last Year . . . *The Bulwark* in the Making," *Book Find News*, II (March, 1946), 6–7, 20–21, and *Theodore Dreiser: A New Dimension* (Norwalk, Conn., 1965). See also Jack Salzman, "The Curious History of Dreiser's *The Bulwark*," *Proof*, III (1973), 21–61.

2. Edgar Lee Masters, *Across Spoon River* (New York, 1936), pp. 329–30.

3. Masters, *Across Spoon River*, pp. 329–30.

4. Swanberg, p. 176.

5. Dreiser made this explicit comparison in a conversation with Mrs. Harris in 1944; Tjader, p. 157.

6. *Book*, pp. 243, 250, 252.

7. Tjader, p. 162. The final sentence in Dreiser's 1914 synopsis is "Orville's request to Etta not to cry, and her answer."

8. *Plays of the Natural and the Supernatural* (New York, 1926 [1916]), p. 172.

9. "Elizabeth," "This Madness—An Honest Novel About Love," *Hearst's International-Cosmopolitan*, LXXXVI (April, 1929), 81–85, 117–20; (May, 1929), 80–83, 146–54.

10. He derived his principal "invented" plot incident, Stewart's crime, from a newspaper story. (Tjader, p. 179.) The incident appears in Dreiser's 1914 synopsis of the novel.

11. In Dreiser's earliest drafts, Solon is from Opdyke, north of Philadelphia, near Trenton, and Benecia is from Dukla (also called Douglas), south of Philadelphia, near Wilmington. In later drafts, he coalesced both settings into Dukla and placed it approximately at the site of Newtown, Pennsylvania, twenty-five miles northeast of Philadelphia and nine miles west of Trenton. The Llewellyn and Franklin Hall of the novel are Bryn Mawr and a composite of Swarthmore and Haverford.

12. It is difficult to date Dreiser's acquisition of books, but among those in the Dreiser Collection which he probably acquired at the outset of his work on the novel are Allen C. Thomas and Richard H. Thomas, *A History of the Friends in America* (Philadelphia, 1905); *Biographical Sketches and Anecdotes of Members of the Religious Society of Friends* (Philadelphia, 1871); and *Discipline of the Yearly Meeting of Friends for Pennsylvania, New Jersey. . . .* (Philadelphia, 1910).

13. Dreiser to Lengel, July 1, 1942.

14. The dummy is in the Columbia University Library.

15. The announcement occurs in John Lane's promotional pamphlet *Theodore Dreiser: America's Foremost Novelist* [1916].

16. The carbon, which is among the Estelle Kubitz Williams papers in the Dreiser Collection, can be dated by reference to Swanberg's comment that Dreiser worked with Miss Kubitz on the novel during the summer of 1917 (p. 219) and by Dreiser's letter to May Calvert Baker, July 23, 1917, in which he noted that he had completed twenty-eight chapters of *The Bulwark*.

17. Chapter III, p. 1.

18. Chapter V, p. 8.

19. Chapter VIII, p. 7.

20. Dreiser to Mrs. Campbell, November 25, 1925; *Letters to Louise*, p. 27.

21. *Letters to Louise*, p. 32. In a letter to Griffith Dudding, October 20, 1965, Mrs. Campbell recalled that she received two holograph manuscripts—one on small sheets, the other on large ones. These would seem to be Dreiser's original drafts of the 1914–16 and 1917 versions of the novel. Since he still had these versions available either in typescript or in revised form in his 1920 draft, he apparently did not miss the holographs when he began work on the novel again in early 1942. In July 1942, Mrs. Campbell accidentally discovered that the holographs were in her possession and returned them to Dreiser.

22. The Jones-Dreiser relationship, as well as the related subject of the influence of Woolman's *Journal* on Dreiser, is well surveyed in a series of articles by Gerhard Friedrich: "A Major Influence on Theodore Dreiser's *The Bulwark*," *American Literature*, XXIX (May, 1957), 180–93; "The Dreiser-Jones Correspondence," *Bulletin of Friends Historical Association*, XLVI (Spring, 1957), 23–34; and "Theodore Dreiser's Debt to Woolman's *Journal*," *American Quarterly*, VII (Winter, 1955), 385–92.

23. See Dreiser to Warner Clark, July 9, 1934 (*Letters*, II, 679) and Dreiser and John Dos Passos, "A Conversation," *Direction*, I (January, 1938), 2–4, 28.

24. Dreiser to Jones, December 1, 1938; *Letters*, III, 822. The three books, heavily marked, are in the Dreiser Collection. Also in the collection is Dreiser's marked copy of Woolman's *Journal*.

25. *The Trail of Life in the Middle Years* (New York, 1934), p. 40.

26. *The Trail of Life in the Middle Years*, p. 129. The marginalia was noted by Griffith Dudding, "A Note Concerning Theodore Dreiser's Philosophy," *Library Chronicle* of the University of Pennsylvania, XXX (Winter, 1964), 36–37.

27. "Presenting Thoreau," *The Living Thoughts of Thoreau* (New York, 1939), pp. 1–32. Although Dreiser's secretary Harriet Bissell did the preliminary editorial work for this volume, there is no doubt that Dreiser read her selection of material and that he wrote the introduction. See Swanberg, p. 456.

28. Dreiser, *The Living Thoughts of Thoreau*, p. 15.

29. Tjader, pp. 72–73.

30. Tjader, p. 77.

31. Dreiser wrote Mencken on March 8, 1943, just before putting aside the novel, that he was working on Chapter 34; *Letters*, III, 979. This thirty-five-chapter fragment of Part One is in the Dreiser Collection.

32. Mrs. Harris (Tjader, pp. 158, 193–94) recalled a long separate introduction on Solon's Maine boyhood which Dreiser had written in 1942–43 and which he worked into the opening chapters of Part One in 1945. Dreiser's 1942–43 draft of Part One, however, reveals that the "introduction" was merely a more extended version of the opening chapters of the published novel and not a separate fragment. Helen Dreiser's remark in a letter to Mrs. Campbell, postmarked May 20, 1946, that in 1942 Dreiser "started the book over with a new beginning," is the more accurate recollection of Dreiser's 1942 work.

33. In her *Theodore Dreiser*, pp. 159–60, Mrs. Harris designated the two major versions which she and Dreiser drew upon for their rough draft as the Financial Version and the Family Version. She notes as well that they used the Family Version as their principal text,

adding financial material to it from the Financial Version as necessary. This designation misleadingly suggests that Dreiser had two different conceptions of the novel during its pre-1942 history. In fact, the Financial Version was Dreiser's 1917 draft, the Family Version his 1920 manuscript. The first, though it contains a more extensive account than the second of Solon's business experiences, also has a full history of his personal life. Dreiser chose the 1920 manuscript as a base text not because it was a "Family Version" but because it was his longest and his last full attempt to write the novel and therefore offered the most useful framework for revision and for the inclusion of material from earlier and later versions of the novel.

34. The physical state of the 1945 rough draft of *The Bulwark* reflects to a considerable degree the history of the composition of the novel. Part One is on yellow sheets with pica type. Part Two consists of approximately equal portions of faded blue sheets with pica type, white sheets with blue elite type, yellow sheets with elite type, and white sheets with elite type. Part Three is primarily on white sheets with elite or pica type, but Chapters 60–61 and part of Chapter 64 are on yellow sheets and elite type, and Chapters 56–57 are on faded blue sheets with pica type. All three parts contain passages in Dreiser's hand.

Part One was typed by Helen at her insistence, after an argument with Dreiser and Mrs. Harris, because she had worked with Dreiser on this portion during 1942–43 and felt that she should be permitted to contribute to its final preparation. (See Tjader, p. 194.) Mrs. Harris, who had an elite typewriter, prepared most of the rest of the manuscript, apparently choosing to use yellow sheets for the material which she and Dreiser had distilled from earlier versions of the novel and white sheets for newly written material. The blue sheets are in sections of the novel which deal with Solon's financial affairs and are from the 1917 typescript, and the white sheets with blue elite type in Part Two are from the 1920 typescript.

35. Brief accounts of this phase of the genesis of *The Bulwark* can be found in *Letters*, III, 1030 n18 and Swanberg, p. 519. All the manuscripts of this period are in the Dreiser Collection: Dreiser's carbon of the version prepared by Mrs. Harris and himself; Mrs. Campbell's heavily revised carbon of this version which was the basis of her clean typescript; the printer's copy prepared by Elder from the original of the Dreiser-Harris version and Mrs. Campbell's clean typescript; and revised galley.

36. Mrs. Campbell to Robert H. Elias, February 19, 1949; Cornell University Library. See also *Letters to Louise*, p. 117.

37. Dreiser to Mrs. Campbell, May 21, 1945, and Dreiser to Farrell, May 26 and June 20, 1945; *Letters*, III, 1018–21.

38. Farrell to Dreiser, June 25, 1945.

39. Helen to Mrs. Campbell, reporting Dreiser's wishes, June 28, 1945.

40. Dreiser to Mrs. Campbell, July 27, 1945; *Letters*, III, 1022–23.

41. Dreiser to Elder, August 31, 1945, and Dreiser to Mrs. Campbell, September 1, 1945; *Letters*, III, 1027, 1028–29.

42. Elder to Dreiser, September 20, 1945.

43. Dreiser to Elder, September 22, 1945 (telegram).

44. Elder to Farrell, October 11, 1945.

45. Elder to Elias, April 4, 1949; Cornell University Library.

46. Dreiser to Elder, December 22, 1945; *Letters*, III, 1033–34.

47. Tjader, p. 235.

48. Mrs. Campbell wrote to Helen Dreiser on April 8, 1946: "I feel a sense of pride and gratification when I read critiques of *The Bulwark* commenting on its clarity and the fact that it covers the ground more swiftly, because I feel I had a part in bringing that about."

49. Farrell to Dreiser, June 25, 1945, and Helen to Mrs. Campbell, July 11, 1945.

50. Farrell to Dreiser, June 25, 1945.

51. The best critical discussions of *The Bulwark* are by Sidney Richman, "Theodore Dreiser's *The Bulwark*: A Final Resolution," *American Literature*, XXXIV (May, 1962), 229–45 and Jonas Spatz, "Dreiser's *Bulwark*: An Archaic Masterpiece," in *The Forties* . . . , ed. Warren French (Deland, Florida, 1969), pp. 152–62.

52. The incongruous verbal irony in the chapters devoted to Solon's business affairs

derives from Dreiser's reliance upon largely unrevised 1917 material; see p. 370, n34 above.

53. For "My Creator," see *Notes on Life*, ed. Marguerite Tjader and John J. McAleer (University, Ala., 1974), pp. 327–33.

54. The three earlier instances are: page 124, when Solon's "respectability and prosperity" cause his neighbors to consider him "a good man—one of the nation's bulwarks"; page 283, when his fellow bank directors, after recalling his reliability and integrity, affirm that he is "a bulwark in that respect, and they needed him, now more than ever, to hide behind"; and page 302, when his colleagues at the bank again find him "the picture of solidity and worth. They saw in him a bulwark of the older and better order of things."

Part Four: *The Stoic*

1. Dreiser to Mencken, May 26, 1912.

2. Dreiser wrote Sergei Dinamov on October 14, 1928, that he was about to begin work on the novel; *Letters*, II, 477. Although he wrote Otto Kyllmann on May 6, 1931, that he was working on *The Stoic*, it is unlikely that he did any actual writing before early 1932.

3. The original typescripts of the summaries and the plot synopsis are in the Lilly Library, Indiana University; the carbons are in the Dreiser Collection.

4. See Dreiser's clippings "The Materials of a Great Novel," *New York World*, February 4, 1906 (folder 1, page 2, of his notes for *The Stoic*) and "Little Now Left," *New York World*, June 14, 1913 (folder 2, page 1).

5. On July 31, 1932, Dreiser wrote Louise Campbell that he was at work on Chapter 54; *Letters*, II, 593. The last entry in the running summary of the plot prepared by Dreiser's secretary Miss Evelyn Light (see note 6 below) is for Chapter 53. Miss Light's typescript itself concludes with Chapter 55.

6. Miss Light's summaries, dated from June 6 to August 1, 1932, are in the Lilly Library, Indiana University (the originals) and the Dreiser Collection (the carbons).

7. See Dreiser's letters to Mrs. Campbell during the spring and summer of 1932; *Letters*, II, 585, 589–93, 599.

8. Lengel to Dreiser, August 12, 1932.

9. Miss Tatum's edited copy of the 1932 typescript of *The Stoic* is in the Dreiser Collection. Fragments of Miss Tatum's work on *The Stoic* manuscript are also in the Lilly Library, Indiana University. One such fragment contains an initialed query by her dated May 21, 1933. Also see Swanberg, p. 404.

10. See Tjader, pp. 200–202.

11. Since Mrs. Harris worked closely with Dreiser during May 1945 on his plans for completion of *The Stoic* and since she does not mention this major change in direction, it can be assumed that the idea for it occurred to Dreiser in the summer of 1945, after her departure for the East and before he again began to work on the novel.

12. The clipping, first noted by Philip Gerber—"The Alabaster Protégé: Dreiser and Berenice Fleming," *American Literature*, XLIII (May, 1971), 228—is on page 1, folder 2, of Dreiser's notes for *The Stoic*.

13. Helen Dreiser, pp. 150–57.

14. There are three such instances among Dreiser's books. His copy of Arthur Waley's *Zen Buddhism and Its Relation to Art* (London, 1922), p. 25, contains the underlined statement, "Quakerism, like Zen, is a non-dogmatic religion, laying stress on the doctrine of Immanence." In his copy of Harendranath Maitra's *Hinduism* (New York, 1922), p. 32, he queried "Quakers?" in the margin next to the comment that "It is only in Hinduism, I think, that we find the conception of God assumed in *all* the human relations of life." And in his copy of the *Bhagavad-Gita* (Hollywood, 1944), p. 17, he underlined Aldous Huxley's remark, in his Introduction, that "John Woolman, the American Quaker, provides a most enlightening example of the way in which a man may live in the world, while practicing perfect non-attachment and remaining acutely sensitive to the claims of right livelihood."

15. Tjader, p. 230.

16. The book—*Bhagavad-Gita: The Song of God*, trans. by Swami Prabhavananda and Christopher Isherwood, with an Introduction by Aldous Huxley (Hollywood: The Marcel Rudd Co., 1944)—is in the Dreiser Collection. For Dreiser's verbatim use of this edition, compare *The Stoic*, pp. 275–76; 286; 291; 294; 299 and the *Bhagavad-Gita*, pp. 149; 167; 161; 103; 61.

17. Dreiser's heavily underlined copy of this work (New York, 1922) is in the Dreiser Collection.

18. Dreiser to Elizabeth Kearney Coakley, October 13, 1945; the Huntington Library.

19. The epilogue was a condensed version of Dreiser's essay "Good and Evil," *North American Review*, CCXLVI (Autumn, 1938), 67–86.

20. Dreiser to Farrell, December 3, 1945; *Letters*, III, 1032.

21. Dreiser to Farrell, December 14, 1945.

22. Farrell to Dreiser, December 19, 1945.

23. Dreiser to Farrell, December 24, 1945 (*Letters*, III, 1035) and Dreiser to Donald Elder, December 22, 1945 (*Letters*, III, 1033–34).

24. Helen Dreiser to Farrell, January 8, 1946.

25. Helen Dreiser to Mrs. Campbell, March 2, 1946 (relaying Elder's concern) and April 22, 1946. The typescript sent to Mrs. Campbell contained the first of Dreiser's two final chapters (Chapter 90) but lacked the second and the epilogue.

26. Helen Dreiser noted Elder's request in a letter to Mrs. Campbell, April 22, 1946.

27. Donald Elder to Helen Dreiser, August 5, 1947. In a telegram to Helen on June 17, 1947, Elder had declared Mrs. Campbell's version "excellent."

28. In all, Elder restored only 15 pages of Dreiser's original typescript in a printer's copy typescript of approximately 525 pages.

29. Donald Elder to Helen Dreiser, September 8, 1947, and Marjorie Pieri (of Doubleday) to Helen Dreiser, September 22, 1947. The editor's note, however, is misleading, since it implies that Chapter 79 was the last which Dreiser wrote and that Helen reconstructed all of the Appendix from Dreiser's notes. In fact, as I have already noted, the Appendix consists of a compressed version of what was indeed Dreiser's last chapter and Helen's brief summary of Dreiser's plans for an additional section devoted to Berenice's soliloquy.

30. For Dreiser's faulty representation of Hindu philosophy, see R. N. Mookerjee, "Dreiser's Use of Hindu Thought in *The Stoic*," *American Literature*, XLIII (May, 1971), 273–78.

INDEX

INDEX